This book meticulously unravels the tragic story of New Zealander John Mulgan in Nazi-occupied Greece, as he struggled to come to terms with the role of the British-led commandos among whom he served and to find his own political conscience. It is at once an important contribution to the history of New Zealanders in Europe during WWII and to the still-contested story of the Greek Left in and after the Greek Civil War of the 1940s.

—**Roderick Beaton**, Emeritus Koraes Professor of Modern Greek & Byzantine History, Language & Literature, Department of Classics, King's College London

Every generation has found something of its own debates in Man Alone *and John Mulgan's complex legacy. C. Dimitris Gounelas and Ruth Parkin-Gounelas, in this scrupulously scholarly and utterly absorbing bi-focal exposition of Mulgan in the Greek crisis, give us a figure for our own day: enmeshed in an under-recognised anti-colonial struggle, caught and bucking against the political compromises of war, and drawn into the currents of the Greek left. An intimately detailed account of Mulgan's then, this story of austerity, resistance, and bureaucracy has much to teach our now.*

—**Dougal McNeill**, Programme Director, English Literature, School of English, Film, Theatre, Media Studies, and Art History, Te Kura Tānga Kōrero Ingarihi, Kiriata, Whakaari, Pāpāho, Tāhuhu Kōrero Toi, Victoria University of Wellington, Te Herenga Waka

John Mulgan and the Greek Left

A REGRETTABLY INTIMATE ACQUAINTANCE

C.-Dimitris Gounelas

Ruth Parkin-Gounelas

TE HERENGA WAKA
UNIVERSITY PRESS

Te Herenga Waka University Press
PO Box 600, Wellington
New Zealand
teherengawakapress.co.nz

A catalogue record is available from the
National Library of New Zealand.

ISBN 9781776920679
Published with the support of

ARTS COUNCIL OF NEW ZEALAND *TOI AOTEAROA*

Printed in Singapore by Markono Print Media Pte Ltd

Contents

Plates

Following page 174.
(Note: Spyros Meletzis [1906–2003] was the eminent photographer accompanying EAM to whom many of these images are credited.)

Maps

Note on transliteration

The spelling of Greek names can cause confusion as there is no internationally accepted system for representing the sounds of the modern Greek language in the Latin alphabet. In general we use a system based on a compromise between pronunciation (the sound of the word in modern Greek) and the Greek spelling. This means, for example, that the Aegean island that used to be spelt Euboea we write as Evoia (following both the sound 'Ev' and the Greek spelling of the second diphthong, 'oi'). The names that Mulgan would have had on his maps at the time often follow another system—e.g., the place that would normally be transliterated today as Domokos is written by Mulgan as Dhomokhos. First names tend to be historically specific—e.g., the 1930s dictator Ioannis Metaxas, as opposed to the modern poet Yannis Ritsos. Where confusion might arise, we sometimes give alternative spellings.

Unless otherwise stated, all translations from the Greek are ours.

Acknowledgements

This book is the result of a convergence of our two separate interests: Dimitri's research into the history of New Zealanders in wartime Greece and Ruth's interest in British and European literature of the 1930s–40s. A shared admiration for Mulgan's writing as well as his remarkable contribution to the Greek resistance was the catalyst. Often throughout the eight or so years this book has been in the making we have reflected on the affinity between Greeks and New Zealanders, a bond which left a deep impression on the men who served in the New Zealand forces in Greece, many of whom were concealed and protected after the Axis invasion. This affinity has continued for us in ways that Mulgan himself acknowledged when he wrote about the kind of re-education that results from prolonged contact with the other's culture.

From the start of our research Vincent O'Sullivan has offered generous assistance and advice on many occasions. We are deeply indebted to him for his support and encouragement.

Our thanks to Richard Mulgan for permission to access closed files in the King's College London Military Archives and the Alexander Turnbull Library in Wellington.

The staff of the Turnbull Library have been exceptionally helpful in replying to questions and sending files from the Mulgan and other papers. On many occasions, individual library research assistants, too numerous to name, spent considerable time and energy searching out material for us. Thanks also to the staff of the Hocken Collections, University of Otago, for supplying documents. In Athens, the staff of the Benaki Historical Archives in Kifissia, the Library of the Communist Party of Greece, Perissos, and the Directorate of Military History of Greece, have all been very helpful. The staff of the many libraries of Aristotle University, Thessaloniki, have assisted us in locating material on numerous occasions. In the UK, the Liddell Hart Centre for Military Archives (King's College London) as well as the National Archives (Kew, London) have provided us with rich sources of unpublished material. Much of our reading derives from the holdings of the copyright library at the University of Cambridge.

For patient work on the photographs, we are grateful to Kostas Arampatzis. Many thanks to Tasos Paschalis for drawing the maps.

From the village of Kataraktis in Tzoumerka and its small library, our thanks to Christos Makrygiannis and Athanasios Salamouras for information about Kostas Tsamakos.

Many individuals have helped shape our thought along the way by sharing information and ideas. We have greatly valued conversations with Tassos Anastasakis, Gerassinos Contomichalos, Nicolas Contomichalos, Odysseas Maaita, Argyrios Mamarelis, Clare Mulley, Kyriakos Papoulidis, Anna Wirz-Justice and Simon Worrall, among many others.

The professionalism and support of our editor at Te Herenga Waka University Press, Anna Knox, has eased things for us considerably through the process of production.

Our children, Angelika and Fragiskos, have played an important role in sharing the enthusiasm and understanding the dedication that has gone into this book.

Foreword

It is remarkable how a man who was so impressively pragmatic, whose life was committed to worthwhile things decently done, and convincingly direct in his loyalties and values, may still seem so elusive, so enigmatic, eighty years after his death. While what Mulgan wrote similarly takes us to more diverse readings of what he himself so modestly regarded. All he claimed for his prose was that it was written without pretension. As he wrote to Charles Brasch about his one short novel, a now inescapable cornerstone of New Zealand fiction, 'I feel myself that it was formless, unpractised and to be honest, a little dull.' It is certainly a work which is harsher about his own country, than any attempt to applaud it. Its title, *Man Alone*, was far more a lament for a society crumbling without communal values, than it was anything like the celebration of individualism and enterprise so many wanted it to be. In *Report on Experience*, he would write with compelling eloquence of meeting up with his fellow New Zealanders at El Alamein, and the pride he took as he watched them from the ranks of the British Army. Yet in that same letter to Brasch, written from Coleraine in Northern Ireland, shortly before leaving for North Africa, he noted 'What a lonely desolate place New Zealand seems to me now. I feel a sense of such tragedy in all the people I like there much more deeply than over here. I am loving Ireland, even if it is the unregenerate north.' For all the clarity of Mulgan's prose, how often the reader can be pulled up with— what is it? Not wanting to say too much? A deft turn that prevents an easy answer to a puzzled query?

The details of Mulgan's life, not surprisingly, become more complicated, his personal views far more difficult to trace, once he had left the British Army to join the Special Operations Executive, with its mandate to work what confusion it could behind enemy lines. He was parachuted into Greece in September 1943, to work with other SOEs in assisting the Greek resistance. Few populations, apart from the Poles, endured as much as the Greeks during occupation. They were resilient under starvation and random brutality and punishing winters. While during the time Mulgan was with the *andartes* in Thessaly, the painful paradox unfolded that the conception of freedom the majority of Greeks held for their country would be subverted by British post-war intentions, and Churchill's insistence—part prejudice, part ignorance—on the assumed right of a Great Power to decide what was best for smaller nations. This study now makes clear how Colonel Chris Woodhouse, who recommended Mulgan for his Military Cross and later wrote of him as his most effective operative in the field, also advised, once the Germans withdrew, that he be directed to work away from further SOE involvement, not because Mulgan was 'burned out', as was sometimes assumed, and as his suicide might retrospectively seem to confirm, but because of his political loyalties.

The Greeks already knew, well before the end of the war, that a promised referendum would not take place, and an unpopular King and right-wing Government-in-exile would be imposed. The civil war that followed the withdrawal of German forces was inevitable. A subsequent decision by Peter Fraser that no New Zealand troops were to be used in British deployments against their recent *andartes* allies was, and remains, a decision New Zealanders and Greeks take pride in. A confidential report that Mulgan was asked to provide for the Labour Government in Wellington, and that he wrote in the last weeks before his death, was significant in his own country's attitude to Greek affairs.

So much relating to Mulgan personally, as well as to his work in Greece, is a tangle of allegiances and commitments that is daunting for any researcher. Files are incomplete and dispersed, some directly relating to Mulgan stay unavailable, and there is the forbidding fact that so much that is relevant demands working with Greek sources. It could not be more fortunate for any study of his politics, and those of Greece generally, that the present authors are so uniquely placed to do so. The Mulgan we take from their pages is one of remarkable independence and integrity; the personality we now know so much more about is sympathetic, troubled, yet at times still curiously elusive. But we read of him against a background so much more informed than has been possible until now, and with a more closely detailed foreground of his day-by-day work.

Dimitri Gounelas grew up in Kifissia, a town a little north of Athens, on a main road where the constant business of war impinged on his childhood. He followed an older sister, already married to a New Zealand doctor, to Wellington in the 1960s, where he married Ruth Parkin. From Victoria University, they went on to doctorates at King's College London and Oxford University, and to professorships at the University of Thessalonika. You see what I mean when I speak of an ideal authorial matching. Each has published significantly in their own academic fields, but what began as a shared casual interest in Mulgan, led to research on a scale that so substantially alters what might be said of him.

The massive and intricate tensions that cover this period in Greek social and political history cannot be simplified, without losing so much that is essential. The Gounelases assume their readers are serious about what needs to be known, as they are serious in providing it. They are careful in what they explain, and are generous with what they draw on. Most of all, their own passionate interest in the man, their knowledge of his own earlier years in Auckland and at Oxford, and then the country he finally arrived at, drive a deeply informed story.

Since the first news of Mulgan's death in April 1945, conspiracy theorists have run fast and loose. General Freyberg was quick to spike a number of rumours, and sent his legal advisor, Thaddeus (later Sir) McCarthy to Cairo, to be assured that the British authorities had dealt with evidence and inquests in a correct way. But if not the death itself, then certainly the circumstances immediately preceding it, continue to raise questions. The Gounelases are conscientious and fair in presenting them. But their startlingly fresh fact is that the Polish woman Christine Atherton, who was living in the Continental

Hotel in Cairo at the same time as Mulgan, to whom he wrote one of his last letters, and who was emotionally close to him, was the same Christine Granville, and before that, Krystyna Skarbek, the most decorated and legendary of SOE's undercover agents in Europe.

You can see how the door now swings wide. Was Mulgan aware of her identity, a woman so famous for concealing it, and who lived under numerous names? Surely Mulgan's commanding officer in Cairo, and the recipient of his last long letter, who presented as an English officer but was in private life a Polish Count, must have known? And yet nothing of this is mentioned in the inquests, or in other documents. The shadowy woman who gave evidence of their friendship, and last spoke with John a few hours before he took his life, faded away, until this book so convincingly identified her. But as an aside, almost, to that much more ardent tracing of his constant engagement with Greeks, and the depth of his Greek commitment. How finely Dimitri and Ruth Gounelas have gifted us with that, and much else. And one detail I love. There is certainly no other SOE who so deserves to be remembered in a Greek folk song, and to survive in its lines:

> *Fine fellow from New Zealand*
> *Who came to our house to hide*
> *You'll find affection, love and friendship*
> *As if you're in your own home.*

Refrain

> *Put on my son's clothes, he's been killed,*
> *And don't be afraid, no one here has been betrayed.*

—Vincent O'Sullivan, April 2023

Abbreviations

Military and political organisations

AMM: Allied Military Mission (to the Greek resistance)

BLO: British Liaison Officer

BMM: British Military Mission (to the Greek resistance)

EAM: Ethniko Apeleftherotiko Metopo (National Liberation Front)

EDES: Ethnikos Dimokratikos Ellinikos Syndesmos (National Republican Greek League)

EKKA: Ethniki kai Koinoniki Apeleftherosis (National and Social Liberation)

ELAS: Ellinikos Laikos Apeleftherotikos Stratos (Greek People's Liberation Army)

FO: Foreign Office (Britain)

KKE: Kommounistiko Komma Elladas (Communist Party of Greece)

PEEA: Politiki Epitropi Ethnikis Apeleftherosis (Political Committee of National Liberation)

OSS: Office of Strategic Services (USA)

SIS: Secret Intelligence Service (Britain)

SOE: Special Operations Executive (Britain)

Archives

ANZ: Archives New Zealand, Thorndon, Wellington

ATL: Alexander Turnbull Library, Wellington, New Zealand

BHA: Benaki Historical Archives, Kifissia, Athens

DIS: Diefthynsi Istorias Stratou (Directorate of Military History), Athens

KCLMA: Liddell Hart Centre for Military Archives, King's College London

LCP: Library of the Communist Party of Greece, Perissos, Athens

TNA: The National Archives/Public Record Office, Kew, London

Texts frequently cited

AGM: *A Good Mail: Letters of John Mulgan.* Ed. Peter Whiteford. Wellington: Victoria University Press, 2011a.

Diary: Mulgan's diary as SOE agent in Greece. KCLMA Dobrski GB 0099, 20.

Dobrski: Mulgan's correspondence with Dolbey, etc. KCLMA Dobrski GB 0099.

LJB: *Long Journey to the Border: A Life of John Mulgan.* By Vincent O'Sullivan. Auckland: Penguin, 2003.

RE: *Report on Experience.* By John Mulgan. Ed. Peter Whiteford. London: Frontline Books/Wellington: Victoria University Press/Annapolis, Maryland: Naval Institute Press, 2010.

Introduction

I have a noble and regrettably intimate
acquaintance with EAM-ELAS

—John Mulgan to J.V. Wilson, 20 April 1945

'Intimacy' was not an emotion that came easily to John Mulgan. He had an open, friendly manner, a winning smile and a knack of putting people at their ease; everybody liked him. But he was not the sort to use the word 'intimate' readily to describe personal relations, least of all his own. So it's striking that on one of the rare occasions he does use the word, it's to describe his relationship with something as seemingly remote as a radical left-wing political organisation in Greece. Characteristically, to deflate the emotional potential of the confession and maintain the self-deprecating ethos required of New Zealand masculinity, the assertion is hedged with qualifications: the mock-heroic 'noble', as well as the ambiguously disapproving 'regrettably' (whose is the regret? his own? that of others?). But within the context, the phrase 'intimate acquaintance' suggests something private and personal. Beneath the ironic undercutting is an earnest but necessarily guarded statement of allegiance, written at a hyper-sensitive moment in the war to a close friend, a man at a safe distance in New Zealand to whom

1

Mulgan felt he could risk a guarded political confession.

How had a 33-year-old from a comfortable liberal New Zealand background got to this point of allegiance to a band of revolutionary left-wing partisans (ELAS, the Greek People's Liberation Army) based in the rough and isolated mountains of central mainland Greece? What lay behind this trajectory? These questions may not have puzzled his contemporaries quite so much, given the anti-fascist turn taken by many Western intellectuals in the immediately pre-war years—although by 1945 most would have found his choices odd, if not reprehensible. To a reader today, however, his situation is both more and less difficult to understand. On the one hand opportunities for radical political commitment of this kind are almost certainly less frequent in the West today. On the other hand, the twenty-first-century reader has access to a huge number of accounts of pre-war and wartime attitudes and activities—in both New Zealand and Greece. From out of a vast bibliography, it is now possible to account for many of the causes and implications of passionate political engagement at the time. This is not to say, however, that there is consensus on John Mulgan's political views or (even less) on the events in which he became embroiled.

This study sets out to trace the way that Mulgan's 'acquaintance' with ELAS and its political wing, EAM (the National Liberation Front), soon developed into a form of identification, and to argue that, for all its qualifications, 'intimacy' should be read here in a strong and positive sense. The historical focus will be on the period from September 1943 to April 1945, the years of his engagement with the Greek situation, but what we will be treating as Mulgan's predisposition to this identification had been well prepared, especially from the time of his arrival in 1933 in Britain, where his six years in Oxford laid the groundwork for a radical and enduring left-wing orientation. For many from the red Thirties, the onset of war and the developing mistrust of Soviet intentions led to a rapid disillusionment with left-wing ideals. But for Mulgan the experience of living in the mountain villages of central mainland Greece and coming to terms with the reformist objectives of their partisans only added a deeper layer to his politics. This was socialism in action, what he came to call 'practical communism', as he envisaged it on the world stage. This confession of intimacy to J.V. Wilson just before leaving the British army was a rare moment, an opportunity to express openly his qualified support for communism: support for its egalitarian, anti-capitalist and anti-imperialist ideals as he saw them in the 1930s and early 1940s, with a clear-eyed view of what needed reforming in the movement. In Greece he was to witness the movement's struggles and miscalculations, but never to lose faith in its ideals.

His was not to be a straightforward story. Mulgan was serving in Greece under the British, carrying out sabotage and intelligence work with the Special Operations Executive (SOE), under oath to the secret services, for whom confidentiality and allegiance were paramount. Free expression of his political views was out of the question. This was manageable, so long as Britain's military aims coincided with those of its Greek allies—including, initially, the ELAS partisans Mulgan was working with. However, from the time of his arrival in Greece in September 1943—a crucial turning point in the war as Russia began to represent a threat rather than a heroic ally—British policy began to shift, and support for the ELAS partisans to be withdrawn, leaving Mulgan with a personal and professional dilemma that he struggled to resolve.

The challenge, when exploring Mulgan's thoughts and activities at this time, is to reconcile the widely varying accounts of the different political and military aims, both at the overall strategic level and on the ground. Until recently, the narrative, at least from the Anglophone point of view, has been dominated by British (and to a lesser extent American) accounts. (The experiences written up by or about New Zealanders also serving with SOE—men such as Arthur Edmonds, Tom Barnes, Don Stott, William Jordan or Dudley Perkins—tend to be more anecdotal but generally follow the British line of rapidly increasing mistrust of left-wing politics.) On the other side are the Greek accounts of what happened, which are often starkly at odds with Anglophone narratives, and are themselves far from unified.

Much of this has to do with perceptions of the political in Greece, as opposed to in Britain (and Commonwealth countries). Mulgan was to notice how, due to centuries of occupation and instability, Greeks are politicised early and grow up with politics as their 'alphabet', as he put it in *Report on Experience* (RE 138). But to suggest that the British approach to the Greek situation was *a*political would be a serious error—one which, however, many of those in the Allied forces set store by. With the end of conflict in sight by late 1943, both sides—the British Mulgan was serving under and the partisan forces he was serving with—were jostling for position in the post-war arena that was beginning to be staked out. Much of this had to do with the Soviets, who were slowly making their way in a south-westerly direction, towards the Balkans and the Mediterranean, and causing considerable alarm in Western quarters.

Cold War perspectives have shaped Mulgan's story as much in his own time as subsequently. But with the lifting of this deeply political shadow (or perhaps, some might argue, its replacement by others) towards the end of the last century, historiography took a new turn in its approach to the war in Greece, and its partisan liberation movements have been examined in a new light. Much of this was initiated in Greece itself. The fascist junta between 1967 and 1974 produced a sufficiently strong rebellion, from Greeks both within and outside the country, to result in an outpouring of revisionist histories and a strong appetite for a revised understanding of the aims and achievements of the Greek left. At the turn of the 21st century, younger British historians like Roderick Bailey, Mark Seaman and Neville Wylie began to challenge SOE's claim to strictly military rather than political motives for its intervention in the Balkans. One of the many fascinating aspects of Mulgan's story today is the way he straddled both sides, never quite 'going native' among the Greek guerrillas but remaining constantly alert to the mistakes and dangers of the policies he was supposed to be serving.

His prescience was remarkable. What we describe as this bi-focal perspective, however, would have put him under considerable strain. Throughout his time in the mountains, he was called upon to account for his views and actions, both in reports to British Headquarters in Cairo and when questioned by the visiting head of the Allied Military Mission, Chris Woodhouse. Well aware of the impossibility of open challenge to his commanders on the ground and in Cairo if he wanted to retain his much-loved post, he wrote carefully worded reports, sometimes hinting at but ultimately avoiding open opposition to British policy. It is one of the ironies of this bi-focal stance that he has even occasionally been cited as speaking out against the horrors of the Greek left. All this time, his resistance work with his Greek comrades allowed him to achieve a continued degree of collaboration and success which was described by many as unique in the country. To detect Mulgan's more nuanced views and feelings beneath his official statements requires a strong critical microscope.

Reading the Greek alongside the Anglophone accounts of these events can sometimes feel like moving between two parallel universes. As far as most of the British Liaison Officers (BLOs) serving with SOE saw it, all decisions were taken by and operations co-ordinated from headquarters in Cairo. But for those in the ELAS forces or its administrative wing, EAM, this was their war, with its own specific and often very different objectives. One Greek account we have resorted to frequently is the hefty book by a man Mulgan referred to affectionately as 'the general' (in lower case: like George Orwell, a fellow traveller, Mulgan was wryly sceptical of military titles and hierarchies). Carefully buried in anonymity in Mulgan's accounts because of his high profile and vulnerability to German capture, 'the general', it turns out, is none other than the Commander-in-Chief of ELAS, Stefanos Sarafis,[1] a name that still evokes strong reactions in Greece today. To those on the Greek left, his name represents heroic self-sacrifice and leadership of a movement that was attempting to expel both the occupying Germans and the fascist elements that had dominated national politics for decades. This Sarafis was immortalised on his death in 1957 by the well-known poet Yannis

---

1   Unlike many in the top positions of the movement, Sarafis managed to survive the war to write it all up. He was not to last for very long, however.

Ritsos as 'Our General, humane and modest [. . .] / who shared your bread and your courage / with the harassed Republican/Democratic cause' [me tin kinigimeni Dimokratia]'.[2] For those further to the right, however, he was a harbinger of horrendous things to come: the violence of the civil war that was beginning to threaten in the country at the time of Mulgan's arrival.

Mulgan, it is now clear, worked in close collaboration with Sarafis throughout his time in the Greek mountains. They shared the same area of operation, the area variously called Thessaly or northern Roumeli, to which Mulgan had been sent and which also happened to be the centre of ELAS operations in the country. Through his regular contact with Sarafis, and unlike the BLOs in other parts of Greece—those in the Peloponnese in the south, or in Macedonia in the north—Mulgan was at the absolute heart of ELAS decision-making and activities. But despite this regular contact between the two men, Sarafis's book, *ELAS* (1946), makes only one passing reference to Mulgan, as a 'British major' (all BLOs were referred to as 'British' or even 'English'),[3] and in his detailed account, collaboration with SOE is only briefly referred to. There were good reasons for this. Like most 'Elasites', Sarafis suspected the British of ulterior motives in their collaboration—that his movement was being used but would be discarded or betrayed when the time came. He would be proved correct. But Mulgan seems to have been regarded by all the left-wing combatants—professionally trained officers like Sarafis as well as resistance conscripts—as an exception, someone who not only understood their aims but empathised with their ideological commitment.

The details of the relationship with Sarafis are difficult to detect. Mulgan, for his part, avoids direct reference to the identities of the 'chiefs' of ELAS, for reasons of security. Their identities and whereabouts, if revealed, would have exposed them and their troops

2   katiousa.gr/logotechnia/poiisi/dike-mas-archistratige-sarafi-4-poiites-ymnoun-ton-doksasmeno-stratigo-tou-elas-stefano-sarafi/. Date of access 3 Dec. 2021.

3   Editing the translation into English of his book 23 years after Sarafis's death, his wife Marion, who would not have known him, refers to Mulgan in a footnote as 'Australian' (Stefanos Sarafis 1980, 292n1).

to brutal German reprisal. Unable to write home about his activities in these covert operations, the only personal writing he did during these thirteen months was in a tiny diary now held in military archives in London. The ink is often washed out, either by censors or perhaps by another dunking in the river, and when legible the diary entries, according to military protocol, are confined to cryptic geographical and strategical notes. A close reading in parallel with the accounts of others, including Sarafis, however, reveals the extent to which Mulgan's activities coincided constantly with those directed from nearby ELAS HQ. Exceptionally, Mulgan does make direct reference to the head of the ELAS division in his immediate area, Kostas Tsamakos, subordinate to but a close ally of Sarafis, both in the diary and then later in *Report on Experience*, where he expresses well-founded anxiety about the fate of his friend in the immediate future. Others of a higher profile, whose names will appear regularly in the pages that follow (Aris, Psarros, Bakirtzis, Svolos, Siantos, Tzimas and Karagiorgis, along with Sarafis), are rarely or only cryptically mentioned by name in the diary but are clearly part of Mulgan's everyday life.

One of the issues that starkly divides SOE and EAM-ELAS narratives is the extent to which the ELAS guerrillas were involved in fighting the Germans. In most SOE accounts the reader is given to understand, as the New Zealand BLO Bill Jordan put it (with flagrant inaccuracy, it has to be said), that the only 'bona fide resistance army in Greece' was that of the fully British-backed and pro-monarchist group EDES.[4] ELAS fighters, Jordan contended, were 'louts' or 'villains [. . .] with the wrong politics', who 'sat on their backsides and talked all day' (1969, 96, 110, 57 and 62). Jordan had strong personal reasons for his animus against what was in fact at its peak a highly organised fighting force numbering over 100,000, but the prejudice was common among his fellow Kiwi operatives in SOE, including Tom Barnes and Don Stott (Arthur Edmonds had a more equitable approach). And for a long time,

---

4   By the end EDES numbered roughly one sixth the size of ELAS's volunteer forces. Apart from the early involvement of an EDES group in blowing up the Gorgopotamos viaduct, EDES did little to hinder the Germans.

British voices that carried weight on Greek issues continued to replicate these opinions despite increasing historical evidence for the extensive success of the ELAS resistance fighters. One example here is Patrick Leigh Fermor, a former BLO known for his and Bill Stanley Moss's ill-advised kidnapping of a German General on Crete (dramatised in the book and film *Ill Met by Moonlight*), as well as for his later books on Greece, including one often quoted about the area in which Mulgan spent much of his time in Greece, *Roumeli* (1966). For Leigh Fermor, the ELAS fighters 'wrought chaos on the mainland' and left only 'the scum' to continue the fight (1983, 142). The picturesque and 'charm-filled radiance' of Leigh Fermor's post-war descriptions could not be further from Mulgan's Roumeli. Romantic classical throwbacks have no place in *Report on Experience*. And, it must be stressed, Mulgan certainly didn't romanticise his fellow fighters. But he came to the task from a very different ideological perspective and understood the difficulties: their lack of military training, the fact that they had very little ammunition, the knowledge that when the inevitable German reprisals would occur, it was the families of these men and women, not of the BLOs, who would be shot and have their villages burned. Most importantly, he understood the long-term national project that many Greeks had at the forefront of their minds. Like Harold Laski, the radical political theorist he admired, Mulgan had taken to heart the view that 'a nation that is deprived of the right to determine its own way of life suffers an abridgment of personality which, sooner or later, issues in violence' (Blaazer 1992, 122). Because Mulgan was such an anti-romantic, averse to exaggeration or self-reference, it's easy to miss the depth of his ideological orientation. Throughout, he was exceptional among SOE operatives for the way he continued to pay tribute to the aims of ELAS, to both its heroic but often ill-disciplined fighting and its constantly tragic sacrifices, first against the Italians and then—when the Germans took over—despite the stark inequality of their forces and arms. He also understood—and this is an important theme in both *Report on Experience* and his reports to

HQ in Cairo—that guerrilla fighting needs to employ very different tactics from those of regular warfare, that direct confrontation is out of the question and hit-and-run operations the only option. Having followed Tom Wintringham's programme for the Home Guard as a revolutionary people's militia in British towns preparing for German invasion in the late 1930s, as well as the successes of Orde Wingate's guerrilla operations in Abyssinia against the invading Italians, Mulgan was well primed to understand and support the particular forms of resistance that were available to himself and his Greek comrades.

Another issue that divided (and sometimes continues to divide) accounts is the extent to which the Greek movement was in thrall to the Soviets. At the time, the British view was that the Greek 'Communists', controlled from Moscow, were preparing to take over the country the moment the Germans withdrew, and that their movement, far from being democratic, was as totalitarian as the fascist forces occupying the country. More recent historical publications disprove this view. Reinforcing this divide are attitudes to the British involvement in the fighting on the streets of Athens in December 1944, known today in Greece as *Ta Dekemvriana*. Were the British 'rescuing' the Greeks from a fate (communism) worse than they understood, or were they pursuing an imperialist policy of their own, to secure influence in the eastern Mediterranean in the post-war era? These debates brought Mulgan into direct conflict with his commanding officer, Chris Woodhouse—whose views, however, he was only able to challenge indirectly.

Our attention will often be focused on the different forms of communism to which Mulgan was responding: Soviet, Continental, Greek and British. As *Report on Experience* illustrates, much of his adult thought circled around these distinctions. To lift the Cold War carapace that covered the history of the second half of the last century is to reveal not a fixed dogma but a maelstrom of shifting political philosophies and practices in Europe in the 1930s and early 1940s which resulted in a wide range of political positions, along with a great deal of optimism. Another young (British) SOE officer of left-wing persuasion, Frank Thompson, spoke of a 'chemical change' taking place in Europe[5] out of this ferment of pluralistic activism. A central difficulty in interpreting the Mulgan story is the fact that the EAM-ELAS movement was often referred to *en bloc* as 'communist', whereas a large proportion of its supporters would more accurately be described as socialist, republican or generally centre-left. Mulgan did not flinch from the communist label in the way many did, but rather concentrated, both during his time in Greece and prior to that, in Oxford, on exploring its strengths as well as differentiating his views from those of others on the left. He approached communism, in other words, in much the same way he approached everything: with open eyes and a large dose of pragmatism. We will be exploring the ways in which Mulgan had what could be called a critical admiration for the communist project, both on the theoretical level and as being implemented in the Soviet Union, a predisposition which prepared him to take many of EAM's aims on trust, all within an environment (among his military superiors) which was becoming hostile to the point of paranoia. His story was unusual but not unique: a few other British operatives, like Frank Thompson (or Rufus Sheppard, in Greece), followed the same ideological trajectory.

These men had emerged from a very specific political environment, that of the movement called the Popular Front. With the rise of fascism, the Communist International had decided in 1933 to approach socialist-inclined groups throughout Europe to join forces against the common threat. Within two to three years, Popular Front governments had been elected in Spain and France which combined several different parties left of centre along with the Communist Parties. Plurality in unity was called for as national economies struggled against mounting unemployment and the growing threat to the international order. By 1941, SOE London was in contact with Greece via Evripidis Bakirtzis, a member of what the British, setting out plans for resistance and sabotage operations within occupied Europe, saw as a promising anti-Axis group called

---

5   T.J. Thompson and E.P. Thompson 1947, 140. For more on this view of Thompson's (and Mulgan's), see the last chapter.

the Laiki Dimokratia (Popular Democracy). An amalgamation of communist, agrarian and socialist parties, this movement was by the following spring calling itself the National Liberation Front (EAM: Ethniko Apeleftherotiko Metopo).[6]

The Popular Front had engaged Mulgan's attention to a considerable extent in Oxford, as evidenced by a body of his writing that has so far attracted little attention. In 1936 he and fellow New Zealander Geoffrey Cox suggested a series of columns for newspapers back home which would give a deeper, more informed picture of what was happening in Britain. 'Behind the Cables', published in the *Auckland Star* and the Wellington *Dominion*, ran from early 1936 to mid 1937, on a fairly regular fortnightly basis. Beginning rather cautiously, Mulgan and Cox soon settled into their comfort zone and sent off a series of scathing denunciations of British policies at this time of crisis. Their main interest was in foreign policy, issues such as the Hoare-Laval pact that had attempted to betray the Abyssinian Government under invasion from Mussolini's forces the year before, and the disastrous 'isolationist' position on the European stage which left the Spanish Government at the mercy of Franco's take-over, as well as the compromises being made by Baldwin's National Government on issues such as unemployment and poverty, and the way the huge increase in the armaments trade was benefitting the rich. Behind these salvos lay the political programme of the Popular Front, particularly that of the government of Léon Blum in France—its support for the collective security which Mulgan and Cox deemed vital and the significance of the egalitarian initiatives of French and Soviet economic policy. 'Behind the Cables' dedicated several sections to the Popular Front as its appeal spread. In Britain itself, the New Zealand duo record, many on the left were uniting against government policies; their columns read like a political history of radical left debate in this 'millennium year of 1936', as Mulgan was later to call it (RE 67). What was increasingly referred

---

6   For the early history of EAM, see Hajis 1980. For early British contacts with Bakirtzis ('Prometheus'), see Sweet-Escott 1975, 10. Sweet-Escott stresses that 'There was no suggestion whatever that at this time E.A.M. was dominated by the Communist Party of Greece, the K.K.E.'

to by these thinkers as the 'fascist-imperialist' drive in international politics would preoccupy Mulgan in the years ahead, in a growing critical distance from official British policies. Many others shared his views. As George Orwell put it in his 'Letter from England' to the American *Partisan Review* in January 1943, 'The average English intellectual is anti-British' (Orwell 1971, 319). For all this, it was almost certainly a Eurocentric commitment in Mulgan's thinking which led him to join the British army rather than the New Zealand forces. The decision was to have serious consequences.

Writing in these columns for a New Zealand readership, Mulgan and Cox sometimes refer to topics related to the dominion, from dairy imports to Japanese activities in the Pacific. Significantly, on a couple of occasions they note how the policies being implemented by Blum's Popular Front government were in fact close to what was being attempted by Michael Joseph Savage's new Labour government. But what is striking about the viewpoint is its Eurocentrism, the way the authors convey an excitement at being at the centre of things on the world stage. The outbreak of the Spanish Civil War that year had a profound effect on Mulgan's consciousness—as it did for a great number of left-leaning people at the time. Eventually, over 40,000 young foreigners, from over 50 countries, would flock to fight for the Republican cause, and 20,000 others served in medical or auxiliary units. Mulgan's political trajectory may be viewed within the context of what used to be called 'the Auden generation'. He certainly shared W.H. Auden's early enthusiasm for left-wing causes and worked closely with the poet on several projects in Oxford. Orwell's political orientation, too, though outside this refined academic atmosphere, offers many points of comparison. Also of comparative interest are political activists still further to the left like Frank Thompson and James Klugmann, who, unlike Auden and Orwell, continued to hold faith with communism into the 1940s.

* * *

Part I here outlines the immediate background to the focus of our study: first Mulgan's intellectual development in Oxford within the context of its time, and then the history of Greece immediately preceding his arrival there. Part II, which explores the details of his engagement with EAM-ELAS under British command, traces his activities on the ground and daily dealings with the Greek *andartes*. Part III begins with what is in some ways the central chapter in that it attempts a reading of *Report on Experience* as what we are calling its bi-focal exposition of the Greek crisis. With only one reference to EAM-ELAS, and that an indirect one, the book has not usually been read in terms of Mulgan's opposition to British policies. Mulgan, we argue, had become an adept in subterfuge to evade the censors he knew would work through his text with a fine-tooth comb if it was to be published in the post-war years. The extent to which his views were subversive of the policies he was expected to be implementing can be more clearly understood by comparing his text with that of the official history of the occupation in Greece from the British point of view, Chris Woodhouse's *Apple of Discord*, published the following year (1948). But this conflict of viewpoints is never played out openly. Mulgan's oppositional tactics involved sophisticated rhetorical strategies that gave safe cover to his underlying beliefs. Most of his book was written after the liberation from Axis occupation, but Mulgan knew this was not a liberation for Greece. For all its seeming lucidity which has made it a popular point of reference in Anglophone accounts of SOE, *Report on Experience* is far from a straightforward read.

The final chapters of the book, dealing with events in Athens and Cairo, open out to posthumous and more speculative issues. Chapter 10 puts forward a hypothesis which seems to us highly plausible, but which only further evidence could validate. Much of the Mulgan story has concentrated on his death, with the suicide thesis shadowing his significant achievements in the Greek resistance. (The official New Zealand history of 'Special Service in Greece' in the war, for example, lists only Mulgan's death, after generous accounts of the daring exploits of Barnes, Stott and others [McGlynn 1953, 32].) Our study offers some suggestions but no final answers about what remains the mystery of Mulgan's death. Its main aim is to explore a political journey, the way the service of a New Zealander under British command in Greece developed into a profound engagement with a cultural phenomenon so different from his own. In all this the 'noble and regrettable' intimacy with EAM-ELAS described to J.V. Wilson was absolutely characteristic of his habitual mode of expression. The intimacy was genuine and deeply felt, but its expression was veiled by ironic deflation and ventriloquised disapproval.

One final question may dominate readers' minds as they follow Mulgan's story to its conclusion. Wouldn't he soon have renounced his radical political position if he had survived, as so many of his peers did in the Cold War era? After fighting with the Workers' Party of Marxist Unification (POUM) in Spain, George Orwell soon became a prominent critic of Soviet totalitarianism, as readers of *Animal Farm* (1945) and *Nineteen Eighty-Four* (1949) will know. Likewise Stephen Spender, at one point clearly a hero of Mulgan's. As a climax to the volume of poems he edited in the period of euphoric solidarity during the Spanish Civil War, Mulgan had anthologised Spender's poem 'It is Too Late Now', a radical call to the 'fiery soul' of comrades to renounce comfort and 'advance to rebuild and sleep with friend on hill / advance to rebel' (Mulgan 1938, 177). A decade later, however, Spender was being anthologised within a very different context, this time along with Arthur Koestler and others in a volume entitled *The God that Failed* (1949) dedicated to the views of those who had lost faith in communism.

Would Mulgan have done the same? He would certainly have continued to criticise criticise Stalinist communism's abuses, as he did in Greece. At the same time, never having elevated communism to a 'religion', as he accused his New Zealand friends Ian Milner and James Bertram of doing, he was able to hold on to some of its ideals while rejecting the actions that betrayed them. The inclusiveness of the Popular Front, which incorporated what were sometimes called communists along with the Communists, underpins everything he believed in the last decade of his life. There is no doubt that Lenin's founding denunciation of capitalist imperialism continued to the end to be an article of faith with Mulgan. He would certainly have joined those voices on the left that held Britain responsible to a large extent for the tragedy of Greek politics in the post-war decades. And the united 'Front' of EAM, whose history he had shared so intimately, would have made it difficult if not impossible to accept the simplicities of Cold War ideology already evident by 1943— the polarisation of communism and anti-communism with little in between. Within today's political climate, with its rapidly shifting parameters, Mulgan's challenges and resistances seem to us to give his voice greater clarity than ever.

I | Prelude

CHAPTER 1

European Socialism in the 1930s

*There is a spirit abroad in Europe which
is finer and braver than anything that
tired continent has known for centuries,
and which cannot be withstood.*

—Frank Thompson's 'Christmas message' to his family, 22 Dec. 1943
(T.J. Thompson & E.P. Thompson 1947, 169)

In the early hours of 11 September 1943, in near full moonlight, Major John Mulgan, a New Zealander in the British special services, was parachuted under cover into remote mountain terrain in western Thessaly, in the centre of occupied Greece. It was a dangerous mission but he was well prepared: codes and silk maps concealed in trouser seams, dollars in the heels of his boots, a money belt with 50 gold sovereigns, a compass sewn into one of his fly buttons, cyanide capsules in case of capture and a Colt 45 pistol in a leather holster.[1] There would have been fear and a lot of adrenalin, but Mulgan described the moment in terms of exhilaration, citing 'a delight and inspiration' (RE 124) at the prospect of using all his skills and knowledge to sabotage and halt the progress of Greece's fascist-imperialist invaders. Having already served in the regular army for nearly four years in Ireland and then North Africa, he was confident

---

1 These details are courtesy of Simon Worrall, whose father Philip was parachuted into Greece with Mulgan.

19

the SOE posting would offer greater opportunities for initiative and cultural engagement—rather than obedience to military protocol, which he hated. He had an enormous amount to learn but at the same time could not be called a novice to Greek affairs. For his degree in English back in Auckland, he had done courses in history and ancient Greek, and he had just come from a programme of intensive training at the British camp for SOE commandos in Palestine. There, in addition to learning about parachutes, explosives and wireless transmitters, he had studied the geography, history and language of the Balkan country that was to be his home for the next thirteen months.

On landing, Mulgan and Major Philip Worrall, the Englishman who was dropped with him, were met by a small band of the region's left-wing resistance fighters calling themselves the Greek People's Liberation Army (ELAS), men who were at home in this rugged environment of the Pindus ranges inaccessible to enemy penetration. That same day, as Mulgan recorded in *Report on Experience*, he sat on a hill overlooking the plains below and the nearby town of Trikala, talking to a Greek 'general' who was later to figure prominently in his daily life as one of the partisan 'chiefs'.[2] Stefanos Sarafis, who was in his early fifties by this time, found he could talk comfortably to the new arrival, in spite of some language difficulties. Mulgan remembered it as a rather one-sided conversation, and that as a novice to the situation he 'found the military situation so strange as to be not possibly affected by any remarks of mine' (RE 137). The humility was characteristic, fundamental to Mulgan's readiness to listen and learn.

It was to be a long day, this first day in Greece. To capture its atmosphere and absorb the totality of what lay before him, Mulgan

2   Working closely with Rufus Sheppard (code-named 'Hills'), Sarafis would have been expecting him. The only 'General' at the time in the ELAS forces, Sarafis describes being in Porta (where Mulgan describes himself sitting in a café on the day of arrival) with Aris Velouhiotis, Chris Woodhouse and 'Hills' to negotiate with the British and an EDES delegation over what was to be done with the Italians, who had just surrendered (on 8 September) (Stefanos Sarafis 1980, 182). Sarafis was 52 at the time and spoke some English, just as Mulgan was now able to speak some Greek. The 'general' also appears in *Report on Experience* on pages 143 and 144 and many times in Mulgan's diary.

roams cinematically in his descriptions, as if in a long take, from distant mountains to a local child coming around chanting 'EAM-ELAS'. The Italians, who have just surrendered in huge numbers, are moving up into the hills under ELAS and Allied protection; the Germans, with their massive machinery, are surging into the fertile plains; later, in a makeshift café in the burnt-out village of Porta while continuing the military 'conference' with Sarafis, he watches the bearded *andartes* pouring in on all sides. At the end of the day, with the ouzo racing in his blood and reducing it all to a blur, the *andartes* begin to sing. All of this, Mulgan writes, 'was partisan warfare as one might have hoped to find it, friendly, and picturesque' (RE 139).

Over the next five days in Porta, however, he would have begun to pick up on the tensions beneath the surface: the uneasy relationship between the British (represented by Chris Woodhouse) and ELAS (represented by Sarafis) (Stefanos Sarafis 1980, 182). And as the Germans approached, he and fellow left-wing agent Rufus Sheppard had to escape for safety into 'the twisted ranges of the Pindus, rugged and tortured' (RE 137). The 'picturesque' delusions quickly evaporated.

Mulgan was to form a strong bond with this landscape and the people who inhabited it. Working with the *andartes* gave shape to an identity that his life thus far seemed to have prepared him for. Much of this had to do with politics.

* * *

His political views, when discussed by critics and biographers, have generally been described as left leaning but fundamentally liberal, with an emphasis on democracy and individualism. Mulgan's father Alan, a staunch pro-British liberal,[3] was instrumental in emphasising this line, which was continued, with greater nuance, by Mulgan's

---

3 In his 1958 memoir *The Making of a New Zealander*, Alan Mulgan describes how after WW1, 'I found myself moving to the Left [. . .] but I have never surrendered what I believe to be the Liberal creed' (120). Earlier, perhaps with his son in mind, he remarks that 'A visit to England has pushed many a colonial to the Left in politics' (112).

biographers Paul Day and Vincent O'Sullivan. Evidence for such a position can certainly be found in his correspondence and writing. In *Report on Experience*, completed by Mulgan in the last months of his life,[4] Chapter 3 is dedicated to his political views, and here the retrospective summary of his involvement with communist groups in Oxford contains considerable critical distancing.[5] In the same breath, however, he draws attention to the wide range of positions within the communist movement, making a clear distinction between the 'soft' communism of his fellow students in Oxford, the hard-line Stalinist position that avoided criticism and subsequently left many comrades feeling betrayed after the Molotov-Ribbentrop pact in 1939 (RE 67), and something quite different that he was to engage with on the Continent of Europe. These 'practising Communists' whom he fought alongside in Greece were a different breed altogether, 'remote from the theories of those pre-war days' (RE 69). Greece, and his experience of engagement with the revolutionary project there, stimulated and gave practical relevance to aspects of Mulgan's radicalism that had until then been mainly theoretical.

It was at Auckland University College, where he studied English, classics and history in the early 1930s, that Mulgan began to develop a tendency towards radical politics. With the Depression beginning to bite, rioting by unemployed workers in April 1932 in which he became caught up left Mulgan with an acute awareness of the importance of equality and justice, a theme which, as Dan Davin puts it, is at the root of all his writing (1962, 373).[6] Fellow student James Bertram, who also witnessed the riots, later said that the only

---

4   The memoir, finished in Athens in early 1945, was sent in March 1945 to Mulgan's wife Gabrielle in New Zealand. This manuscript was published by Oxford University Press in 1947. In 2010 a new edition came out with annotations by Peter Whiteford, Preface by Richard Mulgan and Forward by M.R.D. Foot. All quotations are from this second edition.

5   For example, he writes that 'Even if the party was always right—an unlikely contingency, men and politics being what they are—their treatment of individuals was too coldly impersonal to offer much hope of a free and fair world'; also, 'it may be true that the individual has no place of importance in the fatal evolution of our times; but it is not hard to see the defects in a system which lays claim so coldly to individual men, and, being itself without humour or humanity, sets out to legislate for mankind' (RE 68–69).

6   Davin wrote, in a review of *Report on Experience*, that the Queen Street unemployment riots 'seized his imagination and his sympathy and turned his mind towards the problem that is at the root [. . .] of his writing [. . .] how men are to live together' (1962, 373–74).

time he ever saw the habitually imperturbable Mulgan show real anger in his life was during these events, when he changed allegiance from the establishment to the hungry and desperate workers. The generation of young New Zealand men who left to study in Oxford around this time were all shaped by this climate of protest. Bertram, Davin, Cox, Milner and Mulgan—the 'Peacock' group analysed by James McNeish—all went on to engage with radical politics abroad in the years ahead. As McNeish puts it, 'They were the most political generation New Zealand had ever seen and in England they joined the most political generation in the history of Oxford' (2003, 66–67). Tremors from the Russian Revolution were being felt across the world. In New Zealand the Labour Party which eventually came to power in 1935 under Michael Joseph Savage had had a turbulent history, especially with its previous socialist leader, Harry Holland, who had spent time in gaol for his activities. Keith Sinclair's description of the context has been frequently cited:

> When the depression settled on New Zealand like 'a grey and ghastly visitor to the house'—as John Mulgan wrote in *Report on Experience*—a good many people wanted to know who had let him in. There was a quite extraordinary amount of speculation and controversy on economic questions. Marx, Keynes, the Russian Revolution, the 'New Deal', were scrutinized from every angle, not merely in academic institutions, but at trade union and farmers' meetings, and in the clubs and pubs. (1980, 264–65)

As Mulgan's novel *Man Alone* would show, these debates touched its author closely. The year after the Queen Street riots he took a stand with other students against a bid to inhibit freedom of speech for university staff—at a time, as his father Alan put it, when 'there was much fear of what was called Bolshevism'. As a result of this John may have come to be regarded in some quarters as 'a dangerous fellow', causing him to miss out on the Rhodes Scholarship which it had been assumed he would get (Day 1968, 138–39n10), although

C.K. Stead doubts this was the reason.[7] In October 1933 he left for Oxford anyway, where he had been offered a place at Merton College, on funds borrowed from his parents.

Like the many colonials who have been to study at Oxford Mulgan found the university aesthetically seductive and academically stimulating. He refused, however, to be overwhelmed by it, writing home on 4 May 1934: 'I *will* not subscribe to the feeling that old things are ipso facto beautiful & to be admired' (AGM 42). At the same time he began to distance himself from what he saw as the parochialism of New Zealand politics, telling his parents rather loftily that 'the average N.Z. revolutionary intellectual is a very lonely & useless figure [. . .] out of touch with the working class & with their own class'. His concluding remark can not have been of much comfort to his parents: 'I should love to be coming back to do something in it—because I think that as at College, I can talk with both sides—but I don't think I shall' (41). After only six months in England, his identification as European seems to have been well under way. The other New Zealanders in Oxford noticed how Mulgan's friends tended to be English grammar-school boys from working-class backgrounds on county scholarships: 'not a single public-school boy. And no Kiwis', one of them noted (McNeish 2003, 87). It was a pattern that would continue.

Red Oxford

1933, the year of Mulgan's arrival in Britain, was a crucial moment of political reappraisal after Hitler's rise to power that year. Much of this had to do with the broadening appeal of European communism. The Cambridge communist and contemporary of Mulgan's James Klugmann records that in the period 1927–32

---

7   This issue caused an acrimonious debate after the publication of Stead's essay on Mulgan in *Islands* in April 1979. In Postscripts to his essay in 1981 and then 2001 Stead details the challenges but refuses to back down on his opinion that the reason was Mulgan's weaker grades. In spite of this, his essay argues convincingly in favour of regarding Mulgan, from his time in Oxford onwards, as an unequivocally left-wing writer whose 'tone and [. . .] purpose [. . .] owes a good deal to Auden' (2013, 164).

democracy had been almost a 'dirty word' in the communist movement (1979, 25). But now, with Hitler ratcheting up a vast war machine and violating human rights with impunity, the importance of developing a concept of socialist democracy became a dominant focus of the left. Another issue that needed radical reappraisal was nationalism, which fascism was perverting for its own ends. At the Seventh Congress of the Communist Assembly in July and August 1935, definitions of democracy were revised and Marxist-Leninist concepts of nationalism and internationalism re-established. As Klugmann puts it, with international fascism gathering momentum there was an urgent need to combine patriotism with a popular and proletarian internationalism (25). This enabled many on the left who were concerned that pacifism was no longer an option to join forces on a pan-European platform. Appeasement to Hitler risked unleashing fascism on a global scale. These revised policies struck a chord in increasing numbers of people from the working class, the student population and the liberal left. Membership of the British Communist Party, numbering 2,500 in 1930, had by 1936 increased to 11,500, and then to 17,500 in 1939 (reaching 56,000 in 1942) (Klugmann 1979, 27). (The Communist Party of New Zealand had around 2,000 members in the early 1940s [Parker 1998, 16].) With unemployment at nearly three million in Britain, huge support by students in Oxford, Cambridge and other cities had been given in 1932 to the hunger marches. Klugmann records that when Scottish unionist leader Willie Gallacher visited Cambridge to speak to the growing body of Communist Party students in 1934, he issued a warning against students dropping their studies to join working-class movements. With the injunction 'Every communist student, a good student', he urged crowds to train to contribute to society on all levels. The advice, Klugmann adds, led to a significant rise in the number of first-class degrees among communist students at Oxbridge in the years that followed (34). Mulgan, graduating with a first the following year, was part of this process. Later, in *Report on Experience*, he describes himself in his Oxford period as a 'keen [. . .] reader' of Trotsky and Tom Wintringham, a prominent British Marxist journalist and founding editor in 1934 of *Left Review* (RE 84).[8]

Also at Merton College in the mid 1930s, reading for a doctorate in philosophy as a mature student, was the German intellectual who would soon become an international authority on Eurocommunism, Theodor Adorno. Adorno would later describe Mulgan to his friend Walter Benjamin as 'a rather interesting character [. . .] and a Marxist' (Adorno and Benjamin 1999, 150).[9] What Adorno meant by 'a Marxist' at this time is worth examining. The definition was shifting rapidly in response to international events and varied considerably from place to place; pinpointing it in relation to Mulgan's developing European identity is important at this stage.

Of the many forms of Marxism, Adorno's was perhaps the most 'Continental', embodying as it did the thought of the Institute of Social Research at Frankfurt University (the famous Frankfurt School), which had been forced to relocate to Geneva in 1935 (and later to New York) after the Nazi rise to power. Both Adorno and Benjamin were associated from a distance with the School at this time and were corresponding frequently about new forms of social organisation free of economic exploitation and the brutality of the totalitarian state. Both were Hegelian Marxists, less interested in party struggle than in the humanist-utopian aspects of Marx's work. Critical of recent Soviet abuses of Marx's theories, they shared the Frankfurt School's prioritisation of the writings of Marx on social and economic theory. Benjamin, who was based at this time in Paris, was working on what was to become his famous 'arcades' project, exploring the fetish nature of the commodity, a key aspect of the capitalist economy as laid out by Marx.[10] Adorno's theory of

8   In subsequent years in Oxford Mulgan would have become aware of Tom Wintringham's role in the Spanish Civil War. At the start of the war in the autumn of 1936 Wintringham went to Barcelona as a journalist for the *Daily Worker*, but soon joined and then commanded the British Battalion of the International Brigades. Wounded in February 1937, he befriended one of Mulgan's favourite novelists, Ernest Hemingway, who used Wintringham as a character in *For Whom the Bell Tolls* (1940). Wintringham was again wounded in August when he returned to fighting.

9   On his way back from Geneva in 1936 Mulgan shared a train journey from Paris to Dieppe with Adorno. The two got on well, it seems: Mulgan wrote to his parents that they had 'talked until we were at Dieppe' (LJB 172).

10   *Passagenwerk* or *Arcades Project* was begun in 1927 and left unfinished due to Benjamin's

the 'culture industry' would be developed over the next decade. At this time, however, apart from his doctoral thesis on Husserl he was also working towards the writing of *Dialectic of Enlightenment* with Max Horkheimer (first published privately during the war, in 1944), which explores the rise of bourgeois subjectivity; other work at the time included articles on the social function of jazz.

Although it would be stretching it to argue that Mulgan wrote from the same historical-materialist standpoint as Adorno, he was undoubtedly influenced by university debates about how literature needed to be written and analysed. Reading English at Cambridge at the same time as Mulgan in Oxford, James Klugmann noted the way impatience was mounting in the 1930s in opposition to literary criticism as gossip about the author rather than 'the reciprocal relationship of literature and society', 'the influence of everything on everything' (1979, 34). After finishing his studies, Mulgan worked at the Clarendon Press (the scholarly branch of Oxford University Press), where he gained experience in anthologising literary texts as mediated through their historical determinants. And the novel he was to write himself in the next few years, *Man Alone*, could be interpreted as playing out, in the Adorno-Horkheimer manner, 'a model of experience in which the subject might be seen to engage with the object [society] without either being reduced to the object or choosing in Sartrean manner its own mode of experience' (Brian O'Connor 2000, 15). Mulgan's Marxism, like Adorno's, is somewhat different from Sartre's, with its insistence on the freedom of individual choice, and is more inclined to put the subject in dialectical relation with the prevailing power structures. In a spirit similar to Adorno and Horkheimer's humanist socialism, Mulgan shared with many Continental Marxists the attempt at this time to steer a course between mechanistic interpretations of Marx adopted by the Soviets and a decaying Western capitalism. For the Frankfurt School, as much as for him, however, the immediate enemy was fascism. Adorno would also go on in the years ahead to devise

suicide in 1940. It consists of a huge collection of writings on Paris in the nineteenth century. The full text of the unfinished work was finally published by Harvard University Press in 1999.

what he called the F-scale, which charted the degrees of fascist traits in different human personalities.

Mulgan's work at the Clarendon Press gave him plenty of opportunities to express and develop his political views. A significant collaborator was W.H. Auden who, along with others like Stephen Spender, Cecil Day Lewis and Louis MacNeice, had prepared the ideological ground at the university a few years earlier. After graduating, Auden undertook some of the country's most radical experiments in committed, left-wing literature. One lesser-known example is the play he wrote with Christopher Isherwood, *On the Frontier*, first produced in October 1938 at the Cambridge Arts Theatre by the London Group Theatre, with music composed by Benjamin Britten. The play depicts the outbreak of war between two fictional European countries and highlights some of the major features of British politics in the mid to late 1930s: workers' agitation and strikes, student radicalism, the lure of pacifism, bourgeois disdain for the 'never-never land' of socialism, the manic rhetoric of the fascist leader, and the bigotry and greed underlying the 'patriotic' drive to war. Along with the fascist called Leader, the villain of the piece is the smooth industrialist Valerian, who plans (unsuccessfully) to sit the conflict out and get richer in the process, prompting the Second Leftist to warn that 'The country is in danger / But not from any stranger. / Your enemies are here / Whom you should fight, not fear' (Auden and Isherwood 1958, 154). Clearly reminiscent of Brecht and Weill's *Threepenny Opera* in its socialist critique of capitalism as well as its musical format with fragments of prose, verse and song, the play reads like a pastiche of voices on the left at the time. It ends, however, with a song between the two lovers who are attempting to escape it all— just as Auden and Isherwood would soon do in their flight to the United States.

Auden was to renounce his socialist writings in later years, but when he was collaborating with Mulgan at the Press, between 1936 and 1938, his charismatic personality and opinions struck a strong chord in Mulgan, who told his parents he found the Englishman 'extraordinarily attractive both to look at and to talk to' (LJB 184). Vincent O'Sullivan gives a fascinating account of Mulgan's first collaboration with Auden over the latter's edition of *The Oxford Book of Light Verse* (1938), with citations from the correspondence between the two men held in the Oxford University Press archives. Auden was pursuing what was to become a life-long passion for popular verse: ballads and nursery rhymes, nonsense verse and doggerel, going back to medieval times. Some of the material was rather too close to the edge for respectable taste. O'Sullivan describes the 'ticking off' Mulgan got from those in higher places in the Press, partly for sloppy checking of references but more seriously for allowing through some irreverent and indecent material. Auden was used to this sort of reaction. 'The English are like that', he joked with Mulgan in mid 1938: '*Not* New Zealand I hope. Fukkit passes because it is medieval and scholars are past hope' (LJB 183).

It was around this time, with the defeat of the Republican cause in Spain and the seeming capitulation of the British to Hitler's continuing imperialist drive in Europe, that Mulgan started writing what O'Sullivan calls 'railing' letters home, abandoning his habitual mode of reasoned debate. His quarrel was with 'the great wet mass of middle classes of whom [D.H.] Lawrence prophesied that they would go soft inside', whose only interest was self-interest. Liberty, he wrote, could no longer be guaranteed them: 'I have never before felt myself so much out of sympathy with England as a whole', he wrote home on 10 October 1937 (LJB 185–86). A few months later, his fury at what he described as British 'capitalism destroying itself' had reached such a pitch that he was writing:

> At times I've looked forward with a sort of gloomy pleasure to the destruction of this country and its selfish intolerant ruling classes. As it comes nearer, I can see how much that might have been enlightened and fine is going to be lost. As you look back to 1935, saw how they sabotaged the League [of Nations]—rather than risk communism in Italy—how things have got worse ever

since, how the democracies throughout Europe feel themselves betrayed, the Americans turning away disgusted, the splendid fight that the Spanish people put up going for nothing—it isn't any real satisfaction to know that all these people will destroy each other. (AGM 133)

Mulgan was to get very good at keeping the lid on such rage in the years ahead, but occasional outbursts to those closest to him indicate that his hostility to the British ruling classes (Auden's 'The country is in danger / But not from any stranger') was to be a recurrent theme.

There is an Audenesque disdain to this new impatience. Like many on the left at this time, Auden's focus was primarily Continental European. His time in Berlin in the late 1920s and early 1930s had given him a perspective on English conservatism, including (and perhaps predominantly) its repressively normative attitude to sexual identity, that resulted in liberation from a sense of national identity and a surge of political writing. In his landmark study of the decade entitled *The Auden Generation* (1976), Samuel Hynes wrote (with some resonance for our post-Brexit era): 'A sense of community with Europe has not, traditionally, been an English feeling, but by 1935 many Englishmen felt it' (176). The readiness with which Auden cast off his Englishness would have appealed to the young Mulgan, already fairly advanced along the path to a post-colonial radicalism.

The next collaboration between the two men was for the left-wing publisher Victor Gollancz, a poetry anthology to be entitled *Poems of Revolt*, edited by Mulgan and with an Introduction by Auden. Their brief was to offer the reading public a survey of poems, past and present, which challenged the status quo and gave voice to the drive towards equality and justice. Many of the poems Mulgan chose are concerned with class difference and rebellion, from literature of the Peasants' Revolt of 1381 to the poem he singles out for particular attention, William Morris's 'Death Song', written after the police violence against demonstrators in Trafalgar Square in 1887. In his Editorial Note, Mulgan praises the way Morris 'wrote his socialist poems deliberately and conscientiously for a popular audience' and quotes: 'We asked them for a life of toilsome earning, / They bade us bide their leisure for our bread' (Mulgan 1938, 12). This was noticed by Australian-born Marxist writer Jack Lindsay, who reviewed the volume for *Left News*. Mulgan deserves praise, he wrote, for the way he keeps class-consciousness in focus as well as the way the poems speak 'from the humanist core of revolt against a world where money-values crucify the individual' (LJB 186). Auden begins his Introduction to the volume somewhat defensively, indicating the way his focus by this time was shifting from social protest to psychological impact (he was reading Freud).[11] 'Reading this anthology will teach no one how to run a state or raise a revolution', he writes. But he repeats what had become axiomatic for many: the need to record the history and presence of oppression in English society:

> The details of our circumstances of injustice change, so does our knowledge of what is unjust and how best to remedy it, but our feelings change little. [. . .] The primary function of poetry, as of all the arts, is to make us more aware of ourselves and the world around us. (Auden 1938, 8–9)[12]

But the timing for the volume's reception was not favourable. Assessing the reviews a few months later, Mulgan wrote to his father that although the *Times Literary Supplement* had reviewed it 'very fairly', he wasn't surprised that, given the climate, other publishers 'tend to boycott Gollancz' more political publications' (AGM 147). As war became increasingly likely, the mood was changing fast; late in the day, Gollancz thought it wise to change the title from *Poems of Revolt* to *Poems of Freedom*.

---

11 Auden's well-known essay on 'Psychology and Art To-day' (1935) outlines the therapeutic function of poetry, for both poet and reader.

12 Auden's biographer writes that given Auden's prominence as a Marxist poet, Mulgan could have expected a more radical thesis from his collaborator (LJB 186).

The Eurocentric turn and
the 'millennium year of 1936'[13]

It was during the four years between finishing his degree and joining
the army that Mulgan's political views were most significantly
consolidated. The wider Oxford environment brought him into
contact with many like-minded writers and activists, and his reading
and contacts at the time provide an impressive record of what
energetic networking and enthusiastic commitment could achieve.

Probably the best indication of Mulgan's political thinking at
this time is the series of 'Behind the Cables' columns he wrote with
Geoffrey Cox for the *Auckland Star* and the *Dominion* between
January 1936 and July 1937, some 43 articles published on a roughly
fortnightly basis. As O'Sullivan records, the two men held very
similar views on the political situation and took turns to write the
column, with the author's name appearing first on the by-line (LJB
162). This was a period of intensely optimistic left-wing activism in
Europe, and although their brief was to send a more sophisticated
account of British affairs than was available from the cable news
most New Zealand papers depended on, the interest of both men
was primarily in foreign policy, in particular European politics.
They were, in a sense, in the eye of the storm. From October of the
previous year, Italy's forces had been invading Abyssinian territory,
a conflict which was to draw Europe's attention to the dangers of
fascist-imperialist aggression. And then in the middle of the series (in
July 1936) the Spanish Civil War broke out, galvanising the whole
of European political attention. Both conflicts had a profound effect
on Mulgan in this immediately pre-war period.

In the first 'Behind the Cables' column, the Abyssinian crisis
featured as representing the failure of the British and French
governments to intervene and halt Mussolini's aggression. The next
month the authors expressed disappointment in Anthony Eden
who, as a young Foreign Secretary, had held out promise of a tough
stand against Italy through oil sanctions but had now seemingly

13   RE 67.

been 'curbed by the older statesmen' in the Conservative Party.[14] A repeated point of reference throughout the columns is the Hoare-Laval pact, the notorious secret agreement between Britain's Sir Samuel Hoare and the French Prime Minister, Pierre Laval, partially to dismember Abyssinia in Italy's favour. The plan, leaked to the press, had caused a major scandal the previous December. By May, Geneva, seat of the League of Nations, was being described by the New Zealand pair (Mulgan writing) as 'a name of ill-omen at the moment—home of abandoned causes and lost ideals', with calls from the left 'to restore Britain's lost prestige' and 'save the principle of collective security' (21 May 1936).

The 'collective security' versus 'isolationism' debate, initiated by the Abyssinian crisis, was to reverberate throughout their columns. Mulgan and Cox's view was that those countries (like Britain) holding to an isolationist position were simply seeking to further their own interests at a time of approaching disaster when the only hope was in a pan-European collectivity capable of resisting fascism. After the Germans broke the Treaty of Versailles and occupied the Rhineland on 7 March, most people continued pandering to Hitler. Only the communist *Daily Worker*, Mulgan wrote, 'stood against our holding out the hand of friendship to Germany.' All the other newspapers were 'speaking with one voice' on the opposing side (7 April). Mulgan and Cox had a particular axe to grind with two aristocratic newspaper magnates in Britain: Major Astor, a Tory MP and hugely wealthy proprietor of *The Times*, and Lord Rothermere, proprietor of the *Evening News* and the *Daily Mail*, Britain's top-selling newspaper. Attacks on 'Bolshevism' in these papers, they record, regularly reached hysterical levels. Lady Nancy Astor, Major Astor's sister-in-law and someone in a position to influence newspaper policy, is mocked as the sort for whom communists are 'large people who eat babies for breakfast' (1 August 1936, 8). In Lord Rothermere's papers, 'every rumour of a rumour of an atrocity becomes headline news'—provided it is committed by 'the Reds'

14   'Behind the Cables', *Auckland Star*, 31 Mar. 1936, 6. paperspast.natlib.govt.nz/newspapers/
     AS19360212.2.41. (All further references to this column in the text are to this site. Unless
     otherwise stated, the column appeared on page 6.)

(2 September). Such tactics would become familiar to Mulgan later in Greece, where a government-controlled press attributed all atrocities to the left. Equally prescient are Mulgan's observations about Hitler's manoeuvrings. Given the severely weakened state of the German economy in 1936, he wrote, Hitler will have to go on 'try[ing] out the method which so many dictators have employed when discontent grows at home—the pursuit of triumphs in the field of foreign affairs'; 'He will have to go on having these circuses to hide the fact that there is too little bread' (15 April).

By July, however, all other topics had been swept aside by the outbreak of civil war in Spain. From the start, Mulgan and Cox interpreted this war in ideological terms, as between left and right, between Spain's elected socialist government and Franco's fascist challenge to it. This divide, they wrote, will split Europe 'into two sections hostile beyond all possibility of reconciliation.' By now, they viewed the League of Nations as 'bankrupt and impotent', unsupported by an apathetic Cabinet of the National government of 'tired [. . .] elderly men' (Stanley Baldwin, Ramsay MacDonald, Neville Chamberlain) with no one to replace them, least of all the Opposition. The only hope was a 'radical reconstitution of the Ministry' before the autumn (24 August).

Mulgan had the opportunity to verify things first hand when he was selected to represent New Zealand as an observer at the League in September. The fortnight in Geneva attending meetings of the Assembly did little to raise hope of meaningful action. At briefings in London before they left, the New Zealand delegation 'sat around', Mulgan wrote to his parents, 'and talked gloomily about Fascism and how England had wrecked the League' (LJB 166).[15] In *Report on Experience* nearly a decade later Mulgan referred to the Abyssinian crisis as a watershed moment of betrayal of international justice. As economic interests drove the world forward to war, he recorded bitterly, 'Passengers dropped by the way were the Negus of

15   The New Zealand group attributed this pessimism in part to 'the shadow cast by the recent great failure of the League in the Italian-Abyssinian dispute' (report on the League of Nations Assembly to the New Zealand Parliament by High Commissioner to London Bill Jordan, cited in LJB 168).

Abyssinia, several million Chinese, and the Spanish people' (RE 48).
In Geneva the Spanish delegate Del Vayo protested about the lack
of international solidarity for his country and Mulgan was appalled
at the way 'everyone is getting ready to recognise the new fascist
government' in Spain. 'It doesn't look very pleasant', he wrote to his
parents again on 28 September,

> to see [British Foreign Secretary Anthony] Eden coming into
> the assembly, cold-shouldering Del Vayo, chatting cheerfully
> with the Portuguese [who, as he and Cox were reporting, were
> supplying the fascist rebels with arms].[16] It sounds absurd but
> Whitehall would rather have a fascist Spain, and lose Gibraltar
> and the Mediterranean, than have what they call the Moscow
> peril coming near them with its threat to their own property and
> regime. (AGM 108)

These betrayals were sharpening Mulgan's nerve for future
encounters. But the tide of apathy seemed to be turning. As George
Orwell was to put it in *Homage to Catalonia*, although 53 nations
had merely made 'pious noises "off"' when Mussolini bombed the
Abyssinians, the recent rebellion of the Spanish people seemed to
hold out new hope of stronger international support (2000, 199).

The Spanish conflict became the kernel of what Mulgan thought
World War 2 would really be about: first confronting fascism, but
then, more fundamentally, the need for international solidarity in
the struggle against capitalist exploitation. In *Report on Experience* he
ponders the way future generations would judge those like himself
who failed to join Orwell and Tom Wintringham: 'They will ask why
we didn't get killed in Spain' (RE 64). His inactivity seems to have
left residues of unresolved remorse; it was a common feeling at the
time.[17] Greece, in the end, was to be Mulgan's Spain, the opportunity

16 At the end of the column for 21 September 1936, Mulgan and Cox record that Germany and
    Italy, despite a professed commitment to neutrality in the Spanish conflict, 'are still sending
    arms to Portugal, which is openly in sympathy with the rebels [under Franco].'
17 McNeish records a conversation between Mulgan and Geoffrey Cox in Oxford soon after the
    outbreak of the war: 'Cox [. . .] felt sick over Spain. Like Mulgan he was filled with remorse

he craved to take an active stand against different forms of fascism and capitalist imperialism: that of the occupying Axis powers, as well as of a home-grown Greek variety increasingly supported, as the war went on, by the British furthering their own imperialist interests. 1936 was the year of reckoning. As events in Spain dominated headlines, Cox and Mulgan reported that 'A military dictatorship in Greece, set up to break an abortive stay-in strike, threw another stone this week into the troubled European pool; so far there have been few international repercussions' (27 August). From spring onwards, Greek workers had been demonstrating throughout the country, calling for a decent living wage. In response the Greek king (George II), who'd been returned to Greece only the year before, gave Prime Minister General Ioannis Metaxas a mandate to suspend Parliament and in effect become dictator. Ripples of this brutal anti-communist regime were to spread well into the already turbulent European pool and parallels with Spain would become all too evident in the decade ahead. As well as an agrarian economy, Spain and Greece shared a social fabric plagued by fascist elements strongly resisted, however, from within—all of which would play out tragically in a prolonged and brutal civil war.

Writing about Spain: Mulgan with Orwell and Auden

The first reference Mulgan makes to writing a novel comes in this very month (August 1936), when he told his parents it was 'about half done' (AGM 102). As if spurred into action by news from the Iberian Peninsula, he began working memories of his homeland into a new frame: the call to political responsibility, distant yet ultimately inescapable. His novel would be finished and sent for publication in 1939. In the three years of intermittent writing before the outbreak of war, he would have come across other literary representations of this same call. Two in particular may have left their mark on him in different ways.

and felt he should be there.' Cox eventually did go, as a reporter for the *News Chronicle* in October 1936. 'I'd rather go and fight', Mulgan is recorded as saying (McNeish 2003, 95).

One was *Homage to Catalonia* (1938) by George Orwell, whose voice from the left reverberated prominently in this decade. Written immediately after his return from six months' fighting in Spain alongside the partisans of the Workers' Party of Marxist Unification (POUM: Partido Obrero de Unificación Marxista), the book opens with an arresting description of a fellow volunteer, a young Italian he met on arrival at the Lenin Barracks in Barcelona:

> He was a tough-looking youth of twenty-five or -six, with reddish-yellow hair and powerful shoulders. His peaked leather cap was pulled fiercely over one eye. He was standing in profile to me, his chin on his breast, gazing with a puzzled frown at a map which one of the officers had open on the table. Something in his face deeply moved me. It was the face of a man who would commit murder and throw away his life for a friend—the kind of face you would expect in an Anarchist, though as likely as not he was a Communist [. . .] obviously he regarded map-reading as a stupendous intellectual feat. I hardly know why, but I have seldom seen anyone—any man, I mean—to whom I have taken such an immediate liking. [. . .] As we went out he stepped across the room and gripped my hand very hard. Queer, the affection you can feel for a stranger! It was as though his spirit and mine had momentarily succeeded in bridging the gulf of language and tradition and meeting in utter intimacy. (Orwell 2000, 1–2)

Here's that word 'intimacy' again. This almost visionary moment is unusual in Orwell's writing: most of the book keeps closely to a terse record of the daily trials and tedium, the progress of the war and the political manoeuvrings. But as it was to be for Mulgan in Greece, it was such moments that defined his allegiances and identification with the revolutionary cause. Words like 'Queer' and 'I hardly know why' point to the unconscious nature of such identifications. Many in their position were drawn to such causes, although few (including Orwell himself) retained the commitment despite disappointments and setbacks. Like Orwell, Mulgan was often to experience intense exasperation in the face of 'the gulf of language and tradition' between himself and the comrades, and the brutality, betrayals and factionalism that crept in as time went on, particularly as outside forces became involved. But what distinguished both men from others was a willingness to enter into the comrades' mental and physical space, to relate with trust to others in the group, and to be deeply touched by their basic 'decency', as both men repeatedly call it.[18] Both were passionately anti-hierarchical. Orwell writes often about his enthusiasm for the egalitarian atmosphere among the POUM militia, where men could and often did challenge officers on policy. Five years later, chafing under the hierarchies of the regular British army in the North African desert, Mulgan would throw it all in and seek a new kind of commitment. What he would find in southern Thessaly was another model of equality and fraternity; he was to be one of very few British Liaison Officers to refer to the *andartes* as 'comrades'. Like Orwell's Barcelona, the Government of Free Greece in the mountains (PEEA) would represent for Mulgan 'a microcosm of a classless society' (Orwell 2000, 88). What Orwell writes about his experience on the Aragon front in 1937 could have been written by Mulgan about his experience in the Greek mountains a few years later:

> I had dropped more or less by chance into the only community
> of any size in Western Europe where political consciousness and
> disbelief in capitalism were more normal than the opposite. Up
> here in Aragón one was among tens of thousands of people, mainly
> though not entirely of working-class origin, all living at the same
> level and mingling on terms of equality [. . .] the prevailing mental
> atmosphere was that of Socialism. Many of the normal motives
> of civilized life—snobbishness, money-grubbing, fear of the boss,
> etc.—had simply ceased to exist. The ordinary class-division of

18   Freud explains this in terms of a horizontal and egalitarian identification among people in a group, as opposed to that other tendency in group dynamics, the vertical and hierarchical subordination to a leader. The main exploration of these phenomena comes in Freud's 'Mass Psychology and Analysis of the "I"' (Freud 2004, 15–100). For a fuller psychological reading, see Parkin-Gounelas 2012.

society had disappeared to an extent that is almost unthinkable
in the money-tainted air of England. [. . .] Of course such a state
of affairs could not last. [. . .] But it lasted long enough to have its
effect upon anyone who experienced it. However much one cursed
at the time, one realized afterwards that one had been in contact
with something strange and valuable. (87–88)

There is no evidence that Mulgan read Orwell's book although,
given his voracious reading in the Oxford period, it is not unlikely.
But the 'spirit abroad in Europe' described by Frank Thompson
was in the air, stirring deep instincts that would find conscious
expression in many at the time. James Bertram was to have a similar
experience of socialism in action at Mao's headquarters in Yenan in
1937, described by McNeish as 'a cross between a mass mobilisation
centre and a democratic Marxist kibbutz' (2003, 143–44).

W.H. Auden's literary response to Spain, a poem written after his
return in the early stages of the Civil War, was to become something
of a *cause célèbre* at the time. His departure had been applauded
by many on the left in Britain who had come to feel that joining
the International Brigades represented a last stand against fascism.[19]
Auden was not to take Orwell's approach; he volunteered to drive
an ambulance but ended up giving a few broadcasts in English for a
Republican radio station and stayed only two months. But his poem
'Spain' continues to this day to stand for the political fervour of
that struggle, despite Auden's own later denunciation of it. Orwell's
initial reaction to the poem was not enthusiastic either. But by the
end of the 1930s he conceded that it was, after all, 'one of the few
decent things that have been written about the Spanish war' (Bryant
1997, 100). First appearing in May 1937, the poem was an early
response, when its author was hardly in a position to predict the
outcome of the war. It was not, either, an eye-witness account from
the front line, raising scorn in some quarters as to its credentials.
Its appearance as a single-poem pamphlet with proceeds going to

---

19   Among these was a writer for the *Daily Worker* on 12 January 1937, who referred to Auden as
'the most famous of the younger English poets [. . . and] a leading figure in the anti-Fascist
movement in literature' (Hynes 1976, 251).

Medical Aid for Spain,[20] however, made its commitment clear. As a result the poem was to raise political and aesthetic questions which define many of the debates of the era.

Auden frames his poem with an historical survey: the invention of cartwheels and clocks, Chinese trade routes, the trials of heretics and witches, the 'construction of railways in the colonial desert' (Cunningham 1986, 1). All this was 'Yesterday', the word intoned on every second line in the first six stanzas. Yesterday's inventions and superstitions defined human aspiration. But from the fourth stanza, the present enters history in counterpoint: 'but to-day the struggle'. Something has stirred people, internationally, a rallying cry producing Frank Thompson's 'chemical change' in forces of nature beyond individual choice. For Auden it was like a biological drive, deeper than consciousness:

> Many have heard it on remote peninsulas,
> On sleepy plains, in the aberrant fisherman's islands
> Or the corrupt heart of the city,
> Have heard and migrated like gulls or the seeds of a flower. (3)

We remember Auden's words about oppression in his Introduction to Mulgan's volume, how 'our feelings change little', in spite of the different forms oppression has taken throughout history. In his other politically committed poem of the period, 'September 1, 1939', he again invokes the mismanagement of democracy and dictatorship, which Thucydides warned must be endured over and over again, the lesson never learnt. In that poem he is inclined to lay the blame at the door of capitalism, or rather of Luther, whose theology initiated the 'competitive excuse' that 'has driven a culture mad'.[21] In 'Spain', his theme is not continuity but the break in history, the way the war ('to-day') represented an indelible line between yesterday and tomorrow. The 'Tomorrows' of the penultimate stanzas offer an

---

20   Auden revised and reprinted the poem as 'Spain 1937' in *Another Time* (1940).

21   Auden, 'September 1, 1939', poets.org/poem/september-1-1939. Date of access 19 Feb. 2019.

uneasy reassurance, at best 'all the fun under / Liberty's masterful shadow', or the illusions of democracy dominated by industry and capital: 'The eager election of chairmen / By the sudden forest of hands' (3–4). The poem catalogues bourgeois addictions such as 'the medicine ad', 'the brochure of winter cruises' and 'the chain-store' (3). In this way, as critics such as Stan Smith have noted, Auden undermines the false 'liberal antithesis' between public and private experience, one ultimately impossible to maintain, as the current climate was demonstrating. This makes 'Spain' what Smith calls 'an interventionist polemic' attacking western culture's inability to link the personal to the encroaching context of history and politics (Bryant 1997, 105). Later, in the post-war period, Auden did not welcome being labelled a 'polemicist' and would insist that his dedication was to language alone. (He excluded both these poems from all collections of his poetry after 1945.) But as a recognised Marxist at the time, in a poem dedicated to the cause, he could not prevent 'Spain' being read in terms of commitment, could not avoid invoking history's power to determine meaning. Its context defined it. The last words of the poem may state that history 'cannot help nor pardon' (4). Its power to determine a response is nonetheless an inevitable product of the moment ('to-day'), of its inscription in art. Auden may have denounced his poem, but it made its way without his endorsement.

The challenge of balancing the demands of the aesthetic against the call of political commitment was one that Mulgan too was negotiating in the months between 1936 and 1939 as he worked to finish *Man Alone*. There has been considerable debate about the extent to which it can be read as a Marxist novel, not least because Mulgan frames the narrative within the Spanish Civil War, which the protagonist, the Englishman Johnson, ends up going to join on the side of the Republican Army. Dougal McNeill is right to argue that the link between Mulgan and Marxism has been made 'too glibly', that critics of *Man Alone* have failed to clarify whether it is a matter of form or content or something else, which is at issue (2012, 3, 7–8). Its 'Hemingwayesque' style (the phrase is Mulgan's own [AGM 147]) of terse narrative and exteriority of speech and action was noted by James Bertram in an influential review in 1940 (1985, 41), and invites comparison with socialist realism. But when Mulgan apologised to his father in March 1939 that it was 'a very political novel, I fear' (AGM 147), he was probably referring to thematic issues such as the explicit empathy for the unemployed and exploited farm labourers in New Zealand. This comment to his father shows Mulgan's tendency in his most committed personal statements (as with that about the 'regrettable intimacy' with EAM-ELAS) to duck behind a coy façade. He repeatedly referred to his novel, which was to take on iconic status both at home and abroad (where it has been taught in courses on post-colonial literature), as 'dull' and 'lack[ing] conviction' (AGM 152, 175). Few readers would agree.

Some analysis of the novel has focused on the 'man alone' theme, on 'individual endurance and independence' as defining the national (masculine) character and forming the 'foundation of the good society' (Day 1968, 111, 109). But this interpretation fails to recognise that most individuals like Johnson are products of the Great War and, like the 'tired' and 'elderly' politicians in the British Cabinet, have adopted a stance of defensive isolationism in response to its horrors. Mulgan often talked about the antagonism between this generation and his own.[22] These men, as he put it in an essay in the mid 1930s, 'did not see themselves as part of a system, and they had not been born to accept the world'.[23] 'It is only in the new countries' (like New Zealand), Mulgan continues, 'that you can live like that and the chance may go from there in time' (2011b, 62). As Johnson lies in bed at the end of *Man Alone* 'trying to work out in himself what it was beyond [. . .] that he could want', he finally rejects the life of these 'quiet soft-spoken, and honest' men in favour

22   See, for example, *Report on Experience*, where he describes how the Great War 'tired out those who survived' and who subsequently 'played for safety', setting them in opposition to the next generation, 'who wanted action and belief and found neither'. Between these generations, he writes, 'there grew up a genuine hatred, rare and peculiar to those times.' Then, as if describing the inter-war British policies summed up in the 'Behind the Cables' columns, he continues: 'It was the era of prevarication, of the smooth parliamentary reply, the government commission, the committee of reference' (RE 63).

23   The essay, entitled 'Rustic Witness: An Interlude' and included at the end of *Journey to Oxford*, describes a conversation with a war veteran, a solitary farm labourer, in a pub in Buckinghamshire.

of 'a life active [. . .] and men moving, making something together' (Mulgan 2021, 212–13)—collectivity and solidarity, in other words, as against a life of isolation, however alluringly idyllic it may seem. Vincent O'Sullivan's reading of the novel strikes exactly right. Its concern, he writes, is with the horrors of isolation in a country 'dislocated by capitalism's failure', which has driven a 'wedge between man and man' (LJB 192–93). Mulgan's protagonist, he continues, shares his author's 'existential drive to press value from the grit of immediate experience', his realisation that it is 'only in working-class solidarity, and in shared radical enterprise' that society can hold out some satisfaction (LJB 195–96). It would be another five or so years before Mulgan had the opportunity to put this conviction to the test in his own life, when he joined the left-wing partisans in Greece.

C.K. Stead described *Man Alone* as 'basically Marxist in structure' (2013, 162). But the problem, as McNeill demonstrates, is not just with style or theme or structure but with the slipperiness of the term 'Marxist' itself, which could include anything from Stalinism to Eurocommunism, as well as a New Zealand version of socialism, all terms taking on different shades of interpretation at the time. Mulgan's position within this spectrum was never straightforward but he certainly retained from his Oxford days a Continental 'humanist (democratic) socialist' emphasis based on the economic teachings of Marx and Lenin. Like so many at the time, he had lost faith in free-market liberalism, noting the way its abuses across the British Empire were fuelling anti-colonial reaction. His experiences in Greece were to reinforce this position. Mulgan himself thought, wrongly, that his novel would interest only 'my family and left-wing friends', as he wrote to his wife Gabrielle in June 1941 (Day 1977, 26). He was underestimating the appeal its gritty, low-key realism and evocation of the New Zealand landscape and ethos would have in the post-war climate. But for all this, as the novel shows, New Zealand is ultimately a place to be escaped from, as Mulgan himself certainly felt at this time.[24] What is important from the perspective of this

---

24   He wrote to Gabrielle in Canada in July 1940: 'I feel strangely about New Zealand. I don't think it's any place to go to, never want to go back to it myself, it's an unreal place that won't endure these times, it was like being brought up in a national park owned by England to come

terrifying moment in history, when war was about to be declared, is the way *Man Alone* ends not in gloom or escapism, like so much other fiction of the time, but rather with a bracing resignation underneath it all (in Johnson) offset by the politically radical O'Reilly's optimism about the possibility of a different social organisation in the future, after the Spanish war was over. Johnson feels he's 'knocked around' in life; the socialist and union man O'Reilly, who's fought with the IRA, counters that he's '*been* knocked around, that's what you've done' (Mulgan 2021, 219, emphasis added). In this dialectic between knocking around and being knocked around, it is suggested, what can't be killed is not so much Johnson the individual as his stubborn expectation of something bigger, 'a life active' with 'men moving, making something together.' Although the novel shares a sense of 'tense irresolution' which Peter Widdowson defines as characteristic of much English fiction of this period (1979, 134), it leaves us in no doubt that the forces Johnson has been unwittingly engaged in will be carried forward. The inward turn in Modernist fiction of the 1920s (Lawrence, Joyce, Woolf) had given way to the story of a man with little interiority, a figure more consonant with the Frankfurt School's perception that humans are the product of society down to their innermost core. Personal anxiety was a luxury the time could ill afford. These impulses have their roots in a politics which would guide Mulgan through the much larger war ahead of him.

The Popular Front

With the outbreak of the Spanish Civil War in July 1936, pacifism on the left declined rapidly as most progressives began to understand that appeasement was no longer an option. With left and right increasingly polarised and existing political parties fast changing shape, left-wing socialists like Mulgan were confronted by a wide range of conflicting or overlapping political affiliations. It was out of this maelstrom of shifting definitions that a movement which

from there, I would like Richard [their son] to grow up in Canada or the States or Russia, one of the big places, for even in that last God forsaken country there is something that will endure & they will be reading Marx long after we are dead' (AGM 175–76).

sought to unite everyone on the left emerged: the Popular Front.

On 16 February 1936, the month Mulgan and Cox's first 'Behind the Cables' column was published, the Frente Popular, a coalition of left-wing republicans and workers' organisations, was elected into office in Spain. Mulgan and Cox followed its progress with intense interest and when, three months later, the French Front Populaire won a landslide victory in the legislative elections, the tone of their reporting warmed to the point of fervour. On 18 June, Mulgan concluded the last of ten consecutive columns he himself had authored with a section on the Popular Front, stating that though these were still early days, 'bigger things may come from this small beginning.' From June 4 the Front Populaire government was headed by the charismatic Léon Blum of the French section of the Workers' International (SFIO). From this point on, 'Behind the Cables' began to refer to the Franco-Soviet approach as providing reasons for optimism, in particular its 'determin[ation] to do something to improve the lot of the workers'. Blum, the authors noted, had been drawn to socialism through friendship with Jean Jaurès, the prominent socialist leader who was assassinated in Paris at the outbreak of WW1 and whose heterodox version of Marxism opened the philosophy up to broad European appeal. France is one more reminder, they wrote, 'that the situation in Europe is coming, more and more clearly, to appear as a series of contests between Communism and Capitalism.' Intensifying government control, in the direction of either fascism (in Germany), 'standing for the protection of the capitalist system', or socialism (in Spain, France, Denmark, Belgium and Russia), 'aiming at building up a new, more internationally-minded economic order', was forcing the Continent into two factions of irreconcilable opposition. Meanwhile, the authors concluded with a trace of derision, these movements, though rumbling underneath, 'seem to trouble the surface of English life little,' with cricket and Wimbledon at the centre of attention (1 July 1936).

Though more tentatively, similar attempts to unite the left against capitalism *were* beginning to bear fruit in Britain. Mulgan and Cox describe these against a backdrop of disillusionment with the Labour Party, the traditional home of the left. In a column on April 7 recording Germany's takeover of the Rhineland, a hysterical speech by Hitler denouncing Bolshevism and a report indicating that half the population of Britain is malnourished, Mulgan complains about Labour's lack of 'courageous and intelligent leadership' in both foreign and domestic policy. Only an 'uneasy association' between the Communist Party and a few Tories like Churchill, he records in the next column on April 15, is following the 'Franco-Soviet view' and expressing concern about Hitler's intentions. Britain's so-called National Government, a Tory, Liberal and Labour coalition, was being overtaken by Tories, Mulgan complains on 18 June, with the Tory leader Stanley Baldwin giving only a pathetic 'smiling' response to fierce denunciations from the Labour party and Tory backbenchers alike. But more positive initiatives had already begun to gather pace.

Two and a half years earlier, when Mulgan first arrived in Oxford, he had attended a meeting addressed by Harold Laski from the London School of Economics, an influential Marxist in the interwar years who had close links with members of the Institute of Social Research (the Frankfurt School) such as Adorno. The meeting 'was extraordinarily interesting', Mulgan wrote to his parents, 'a protest against Fascism called by [A.D.] Lindsay, Head of Balliol. Laski is a brilliant speaker—one of the best that I have ever heard'. He continued:

> The feeling down here is very tense—knots of fascists & communists ready to fight at any moment. Campbell, editor of the 'Daily Worker' spoke at the end of the meeting—a small, worn man with burning eyes—most impressive. I feel as if things are going to happen. (AGM 28)

Within a couple of years things were indeed happening—in limited pockets of activity. Many on the Labour left joined the Independent Labour Party (ILP), which had disaffiliated from Labour that same year (1933), and it was this group which expressed most enthusiasm for the Popular Front.

'The Communist party is now seeking affiliation', the 'Behind the Cables' duo wrote in their 27 August 1936 column; the Front was not only radically broadening its base but was proving to be 'a movement now, pressing for a vigorous foreign policy [. . .] avoiding regional pacts, aiming at the resuscitation of the League, or something like it, and disarmament. With this would go certain measures of social reform, possibly nationalisation of transport, the mining industry, etc.' With Labour trade unions dominated by leaders on the right,[25] an injection of elements from an international forum capable of breaking up hidebound allegiances was needed. The Front's readiness to incorporate the Communist Party, and its openness to economic and social initiatives further to the left, encouraged those frustrated by Britain's political apathy to look for new ways forward. Mulgan's enthusiasm for Harold Laski is instructive here.

Laski, who had joined the ILP in 1920 and for a time supported the Popular Front, was part of a British tradition of radical thought that included figures like H.N. Brailsford, J.A. Hobson and Sir Stafford Cripps, all of whom appear in Cox and Mulgan's columns and who were negotiating the fluid boundaries between the Labour left and communism. Laski in particular represented a new generation of radicalism which looked to Russia for political guidance. In an essay published in the *New Clarion* a few months before Mulgan attended his talk at Oxford, the 40-year-old Laski had argued that although 'Russian policy in relation to freedom has been full of grave errors of judgement', Lenin's views on the classless society would eventually bring 'a freedom far more profound and effective' than the freedom of capitalist states (Blaazer 1992, 165–66). In his book *Communism* (1927), Laski wrote that the Bolshevik regime may be a 'new and more powerful tyranny' than Tsarism, but it was at least 'a tyranny conceived in the interests of the masses' rather than those of

25 In their column for 6 October, Cox and Mulgan covered the recent TUC meeting in Plymouth and accused its leaders of being out of touch with the growing left-wing sentiment among the rank and file of British workers.

international financiers (143). This preparedness to hold faith with the Soviet experiment, quickly abandoned by most on the left in coming years, would characterise Mulgan's thinking during his time in Greece. For him it was a matter of pragmatism rather than party dogma, policies that might enable oppressed societies to break old tyrannies and regroup in new, more egalitarian ways.

Along with Victor Gollancz and John Strachey, Laski had been instrumental in the founding of that other important pocket of commitment to the Popular Front in Britain, the Left Book Club (LBC).[26] After the Front's victory in France with the support of the Communist Party, the first book chosen by the LBC for distribution in 1936 was *France Today and the Popular Front* by Maurice Thorez, General Secretary of the French Communist Party. G.D.H. Cole, another representative of the new Labour-left generation, had his book *The People's Front* selected by the Club for June the next year. A stream of books followed: 'England is book club crazy at the moment', Mulgan wrote his father in April 1938 (AGM 136). His own publication in the LBC format, *Poems of Freedom*, was one of many that showed it was possible to be anti-fascist but not necessarily communist, communist but not necessarily anti-democratic, and democratic but not necessarily capitalist.

With their New Zealand readership in mind, the 'Behind the Cables' authors compared the Popular Front for decisiveness with measures taken by Michael Joseph Savage's new Labour government back home. Like Savage, Blum had 'raised wages, improved working conditions, introduced a 40 hour week, [and] extended national control of the Central Bank'.[27] In France,

---

26   The Left Book Club, founded in May 1936, dedicated itself to publishing a book a month as part of a programme of 'political education' to fight fascism. By autumn 1937 the Club had more than 50,000 members and in all circulated around a million books (among them four titles by Orwell)—at affordable prices and with the distinctive yellow or orange covers (Hynes 1976, 208–10).

27   This column was authored by Cox. In his own column of 24 September, Mulgan points out how the *Manchester Guardian* (mouthpiece of the radical left at the time) was praising New Zealand for its proposals to the League of Nations, due to meet shortly in Geneva. These proposals, he continues, are close to those of political thinkers like Herbert Morrison and H.N. Brailsford. But British politicians continue to turn the other way and focus only on the meeting of the Locarno Powers (the big powers, who seem unable to agree). 'There is a wide

Other trouble will come only if the Blum Government shows itself weak and indecisive. And in the past few weeks M. Blum has taken a definitely strong line. He settled the serious Lille textile strikes, made an able radio speech in response to Herr Hitler's Nuremberg orations, and has now courageously devalued the franc. If he continues in this manner France's internal peace is safe for the present. (22 October)

Optimism, based on holding one's nerve, still seemed possible in 1936.

As David Blaazer details in a book on the Popular Front, among the Labour left in Britain there was a wide variety of attitudes to the Soviet Union, the Comintern and the Communist Party of Great Britain (CPGB) (1992, 6). This flexibility suited Mulgan, who had an instinctive mistrust of what he saw as a 'religious' tendency in party politics. The fanatical adherence to anything Russian of his New Zealand friends Milner and Bertram seemed a sad thing, he told his parents in March 1940. The best people, to his way of thinking, were those like 'my friend GT Garratt', who organised relief for the left-wing Spanish government but then did the same for the Finns when they were invaded by the Soviets, 'without any sense of contradiction' (AGM 164–65).[28] Expediency, the practical struggle for equality on both the individual and the national level (the right of nations to self-determination, fundamental to a just internationalism) were his only abiding obsessions. This pragmatism left Mulgan free to admire Russia's revolutionary economic and social innovations to the end. Not having embraced the country's political trajectory *en bloc* protected him from the disillusionment of so many on the left after 1939. But this alignment *across* party lines was common on the left in the 1930s. Even within the fascist states themselves, Mulgan noted, there lurked a united force of 'men

gap between this point of view', Mulgan concludes, 'and the policy expressed by the "Popular Front" in England and by the New Zealand Government.'

28 Geoffrey Garratt (1888–1942) was a British journalist and political activist, an active member of the Independent Labour Party and a vocal critic of the British Raj. His book *Mussolini's Roman Empire* (1938) expresses many views echoed by Mulgan in the last decade of his life.

who were once socialists, Communists, liberals, just waiting'—as he himself seemed to be (AGM 128). The tendency of the British press to dismiss Spain's Republican government as 'Communist', failing to recognise it as a genuinely broad-based left-wing movement, was an error the 'Behind the Cables' duo noted several times. Mulgan would later be confronted by an identical misconception in his dealings with EAM-ELAS in Greece.

But to support the anti-fascist cause without dismantling capitalism was futile. Both the Communist Party and the Labour left shared Lenin's belief that fascism was the outcome of the imperialist phase of capitalism based on the need to create markets in other countries to absorb surplus products. The Boer War of 1899–1902 had turned the attention of many like John Hobson, and Lenin after him, to the evils of imperialism; anti-imperialism became one of the defining characteristics of the new 'collectivist' progressivism in Britain in the first decades of the twentieth century.[29] Lenin's *Imperialism: The Highest Stage of Capitalism* (1916), appearing in English translation in 1926, continued to shape Mulgan's thought in the coming years. For his part, Lenin repeatedly acknowledged his indebtedness to the work of the British economist John Hobson, whose *Imperialism: A Study* (1902) had a profound influence on the whole generation of political theorists who formed the backbone of the ILP. Via these thinkers, the Labour left and communism were able to share a common language in opposition to the ruthless territorial ambitions of fascism at the time. Most agreed with Brailsford, following Lenin, about the pernicious effect of arms manufacturing, and that since WW1, power had 'passed unquestionably from the industrialist to the financier' (Blaazer 1992, 150).[30] For Mulgan, international solidarity needed to have an economic basis. In England, before he

29   In the 'Behind the Cables' column of 24 September, Mulgan, soon to leave for Geneva, praises the work of Norman Angell, another theorist on the Labour left, who in his influential book *The Great Illusion* (1911) had debunked the idea that one country can defeat another through war, given that all countries are economically inter-dependent.

30   In this respect, Liberals, with their underlying support of capitalism-imperialism, did not always fit comfortably into the Popular Front, although they were eventually incorporated into it in 1938.

left for war, a good part of his thought and activity went into the planning of a new economics journal appropriate for the historical moment. Vincent O'Sullivan gives a detailed account of some of the economists Mulgan approached in his attempt to persuade his bosses at the Press that something less abstract and theoretical was needed than what was being produced by Oxbridge academics (LJB 198–200). One economist Mulgan connected with was John Jewkes, who had been published in Gollancz's LBC series.[31] In his research at Manchester University in the 1930s and 1940s, Jewkes focused on local economic problems such as unemployment and poverty in Lancashire. Mulgan was drawn to this empirical approach in the social sciences, which were then in their infancy. In spite of his hard work, the new journal was put on hold as war approached. But Mulgan did get the Press to back H.D. Dickinson's *Economics of Socialism* (OUP, January 1939), which, for all his reassurances to his employers that the book 'is entirely academic and non-political as far as I could see' (LJB 198), gave direct expression to the Popular Front politics of Hobson, Cole, Laski and others (including Lenin and Marx) that Mulgan was following. This was the proselytising phase of his political career, when he was in a position to speak out. It was probably this energetic fervour that lay behind his complaint to his parents in June 1939, just after *Man Alone* had been sent off to the publisher, that the novel 'lacks conviction' (AGM 152). Now, more than ever, it was a question of 'the importance of a political meeting, of persuading as many people as possible in the short time that's left which side they should be on' (AGM 136). His proselytising days were nearly over, but ahead lay a long stretch of time to put into practice the principles that had been solidly established.

* * *

Soon after war broke out, Mulgan wrote his parents what was perhaps his most serious statement of political intent—probably, as

---

31   John and Sylvia Jewkes, *The Juvenile Labour Market* (London: Gollancz, 1938).

McNeish puts it, 'as close as Mulgan gets to a personal credo' (2003, 104). It was certainly prophetic for him personally, in ways neither he nor anyone around him could have predicted:

> it's this fascism business that gets me down. You can see it all happening so clearly in Spain. There, as in Germany, the capitalists—like March and Gil Robles—have hired the [Franco's] army to beat down the lower middle classes, workers and peasants [. . .] Nearly all conservative sympathy [in Britain] is with the army and their Moorish legions in Spain—quite good authorities, like the Manchester Guardian, publish evidence of loans having been made from London to them—'as an insurance against communism'. [. . .] [The English middle and upper class today] won't stand socialism because it stands to lose too much by it. I don't believe in communism myself much—I'd like socialism by evolution—but if we're not going to have it, I know that I would fight with the communists—it's fundamentally much more decent than this other murderous and selfish repression. (AGM 103–4)

As it turned out, this was to be no mere posturing.

In July 1939 Mulgan enlisted in the British army as Lieutenant and ended up serving for nearly two years on garrison duty in Northern Ireland. After being promoted to Major, he was sent to Egypt and took part in battles in the Western Desert, including at El Alamein. Soon after this, in mid 1943, he applied for transfer to Force 133, the commando unit of SOE, and joined up at the training camp in Palestine. Two months later he was parachuted into Greece. By this time, his political views were naturally shifting in relation to events. Like many on the left in the years leading up to the war, he 'unconsciously shared [their] pessimism' about the possibility of a socialist alternative to fascism, sensing that the war would be won on nationalist rather than ideological grounds. But after 1940, he reflected in *Report on Experience*, the mood passed and 'the nagging search for [an ideological] faith returned' (RE 115). Lenin's '*c'est la guerre capitaliste*' about World War 1 is cited with some equivocation in the early pages of *Report on Experience* (61). By the end of the war Mulgan had learned a great deal about the way capitalist imperialism had shaped its final outcome in Greece. He had also had a lot of practice in using equivocation as a rhetorical strategy—as had many on the left, caught up as they were in the divisions and conflicting priorities of the Allied cause.

Greece in 1941-44

CHAPTER 2

The War in Greece 1941–43

This war will last as long as it can. But
every passing day brings a loss of blood
for everyone of us, which nobody knows
when our people will be able to recover

—Poet Giorgos Seferis to novelist Henry Miller, 3 Dec. 1941
(Seferis 1993, 170)

The occupation of Greece by Axis forces is one of the most harrowing chapters in the history of World War 2. From the time of the German invasion in April 1941 until the final evacuation three and a half years later (in October 1944), the country suffered 'a loss of blood' as well as material destruction on an almost unprecedented scale.[1] Much of the hardship and brutality was the result of reprisals against the fierce and determined resistance of the Greek population, a resistance in which Mulgan was to play an important role.

His arrival came at a time of particular turmoil and suffering. By September 1943 the country had been under German, Bulgarian and Italian occupation for two years and had lost more than 300,000 civilians from starvation alone. Earlier that year, over 60,000 Greek Jews, most of them from Salonika (Thessaloniki), were deported in

---

1   The human loss from the war in Greece was, according to Woodhouse, 8 percent of the population (well over half a million out of a total population of around seven million), as opposed to 0.8 percent in Britain (2002, 161). For a detailed account of the famine, see Mazower 2001, 23–52. Mazower (40) estimates that in the winter of 1941–42, in Athens and Piraeus alone, mortality rates were between five and seven times higher than in the previous winter.

cattle trucks to Auschwitz-Birkenau, where as many as 90 percent of the country's long-established Jewish community were exterminated (Mazower 2001, 256). By June '44 nearly 900 towns and villages had been raided then completely destroyed, leaving over a million people homeless. What has been called 'one of the most virulent hyperinflations ever recorded' was also taking hold, so that by 1946, price levels were over five trillion times what they had been in mid 1941 (Clogg 2012; Grigoriadis 2011, IV, 27–30). Further calamities were to follow.

Greece had entered the war reluctantly, with its dictator leader Ioannis Metaxas attempting to maintain Greek neutrality. But on 28 October 1940, in rejecting an ultimatum from the Italians to surrender, Greece was forced into conflict. Its successful expulsion of the Italians more than fifty kilometres back into Albania was a brief moment of national triumph. By early the next year, Britain had set in motion its plan to establish Greece as a wall against further German invasion southwards, to turn Greece into the main theatre of conflict in Europe; at the time Greece was the only nation on the Continent to have successfully repelled Axis aggression. The British war Cabinet had endorsed Churchill's plan on the grounds that the geographical position of Greece, along with the enthusiasm prevailing after the Albanian victory, held out the best hope for a strong defence. They counted, of course, on support from the Greek army. Meanwhile, the contingent of New Zealand and Australian Expeditionary Forces had started arriving on the mainland of Greece in early '41, with approximately 16,000 and 17,000 troops respectively. By the end of March, the total British and colonial presence comprised around 64,000 troops, under the command of General Maitland Wilson. Some historians have claimed that Churchill's plan in waylaying the Germans in Greece was to delay their invasion of the USSR, although this view has been disputed— by, for example, the eminent historian of military strategy Liddell Hart (2011, 166–67). As it turned out, however, the resistance against Axis forces in Greece did indeed delay the German offensive in the Soviet Union by more than a month. Instead of starting on

15 May, as planned, the Barbarossa Operation began on 22 June, eventually stranding the German army in severe winter conditions with catastrophic loss of life.

Churchill's strategies for Greece rarely went according to plan. The head of the Greek army, Field Marshal Alexandros Papagos, along with Prime Minister Metaxas (before his death on 29 January 1941), demanded guarantees of greater support from the British, which did not materialise, and Papagos delayed joining the Allied effort until the last minute. As a result, the Greek army did not participate as expected in the defence (except for the limited support of two reduced Greek regiments in the first battle in the Vevi-Kleidi area near the border with Yugoslavia on 10–12 April). Stranded in the centre of mainland Greece, the Allies were left to fight alone and erect rapid defences in narrow passes (Vevi-Kleidi, Aliakmon, Platamonas, Tempi, Thermopyles, Korinth) so as to gain time for evacuation further south. After the crushing defeat of the Italian army in 1940, Papagos had appeared on the 16 December cover of *Time* magazine as a European hero; his failure to collaborate successfully with the Allies, however, rapidly tarnished his reputation.

In spite of this, on 6 April Papagos had ordered the Second Greek Army to fight independently from the Allies at the Metaxas defence line along the borders with Yugoslavia and Bulgaria. The Greek army of around 70,000, however, was no match for the massive German forces that had advanced: in total approximately 680,000 troops, 700 aircraft and 1,200 tanks. The core of the Greek defence at the Rupel fortification surrendered within three days and gradually the whole front collapsed. Concurrently, the First Greek Army, a force of more than 350,000 which had routed the Italians in Albania, was lying low in the west, and on 20 April negotiated its own surrender to the German commander, Sepp Dietrich of the SS Division. The mainland of Greece had been taken by Wehrmacht forces in just twenty days. The Allies, meanwhile, barely managed to evacuate their troops from southern ports (Porto Rafti, Nafplio, Tolo, Monemvasia and Kalamata) before the end of the month.

From here on the Allied defence was concentrated in the far

south, on the island of Crete, where most of the evacuated troops had ended up. A British contingent, the Mobile Naval Base Depot Organization, had been sent to Crete in November 1940 but failed to establish any serious defensive structure, mainly because it was not clear for some time whether the Germans would attack. Hasty preparations were now made by New Zealand's General Bernard Freyberg, who was given command of the island's defence at the end of April '41. Freyberg had less than three weeks to organise his troops before the main German assault on May 20. Under his command was a force of around 58,000, which included approximately 10,000 newly recruited Greeks, to cover the long stretch of the northern coastline from Maleme (west of Hania and the port of Souda) to Herakleion. This time the offensive came from the air, with parachutes and gliders rendering the invaders vulnerable.[2] With the help of local Cretans, fighting sometimes on their own initiative with knives and pitchforks, more than 5,000 Germans were killed in the Battle of Crete. However, as many commentators, including Dan Davin who took part in the battle, have pointed out, 'the area between Kastelli and Maleme through lack of men and time was virtually undefended', and indeed it was here that the Germans managed to penetrate (Davin 1953, 459).[3] If it hadn't been for tactical misjudgements and possibly poor communications, Crete might have been saved.[4] As it was, the retreat and evacuation of Allied troops began within the next five to six days, mainly from the south of the island.

The Battle of Crete left scars on the national memory in New Zealand that have endured to this day. More positively, the Allied retreat left behind quite a few New Zealanders who couldn't or wouldn't leave and who ended up joining the resistance. Some, like the legendary 'Kapetan Vasili' (Dudley Perkins), returned to Crete

---

2   The German attack included around 500 junkers, 80 gliders and over 15,000 troops. It had also been planned, in addition to airborne troops, that 7,000 men would arrive by sea. See Stroud 2015, 22.

3   For a recent reassessment of Davin's account (and that of many others) of the Battle of Crete, see Bell 2015.

4   See, for instance, Beevor 1991, 230–33; also Filippidis 2007, 428 ff.

to continue the fight after recovering from injury (Elliott 1987). Others, like Lou Northover, survived on the run in the mountains on the mainland; Northover ended up working closely with Mulgan.[5] It is such types who have entered the cultural imaginary in Greece and crop up in local memory and folk songs—like the following by the well-known lyricist Kostis Virvos, who himself joined ELAS in Mulgan's area in 1944.[6]

The New Zealander

Fine fellow from New Zealand
Who came to our house to hide
You'll find affection, love and friendship
As if you're in your own home

Refrain
Put on my son's clothes, he's been killed
And don't be afraid, no one here has been betrayed.

Ο Νεοζηλανδός

Λεβέντη απ' την Νέα Ζηλανδία
Στο σπίτι μας που ήρθες να κρυφτείς
Θα βρεις στοργή αγάπη και φιλία
Και σπίτι σου πως είσαι να θαρρείς

Ρεφραίν

Βάλε τα ρούχα του παιδιού μου που σκοτώθηκε
Και μη φοβάσαι εδώ κανένας δεν προδόθηκε.[7]

5   For a detailed history of New Zealanders in wartime Greece, see Gounelas 2018.

6   Virvos, who joined EAM in 1943, was interned in 1944 and then on his release joined Aris Velouhiotis in the mountains. His lyrics here give a touching depiction of the way the New Zealanders on the run from Axis forces were never betrayed, replicating Mulgan's account in *Report on Experience* (147). Virvos wrote over 2,000 original folk songs.

7   Lyrics: Kostas Virvos, Music: Christos Leontis. From the CD entitled *Katahnia* youtube. com/watch?v=J95Iq81LgHk. Date of access: 9 Jan. 2023.

Mulgan, meanwhile, on the eve of the Battle of Crete, was settling comfortably into the comparatively 'restful' life in a camp seven miles from HQ in Northern Ireland—'just like camping out or going hiking except that you never get any sleep'. It was a relief, he wrote home, not to be 'living on the end of a telephone'. Following events in the Mediterranean, he confessed to his English wife Gabrielle, who had finally arrived in Wellington with their infant son Richard, to feeling embarrassed to be 'sitting here in peaceful Ireland getting promoted while the war goes on everywhere else' (AGM 197, 194, 196). It was to be another year before he would see active service.

Two (nearly three) Greek governments

By this time the Greek government, along with the king (George II), had fled, first to Crete and then to Egypt, taking with them the contents of the treasury.[8] From now on, Greece was nominally governed, at least according to the Allies, by this 'government-in-exile'. Hitler and Mussolini were quick to reach an agreement to divide Greece up, the Germans taking the cities and a few islands of strategic importance, the Italians the mountain terrain of the mainland and the Peloponnese along with the rest of the islands. The Bulgarians, newly attached to the Axis powers for allowing the German offensive to pass through, were given Greek eastern Macedonia and western Thrace. Administration in Athens was taken over by a collaborationist government appointed by the Germans, which ironically comprised the very military generals who had successfully defeated the Italians in Albania. Georgios Tsolakoglou, the most senior among them, initiated the surrender on 20 April 1941, and became Prime Minister.[9]

But the Greeks soon got themselves organised. In Athens, where

---

8   This ended up in Pretoria; only a small proportion of it returned to Greece after the war.

9   The surrender was supported by the influential Bishop of Ioannina, Spyridon, who argued that to continue confrontation with the Axis forces would mean devastation for the Greek people.

300,000 had starved to death in only two months over the winter of '41–'42, popular fury had been mounting. In early '43 Hitler sent directives to the collaborationist government to organise a campaign for civil mobilisation, enlisting Greek men between the ages of 16 and 45 into the German workforce. Soon the walls of the capital were covered with red-lettered EAM slogans: 'Mobilisation equals death; *andartes* everyone' (Mazower 1995, 113). On February 24, a crowd of workers, civil servants and students took to the streets in protest in huge numbers. The demonstrators flooded into Syntagma (Constitution) Square then stormed first the former royal palace, serving as government headquarters, then the Ministry of Labour, where many were mown down by the Italian carabinieri. The next day, public service employees, organised by EAM, went out on strike and, although arrested, managed to get away. Finally, on the 28th, around 3,500 people gathered in Omonia Square to protest the Nazi New Order. The Axis occupiers were forced to back down and the civil mobilisation order was eventually withdrawn.

By early 1942 increasing numbers of Greek men and women had already begun to answer EAM's call and join the resistance. As was inevitable in a population that grew up with politics as their alphabet, guerrilla bands quickly divided along ideological/political lines, resulting in two major groups: EAM-ELAS, identifying as left-wing/communist, and EDES, identifying as centre-right/liberal.[10] Both bands, at this stage, favoured republicanism. This same split along political lines had occurred with the guerrillas in neighbouring Yugoslavia and Albania. In these two countries the British quickly decided, for military and strategic reasons, to support the left-wing/communists while giving up on the right-wing/liberals (the Balli Kombëtar in Albania and the Chetniks in Yugoslavia). In Greece

---

10   EAM (Ethniko Apeleftherotiko Metopo: National Liberation Front) was the administrative body of the organisation based in Athens, to which the Communist Party was attached, and which issued political directives. ELAS (Ellinikos Laikos Apeleftherotikos Stratos: Greek People's Liberation Army) was the fighting wing of the movement, whose leading *Kapetanios* was Aris Velouhiotis. EDES (Ethnikos Dimokratikos Ellinikos Syndesmos: National Republican Greek League) was the main rival to EAM-ELAS and (unlike EAM-ELAS) given full support by the British. For a fuller description of the activities of these bands, see Chapter 4.

the picture was more complicated. Despite vastly superior numbers in ELAS, shortly before Mulgan's arrival, and with consequences which were to affect him profoundly, the British had a change of heart. Increasing apprehension about Soviet strength in the region after what now seemed the inevitable German defeat meant that by the time of liberation a year later, most British support had shifted to EDES, paving the way for the return of the king and thus British control in the eastern Mediterranean. This policy ran counter to the wishes of most of the Greek population, who retained vivid memories of the way the king was responsible for the dictatorship in the previous decade. From mid 1936, as Haris Vlavianos explains, the dictator Ioannis Metaxas, appointed by the king, had left an indelible stain on the country:

> the king [. . .] signed decrees declaring a state of emergency, suspending the constitutional provisions for personal liberties, and dissolving parliament, without fixing a date for new elections. A police state soon began to impose a carefully controlled reign of terror, directed primarily against the Communists, trade unionists, intellectuals, and others known for their strong republican leanings. Monarchy had been transformed into Crown-sponsored dictatorship. The king emerged as the symbol of an oppressive dictatorship which presided over the death of democracy in Greece. (1989, 163)

It was a capacious left-leaning group of workers, peasants, intellectuals and republicans that united under the umbrella of EAM-ELAS and 'took to the mountains' as armed resistance bands, as the Greeks had done so often in earlier times, in the spirit of the *klefts*. The word *klephtes* in Greek means literally 'thieves', which mountain brigands certainly were in the eighteenth century. But in the eyes of most Greeks the *klefts* were also part of a heroic tradition, particularly in areas like Mulgan's Roumeli, where the reputation of local bands of like-minded *klarites* (those 'out on a branch') dated their resistance back to Ottoman rule in the 1820s, and more recently to the Metaxas dictatorship. Churchill would notoriously refer to ELAS as *banditti* in contempt for this tradition. But Churchill had a different agenda for Greece, no doubt partly in response to the way the king had been instrumental in allying Greece to Britain rather than to the fascist states of Germany or Italy, and continued to support the royal claims long after it was clear that most of the country were anti-monarchist. As Nicolas Svoronos puts it, in the minds of most Greeks, the war they'd fought against the Italians in Albania had been as much about opposition to fascism as it had been about patriotism (1981, 8). The years ahead, as German defeat became inevitable, presented a long-desired opportunity for change. Plans were beginning to take shape in the mountains for a new and democratic government, free of foreign control. PEEA, as it was to be called, was instituted during the period of EAM-ELAS's greatest strength, at the centre of Mulgan's area of activity.

Working with the British Mission

By mid 1943 history-changing geopolitical decisions were being taken on a broad scale, when Churchill and Roosevelt agreed at the conference of the Allies in Quebec, and later in Tehran, that Greece was to be the bulwark against the probable advance of Soviet communism, with the Greek king as its token head. Anti-monarchist to its core, EAM-ELAS demanded there be a plebiscite immediately after liberation to determine whether the Greek king had popular support to return. Many EDES supporters also held republican views at this stage. But in March its leader, Napoleon Zervas, had been pressured by the British into supporting the king, and eventually sent a message to the exiled Greek government stating that 'If England, for wider reasons, and even without people's wishes, wants the return of King, we, fighting for liberation, will not oppose it' (KCLMA, GB 99, 1–6/9).[11]

---

11   Chris Woodhouse, at the time second-in-command of the British Military Mission (BMM) under Myers, was instrumental in persuading Zervas to send this message, which Zervas hid even from Pyromaglou, his second-in-command (Grigoriadis 2011, II, 84–85). In *Apple of Discord* Woodhouse admits that 'In retrospect I am inclined to regard this as a mistake' (1948, 74n1).

In the meantime, the British were forging significant links with the guerrilla bands via their undercover (SOE) agents, with SOE HQ in Cairo pressing the Foreign Office in London to ramp up support. The famous destruction of the Gorgopotamos viaduct in November 1942 had proved that collaboration with the Greek partisans, all working together, had great potential. On 30 September that year, two SOE contingents of four members each had been parachuted into mainland Greece.[12] Among the officers were two New Zealand sappers, specialised in explosives (the British Commander-in-Chief, General Harold Alexander, specifically requested that New Zealanders be included) (McGlynn 1953, 3). Rommel was preparing his final offensive in North Africa—with Mulgan at last in action (with the West Kents Fourth Battalion) among those attempting to obstruct him. This first SOE sabotage operation in Greece, named 'Harling', involved around 150 Greek guerrillas from both ELAS and EDES and was a resounding success: the ruined bridge took the enemy nearly six weeks to rebuild and supplies to Rommel from Germany were significantly delayed. After this, the small SOE contingent was instructed to stay on in Greece to plan further sabotages by organising and arming the Greek resistance. The two New Zealanders, Arthur Edmonds and Tom Barnes, became leading liaison officers of ELAS and EDES respectively and were to play important roles to the very end of the war in Greece.[13]

But from the summer of 1943, Cold War hostilities began to affect the operations of the British Mission in Greece and to entangle BLOs like Mulgan in politics. Shortly before his arrival in September, ELAS was becoming increasingly resentful that, despite its huge support throughout the country, most of the arms and ammunition from the Allies was going to the by now pro-royalist EDES. By this time ELAS had a mostly steady force of at least 15,000 *andartes*, growing by the month, whereas EDES had fewer

---

12   Due to bad weather, a third was dropped two weeks later.

13   The participation of Barnes and Edmonds is well documented in Gounelas 2018, 205–38, Barnes 2015 and Edmonds 1998.

than 5,000. Vulnerable to ELAS hostility, EDES began turning for support to the collaborationist government and even to the enemy. There is now clear evidence that between the end of 1943 and mid 1944, the band came to an unofficial 'gentleman's agreement' with the German command in Greece to refrain from conflict.[14] Widespread suspicion of this development boosted the standing of ELAS in the eyes of the Greek people and encouraged its leaders to initiate hostilities against EDES, whose support by the British at this stage seems to have been mainly as a hindrance to ELAS. By this time, as well, tensions *within* British policy over Greece were running high, concentrated around the support for EAM-ELAS. Anthony Eden, Minister of Foreign Affairs, had been charged with curtailing SOE support for the left-wing organisation, with the aim of suppressing it altogether.[15] These developments coincided with the beginning of the German army's defeat in the USSR, after which communism began to be considered a threat equal to or even greater than that of Germany. Quick to exploit this anxiety, the Germans took every opportunity to whip up anti-communist sentiment. In June 1943 the Prime Minister of the collaborationist government in Athens, Georgios Rallis, set up a force of Greeks of dubious political or moral character called the Security Battalions, whose role was to attack the left-wing forces with the support of the enemy.[16] After his arrival, Mulgan was to report on the activities of these Battalions in his area with carefully worded indignation.

Meanwhile, events were moving fast elsewhere in Europe. On 25 July 1943, two weeks after the landing of the Allies in Sicily, the Grand Council in Rome was taken over by Marshal Badoglio. With

14　For an analysis of this agreement and the dealings between EDES and the German forces in Epirus, which also involved the New Zealander Tom Barnes as chief SOE operative in the region, see Richter 2009, 114–31. See also Mazower (2001, 142 and 178), and Fleischer (1981, 59).

15　In March 1943 Eden had decided that operations in Greece should be influenced by someone capable of enforcing British interests more strongly and had replaced the British Ambassador to the Greek government-in-exile, Michael Palairet, with Reginald Leeper. Ambassador Leeper was in diplomatic control of developments in Greece for the following crucial three years.

16　On the Security Battalions, see Grigoriadis 2011, II, 108; Kalyvas 2008, 131 ff; Mazower 2001, 323 ff.

the official collapse of the Italian government two months later, the 11th Italian Army of around 140,000 men was left stranded on the Greek mountains. Although most managed to return to Italy with the help of the Allies, a large number from the Pinerolo Division along with most of their arms fell into the hands of ELAS. The area Mulgan came to be based in was dominated by these newly armed left-wing *andartes*.

Of the British Liaison Officers preceding Mulgan in Greece, one of the most significant was Major Rufus Sheppard, with whom he had a lot in common. After reading English at Oxford, Sheppard had become Professor of English at the University of Egypt in Cairo. At the outbreak of war, he was commissioned in the army and distinguished himself fighting in Abyssinia as Company Commander with the Ethiopian Army in the guerrilla campaign of 1940–41 led by Orde Wingate against the occupying Italians (Ogden 2012, 187). This campaign was of great interest to Mulgan as a model of anti-fascist and anti-imperialist resistance, and Sheppard's experiences in the Abyssinian war no doubt inspired some of Mulgan's reflections on the campaign in *Report on Experience*. Sheppard had arrived in Greece in February 1943 and quickly began his successful collaboration with ELAS, working closely with Kostas Karagiorgis.[17] As a recognised left-wing sympathiser, unusual among SOE operatives,[18] Sheppard had almost certainly been appointed to this particular area by SOE Cairo to dispel concern among the partisans there about SOE's antagonism. This sympathy for ELAS,

17   Karagiorgis (real name Gyftodimos), a journalist, had travelled widely and lived in the USSR from 1934 to 36. Although critical of Stalin's show trials, he was a member of the Greek Communist Party (KKE) and in 1943 arrived in Thessaly with his wife, Maria Agrigianaki-Gyftodimou, also a communist, who had studied philology and took over responsibility for the Women's Organization of Thessaly. As *kapetanios* of the 10th ELAS Division then responsible for the organisation of the resistance in Thessaly, Karagiorgis would have come into fairly regular contact with Mulgan in 1943–44.

18   See Clogg 2000, 67 and 90. Sheppard had initially been instructed to remain independent of other SOE missions in Greece. In May 1943, Myers, commander of SOE on mainland Greece, accused Sheppard and his mission in Thessaly of 'becoming EAM yes-men, not troubling to investigate deeper than E.A.M. desire' (Clogg 2000, 90). Sheppard's sympathy for EAM-ELAS was also noted by Woodhouse, who accused him of being 'naïve and stubborn' (Woodhouse 1982, 55); see also Woodhouse's report, TNA HS 5/363; also Pashalidis 1997, 59. Woodhouse was later to recommend Sheppard's removal from SOE.

to which the Foreign Office was opposed, did not necessarily concern the SOE command in Cairo, whose focus (at least up until the time of Mulgan's arrival) was on effecting sabotage operations with the help of ELAS, spread as the band was over a wide area of the country where the main communications lines from north to south could be sabotaged. But before long Sheppard's politics raised considerable concern amongst his military commanders.

Tensions between SOE Cairo and the Foreign Office came to a head in August, the month before Mulgan's arrival, when the commanding officer in the area, Brigadier Eddie Myers—of whom the Foreign Office was becoming openly critical on account of the growing strength of EAM-ELAS—had taken a bold decision. Calculating that unity and dialogue were to the benefit of all, he agreed to the *andartes'* request that representatives from all three bands (EAM-ELAS, EDES and a smaller group, EKKA) be flown to Cairo to negotiate their recognition as branches of the official national army. The reaction of Churchill, the Foreign Office and the Greek government-in-exile was a predictable fury. Myers was called a 'complete disaster' and 'a very dangerous fool' by Reginald Leeper, British Ambassador to the government-in-exile in Cairo,[19] and was removed from his post—to be replaced by Chris Woodhouse. With sympathies, in time, more towards the Foreign Office rather than SOE, Woodhouse had been given a new objective: to replace Myers' impartial support for whichever band offered resistance to the occupying forces with open support for EDES and opposition to EAM-ELAS.[20] Myers' opinion of EDES and its leader Zervas was far from flattering. He later confessed: 'if while I was commander of the Mission we had asked him to stand on his head, he would willingly have stood on his head' (Marion Sarafis 1980b, 109). Woodhouse, however, reported to SOE HQ, at

---

19 Quoted in Clogg 1975, 173. For a full account of the delegation's trip to Cairo and its aftermath, see Myers 1985.

20 Stefanos Sarafis 1980, 169–70. Woodhouse's status as 'enemy' of ELAS is charted by Ogden (2012, 98), as well as in his own writings where he admits that 'In the interests of establishing bias, I should add that I was one of the supporters [of the EDES leader Zervas]' (Woodhouse 1948, 82n2).

least in October 1943, that 'almost all British Liaison Officers who have met Zervas have a high opinion of him'.[21] Zervas's servility to the British suited Woodhouse well but appalled ELAS leaders like Sarafis,[22] particularly when Zervas dropped his long-held republican views to back the king. This demand for unconditional allegiance to British policy would have a deeply unsettling effect on Mulgan as he worked to support and encourage ELAS collaboration.

21   Woodhouse report to Keble, 'Recent Crisis in Free Greece', Pertouli, 19 Oct. 1943 (KCLMA Woodhouse 99, 1/12, page 6). For further discussion of the differences between EDES and EAM-ELAS and British policy in relation to these groups, see Papastratis 1997 and Fleischer 1997.

22   Marion Sarafis records that towards the end her husband felt 'an almost physical revulsion' with regard to Zervas's servility towards the British (1980a, lxxiii).

II | In the Greek Mountains

CHAPTER 3

SOE Agent

I am having the most interesting time
of the war, perhaps of my life

—Mulgan to his parents, 10 Dec 1943
(AGM 267–68)

The British administration had been aware for several years before the war, but more urgently from 1938 onwards, that it required new forms of irregular warfare to carry out espionage and stimulate subversion behind enemy lines. Created in 1940 and attached to the Ministry of Economic Warfare in London, the SOE commando force was charged with the task of collaborating with national guerrilla groups in sabotages against the Axis powers.[1] Its initial mandate was to operate in the southern Balkans, to include communist and non-communist bands in Greece, Yugoslavia and Albania.[2] SOE ended up employing more than 13,000 operatives worldwide, of whom around 3,200 were women.[3] Selection to the force brought a prestige coveted by ordinary soldiers for the additional daring and

---

1   For an overall assessment of SOE in Greece and more broadly, see Clogg 2000, 60–77; Bærentzen 1982; Kelly 2007, 130–53; and Bailey 2009, Chapter 1: 'Tip and Run Thuggery', 9–34.

2   SOE collaboration with Yugoslavian partisans had started in autumn 1941, a few months earlier than it did in Greece (Auty and Clogg 1975, 100–1). Albanian-British attempts to build up resistance against surrender to the Italians had started in 1940 but the first SOE mission there took place early in 1943 (Bailey 2009, 44 ff).

3   Around 1,200 of the women employed in various roles were civilians; 1,500 were in the First Aid Nursing Yeomanry (FANY), 450 in Air Training Service (ATS) and 60 in the Women's Auxiliary Air Force (WAAF). Around 400 women held officer status (Crowdy 2008, 13).

independence involved, as well as extra pay. Its operations were top
secret and induced a sense of personal responsibility. Many of those
who volunteered to join, Mulgan among them, were not interested
in the rounds of socialising celebrated by the military brass who
frequented expensive clubs and hotels in Cairo. The missions they
sought required an athletic ethos—a willingness to sleep rough or
trek 30 kilometres a day across treacherous enemy-held territory. It is
as if this was what Mulgan was waiting for; he described his 'delight
and inspiration' as he flew over Greece waiting to be dropped on the
night of 10–11 September 1943 (RE 124).

SOE had been thought out according to a specific left-wing
agenda. Minister of Economic Warfare Hugh Dalton, a member of
the Labour Party,[4] wrote in his diary on 1 July 1940 that 'what we
have in mind . . . concerns Trade Unions, Socialists etc; the making
of chaos and revolution—no more suitable for soldiers than fouling
at football or throwing when bowling at cricket' (Wylie 2007b, 110–
11). Breaking the rules of regular warfare was to be part of the game.
Dalton was appointed to head SOE by Churchill himself on 16 July,
with the famous injunction to 'set Europe ablaze'. Dalton's project
was international rather than strictly national in character. Neville
Wylie quotes from a letter Dalton wrote to Lord Halifax, the then
Foreign Secretary, on 2 July, where he outlined

> the creation of a 'democratic international', capable of employing
> 'many different methods, including industrial and military
> sabotage, labour agitation and strikes, continuous propaganda,
> terrorist acts against traitors and German leaders, boycotts and
> riots'. (2007b, 110)

Wylie notes that Deputy Prime Minister Clement Atlee and Hugh
Dalton 'were both fired by the belief that "special operations" was
essentially a form of political warfare, best waged, in Dalton's
opinion, by the sort of people found in his own constituency—the

---

4   As head of SOE, Dalton dismantled the existing Section MI(R) and incorporated D Section
      from SIS into the new organisation (Seaman 2006, 7–21).

Durham miners' (110). Although this programme came in for much modification as time went on, as head of SOE (until he was moved to the Board of Trade early in 1942) Dalton believed in the potential of proletarian activity as part of war operations. His replacements, Lord Selborne and Charles Hambro, were gradually to succumb to the more right-wing line of the main military mission directed from the Foreign Office. But there is little doubt that Mulgan's allegiances would have lain squarely with Dalton's original project and may well have triggered his decision to join. As he was to discover, to use Wylie's words, 'throughout the war politics was an unavoidable and integral ingredient in SOE's activities' (109).

Like many who applied to join SOE, Mulgan did not respond well to institutionalised military discipline. By the time he came to Greece in September '43, he had already served for over two and a half years with the Oxfordshire and Buckinghamshire Light Infantry—first at a training camp in Oxford and then in Northern Ireland—and then in the North African desert for another year with the Royal West Kents, during which time his battalion suffered appalling losses at El Alamein. He would later recount his complaints against the regular British army in *Report on Experience*: its bungling inefficiency and hidebound hierarchical structure.[5] In April '43 he expressed these views in no uncertain terms to higher authority and was released from the West Kents. It might be assumed that such insubordination would get Mulgan into serious trouble; indeed, he expected as much himself. But it may well have made him a promising candidate in the eyes of the SOE recruiting team in Cairo at this time. The young Englishman Frank Thompson, who had been converted to communism by Iris Murdoch in Oxford a few years after Mulgan was there, just before the war, had a similar experience. Recruited

5   For an assessment of the army's attempt to overcome the often 'feudal' relations between officers and men during the war, see Crang 2000, 58–74. But Mulgan's complaints are still shared by some analysts of the British army today. In a critique of a recent book entitled *The Habit of Excellence: Why British Army Leadership Works*, Simon Akam draws attention to the way 'careerism' and 'deference' are built into the system, with much less tolerance for internal debate than in the American system. It is still uncomfortable, he writes, to think about Iraq and Afghanistan, that 'these were conflicts that cost trillions of dollars and thousands of lives, that sought to remake foreign states and didn't succeed' (Akam 2022, 32).

into the intelligence service with the codename 'Phantom', then later into SOE, he learned that 'reporting obvious inefficiencies or bad work with the High Command belonged with their brief' (Conradi 2013, 157). In any event, it certainly did neither of them any harm, at least in the short run. The two shared a quality of intransigence which they mostly kept to themselves.[6] Another example is that of James Klugmann, who astonishingly remained a member of the British Communist Party but managed to survive in SOE (like Mulgan and Thompson, under the Balkans mission based in Cairo), and indeed assumed a dominant role in its planning.

Recruitment and posting

Ironically, given the concern Mulgan's politics would eventually cause the British, his initial selection for this particular area in the Greek mountains had almost certainly been carefully thought through in Cairo. He would initially join the left-wing Rufus Sheppard, who had himself been sent in, it seems, to pacify ELAS leader Aris Velouhiotis, who was showing signs of hostility towards the British for favoring EDES.[7] Sheppard, code-named 'Hills' in the mountains, was a crucial early mentor for Mulgan. Unlike Eddie Myers, the first head of SOE operations in Greece, Sheppard actively encouraged Greek officers to join ELAS, rather than EDES. Sarafis recounts it as follows:

---

6   Descriptions of Thompson's politics at Oxford read as if they are about Mulgan. Arnold Rattenbury writes: 'Except as linguist, Frank Thompson was clearly no Russophile, nor ever, save perhaps in one sonnet, much wedded to Marxist dogma. He was of course, as his brother [the historian E.P. Thompson] puts it, "committed to a communist cause . . . I say 'a' and not 'the' communist cause since Frank Thompson can scarcely be described as an orthodox communist". Anti-Fascism; a sense of classes at war in a historical direction; a wish to replace impoverishment, cultural as much as economic, with richness; also a Thirties sense that no other grouping was doing much about these things: his Communism was that sort of amalgam, responding to something even larger and more vague' (Rattenbury 1997).

7   80 percent of EDES's arms at this time were supplied by the British, as opposed to 50 percent of those supplied to ELAS. EKKA (the third resistance group, of liberal persuasion) also received around 80 percent of their supplies from the British. According to Lt. Col. Dolbey's concluding report, by 30 September 1944 there had been dropped into Greece a total of 1,706 tons of arms and stores by air and a total of 4,090 tons by sea (BHA, 259, 7).

Lieutenant-Colonel Hills, the British liaison officer with the 1st Division [of ELAS], was the only one to tell the officers from Trikkala, 'If you've come to fight, go to ELAS which has real strength and where you'll be commanding real units, but if you've just come to hang around in a different café, then go to EDES.' (Stefanos Sarafis 1980, 168–69)

Mulgan's first weeks in Greece were spent with Sheppard and the 'general' (Sarafis) at ELAS HQ in the village of Kastania (RE 143–44), and the sympathetic initiation into the left-wing guerrillas' objectives would have been just what he was hoping for. On 20 October the Germans moved in with guns at the ready and they all had to beat a hasty retreat. Although they later separated, moving to adjoining bases, the contact with Sheppard continued: Mulgan's diary for 1 December, for example, reads 'Elato [Elati, just south of Pertouli] with Hills'.[8]

Politics aside, on the practical level, it was recognised in Cairo that New Zealanders were better communicators with the guerrillas, on both sides; New Zealand lieutenant-colonels Arthur Edmonds and Tom Barnes occupied leading positions with ELAS and EDES respectively at this time. Brigadier Keble, who was made Director of SOE Military Operations in the Middle East after Alamein, was by now pressing to expand guerrilla forces to the maximum, taking advantage of Anglo-Greek allegiances wherever possible. At the beginning of 1943 there were around 40 SOE officers in Greece; by the end of the year the number had risen to around 200. In the fast-developing circumstances, major German offensives forced the *andartes* in south Thessaly to disperse and reinforcements were urgently needed. Sheppard moved west with the main group while Mulgan headed east with a smaller contingent. Soon, Mulgan and the ELAS fighters had formed a separate sabotage group code-named 'Kirkstone', which comprised three separate stations under Mulgan's command: one in Fourna from which he could control the other two—one in Tsouka with

Major Pat Wingcate and one in Goura with Major Ian Neville.

Brigadier Cleveland Mervyn ('Bolo') Keble is an interesting figure. He had replaced Brigadier Glenconner as SOE office Chief-of-Staff in Cairo in the autumn of 1942, in order, it seems, to inject more energy into Allied irregular warfare around the time of the victory at El Alemein, a task he took to with relish. With overall SOE command for Greece, Yugoslavia and Albania, Keble played a hugely important role at this time of radical shifts in military and political policy. Bickham Sweet-Escott, who headed the London office of SOE in Baker Street at the time, confirms that a great number of the SOE agents were picked personally by Keble, who constantly 'planned to supplement them by many others' (1965, 172). By autumn '43, according to Sweet-Escott (1965, 170), SOE had around 80 separate missions operating in the Balkans.[9] Keble's unorthodox style of leadership was appropriate for the time and task. Brash, ambitious and a highly effective organiser, helped by the fact that he had access to secret information from broken enemy codes (Foot 2008, 284), Keble ignored SOE general HQ and communicated directly with the ideologues in Baker Street (Sweet-Escott, 1965, 170). This gave him a free hand to bypass the Foreign Office, which favoured support for the right-wing groups in the Balkans.[10] Keble's criteria were close to those originally spelled out by Dalton: to cause 'chaos' for the enemy, in any 'revolutionary' way necessary. In 1943, and especially after Stalingrad, admiration for the Soviet contribution to the war against fascism among military personnel like Keble was not uncommon.

Keble's office employed several highly skilled Russophiles. One was Russian-born Colonel Guy Tamplin, who was in the Polish section. With service in both Russian and Polish intelligence

---

9   Before this Keble had served in the intelligence section at GHQ in Cairo, monitoring supplies to Rommel (Cooper 1989, 265). Glenconner, who according to Sweet-Escott (1965, 170) 'lived in a kind of stratosphere', seems to have been considered insufficiently energetic for the task.

10   For a lively assessment of the rivalry between SOE and the Foreign Office, see the article in *The Herald* for 26 Feb. 2000, 'At war with the enemy within', heraldscotland.com/news/12200046.at-war-with-the-enemy-within/. Date of access 27 Sept. 2019.

sections, Tamplin was fluent in both languages.[11] There is no evidence that he was a left-wing sympathiser: on the contrary he was known to be politically conservative. But another key player in the office, the gifted linguist James Klugmann (the Cambridge contemporary of Mulgan's), had been an influential member of the Communist Party of Great Britain before joining up,[12] and Keble seems not to have minded about this. For him, not unlike Churchill in the early stages of the war, political persuasions were secondary to strategic considerations. He gave unconditional support to Klugmann; in reply to MI5's warning in January '43 about Klugmann's affiliation with the CPGB, he wrote: 'We are not really interested in Klugmann's politics which concern this organization but little [. . .] In any case, are we to stamp on Communism when probably our largest ally is a nation composed of nothing but Communists?' (TNA KV2/788/2/8; also Andrews 2015, 131).[13] Under initial command capable of making challenges of this sort, Mulgan was chosen to go into Greece at a time when (for a short while longer) left-wing sympathies may well have been regarded as an asset for the task in hand.

Early in the previous year SOE Cairo had liaised with the Canadian Communist Party to seek out émigré anti-fascists from Yugoslavia willing to return to their country of origin to infiltrate Mihailović's right-wing guerrillas.[14] This would have been at the initiative of Keble and Basil Davidson, the commander of SOE operations in Yugoslavia (Andrews 2015, 133). Keble, Bailey records, was a 'valuable ally' for Klugmann (2007, 78). When he visited

11   For some details on Guy Richard Tamplin, see 'Special Forces Roll of Honours', specialforcesroh.com/showthread.php?4171-Tamplin-Guy-Richard. Date of access 10 Feb. 2019.

12   For a detailed account of Klugmann's politics and activity in SOE, see Bailey 2007; also Andrews 2015, 131 ff. Cooper argues that there is little evidence that Klugmann was a member of NKVD (the Soviet interior ministry) 'hiding behind a smoke-screen of right-wing credentials', as was sometimes thought (1989, 266). We shall return to Klugmann later.

13   Keble's own motto was 'we will never beat the Russians if we don't beat the Germans first' (Davidson 1980, 114). The British SOE operative Archie Jack, who with Mihailović's partisans had demolished the Visegrad bridge in Axis-occupied Yugoslavia, blamed Keble, Deakin, Maclean and the 'extremely left wing' Basil Davidson for ousting Mihailović's right-wing Chetniks from the field of action (Andrews 2015, 140 and Foot 2008, 295).

14   Approximately 30 Canadian-Croat miners were dropped into Croatia on 20–21 April 1943 (Andrews 2015, 133).

Cairo in January 1943, Churchill was informed by his friend the Oxford historian Bill Deakin about the situation in Yugoslavia, where Mihailović's Chetniks were fighting Tito's left-wing partisans with the help of the Germans. At this time, Churchill received a detailed memorandum from Keble's office which convinced him of the need to change policy and support Tito, increasing the number of planes available to carry supplies to the left-wing partisans. One of the arguments made by Keble, as reported by Davidson, was that '"if this situation continues, either the Russians or the Americans will, for different reasons, take a practical interest". We should therefore step in first' (Davidson 1980, 119). Klugmann had probably advised Keble in writing this memorandum. Although there is no direct evidence that Klugmann was a double agent, there is clear evidence, as Andrews records, that Klugmann was manipulating documents to exaggerate the strength of Tito's partisans in order to increase Allied support for them (2015, 2). Whatever the source, the appeal seems to have hit home, and before long Churchill was on side. An often-quoted exchange between Churchill and one of his advisers on the Balkans, Fitzroy Maclean, took place around this time. Maclean had been sent to Yugoslavia to find out what group was most effective against the Germans. On his return he informed Churchill that it seemed certain that Tito's communist partisans, rather than Mihailović's Chetniks, would oust the Germans and gain control of the country. On asking Churchill whether he'd considered the implications of backing Tito, Churchill is said to have replied with another question:

> 'Are you going to live there?' asked the prime minister.
> 'No.'
> 'Neither am I, so had we not better leave the Jugoslavs themselves
> to work out what sort of system they are going to have?' (Davidson
> 1987, 174)

But it was to be otherwise for Greece, where Churchill had very different designs.

It is also possible that Klugmann had a direct hand in Mulgan's selection. By this time Klugmann, by his own admission as well as that of his superiors, had become indispensable in the SOE office in Cairo, despite repeated warnings from London about his communist sympathies (Bailey 2007). From February 1942, for two and a half years, he received one promotion after another and was consulted continuously on matters of policy. Keble also had command of the training school in Palestine where Mulgan spent two months (unusual for an experienced officer—Edmonds and Barnes, by contrast, were given only a few days' training [Edmonds 1998, 2; Barnes 2015, 17]), giving his commanders ample opportunity for insight into his character and views. It is probable that Mulgan, like Klugmann, impressed his military colleagues as a 'scholar of broad sympathies and a reflective mind', as Foot assesses him (on the basis of *Report on Experience*) (2008, 290). 'Broad sympathies', rather than toeing the line of His Majesty's Government, were all to the good in the climate of early SOE policy.

The time of his life

Mulgan's initiation into irregular warfare was immediate and enthusiastic. The independence as well as the 'company of individuals who stand out sharply after the patterned army life that I've been leading' (AGM 265), individuals like Sheppard, would have been more than welcome. There was little time for boredom, with a great deal to learn culturally and politically as well as occasions of high adrenalin. The narrow escape from Kastania, six weeks after arrival, shows what he was up against— and seemingly relishing. Michael Ward, a British SOE officer who was to cross paths with Mulgan at various stages in Greece, gives a graphic description of what he learned about the incident. One evening, having passed through tiny mountain villages where ELAS units were training, Ward and a few others trudged their way up through forests on the precipitous cliffs in the heart of the Pindus massif to reach the joint BMM-*andarte* HQ in Pertouli, situated at 3,000 feet. Later in the evening, as they were sitting talking with others from the mission,

> we suddenly heard a clatter of boots on the verandah followed by a hubbub of voices outside the door. This burst open and in came two dishevelled figures blinking at the light. They were British officers in battledress and it was clear that they were exhausted from hard travel. They were well known to the others, who immediately clustered round to discover what had been happening to them. I learned that the lieutenant-colonel with the reddish hair was 'Rufus' Sheppard and the clean shaven major was John Mulgan. They had been surprised by the Germans in their base in the village of Kastaniá, some twenty miles to the north, and had escaped by the skin of their teeth by slipping out of the back of their house and up into the woods as the Germans drove into the village. They had been obliged to abandon everything. (Ward 1992, 85)[15]

Not all of Mulgan's time in the mountains was to be this hair-raising. In fact it was, at least until the spring several months later, to be a time of comparative seclusion. As winter descended, the small group of men in the station at Fourna (then from 27 December in Goura, then back to Fourna on 9 February) were often snowbound in these high mountains, well protected by their inaccessibility against enemy incursion. Much of the time they were waiting for 'sorties', drops of supplies of food, clothing, weapons and ammunition from SOE Cairo. During the day, when he could, Mulgan would trek

---

15   Mulgan's diary for this time records just one word, 'Pertouli'. But in *Report on Experience* he gives details of the 'leisurely' arrival of the Germans into Kastania, shooting anyone on sight, burning villages as they went, and the rapid departure of the villagers. As far as his and Sheppard's flight is concerned, he simply records that 'Personally I set out to keep my rendezvous with the general' (RE 142–45). Sarafis, who had gone on ahead, gives a rather different version of the escape. The Germans, he writes, advanced with 'infantry, artillery, tanks and aeroplanes', against which the *andartes* had little defence. The (unnamed) British BLOs stopped to make the necessary pot of tea, were caught off guard and were forced to abandon the mules carrying 80 *okades* (c. 100 kilos) of gold sovereigns. (This may have been the party of Philip Worrall, who was in Kastania providing for the Italians.) Sarafis and the ELAS group, he records, moved south-west towards Krania (Stefanos Sarafis 1980, 205).

or ride along the narrow stony tracks from one station to another, getting his area (Area 3) into order. By early in the new year he had won the confidence of Kostas Tsamakos, Commander of the 16th East Thessaly Division of ELAS, to collaborate in the training of a platoon of ELAS *andartes*. When snow cleared, they planned sabotage operations: how to plant explosives in the area along the Spercheios River, mainly on the north–south railway lines that traversed it. On 21 January, his diary records, he attended an EAM conference. The initiation into local politics was well under way.

By early spring of 1944, his team comprised a group of Poles who had defected from the German army, a handful of British and American Liaison Officers,[16] and a large body of ELAS *andartes*. Anglophone accounts have concentrated primarily on his dealings with other BLOs, but the diary kept throughout his time here, where Greek names occur constantly, suggests a different picture. Many of these ELAS fighters, as Marion Sarafis records, were from an agrarian background[17] that Mulgan understood, farm labourers with little military experience but sturdy bodies. Mulgan found that an appeal to their basic 'decency' generally produced results. In time, such was the prestige of his team that it became known amongst SOE agents as 'John Mulgan and Co' (Edmonds 1998, 232),[18] distinguished from those in other SOE areas for the way it gave full backing to and achieved cohesion among the left-wing partisans. A couple of months into his time, in the company of Greek versions of Rufus Sheppard and other assorted types, he wrote home that he was 'happier in this work than in anything I have done since the war began', and was indeed having 'the most interesting time of the war, perhaps of my life' (AGM 267–68).

16   The number of Poles initially attached to Mulgan's force was around 100 but in February 1944, when they were offered evacuation, only 20 of them volunteered to stay on (Capell n.d., 94). For the Americans in the Greek resistance, see Nalmpantis 2010 and Jones 2007.

17   Marion Sarafis details how, although EAM consisted of a predominance of communist members when it was first founded in September 1941, 'by liberation, as seems eminently suitable for an almost 48 per cent peasant population, its membership had been surpassed by that of the Agrarian Party of Greece [AKE]' (1980a, lii–iii).

18   A summary of Mulgan's military operations and the destruction inflicted on the Germans by his group is given in the biography by Day (1977, 29–42) and by Julian Dolbey in a letter sent to Day in 1964 (KCLMA, GB 0099, 34).

From SOE's point of view, the mountain ranges of central Greece provided some of the best terrain possible for guerrilla operations. Peak after peak of precipitous rock face shrouded in dense foliage, mostly conifer, offered endless opportunities for retreat and cover in villages accessible only by mule track. It is often forgotten that partisan warfare is completely different from its regular equivalent and requires not only different terrain but very different strategies. At the training camp in Haifa in Palestine, Mulgan would have been given the pocket-sized SOE *Partisan Leader's Handbook* written by Colin McVean Gubbins, SOE Director of Operations and Training. There, he was instructed in strategies such as road ambush, the concealment of electric detonators, countering enemy information systems, and silent killing. (He was to describe these sessions to Gabrielle as 'long and intricate lessons, nearer to Hemingway than to the reality of total war' [Day 1977, 29].) But the main advice, repeated throughout, concerned effective use of cover in avoiding open conflict with the enemy. The task, as Gubbins put it (a great deal more delicately than Dalton had done), was 'to embarrass the enemy in every possible way' through small acts of diversion and destruction. Sabotage, agents were warned, 'deals with the acts of individuals or small groups of people, which are carried out by stealth and not in conjunction with armed force.' 'Never,' it was repeated, 'get involved in a pitched battle unless you are in overwhelming strength.' 'Break off the action as soon as it becomes too risky to continue.' And crucially, operatives were instructed, remember that this is a game of hit-and-run; item 2a read: 'A line of retreat must be available which will give all the men a safe and sure way of escape. A thick wood, broken and rocky country, etc., give the best cover' (Foot 2001, 447–55). M.R.D. Foot, official historian of SOE, reprints this from the manual as an Appendix to his book *SOE in the Low Countries* (2001). In spite of this, in his monumental *SOE: An Outline History of the Special Operations Executive 1940–1946* seven years later, he falls back on the common Anglophone viewpoint when it comes to describing the activities of the ELAS *andartes*. The 'Animals' operation in Greece in June–July 1943, he writes, 'as several of SOE's observers noticed, was one of the few times when the Greeks did seem to want to come out from the hills and hit back at their occupiers' (Foot 2008, 289).[19] Mulgan, training and fighting alongside the Greeks in their covert operations, was to challenge this ill-informed dismissal on repeated occasions.

Mulgan seems to have been interested in guerrilla warfare for some time. A key influence already referred to was the British Army officer Orde Wingate (1903–44), who had been very successful in escalating guerrilla resistance in Italian-occupied Ethiopia in the early stages of the war.[20] Historians sometimes claim that WW2, at least in the European theatre, can be said to have started not with the German-Russian invasion of Poland in September 1939 but rather with Italy's 1935 attack on Ethiopia (also known by the exonym 'Abyssinia'). Mulgan certainly highlighted its significance; the Italian occupation of Ethiopia from 1936 onwards had focused his despair about the spread of fascism (7 percent of the country's population was wiped out by the invaders). But Wingate and his troops' success in reconquering the country seemed to offer hope that internally stimulated resistance may be an important answer in the fight against fascism. At one point during Wingate's campaign, in May 1941, an Italian army of 14,000 had been forced to surrender to just 150 British, Ethiopian and Sudanese fighters under his command, pulled off through strategies of ambush and surprise. Developing his ideas around the same time as Mao in China and twenty years before Che Guevara in Cuba, Wingate recognised that counterinsurgency was most effective when tapping into the local cause and developing it into something worth fighting for. This works, he stated, 'only when a large proportion of the civilian population surrounding

19   Foot's account of SOE operations in Greece follows the activities of Nicholas Hammond as characteristic (Hammond, we shall see, resigned in August 1944 in protest at Brigadier Barker-Benfield's support of ELAS) and gives a short description of the sabotage of the Asopos viaduct, which involved no Greeks at all. Foot leaves no doubt as to his position in his ironic account of Barker-Benfield's view that the ELAS troops 'were really splendid fellows, who would fight well in the common cause' (2008, 289). Foot cites Woodhouse's *Apple of Discord* as 'the best summary' of Greek partisan activity (331n12). For an examination of this claim, see Chapter 7.

20   Wingate's activities in Ethiopia are described by M.R.D. Foot as 'the first of SOE enterprises east of the Atlantic that got anywhere worth going' (2008, 216).

the enemy's back areas is friendly to the guerrillas' (Anglim 2014, 117). Wingate's anti-imperialist sentiments in support of Ethiopian nationalism under Emperor Haile Selassie were key to his skill in motivating his co-fighters. (He subsequently became very critical of Britain's attempts to stifle Ethiopian sovereignty, and its refusal to honour those it had used in fighting the Italians.) His views were probably not available to Mulgan in written form and can be accessed today only from recently declassified military reports, but Wingate did give a lecture at a conference in Cairo at the end of 1940 which may have influenced SOE policy. More likely, however, Mulgan was initiated into these ideas through Rufus Sheppard who, as mentioned, had fought as a Company Commander under Wingate in Ethiopia (Ogden 2012, 187). Tim Foley, an Irishman who joined Mulgan in the mountains and later became a close friend, had also seen service there. Wingate's report to HQ entitled 'Ethiopian Campaign' gives some detail about his views. He wrote:

> We had first to convince the Ethiopian, suspicious as he was of all white men, of our bona fides. This meant he must see us fighting not by his side but in front of him. His contact with our young officers must convince him that [. . .] we were not only brave soldiers but devoted to the cause of his liberties. (Anglim 2014, 117)

Mulgan's version of this philosophy influenced his operations throughout his time with the ELAS guerrillas. It wasn't enough just to be expelling the invaders; you had to share the deeper concerns of the *andartes*' revolutionary project. He cites Wingate in *Report on Experience* on developing a 'hard core' of fighters, a small group who have been gradually convinced of your good faith, as a key to success. Standard military discipline doesn't work: 'Wingate said: "Never ask favours, but tell people if they care to help they can come along, that you yourself are going anyway"' (RE 155).[21] He would have understood the Greek concept of *filotimo*, which depends on

---

21　Wingate was later sent to organise guerrilla units behind Japanese lines in India and died in a plane crash there in 1944. He is today most famous, in the UK at least, for his creation of the Long Range Penetration Groups of Indian guerrillas known as the Chindits.

this assumption that a sense of honour cannot be imposed from without but only stimulated when it has been fully internalised. This presented the challenge that Mulgan had been waiting for: to draw on the solidarity of the Greek comrades and work towards a common underlying goal.

Another possible influence on Mulgan, though of a very different stripe, was Lenin, whose 1906 essay on *Der Partisanenkampf* ('Guerrilla Warfare') we will be referring to again in a later chapter. At this point it is worth listening to what Eric Hobsbawm writes about Lenin in his book *Age of Extremes* (1994), to compare it with the ideological challenges Mulgan was coming to terms with in his dealings with EAM-ELAS: in particular the movement's rapid growth and shifts in policy. Lenin's Bolsheviks, Hobsbawm writes,

> grew from a small troop of a few thousand in March 1917 to a quarter of a million members by the early summer of that year. Contrary to the Cold War mythology, which saw Lenin essentially as an organizer of coups, the only real asset he and the Bolsheviks had was the ability to recognize what the masses wanted; to, as it were, lead by knowing how to follow. When, for instance, he recognized that, contrary to the socialist programme, the peasants wanted a division of the land into family farms, he did not hesitate for a moment to commit the Bolsheviks to this form of economic individualism. (Hobsbawn 2002, 61)

This readiness to follow and adapt, shared by irregular warriors of such different political allegiances as Wingate and Lenin, was to guide Mulgan through uncharted territory in the months ahead.

The work continued to give Mulgan enormous satisfaction until the end of his time with the *andartes*.[22] Despite the appalling suffering he was to witness, he never lost a sense of joy in the bonding with

---

22 This was confirmed by his interpreter, Paul Contomichalos, who was not only with Mulgan throughout his time in the mountains but also spent three days with him immediately before his death. 'John Mulgan loved his job', he wrote to Paul Day in 1965, 'and was, I believe, one of the most popular Allied officers in this region' (ATL MS-Papers-7906-42). These details are further explored in Chapter 9.

the comrades. An example of this is described by the resistance photographer Spyros Meletzis, some of whose photos we have reproduced in our illustrations. Meletzis was based in 1943–44 around Fourna and nearby Rentina, the seat of the ELAS officers' training school. Towards the end of the occupation, when the Germans were retreating, 'Mulgan and Co' once again destroyed the German-occupied railway station and line at Kaitsa. Meletzis writes:

> I followed the activities of the mountain artillery when, at dawn, it fired on and destroyed the railway station of Kaitsa where, after the second, third and fourth cannon blast, nothing was left standing. Then the Germans started firing at us with mortars and machine guns, but the *andartes*, meanwhile, had unbolted their cannon, loaded it onto the mules, and all together we returned to Rentina. What a celebration that night in Rentina over the success with the cannon! The English head of the saboteurs unit, Major Mulgan, roasted lambs, offered plenty of wine and beer to the men, even cakes. Everyone was over-joyed. (Meletzis 1982, 34–35)

Area 3

The area Mulgan worked in during his time in the mountains was at the heart of the ELAS stronghold, the expanse of around 8,000 square kilometres encompassing south Thessaly and north Roumeli that SOE called Area 3. Here ELAS held absolute control, although trouble threatened on their borders. At one point after his arrival, from October 1943 to January 1944, ELAS was in bitter territorial and ideological conflict with EDES further to the west, where Thessaly meets Epirus. EDES had dominance over Epirus and down to Agrinion, while ELAS controlled mainly the Pindus mountain range, stretching from north to south (north Epirus, Macedonia, Thessaly, Roumeli), with gradual expansion to many other areas.[23]

---

23   ELAS forces expanded gradually to Thrace, Peloponnesus and some of the islands, including eventually even Crete, which was known to maintain its own political agenda, forming resistance groups based on family solidarity.

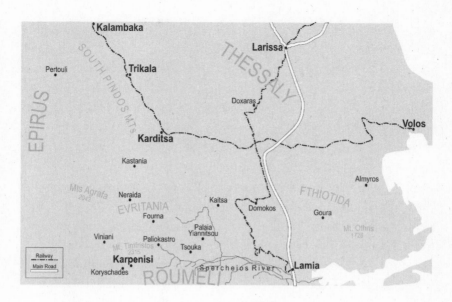

Mulgan writes (as always giving nothing away politically): 'Early in October the Greeks started a civil war, the big party [ELAS] against the small [EDES], but all the fighting was over the mountains in Epirus and did not disturb us' (RE 140). The wider political implications of this civil war would soon become as much a part of Mulgan's war as the resistance against the Axis invaders. Battlelines were being quickly drawn up between ELAS and the British-backed EDES, with none other than New Zealander Tom Barnes as chief BLO with EDES playing a key role as instigator of hostilities. In Anglophone accounts, blame is usually laid at ELAS's door for these hostilities, but Foreign Office archives reveal the extent to which British support for EDES (as well as for EKKA) was intended principally as a means of countering the strength of the left-wing ELAS. Procopis Papastratis records Barnes's 11 December 1943 cable to Cairo: 'Zervas realises he must smash the ELAS so as to be of use to us, which I tell him is our reason for supporting him.' After two attempts in December to persuade Zervas to stand up to ELAS forces under Aris Velouhiotis, Barnes finally succeeded on 4 January (Papastratis 1984, 154). Heavy casualties were suffered on both sides, with EDES eventually pushed back to the boundary of the Arachthos river. Behind the conflict lay the mad scramble for possession of the territories left undefended after the Italian surrender, with the Germans pouring in heavy weaponry to take control. Mulgan had certainly been thrown in at the deep end, into a situation of extreme and interlocking national and international strife.

But for the moment, happily settled in his ELAS bubble, Mulgan's attention was elsewhere. In autumn 1943 when he arrived, the challenges in his area were twofold: to disrupt the Germans enforcing their brutal hold over the country, and somehow to deal with the chaos created by the Italian surrender, which had left their massive forces highly vulnerable in the Greek mountains with winter ahead. After their surrender, nearly two thirds of the Italians managed to evacuate from Greece, but the bulk of the Pinerolo Division and a few other smaller units (approximately 10,000 troops) ended up in Mulgan's area under the supervision of joint SOE and partisan HQ in Pertouli. Philip Worrall, who had landed with Mulgan (carrying 45,000 gold sovereigns), was to become responsible for the care of the Italians in camps further east, near Volos ('the reddest town in Greece' [Eudes 1972, 96]),[24] but Mulgan's base remained in the adjoining mountain area occupied by the ELAS *andartes* of the 16th East Thessaly Division. In the months under snow, with promised SOE planes failing to drop in the much-needed supplies, they could do little but keep themselves and their charges warm and fed. The time was not wasted for Mulgan, who took the opportunity to talk at length with the comrades and learned a great deal about their history, grievances and aspirations.

Longer-term political considerations would have predominated in these discussions. Greek society had been dramatically radicalised by political repression and economic collapse, and the hardship Mulgan witnessed in the mountain villages lent justification to the armed struggle and drive towards social reform being undertaken by EAM-ELAS. In opposition to the Foreign Office in London,

---

24   Eudes writes that the people of Volos, many of whom soon joined Mulgan in the mountains, 'heard the news of the Italian surrender on the radio on the night of 8–9 September. There was an immediate, open, door-to-door mobilization of EAM' (1972, 96).

SOE wisely recognised, at least in the early stage of its involvement in Greece, that their best chance of local support was from groups with anti-monarchist sentiments, as only these would have the motivation to fight a strong resistance with their own post-war future at stake. Along with their political motivation, ELAS now also had the weapons confiscated from the Italians and the incentive to seek national unity through dominance over EDES, particularly as the republican sentiments in EDES began to wane. By the time Mulgan joined them ELAS had increased its popular support to nearly eight times that of EDES, numbering around 35–40,000 nationwide.[25] In gradually putting pressure on SOE to favour EDES, the Foreign Office played an unwitting part in converting thousands to the cause of ELAS, especially as it began to be suspected that the former was secretly supported by the collaborationist government in Athens and that the government-supported Security Battalions were collaborating with the Germans. Politics, as the historian Mark Mazower puts it, began to polarise everything (2001, 93).

As was to be expected of a rapidly expanding popular movement of this size, the policies of EAM-ELAS were far from unified. By late 1943 tensions within ELAS HQ in Mulgan's area were running high. Should the band remain loyal to their British allies, as Andreas Tzimas and Giorgis Siantos of EAM suggested, or should they be wary of becoming instruments of British designs, as Stefanos Sarafis warned? Should their long-term aim be to unite with other Balkan states loyal to the Soviets, as a few believed? Was it not better to follow a broad socialist line (comparable to that of the Popular Front) that believed, as their fighting leader Aris Velouhiotis insisted, that Greece was not ready for communism, that communism was only a distant ideal (Pyromaglou 1978, 84; Woodhouse 2002, 5)? These conflicts were to impact directly on Mulgan's operations as well as his beliefs.

Meanwhile, the insight into left-wing Greek objectives that Mulgan was gaining had to be juggled precariously with directives

---

25   Woodhouse 2002, 38. By the time of liberation, a year later, ELAS numbered 119,000 and
      EDES 19,000, according to Grigoriadis (2011, III, 234–36),

from his commanders in SOE HQ in Cairo. As time went on, he began to chafe under orders he often disagreed with—a situation which set him apart from most other BLOs. Nicholas Hammond in West Macedonia shared the growing anti-ELAS sentiment at HQ; he instinctively mistrusted ELAS and soon resigned, to be replaced by Arthur Edmonds, who was more successful in adhering to the nominal directive to keep out of politics. BLOs in EDES areas, of course, had no such conflict.[26] In Epirus, Tom Barnes sympathised with EDES to the extent of becoming involved in Zervas's attempts to collaborate with the enemy against their left-wing rivals.[27] Barnes even had the dubious distinction of figuring as a prominent denigrator of the left-wing resistance in Louis de Bernières's *Captain Corelli's Mandolin* (1995, 220–21). The novel, which brought the history of the Italian and German occupation of Greece to a wide readership, depicts the ELAS partisans as base and dishonest thugs who robbed the local villagers and raped the women. It caused outrage in Greece (Milne 2000) and the subsequent film version, scripted by Shawn Slovo, rewrote the plot to correct some of the highly fantasised caricatures.

Working with 'the Communists'

Collaborating with the ELAS *andartes*, Mulgan had the opportunity to establish the sort of military relationship that George Orwell had cherished in Spain, one of equality, without reference to class or education. His success in this project was a result of both personality and politics. That it was unique in the country was acknowledged by both Chris Woodhouse, overall commander of the area, and Julian Dolbey at SOE HQ in Cairo. Sabotage operations and harassment of the retreating Germans during the Noah's Ark operation in the autumn of 1944, Woodhouse wrote, were most effective in Mulgan's

---

26   In the Peloponnese, where ELAS fought it out with the Security Battalions, BLOs played only a minor role, collecting intelligence.

27   Richter 2009, 122–78, especially 139, 142–45, 149–78. Throughout these dealings, Barnes often appears to have been acting on his own initiative. For an evaluation of Barnes's role, see Gounelas 2018, 211–13.

area, 'where the mutual confidence established between an excellent group of young ELAS officers and Mulgan's remarkable team . . . reached a higher degree than anywhere else in Greece' (LJB 290). 'Working with' the *andartes* was as much a matter of the assumption of equality, the friendship over an evening drink, as it was of the vitally important organisation and training. More than the other BLOs, especially as his command of Greek improved, Mulgan chose to socialise with the left-wing Greeks around him, and they clearly sought his company. The 20th of February 1944 seems to have been an unusual day without visitors. After a night of 'much drinking', his diary records a 'Quiet sombre languorous day [. . .] Guess the general is sleeping it off'. Then on 24 February: 'General & 2 andartes in for usual tea & drinks'. There would have been much to share by now with the normally reticent and highly disciplined Sarafis. It was this assumption of fraternity that made the difference.

Woodhouse's praise of Mulgan also singled out for notice Mulgan's relations with the commander of ELAS's 16th (and later also 13th) Division, Kostas Tsamakos, which, Woodhouse noted, 'were an example to the rest of Greece' (LJB 290).[28] Tsamakos is a notable example of an ELAS commander who was to pay heavily for his connections with 'the communists'.

Born and raised in the remote mountain village of Kataraktis in Tzoumerka, Epirus, where his ancestors had grazed sheep and goats for generations, Tsamakos fulfilled the destiny of many young Greek men after the humiliating defeat by the Turks in 1897 by enlisting in the newly reformed army which helped to liberate large swathes of Greece from Ottoman rule in 1912–13.[29] Mulgan records how this by now grey-haired veteran had been decorated

---

28   O'Sullivan is quoting from Woodhouse in an internal report on the history of the Allied Military Mission in Greece.

29   After his retirement from military activity Tsamakos wrote and published a vivid collection of stories set in his home village of Kataraktis, many of them with subtle autobiographical references. In the story entitled 'Mitro Kapsalis', a first-person narrator describes how the period from 1909 onwards was a good era to join the army in the build-up to the 1912–13 liberation and says that 'I myself served in that pre-war army in a specialised unit in Athens' (Tsamakos 1949, 40). The plain-spoken, demotic language of the writing would have appealed to Mulgan.

in the Salonika campaign (RE 146), when Greece finally joined WW1: he was wounded, his brother Ioannis records, at the Battle of Skra in May 1918.[30] After this he rose steadily in the ranks of the professional army, but during Metaxas's regime (1936–41) was one of many officers who opted to back Eleftherios Venizelos in his opposition to the fascist-supported monarchy, and was discharged from the army. With his left-leaning republican views, it was natural for Tsamakos to join ELAS rather than EDES in 1943, when the resistance forces were recruiting. Mulgan records good humouredly in *Report on Experience* that he got sick of hearing about the divisions in Greece between Metaxas and Venizelos supporters (RE 167). But the schism, now overlaid by that between right/monarchist and left/republican, was deeply entrenched in Greek society, as he was well aware.

Mulgan's tribute to Tsamakos in *Report on Experience* captures another of those moments of intimacy that stand out:

> If Costa Tsamakos should survive to read this, which I doubt, for his opinions are well known and outspoken, I hope he will still remember our friendship and the long snow-bound hours when we cheered each other in Fourna, passing *tsipouro*—a lower-class cousin of *ouzo*—across the fire and exchanging reminiscences [. . .] we had a great friendship and I think I promised him that if I ever grew to sufficient stature to publish my reminiscences, an unlikely contingency, his photograph, which I still possess, would adorn it. (RE 146)

The photo did not appear in *Report on Experience*, either the first or second edition, but Vincent O'Sullivan does reproduce a fine portrait in the biography. O'Sullivan is right to put scare quotes around Tsamakos's political allegiances when he calls him 'a "communist" of convenience' (LJB 282). Tsamakos, like Mulgan, was never 'a communist' except in the sense used loosely at the time to refer

---

30 Interview published in the newspaper *Empros* on 2 November 1963, 11. Ioannis Tsamakos achieved a certain prominence in Greece as a mountaineer.

to those who, either broadly or narrowly, supported EAM-ELAS. The label 'communist' caused considerable misunderstanding. But the suggestion of 'convenience', that Tsamakos was making opportunistic use of ELAS, can hardly be justified. There seems little doubt, judging from Mulgan's testimony alone, about Tsamakos's 'well known' commitment to the left-wing cause, about which he was prepared to be 'outspoken'.

Mulgan's fear for his friend's safety as the left became increasingly persecuted after liberation was well founded. In the so-called White Terror purges of 'communists' in 1945–46, actual or imagined left-wing supporters and their families were executed, thrown into gaol or sent into internal exile in their tens of thousands.[31] As Polymeris Voglis and others have pointed out, 'Whereas elsewhere in Europe [immediately after the war] prisons were flooded with fascists and their collaborators, in Greece most of the prisoners were members of leftist resistance organizations' (Voglis 2004, 143). In fact, Greece did not pass legislation acknowledging that there had been an anti-Axis resistance until 1984. Tsamakos survived, but on the first page of the newspaper *Rizospastis* on 20 September 1946, nearly two years after the end of the war, he is listed among 32 ELAS officers and leaders sent into exile on the island of Ikaria.[32]

Tsamakos's position in the ELAS forces would certainly have made him a prominent target in the polarised months and years following liberation. In July 1944 he had been promoted by PEEA (the Government in the Mountains) to General and then made Director General to the Secretariat for War.[33] Finally, in September,

31 Voglis writes: 'In 1945, 80,000 warrants were issued, 50,000 persons were arrested and, according to an official report dated the 1 October 1945, 16,700 were in jail'. Numbers of leftists among these vary, but he reckons that 'Perhaps a total of 10,000 leftist political prisoners in 1945' would be an accurate estimate (2002, 57). See also David Close, who confirms these figures and adds that 'various British and American observers confirm that the extent of persecution [of the left] was immense, and that for nine months after Varkiza [12 February 1945] the scale of violence by the Left was insignificant, except in Slav-inhabited areas close to the northern borders' (1993, 164). Mazower gives higher estimates, writing that 'By the end of 1945, some 48,956 EAM supporters were behind bars' (2000, 38).

32 Among those with him were Sarafis, Bakirtzis, Matsoukas and Kalambalikis—see Marion Sarafis 1980a, lxxxii and 1990, 26–30.

33 In this capacity he was chosen on 28 July to welcome the eight-man team of Soviet representatives under Grigory Popov who landed at the Neraida airstrip close to where

Tsamakos was appointed overall commander of the mainland group of divisions of ELAS forces (Stefanos Sarafis 1980, 337, 375, 399). PEEA and ELAS clearly held him in the highest regard.

It is true, however, that like others of those ELAS partisans who were not members of the Communist Party, Tsamakos fell foul of the KKE in the post-war years. In late 1946, when the British-backed Greek government was struggling to reconcile the deeply entrenched hostilities between the left and the right, Tsamakos and a couple of other ELAS officers, including the prominent General Kalambalikis, were released from detention on Ikaria. An undated document, now in the KKE archives in Perissos, Athens, accused Kalambalikis and Tsamakos of selling out and making their peace with the government (LCP, AM 48223).[34] We have been unable to find any evidence, however, for O'Sullivan's further claim that by 1947 Tsamakos had joined the National Army to fight his former comrades (LJB 283).[35] O'Sullivan doesn't give a source for this claim, but it may well have been an ambiguous statement in the undated Perissos document where Kalambalikis and Tsamakos were denounced as waverers, who didn't remain faithful to KKE policy but rather agreed to attempt a compromise with the government. In so doing, the document continues, they 'stood against the Republican/ Democratic Army' ('tethikan antimetopoi tou Dimokratikou Stratou') (LCP, AM 48223), which should almost certainly be interpreted metaphorically rather than literally.

Post-war policy ensured that former ELAS officers were

Mulgan was stationed, their mission being to negotiate with the Greek Communist Party, effectively advising in favour of full co-operation with Allied policy (Grigoriadis 2011, III, 122–23).

34   Marion Sarafis records that Kalambalikis and 'two more ELAS generals', which seems to have included Tsamakos, returned from exile after agreement with the government and (in Kalambalikis's case, at least) in the hope of forming a 'non-communist Left' party (1980a, lxxxii). She insists that the officers had not been denounced by ELAS; their stance, she suggests, should not be interpreted as capitulation.

35   No reference is given to either Kalambalikis or Tsamakos in Thrasyvoulos Tsakalotos's detailed history (1978–79) of the government forces fighting in the civil war between 1946 and 1949. With his anti-communist sympathies, Tsakalotos would surely have crowed about such a capitulation.

systematically excluded from active service.[36] After his return from
exile, according to a witness from his village,[37] Tsamakos lived a
quiet life near his brother in Athens and dedicated himself to writing
fictional accounts of his childhood and youth in rural Kataraktis and
then his early experiences in the military (Tsamakos 1949). These
clearly autobiographical narratives understandably steer well clear of
any political innuendo at this hypersensitive time. He was formally
discharged from the army ('apostrateftike') on 1 January 1948.[38]

* * *

Looking back, commentators today draw attention to the split
within the EAM-ELAS movement, evident from the beginning,
which would ultimately cause its downfall. Mulgan was very aware
that periods of revolutionary fervour (as in Spain) are bound to cause
internal divisions. There was little doubt about which side he was on.

Interesting evidence here comes from Domique Eudes, who in the
1960s recorded oral testimony from several of the leading Kapetans,
some of whom were still living in self-exile from Greece—in places
like Belgrade, Sofia, Prague and Tashkent. A central theme of his
book is the constant tension between those like Aris Velouhiotis
and Tzimas, who pushed for a peasant guerrilla movement, drawing
on support from outside Athens, and the KKE supporters of the
Stalinist-influenced Central Committee of EAM in the capital.
Eudes's summary is worth quoting at this point:

> The image of communism in the mountains was composed
> of various elements: the peasant guerrilla, self-administration

36 The *Lefki Vivlos* (1945b), the KKE's detailed history of the civil war, records that soon after
the Varkiza agreement, and in contravention of its articles, 'not only ELASites but also anyone
suspected of republican/left-wing [dimokratikes] beliefs' were excluded from service (26).
Officers of higher rank in ELAS were placed on 'List B', kept inactive until their retirement
(27). Heinz Richter records how after April 1945, former ELAS members were not considered
worthy to remain on the active list, and that 'Approximately eight hundred former ELAS
officers were put on the demobilisation list' (1985, 156). See also Close 1993, 165.

37 Our thanks to Christos Makrygiannis from the village of Kataraktis.

38 DIS, enkyklio 76/1948.

in the villages, people's justice, decentralization, the national resistance tradition, bearded klephts and, occasionally, priests. The unorthodox nature of this image by comparison with the Stalinist ideal does not make it any less profoundly revolutionary. Its driving force was derived from a peasant reality which had remained largely untouched by industrial upheavals, and which recoiled spontaneously from the centralism and quasi-industrial organization of the orthodox Revolution. The meeting of communism and the Greek Resistance was the local synthesis of a revolution in progress. Certain members of the Central Committee could only see it as a misunderstanding; although the relationship had been useful over part of the course, these individuals were prepared to renounce it at the decisive moment to preserve an abstraction. (1972, 105)

Like Tsamakos, Mulgan identified instinctively with the 'peasant' branch of the movement, and sometimes 'recoiled spontaneously' from directives from Athens. This helps explain his occasional railing against 'the communists', by which he invariably meant the Stalinist hardliners in the capital. Like Tsamakos, he thought in terms of a radical socialism rather than a strict communist programme. Figures published by Andreas Kedros indicate that this was a widespread phenomenon. In 1944 EAM-ELAS included in its ranks '6 bishops, a great number of priests, 30 university professors, 16 generals, 34 colonels and 500 officers of lower rank, all of them non-communists' (1980, 54). As head *Kapetanios* of ELAS, Aris was similarly cautious about the preparedness of Greece for communism. Komninos Pyromaglou, second in command of EDES, records Aris claiming in a conversation at partisan SOE HQ in Pertouli:

A communist revolution in Greece is not yet possible. We know better than anyone, and better than you, what might be the reaction of the people, and what we can expect. In spite of this we will stand firm against the return of the King. (1978, 84)

Mulgan quickly understood the plural constitution of EAM. One of its leading strategists, Giorgis Siantos, was frequently in Mulgan's Area 3. Although Secretary-General of the KKE, he had laid out a Popular Front-style approach early on in EAM's development, and emphasised parliamentary themes rather than the class struggle, despite being himself from a working-class background. (His moderate approach, which included a willingness to tolerate the British presence, later put him out of favour with the harder-line post-war leadership of KKE under Nikos Zachariadis.)[39] Mulgan repeatedly tried to convince his SOE bosses that EAM was not aiming for a Soviet-style government. This was doubted by the British at the time but verified by later historical evidence.[40] Prompted by the Foreign Office in London, SOE Cairo was questioning its BLOs closely about the aims and spread of communism in the country; such was the growing hysteria that most jumped to the conclusion that the Soviets were plotting behind the scenes. Mulgan knew better. In answering a military questionnaire in May 1944, he wrote:

> Communism in Greece is belief of only small minority and then rather its aim is seizure of political point, not re organisation of the country. I have met none of them who had any practical plans for communism in Greece. Greece remains intensely individual country, violently concerned with retention all forms of private property. (TNA HS 5/338)

This assessment is accepted by both Greek and Anglophone historians today, almost without exception. Echoing Mulgan's terms, Polymeris Voglis, for example, writes that EAM 'aimed at

---

39 Siantos had begun as a worker in the tobacco industry and became a leading syndicalist in their union. Sent into exile in the Metaxas period, during the war he occupied senior positions in EAM and PEEA, as well as that of Secretary-General of KKE.

40 A delegation of eight Russians welcomed by Tsamakos came to warn ELAS that the Russian government was not in a position to help them (Kontis and Sfetas 2011, 18). Grigoriadis (2011, III, 124–26) records that the first adviser to the USSR Embassy in Cairo persuaded representatives of EAM, Petros Rousos, and a little later Angelos Angelopoulos to convey to PEEA that they should accept the terms of the Lebanon agreement and send six of their representatives to take up ministries in the government-in-exile.

national liberation and the democratization of the country under
the vague slogan of *laokratia* (people's rule) rather than radical
social change and revolution' (2004, 154). Although Mulgan never
hesitated to express views critical of the excesses of ELAS discipline,
or lack of it, his support for the socialist policies that united most of
the country, for 'our comrades in the hills' (RE 170), never wavered.
What interested him, as it did Orwell, was less the theory of
communism than 'the more important question of its practice; that
is, [. . .] how to start a revolutionary party and [. . .] how to control it
once you have got the party started' (RE 165). SOE Cairo seems not
to have been aware, or perhaps not to have minded, at least initially,
that one of its leading BLOs supported this revolutionary project.
What he encountered in Greece, Mulgan continues in *Report on
Experience*, was an impressive form of political organisation with a
broad socialist inclusiveness:

> The Communists of Greece possessed [...] a very remarkable
> technique for taking and holding power and a considerable ability
> in exploiting this technique. [. . .] The Communists we knew were
> organized to take and hold power and to get orders and to carry
> them out. They would accept any recruits that were prepared to
> accept their discipline and any ideas or slogans that fitted the
> needs of the moment. (RE 168–69)

He would protest about some of these methods and slogans, but
never about the validity of the underlying aims. When Churchill
referred to ELAS cantankerously as 'bandits', nothing could have
been further from the truth. The 'banditry' of the old *kleft* tradition
had been ruthlessly—sometimes too ruthlessly by Aris[41]—stamped

41   Aris's excessive use of force against traitors and those who wouldn't conform to ELAS
     discipline did much to discredit the movement. The mild-mannered Stefanos Sarafis, who
     remained close to Aris throughout, explained (but didn't excuse) Aris's harshness to be a
     result of what Aris had suffered as a member of KKE during his time in prison, where the
     notorious torture methods of Metaxas's Minister of Public Security, Maniadakis, left many
     victims. On one occasion Sarafis asked Aris why he was beating a villager who refused to offer
     some of his sheep to the ELAS mess, adding that 'it was not suitable for the GHQ Captain
     to beat people up'. Aris calmed down but replied: 'Maniadakis never put pepper up your tail'
     (Marion Sarafis 1980a, lxii–lxiii).

out. On one notorious occasion, Aris personally executed a livestock thief as an example to his men. Even Nicholas Hammond, rarely willing to praise ELAS, records that when the RSR (British Raiding Support Regiments) joined them in the mountains in the summer of 1944, they 'contrasted the pilfering in the territory of EDES with the efficiency and discipline of ELAS units' (1983, 158). In 'Free Greece', doors could be left open; 'Locks became a thing of the past.' And with women joining ELAS in increasing numbers, gender relations were carefully regulated, with rape a capital offence. 'You had better understand once and for all,' Aris is reported as telling his men, 'that as long as you are here your rods are just for pissing' (Eudes 1972, 23).

Mulgan wasn't the first to attempt to persuade his military bosses of the need to understand the EAM-ELAS movement in broad and sympathetic terms. Immediately before his arrival, Brigadier Eddie Myers had tried to resolve political tensions among the guerrilla bands by accompanying a delegation of representatives of the three main groups to Cairo, to negotiate their claim to be recognised as a national force. The EAM-ELAS delegation got a hostile reaction from the British administration along with the Greek government-in-exile and the king, and were sent back harbouring significant resentment about their failed petition. Myers's own detailed description of the Cairo trip with the delegates, as well as his subsequent meetings in London, at the very time of Mulgan's drop into Greece, makes instructive reading for its portrayal of Westminster's approach to the Greek left. After three weeks of meetings in the capital with a range of people at SOE HQ in Baker Street, at the Foreign Office, and with the British king, Myers finally lunched with Churchill on 2 October 1943. Churchill informed him that it was not SOE's role to meddle in politics and that he personally looked forward to the Greek king's return to Greece. Myers emphasised Greece's opposition to this but sensed the limits of his power to change the 'Old Man's' mind. He writes:

> One point I could not get into Churchill's head was that the
> andartes were not just 'bandits', but that they represented all

types of Greeks, as well as many Republican leaders. Sarafis had been Military Attaché in Paris. Tzimas had been a Communist Deputy. Kartalis had been Finance Minister in more than one Greek Government. Colonel Psaros was one of the most capable soldiers I have ever met. They were not just 'Tom Wintringhams', which Churchill had more than once called them. I could not convince him that I was in touch not only with the andartes and the mostly poor people in the mountains, but with virtually every element and every thinking body inside Greece, including those in all the big towns. (Myers 1975, 162)[42]

It was Mulgan's (and Greece's) misfortune that Myers, with his broader understanding, was removed from his post after being accused of enhancing the status of the left-wing partisans. (The Greek king, in fact, threatened to resign if Myers was allowed to return to Greece [Myers 1985, 264n].) Chris Woodhouse, who replaced him, had like Churchill an instinctive mistrust of 'Tom Wintringhams', those who had provided a model for many in the 1930s, Mulgan among them, of a new form of social organisation. After the failure of the Cairo trip, British opposition to 'the communists' and determination to restore the monarchy was now out in the open, with ominous implications for the future. Soon after this, as we have seen, renewed hostilities broke out between ELAS and EDES.

By the end of 1943, after the disembarkation of Allied forces in Sicily in July and the withdrawal of Axis forces from North Africa, the tide appeared to be turning in the Allies' favour. One consequence of the new geopolitical picture emerging was that Keble's SOE empire with its eclectic policies was attracting increasing criticism from above. At the end of the year he was replaced by W.A.M. Stawell and

---

42   Myers also insisted (1975, 186) that most Greeks are too individualistic to tolerate a communist government. See also a letter from Keble to the Secretary of the Defence Committee GHQ MEF (8 April 1943), which includes a report by Myers of 7 April 1943 advising against insistence upon the return of the monarchy to Greece. Further to the right than Mulgan, Myers nonetheless urged that 'If H.M. Government publish announcements as advised by me concerning the King and constitutional elections not only [will] EAM establishment of communism be destroyed but most of Greece will remain democratic as they are at heart' (TNA HS 5/338).

soon after that by Brigadier Barker-Benfield. (At this point a section
of the Cairo SOE office moved to Bari in Italy to be closer to support
for the Balkans.) Ambitions for ELAS activity had not been entirely
eradicated from the SOE project. The following August, after Mulgan
had been nearly a year in the mountains, Barker-Benfield, voicing the
tail end of British confidence, visited Nicholas Hammond, who had by
then replaced Chris Woodhouse as commander of SOE in mainland
Greece, at the organisation's HQ in Thessaly. Difference of opinion
between the two men over the role of ELAS led Hammond, who like
his predecessor was suspicious of ELAS's long-term motives, to resign
(Hammond 1983, 170–73; Foot, 2008, 289). As a result, Barker-
Benfield arranged to meet the two New Zealanders, Mulgan and
Edmonds, presumed to be less hostile to ELAS,[43] and after discussion
with both proceeded to offer Hammond's position to Edmonds, who
accepted. Barker-Benfield, according to Hammond, thought that
Edmonds 'had good military ideas' but 'was not much impressed with
him otherwise'. He admired 'Mulgan's directness but did not like his
low rating of the fighting qualities of ELAS' (Hammond 1983, 172–
73). There may have been other reasons for Mulgan's exclusion, and
Hammond rarely missed an opportunity to disparage ELAS, but this
judgement was not inconsistent with Mulgan's views on the military
role and capacities of his guerrilla comrades, as well as on any last-ditch
drive to promote more confrontational ELAS initiatives that would
have devastating consequences for the local people. Although we don't
know what else was discussed, there is no doubt that Barker-Benfield's
mission had been to clarify that ELAS still had some support from
SOE despite mounting evidence from Cairo to the contrary, and
that co-operation with ELAS fighters needed to be ramped up to the
maximum in the face of the imminent German withdrawal from
Greece. He also met up with the EAM leaders Siantos, Sarafis and
Despotopoulos.[44] But this renewed support for ELAS was shortlived.

43 Hammond reveals that Barker-Benfield expressed a very negative view of Tom Barnes, the
    other leading SOE operative (1983, 170–73).

44 At the same time Barker-Benfield refused to meet Colonel Paul West, head of the American
    OSS. Mistrust between the British in SOE and the Americans in OSS at this time is
    discussed in Chapter 8. Clogg describes, however, how some of West's colleagues in OSS

It was around the time of Barker-Benfield's trip to the Thessaly HQ that Edmonds was recommended by Woodhouse for high promotion within SOE while Mulgan was recommended for 'out-posting' from the organisation, suitable only for ordinary regimental or civilian duties.

Mulgan and Edmonds had much in common. Both were hands-on fighters, participating repeatedly and collaboratively with the ELAS guerrillas. Edmonds had been there from the start, having been one of the New Zealand engineers, along with Barnes, specifically requested to be dropped in with Myers to destroy the Gorgopotamos bridge. The two men shared a preparedness to fight with ELAS on its own terms, balancing judgement of its sometimes harsh measures against an understanding of the band's history and political objectives. Based by this time in Roumeli, Edmonds was in frequent contact with Aris Velouhiotis. His description in his 1998 memoir of Aris's often-quoted execution of the miserable livestock thief is remarkable for its absence of emotional hype (Edmonds 1998, 41). Nicholas Hammond, in contrast, describes Aris as 'the traditional Turkish type of bully in Greek legend, a man for whom I had an instantaneous and very deep dislike' (1983, 126). Mulgan's assessment of Aris is characteristically nuanced. In the report he sent J.V. Wilson at External Affairs in New Zealand before he died, he described Aris as 'one good standard type of Balkan Communist',

> a short thick-set man, wearing [...] a black beard, several knives and pistols round his waist, and an expression which always made sensitive persons like myself wish they had chosen some other country to fight in.

This wry self-deprecation, however, is undercut by frank admiration of Aris's ethos:

> were complaining about his subservience to the British. The American Stephen Penrose, head of OSS Secret Intelligence in Cairo, was preparing for a fight with SOE Cairo in August 1944 over the latter's attempt to extract all their secrets to 'enable them to keep us [the Americans] well under control [. . .] aided and abetted by Colonel West [. . .] the British don't like to have free information coming out of Greece without their knowledge, and without their control' (Clogg 2000, 132).

> He differs from certain 'non-political' partisan leaders with whom
> we afterwards had dealings, in that you couldnt [*sic*] buy him off
> with sovereigns or get friendly with him over a drink.[45]

Several others on the scene, and not only those on the left, saw
another side to Aris. Komninos Pyromaglou, second-in-command to
Zervas in EDES, paid tribute to Aris's uniqueness as leader, conceding
that 'he was the one who imposed iron discipline on the ELAS forces
. . . he was everywhere, inspiring admiration and fear, inciting trust
and hope in his *andartes* and despair in others' (Haritopoulos 2003,
349). Panayiotis Kanellopoulos of the government-in-exile summed
Aris up as 'a pure ideologue' (Haritopoulos 2003, 598).

Another similarity between Edmonds and Mulgan was their
profound admiration for the ordinary Greek people, both in their
suffering and in their support for the resistance. Edmonds, in fact,
stayed on in Greece until 1946 and married a Greek. But there were
differences. Edmonds makes a rare statement of overall purpose
around the middle of his memoir when he writes that given the
complexity of conflicting political objectives between the Allies and
the left-wing *andartes*, 'all I could do was to put my energy into
hastening the end of the occupation' (1998, 83). This equanimity
was not an option for Mulgan, given his commitment to the left.

Another New Zealand SOE operative working with ELAS
guerrillas, Don Stott, didn't make things easy for Mulgan. The
notorious 'Stott Affair', described by Mark Mazower as 'one of the
most extraordinary and potentially explosive episodes of the whole
war' (2001, 328), is analysed in detail by the German scholar Hagen
Fleischer. Acting on his own initiative, Stott, who had been decorated
for his role in the destruction of the Asopos viaduct, had like Barnes
become increasingly opposed to ELAS during his mission. In late
1943, via his contacts with right-wing organisations and the quisling
government, he arranged to meet the head of the German Secret
Field Police in Athens to discuss possible joint actions against the
Soviets. When his commander Woodhouse learned of this he

45   Report, 22 April 1945, ATL, J.V. Wilson Papers, MS-Papers-6875-2, 2.

signalled urgent instructions to Stott: 'You should not, repeat not, take any part in political affairs' (Fleischer 1980, 93). The second part of his signal, however, gave characteristically contradictory instructions: 'You should exclude EAM from cells organized by you but do it tactfully without letting them know you are doing so' (100n14). The affair, played down by Fleischer as something of a naïve escapade, nevertheless had the effect, he argues, of convincing the Greek left that, 'in pursuit of their anti-Communist schemes, the British [via types like Stott] did not even desist from collaboration with Fascist Germany' (1980, 107).[46] The indirect implications for Mulgan were probably two-fold. In addition to undermining his efforts to win the trust of the ELAS fighters, it may have made his commander, Woodhouse, just that bit more wary of over-independent New Zealanders taking personal initiative and getting out of their depth, as he would have seen it, on political matters. He would in time pick up on Mulgan's growing anger.

The increase in size and strength of ELAS was making the Foreign Office in London nervous. Gradually, British policy became shaped by Churchill's decision to keep Greece firmly under Western control via the monarchy, despite widespread opposition within the country itself. Within a short time, financial and military support for ELAS began to be withdrawn. Early on, Churchill's instructions had been somewhat ambivalent, recommending support both for the king and for ELAS (as far as it contributed to operational needs), although he can hardly have been unaware of the incompatibility of these two aims. On 18 March 1943, for example, he had advised the Minister of State in Cairo as follows:

> In view of the operational importance attached to subversive activities in Greece, there can be no question of SOE refusing to have

---

46   In her book about Stott, *New Zealand's Secret Heroes*, Gabrielle McDonald gives brief coverage of Stott's 'peace feelers' put out to German command and cites from a resulting report by Hermann Neubacher, Hitler's special envoy to the Balkans, urging for united British and German action against ELAS. McDonald attempts to justify Stott's initiative. 'There is no doubt', she writes, 'that Stott had the best interests of the Greeks at heart' (1991, 43–44).

dealings with a given group merely on the grounds that political sentiments of the group are opposed to King and Government [-in-exile], but subject to special operational necessity SOE should always veer in the direction of groups willing to support the King and Government and furthermore impress on such other groups as may be anti- the fact that the King and Government enjoy the fullest support of HMG. In general nothing should be neglected which helps promote unity among the resistance groups in Greece and between the latter and the King and Government. (Stafford 1983, 124)

Keeping a foot in both camps may have seemed possible in the spring of 1943. As the months and events advanced over the next year and a half, however, SOE's capacity to 'veer in the direction' of pro-monarchy groups became a Herculean task, given that most of the guerrillas were expressing determined opposition. A year after the above injunction, Churchill's patience with SOE had run out. Aware of the mutual hostility between SOE and the Foreign Office, as well as the divisions within SOE itself, he was talking in private about the organisation as 'a nest of intrigues' (Clogg 2000, 120) veering out of central control. 'The firm', as SOE was called among insiders until its name was declassified in the 1960s, was proving an equally frustrating organisation to work for from Mulgan's perspective, though for very different reasons.

Whose narrative?

In both his military reports and *Report on Experience*, Mulgan sometimes followed the tendency of the time in referring to EAM-ELAS members as 'the communists'. While he was well aware that political directives came from the Communist Party (KKE) in Athens, he was equally aware of course of the mixed and broad-based composition of the EAM-ELAS movement. In today's vocabulary, 'radical left' would perhaps be a more appropriate description, though plenty of EAM-ELAS members were more centre-left or simply anti-monarchist, and others had joined for patriotic as much as political reasons.

The blanket term 'communist' has caused considerable misunderstanding, beginning at this time and continuing in subsequent Cold War narratives driven by both Stalin and the Truman administration. Much that has been written about Mulgan's time with EAM-ELAS has been coloured by this misunderstanding. One of the most detailed accounts of Mulgan's military operations in Thessaly is given by Paul Day in an Oxford University Press Writers and their Work series of short monographs in 1977. Having visited the area in 1966, Day was able to trace the precise geography and dates of operations and gives a vivid account of the courage repeatedly displayed by Mulgan in his brutally occupied area. His historical accuracy, however, is skewed by slurs against ELAS[47]—that the *andartes* engaged in 'grandiose talk' but little action (30), 'refused to co-operate' (42) and in fact 'did much [. . .] to hinder' any resolve on Mulgan's part (32). Day was under the mistaken impression that, as he puts it, 'communist doctrine was obligatory for ELAS members' (34). Contrasting the young men and women from the mountain villages who joined ELAS with those left behind, he marvels at the way the villagers 'never showed the slightest sign of [. . .] betraying [. . .] their own worthless partisans who could not protect them' (57).[48] Day even makes the suggestion that the reprisals suffered by the civilian population as a result of Mulgan and the guerrillas' activities were 'completely acceptable to the *andartes*. Atrocities against fellow Greeks were fatalistically accepted' (36). To equate fatalism with heartlessness, however, is to misread the historical circumstances. Mulgan put it differently. In his account of a conversation with a group from

---

47   The main source of Day's account seems to have been a personal communication from Pat Wingate, an SOE operative working under Mulgan. Wingate's service reports to HQ at the time, now held in the Kew archives, give a rather different picture—of repeated co-operation from ELAS, with a few hitches.

48   It's as if Day is deliberately twisting Mulgan's meaning here. This phrase, that the *andartes* 'were worthless and offered them no protection', is in fact Mulgan's own (RE 147) as an example of a German misconception, disproved by the villagers. We shall return to this passage in Chapter 7.

the multiply devastated village of Kaitsa, it is the poignancy of the stoicism of this seeming 'fatalism' which is recognised, an endurance of pain stemming from a history of struggle against occupation and violence. These people made no complaint about what he and the *andartes* were doing.

> When we started to operate again in 1944 above Kaitsa, they sent a deputation to us. [. . .] They had the look of all peasant Greeks, of men who don't expect much fun but are prepared to endure. They didn't ask us to stop sabotaging the railway line, but requested modestly that if we did anything it would be on a scale comparate to the reprisals that would follow. (RE 163)[49]

(Fifty Greeks shot for one German was the general rule.) Mulgan notes elsewhere that the *andartes* in Area 3 had the full support of the population: 'Towards their own fighting men', he observes, the villagers may have shown despair, 'but never hostility' (RE 147). They knew they were being represented. Myers concurred: the Greeks, he wrote, 'were all morally in the Resistance Movement, whether they carried arms or not' (1985, 197–98). This, as Eric Hobsbawm argues in relation to the Vietnam War, is a fundamental prerequisite for successful guerrilla warfare. The guerrilla, he writes, 'must have the sympathy and support, active and passive, of the local population.' Any '"noble" bandit or Robin Hood [. . .] who loses it is dead' (1977, 164).

Behind these observations lies the question: what makes a populace revolutionary? How to explain the mass political mobilisation to EAM membership of some one and a half million Greeks (out of a total population of seven million) in the early 1940s? Part of the answer lies in the way the resistance in Greece was embedded in a deeper movement for radical political and social reform in the country. It was often thought by other BLOs 'that the

49   With similar experience, Myers records the response of the locals in the area when his HQ in Theodhoriana was bombed by the Germans and damage done to local houses. The locals, he writes, insisted the British Military Mission 'were not to blame. They blamed only the "quisling" in Athens' (1985, 197–98).

majority of the rank and file [in EAM-ELAS] were communist by compulsion rather than by choice' (LJB 265). But the accounts of the movement's veterans themselves tell a very different story, returning repeatedly to the sense of a spontaneous reaction, the way people throughout the country flocked to join up—in ways reminiscent of Auden's description in 'Spain' of migrating gulls or seeds of a flower. With mass movements, it's perhaps misleading to dichotomise compulsion and choice, unless we are to interpret 'compulsion' in a deeper, more unconscious sense rather than in terms of external coercion. Instances of manipulation were known and reported, and EAM-ELAS discipline was sometimes ruthless. But this was war, and Mulgan would have understood it; he would, after all, have internalised the instruction from SOE's *Partisan Leader's Handbook* that 'the traitor must be liquidated at the first opportunity' (Gubbins, Foot 2001, 454). This was a struggle which called for full allegiance. More importantly, he knew, as he was to put it, that 'So large a movement could not depend entirely on terrorism'.[50]

That EAM's achievements were to be so tragically short-lived should not detract from their significance. Unlike in France, where Resistance partisans were quickly absorbed into a heroic legend in the post-war period, Greek partisans, along with the social revolution they undertook, were soon to be vilified. It was only when revisionist reassessments of their struggle began to emerge after the fall of the colonels (in 1974) that a different narrative could gradually be pieced together. Along with this shift, Mulgan's views and actions may begin to take on new meaning.

50   Wilson report, 3 (ATL, J.V. Wilson Papers. MS-Papers 6875-2).

CHAPTER 4

PEEA: The Government of Free Greece in the Mountains

After speeches by 'General' [Sarafis] and 'self':
'high drinking & singing but eased off around
10 & to bed, swollen, full of goodwill'

—Mulgan's diary, 25 March 1944

The 25th of March, the day Greeks celebrate their independence from Ottoman occupation, was chosen by EAM-ELAS to mark the beginning of a new independence from foreign control. On that day, the movement officially celebrated the founding of PEEA (Politiki Epitropi Ethnikis Apeleftherosis: Political Committee of National Liberation), the Government of Free Greece in the mountains. In the village of Fourna, along with prominent members of the EAM-ELAS community, Mulgan gave a speech, after which celebrations continued well into the evening. Mulgan was later to write, with considerable nostalgia, of the 'revolution' they had dreamt of at the time, of a 'Free Greece which we had toasted' in the mountains in early 1944 (RE 176). It was a moment of euphoria, an occasion to mark a considerable achievement.

Reference to PEEA could only ever be made obliquely, however, as this new radical government was not recognised by the British, who were backing the monarchist government-in-exile. Occasionally,

Mulgan would use his tiny pocket diary, provided by SOE, to record something more personal. Small and battered, often almost illegible, it is cryptic and sketchy to say the least, mostly recording the names of places he's visited or shorthand references to others he's with.[1] But the occasional expression of communal goodwill, as in the above comment, gives more away about his feelings than was possible in his reports to command HQ.

Though short-lived (it was officially in operation for only eight months), PEEA was one of the most radical social revolutions of its time, and although unable to name it, Mulgan clearly gave full support to this drive for national self-determination. EAM had made several calls to the government-in-exile headed by Emmanouil Tsouderos to negotiate for a government of national unity, but had been outmanoeuvred at every turn. In response, it set about establishing its own government in the mountains—which, indirectly, was soon to topple Tsouderos from power. Like so much in modern Greek history, your opinion of the PEEA project depends on your politics. Those on the left describe it as a brave attempt to rescue a population deserted by its inept leaders—or as what Mark Mazower calls a set of 'social reforms, which now appear years ahead of their time' (2001, 269). Those on the right depict it as a 'bargaining-counter in the political game', 'an amalgamation of amorphous and spurious political parties, controlled by KKE', which was how British BLO Nicholas Hammond described it at the time (1983, 133). Chris Woodhouse wrote of it in terms of 'hoodwinking' and 'hypocrisy' (1948, 184–85). Even recently, centre-right commentators such as George Alexander have described PEEA as part of just another 'round' in

---

1   After Mulgan's death his father attempted to recover any personal papers left in Cairo. On 17 November 1945 he received a letter from a Brigadier A.E. Conway of New Zealand Army Headquarters, Wellington, saying enquiries had been made to Force 133 and he had been informed there was no trace of any such papers. 'We do however hold two small diaries of his, which for security reasons in regard to his work cannot be passed on. They have been read through very carefully and they contain no entries of a personal nature whatsoever. Every entry deals exclusively with his day-to-day work whilst he was in GREECE' (ATL MS-Papers-7906-40). The diary we had access to has entries from 11 September 1943 (the time of his drop into Greece) until 8 November 1944. The second diary may have covered the highly sensitive period from November until his death in April the next year.

the civil war, a ploy by the KKE to gain power (1980, 43–51).

It is important not to idealise the PEEA project, but equally important not to ignore the social and material conditions out of which it was created. By the end of 1943 the population of the Greek countryside was left practically destitute, with its villages burnt and crops wasted. Many thousands of villagers were forced to flee their homes and find shelter in the cities. The capitulation of the Italians had precipitated a barrage of German reinforcements: nearly four full divisions were sent to Greece in an attempt to wipe out the resistance (Skalidakis 2015, 141). As the numbers of Germans increased, the invaders confiscated what they could of the meagre agricultural production to feed their own troops and even deliberately destroyed crops to weaken guerrilla support and morale. The other Greek 'governments' (collaborationist and exile) were doing very little, and the Red Cross concentrated on supporting the population in the cities. Meanwhile the Germans were arming collaborationist forces on the plains to cut off supplies to guerrillas in the mountains. In his diary Mulgan records the deprivation and despair that predominated around him as they waited in vain that winter for drops of stores. On 20 January 1944: 'no blankets black villages'; on 21 February: 'snowed in. General [Sarafis] called confessing to vague depression which I share in view of probable difficulties soon in getting stores from caiques or aeroplanes'; 25 February: 'Increasingly depressed by absence of planes & all stores. Time marches on [. . .] Τι θα κάνουμε? [what's to be done?]'; 4 March: 'Woken 7 am to find one plane dropped near Fourna [. . .] dinner [from] first drop to 16 Div [. . .] All Andartes merry'—and so on. By this time, in his area in Thessaly, ELAS had more than 22,000 fighters, men and women, and 2,500 animals to feed.

The people's government

It was within this context of deprivation and isolation that EAM-ELAS stepped up its efforts to institute systems of welfare, beginning in the mountain villages of the Pindus ranges where Mulgan was based. Earlier attempts had been made in this direction even before the war. Based on fieldwork done in Evritania (Roumeli and Thessaly) in the 1970s, Anna Collard has described the significant progress made in the 1930s towards instituting forms of autonomous government in areas like agricultural co-operatives and agrarian land reform (1990, 225–27). Popular sovereignty was strengthened through local progressive organisations like FED (Karoplesi Union for Progress). Then, at the beginning of the occupation, Panhellenic organisations such as AKE (the Agrarian Party of Greece) and EA (National Solidarity) attempted to compensate for government neglect by providing welfare and support for victims of Axis aggression.[2] Drawing on this experience, PEEA established a governing committee on March 10, 1944, with the official inauguration following on March 25. Other BLOs had been instructed to avoid reference to PEEA at this time.[3] In speaking alongside Sarafis on the day, in the heart of EAM-ELAS territory, Mulgan was at least tacitly registering his support.

The left, according to one of its most eminent historians, David Caute, can only be defined historically and conceptually as 'an absolute based on a minimum demand of one man, one vote' (1966, 30), and from the start the PEEA leaders considered popular sovereignty (*laokratia*) their government's primary aim. Nationwide elections were held to set up a National Council. The following month more than a million and a half Greek citizens aged over eighteen turned out to vote at secret polling stations throughout the country. Women voted for the first time[4] and the turnout was higher than a third of the eligible Greek population (with the exception of the citizens of East Macedonia and West Thrace, who were under Bulgarian occupation). The elected Council, numbering 184

---

2   FED (Filoproödos Enosis Karoplesi: the Karoplesi Union of the Friends of Progress); AKE (Agrotiko Komma Ellados: the Agrarian Party of Greece); EA (Ethniki Allilegyi: National Solidarity).

3   For a fuller account of how GHQ in the Middle East viewed PEEA at this time, see Hammond 1983, 132–34, where he describes PEEA as a shrewdly timed 'bluff [. . .] the [Allied Military] Mission did not recognise the existence of PEEA at all. [. . .] My job was to report on PEEA as well as on ELAS'.

4   Women in Greece were officially granted the right to vote in 1952.

members, then proceeded to elect representatives for each area. The question of how truly representative these representatives were, and the extent to which they were chosen by EAM leaders, has been the subject of some debate. Mulgan felt free to give his opinion only at the very end, as he was leaving Force 133, when he wrote favourably to J.V. Wilson in New Zealand about the fact that EAM had 'their own parliament' in 1944—adding, however, that its members had been 'nominated under the guise of an election'.[5] But conditions were not those of a peace-time Western democracy and the idea was to make a first attempt at popular participation, inviting suggestions for leadership from all professions and classes, especially workers and peasant farmers. As Mark Mazower has argued, although the outcome was the result of 'deliberate, if well-intentioned, political engineering by EAM electoral committees', nonetheless 'the deputies to the Council, who made their way to its session at the village of Koryschades in May, represented a much broader cross-section of Greek society than had been found in prewar parliaments' (2001, 294).[6] Skalidakis, on the other hand, accepts the legitimacy of the procedure but details how, in attempting to represent 'all the people', the approach resulted in a plethora of views that became ultimately impossible to unify (2015, 198–99). At the ideological and organisational centre of PEEA was the Communist Party (KKE), which established a full range of administrative ministries called 'secretariats'—of the judiciary, public order, taxation, the army and civil militia, economic planning, agriculture, elementary education, health and social welfare. Despite its theoretical base in communism, however, in practice the KKE embraced all sections of the political spectrum, including some known to be right wing, and aimed for a government that would be acceptable to the majority of Greeks after liberation. Council meetings now included women, farm workers and priests along with the expected lawyers and journalists. Later

---

5   Wilson Report, 3.

6   Mazower gives some details about the rights and wrongs of these 'revolutionary elections' (2001, 291–95). The most detailed account of the procedure is given by Costas Couvaras, who was an OSS agent on Evoia at the time (we will hear his voice at the end of this chapter). Skalidakis (2015, 189) quotes at length from Couvaras's report.

reminiscences by women in the movement emphasise the way PEEA aimed at full integration of women into social and political life, encouraging education and allowing them for the first time to go out unchaperoned (although sexual relations with fellow fighters were strongly discouraged) (Hart 1990). Such was the prevailing spirit which dominated in PEEA that most of the liberals in the country were persuaded to join. Not least among the aims of this 'people's government' was the emphasis on self-governing cultural activities at district level, to encourage theatrical performances, publication of newspapers, and reform of the country's education system.

PEEA's decrees, drafted in the people's language, *demotiki*, rather than in *katharevousa*, the official language exclusive to the educated, were voted into operation on 27 May 1944 in the village of Koryschades, only 50 kilometres from Mulgan's station at Fourna. Several prominent academics and intellectuals had come to join this new self-proclaimed government, including Alexandros Svolos, a constitutional lawyer, the philosopher Konstantinos Despotopoulos and the journalist Kostas Karagiorgis, along with many civil servants and labour leaders. In tone and reformist zeal the 'Provisions of Operation' read rather like the Preamble to the United States Constitution drawn up by the Founding Fathers a century and a half earlier: 'We the people of the United States, in order to form a more perfect Union [. . .] do ordain [. . .]', etc. The PEEA Preamble reads:

> The Council, comprising representatives of all the Greek people, who gathered to announce their indomitable will to fight, to the last breath, for the liberation of the country, the complete eradication of fascism and the return of national unity and rule by the people, desiring to determine the mode of operation of all powers in free Greece, do vote:
>
> . . . All powers stem from the people and are practised by the people [Article 2] . . . The people's freedom is sacred and inviolable [Article 4] . . . All Greeks, men and women, have equal political and civil rights [Article 5] . . . The official language of all proclamations of public life and at all levels of education is the

language of the people [Article 7] . . . The activities of the National Council will last until the liberation of the country [Article 11]. (Grigoriadis 2011, III, 26–28)

British opposition

EAM repeatedly invited the other guerrilla groups, EDES and EKKA (Ethniki kai Koinoniki Apeleftherosi: National and Social Liberation), to join PEEA and several of their members accepted. Notable here is Evripidis Bakirtzis, who (despite British disapproval) left EKKA to become the first President of PEEA. Bakirtzis had been one of the first successful agents for SOE at the start of the occupation. Along with his friends Stefanos Sarafis and Dimitrios Psarros, Bakirtzis was of centre-left, republican sympathies and had participated in the anti-royalist revolution of 1935, when he was given the death sentence *in absentia* and earned himself the nickname 'the Red Colonel'. Despite this epithet Bakirtzis, like Tsamakos, Psarros and Sarafis and several other ELAS leaders whom Mulgan got to know, was 'less inclined to hold extreme views' than other hardliners in EAM-ELAS, particularly their successors in the movement (Gerolymatos 1992, 229).[7] Of these men Mulgan's closest contact, apart from Tsamakos, was with Sarafis, with whom he had much in common despite the generation that separated them. From his long experience in military, political and diplomatic service, Sarafis had acquired a strong mistrust of the imperial powers which had interfered in Greek politics ever since its liberation from Ottoman rule. A native of Thessaly and Commander-in-Chief of ELAS, which became the military arm of PEEA, Sarafis played a crucial role in the new government's decisions and activities. Mulgan's diary has him riding frequently into various mission stations to share a meal and conversation. It is highly probable that during these conversations, Sarafis felt at ease to share his opinion

7   As Gerolymatos notes, during the period of the *Dekemvriana*, Bakirtzis was commander of the ELAS forces in Macedonia; 'this was one of the few regions that remained tranquil' at the time (1992, 229n29).

of the 'Great Powers who fought out their quarrels at second-hand, using the Balkan countries as pawns' (Marion Sarafis 1980a, xxi). From initially being unable to contribute much in his dialogue with 'the general', by the spring of 1944 Mulgan would have been in a position to express his endorsement of the anti-imperialist project that lay behind the founding of PEEA.

Under strong pressure from the British, both EKKA and EDES refused support for PEEA. Sarafis records that after the (ultimately unsuccessful) Plaka armistice in February 1944, brokered by Woodhouse, where all the bands agreed to collaborate in the national interest, a private meeting took place between Woodhouse, Psarros and Kartalis in which the two EKKA leaders were persuaded not to participate in PEEA and that EKKA should 'ostentatiously abstain from the elections for a National Council' (Stefanos Sarafis 1980, 282). As Woodhouse admits, 'Zervas [of EDES] was advised to oppose the formation of a "single army" at the Plaka Conference, because that would presuppose a single political authority over it' (2002, 75).[8] Although invited to the oath-taking ceremony, the Allied Military Mission refused to attend and never acknowledged the existence of PEEA (Stefanos Sarafis 1980, 271). Following Foreign Office directives, the AMM recognised only the exile (royalist) government in Cairo as legitimate, however unrepresentative it was acknowledged to be. In London, Churchill fumed at the presumption of the Greeks in taking this initiative and wrote a minute on 7 May holding certain SOE people accountable for the gathering strength of the Greek left, which he imagined might be encouraged by the Soviets:

> SOE barges in an ignorant manner into all sorts of delicate situations. They were originally responsible for building up the nest of cocatrices for EAM in Greece [. . .] It is a very dangerous

8   In his diary for 31 December 1943, Zervas had speculated that 'Communists' were preparing to create an independent government in Mulgan's area of Spercheiada, and mentioned the names of Svolos, Glinos, Sarafis, Kartalis and Tsirimokos. Most of these men did indeed later lead PEEA, although Zervas was wrong to assume these men were all communists (Skalidakis 2015, 169).

thing that the relations of two mighty forces like the British Empire and the USSR should be disturbed by these little pinpricks interchanged by obscure persons playing the fool far below the surface. (Goulter-Zervoudakis 1998, 183)

These obscure persons, who with their pinprick activities were disturbing the progress of the mighty forces of the British Empire (as yet, it seems, unaware of its imminent demise),[9] were to challenge imperial British intentions for as long as they were able.

Balkan models

The possibility of setting up a new socialist state without Soviet intervention had been offered by the example of Tito in Yugoslavia. By early 1943, SOE had shifted support from the right-wing guerrillas under the Serbian leader Mihailović to the left-wing partisans led by Tito. As already mentioned, SOE Cairo—where the Greek, Yugoslav and Albanian desks shared a common command—was originally motivated by territorial rather than political considerations and came to back Tito's and Hoxha's communists rather than the nationalist partisans in Yugoslavia and Albania respectively.[10] In the early stages of occupation Tito, like EAM, succeeded in uniting a broad base of the population (peasants and workers, students and intellectuals) against fascism. Like the EAM leaders, he understood that a popular revolt against the occupiers could only succeed if its supporters were convinced they were fighting for national self-determination, resistance to foreign colonisation, and for a fairer, more equal society. Tito had gained sufficient majority support to set up the Anti-Fascist Council for the National Liberation of Yugoslavia (AVNOJ), which comprised both communist and non-communist

---

9   And yet, as Tariq Ali puts it, Churchill by late 1943 'was only too aware that US industry and Soviet manpower and industry had won the war' and that 'The British Empire was bankrupt' (2022, 303–4).

10   See Churchill's letters to Eden on 29 and 30 Dec. 1943 and to Tito on 8 Jan. 1944 in Churchill 1951, 469–71 and 463–66. For more details on British policy on the Balkans and Yugoslavia, see Sweet-Escott 1975 and Barker 1975.

representatives. Its aim was to administer territories under the control of the partisans, and it pledged commitment to democracy, the rights of ethnic minorities, the inviolability of private property and the freedom of individual economic initiative. (By 1945 this had become the Socialist Federal Republic of Yugoslavia.) By contrast with the partisans of Tito or Hoxha, however, EAM, whose roots were based on a broader Popular Front model, did not set up PEEA on specifically communist principles: its leading members, along with the Communist Party, adopted a liberal-left agenda. Although Tito was sympathetic to the EAM project and his partisans exchanged information and intelligence with their southern neighbours, he was in the event unable or unwilling to offer direct help to the Greeks.

Unlike in Yugoslavia, PEEA was up against determined opposition. With promptings from the Foreign Office, the KKE was accused of using PEEA to undermine Greek nationalism and of collaborating with Bulgaria and Yugoslavia as part of a plan to cede Greek Macedonia in exchange for support from other Balkan communists. Eventually, the government in the mountains would fall apart after the manipulations of the new head of the exile government, Georgios Papandreou; in spite of significant compromises from late summer onwards it was gradually closed down by early November. It continued, however, to be active at the local level throughout the country. As Voglis and Nioutsikos have argued, it was through the organisational structure of the by then defunct PEEA that 'after the withdrawal of German troops from [mainland] Greece in October 1944, the EAM-ELAS actually ruled the country (except Athens) until January 1945' (2017, 329).

One of the most committed supporters of Tito's project was the journalist and historian Basil Davidson, who had been James Klugmann's boss in the Yugoslav section of SOE in Cairo.[11] A discreet socialist sympathiser, Davidson was dropped in to fight with Tito's partisans in August 1943, the month before Mulgan landed in Greece. His account of his time there makes instructive reading

---

11   As SOE agent in both Budapest and Cairo, Davidson had come into contact with Christine Skarbek (Mulley 2012, 282), who will appear in Chapter 10.

alongside Mulgan's *Report on Experience* for the way both men took to their co-fighters: their 'decency' and stamina, their assumption of equal terms. Davidson wrote that

> First impressions were very good, they continued to be very good, it was a very fine movement [. . .] very united, at least that was the product that I saw in northern Serbia. They were effectively all farmers, very decent people with a great tradition of hospitality and they took to us, to me and to others who were there in the measure that we accepted their standards and put up with the conditions which they put up with. They were physically very strong, very tough, but they were also morally tough. Any who were captured by the enemy were usually shot without question. (Stafford 2000, 184)

What Davidson records in *Special Operations Europe: Scenes from the Anti-Nazi War*, first published by Gollancz in 1980, reveals the extent to which PEEA almost certainly had one eye on the measures the Yugoslavs were taking across their northern border, not least among which was the attempt to oust a defunct monarch. Davidson writes:

> The democratizing theme may be followed through all the public declarations of the liberation movement. [. . .] In July 1944, for example, it was ordered that democratic administrations were to be created in every liberated zone of any magnitude, and by this time there were quite a few of these. The stress was on democratic representation as an immediate guarantee of mass participation in the struggle during the war, but also as a liberating model after the war.
>
> 'What matters,' said these orders, 'is to create organs of people's power in every village as soon as the nazi-fascists are chased out of it. These organs must emerge directly from the mass struggle and its institutions: from partisan units, peasant committees, factory committees, youth movements, women's defence groups.'

Each local committee was to evoke participation to the possible
maximum. (Davidson 1987, 305–6)

Under shared overall SOE command and in geographical proximity,
the Yugoslav partisans would have been regarded by Mulgan as co-
participants in a common cause. The difference was that his country
command was taking an increasingly hostile stand against the
guerrillas he was supporting, putting him increasingly out on a limb.
Apart from a few exceptional cases, the BLOs in Greece aligned
themselves with official policy—to back Zervas and EDES and
discreetly to sideline and then eliminate ELAS and its revolutionary
schemes to reorganise the country.

Reporting to HQ

The non-recognition of PEEA by the AMM presented Mulgan with
considerable difficulty. Unable to refer to it in official reports to HQ,
let alone in his heavily censored correspondence, he was able only
to skirt around the topic or drop the occasional hint. Fairly early
on in his time in the mountains he was given a questionnaire to fill
out,[12] asking for his thoughts on fourteen different political issues
relating to his area. This 'MOST SECRET' document, completed by
Mulgan in August 1944, contains the cautiously expressed essence
of much of his thinking about EAM-ELAS and its influence. Its
compilers were clearly nervous about the growing strength of the
organisation and asked, from several different angles, whether it was
leading the country towards communism, particularly a form of
communism which might be amenable to Soviet control. Mulgan's
replies are measured in tone, but suggest an underlying irritation, an
impatience with this obsession which bore little relation to what he
saw around him.

In response to the fifth question, about the 'Aims and strength of
E.A.M.-E.L.A.S. both real and apparent' and the 'extent to which

---

12   The questionnaire is dated 8.10.43 but was not completed by Mulgan until ten months later,
      in August 1944. All references are to the copy in TNA PRO HS5/338.

the organisation is under direct communist control or is a genuine "popular front" of left-wing parties', Mulgan makes an important clarification: that although a 'small number of Communists control policy from above' (he would have had in mind the organisation of PEEA, initiated by KKE), the vast majority in the organisation fall under the latter category of 'popular front' supporters in a broad left-wing amalgamation, of which 'Very few [. . .] are Communists'. In his area of East Thessaly, the EAM-ELAS movement, he writes, 'has remained more national', with no opposition from EDES or EKKA—in other words, Free Greece was more or less unanimously supporting the movement. Some of the ELAS officers, who joined from the regular Greek army, 'disapprove of [official EAM] policy but feel unable [to] resist it', he concedes. But this in no way undermines their support for the movement. It is a serious mistake, he writes in conclusion, to denounce the whole organisation as 'communist' and not recognise its broad composition:

> in order to encourage moderate, Venizelist [i.e. republican], democratic, elements in Elas, it is necessary to avoid wholesale denunciations of the party that have so often been made. Propaganda, often untrue, sponsored by H.M.G. through B.B.C. during period of Civil War last winter did us and cause of moderation considerable harm.

In his answer to the third question, about the 'Attitude of the people towards British connexion and attitude of particular groups towards policy of H.M. Government', he states more bluntly that

> Policy of H.M.G. in supporting E.D.E.S., & Greek govt abroad, is continually and openly attacked by EAM-ELAS but they are always careful to distinguish between this policy and ourselves as individuals. Generally, policy of H.M.G. is source of some bewilderment.

Had Mulgan made his own disapproval of Britain's 'bewildering' policies clear to the *andartes*? The plural 'ourselves' here seems somewhat disingenuous (or perhaps just modest) given what he knew about the anti-ELAS sentiments of most BLOs, certainly of their commander in the area, Chris Woodhouse. He finishes his answer by adopting the moral high ground, insisting that it would be well to bear in mind the 'fundamental liking and friendliness of all Greeks towards Englishmen as we move about the country. H.M.G. should perhaps be grateful for this. We are.' Gratitude for Greek tolerance of and generosity towards the British was not always expressed by SOE operatives, and one senses Mulgan wagging a finger at arrogance in command quarters. Later, in *Report on Experience*, he adopts a similar admonitory tone when he wonders

> how we would have felt in occupied England if the Americans had
> come in to us with golden dollars and arms to lead our resistance
> movement, and just how politely we would have reacted to their
> direction. (RE 153–54)

Far less politely, seems to be the implied answer. It was characteristic that he never lost sight of the fact that this was a *Greek* resistance movement, with its own very particular political agenda.

Perhaps the nearest he gets to mentioning the unmentionable PEEA comes in his answer to question six, which solicited his views on the attitudes towards and the strength of communism in Greece. His answer shows him drawing a careful distinction between communism as theory and communist/Popular Front-style organisation in practice as he saw it around him: 'Communism in Greece is belief of only small minority and then rather its aim is seizure of political point, not re organisation [*sic*] of the country. I have met none of them who had any practical plans for communism in Greece'. The 'practical plans' laid out in the PEEA project, in other words, should not be the source of obsessive anxiety in Cairo.

This blueprint for practical socialism guided Mulgan's thinking throughout his adult life. What he saw in operation in the mountains, with all its difficulties, was what, as he wrote in *Report on Experience*, 'the world' needed at that time: a co-operative and democratic system of political organisation 'that is probably not peculiar to Greece, that is generic to the world, and specific in its reflections on the way we [ought to] live now' (RE 168). From gender equality to openness to communist ideals, to co-operative forms of government at all levels, Greece offered an inspiring model. He elaborates further in his book:

> Some elements of Communism might be made suitable to Greece, but it would have to be of a very co-operative and democratic nature to last. The plains of Thessaly and Macedonia and Agrinion would work well as co-operatives, with pooled machinery and marketing. There is a good deal of co-operative law and custom already in the villages, agreement as to grazing rights and forestry, rules for the right ordering of disputes over property. (RE 167)

For his own theoretical elaboration on this PEEA model, Mulgan adds a few 'flippant' recommendations: first that there should be a law prescribing eight hours' work for every man instead of twelve for every woman; second that discussing politics should be prohibited during daylight hours; and third that an inter-village football league should be set up 'to replace Venizelos and Pangalos and Metaxas as subjects for debate' (RE 167). He continues:

> But the Communism we knew in Greece never had any programme. The flippant suggestions [of his own in the] foregoing paragraph would have been revolutionary, if only because they showed a practical interest in what might be done with Greece once the Germans had gone. The Communists of Greece possessed, on the other hand, a very remarkable technique for taking and holding power and a considerable ability in exploiting this technique. (RE 168)

The KKE, in other words, had facilitated the institutionalisation of the blueprint for PEEA but showed no 'practical interest' in its implementation. That was being undertaken by the more socialist-leaning members, who drew on the co-operative structures already partly in place.

Report on Experience (written mainly in the months after demobilisation, at the end of 1944 and beginning of 1945) came next in Mulgan's ongoing assessments of Greek 'communism'. But he had one final report to make in the month he died, to J.V. Wilson in Wellington, and it was here that he offered his most frank assessment of the PEEA project. He begins by repeating his belief that 'The Greek communists [. . .] have not so far been very specific about programmes'. But what he does detect is described in the following terms, still without referring to it as PEEA:

> They [EAM] had their own police [. . .] and kept everyone in line quite effectively. E.A.M. was not only an organisation of the hills but ran through every German-occupied town. They had their own taxation, which kept the partisans going in supplies, and their own justice—rough—and finally in 1944 their own parliament, nominated under the guise of an election. You could dismiss the movement, according to your taste in politics, but could not deny its efficiency. So large a movement could not depend entirely on terrorism, but the appeal to nationalism and patriotism varied in different parts of the country. In Thessally [*sic*], (the part of Greece that I knew best) it was very much a popular movement, shared in and believed in by a majority of the people. In the Peloponnesus, which is conservative and royalist, it was a minority movement that existed by armed force. In Macedonia, it was crossed with anti-Slav feeling, which the E.A.M. leaders, who had strong affiliations with Tito and with Bulgarian communists, had to play down rather uneasily. In Athens it flourished among the dock-workers of the Piraeus and lived a gangster life during the occupation, recruiting young men who killed and got killed during the civil war of December 1944.[13]

13   Mulgan report to Wilson, ATL. J.V. Wilson Papers. MS-Papers 6875–2, 3.

This well-informed analysis of the mosaic of support for EAM and PEEA throughout the country is coloured by Mulgan's experience (from a distance, in Cairo) of the December conflicts in Athens, between EAM-ELAS and the British-backed right-wing Greek militia. Events had moved very fast by this time. He tells Wilson that when he left Greece in November,

> E.A.M.-E.L.A.S. were in control of all Greece except a small circle round the Grande-Bretagne hotel in Athens where the Papandreou government [newly arrived from exile] was functioning. On the whole they were behaving very well but it was quite clear that they were not going to surrender their control peacefully.[14]

As violence escalated and the British raised the stakes in controlling Greece as 'a second grade colony', as he put it in the letter to Wilson on 20 April,[15] things began to get very ugly on both sides. Mulgan wrote to Gabrielle in January '45 of the 'brutality and savagery' now dominating in the resistance bands:

> I wouldn't have any fears personally from Elas, though they may have changed a lot with the events of these last two months and the extremists and communists taken [sic] a firmer hold than they had before. (AGM 288)

What prevailed now was the fascism of the right, driven by the right-enforced Greek army, ranged up against an emerging 'fascism of the Left'.[16] The democratic promise of PEEA was by this time collapsing under the pressure of civil war. Within a year or so many of the ELAS-PEEA leaders were in internal exile (Sarafis, Tsamakos, Kalambalikis); others were dead—either murdered by government security forces or through committing suicide (Aris Velouhiotis and, in early 1947, Evripidis Bakirtzis).

14   Ibid., 4.
15   Mulgan to J.V. Wilson, 20 April 1945, ibid.
16   Mulgan report to Wilson, ibid., 4.

In his letters home at this time Mulgan outlined schemes of government that Vincent O'Sullivan understandably writes off as 'simple to the point of benign anarchy' (LJB 332). His most coherent statement in this regard comes in a letter to his parents of 13 January '45:

> There seems some hope of a [political] settlement [in Greece] but ELAS of course still hold all the country outside Athens and Attica and it will probably take more than arms to shift them. It would be a good thing now if they would throw over the communists, who by the nature of their doctrine can't ever be trusted. I was more sympathetic to communism when I was younger. It was the only religion of my time and they were the only people who were prepared to fight in Spain and elsewhere. [. . .]
>
> Nearly always when we argue about this difficult post-war phase, we say that we must find a form of government that will look after the common people, 'the little people' as Priestley and Steinbeck and everyone else says. Personally I am beginning to think that it is time the little people got up and helped themselves. There are enough of them and no-one else will in the long run. (AGM 286–87)

The first thing to note about this analysis is that Mulgan does not conflate EAM-ELAS with 'the communists' and in fact thinks it would be good if the more moderate members 'thr[e]w over the communists'. As he was at pains to insist on many occasions, only a minority in the movement were communists. Now, with three quarters of the country under EAM-ELAS control, would be the time to 'throw over' the extremist elements on both sides. As for his suggestion that 'it is time the little people got up and helped themselves. There are enough of them', we need to remember that for over a year he had been living in a community that had done exactly that.

* * *

A fitting conclusion here, we feel, is to listen to the voice of another member of the Allied Military Mission who had gained the trust of EAM, whose testimony from inside the PEEA Council meetings in Koryschades brings the optimistic spirit of the new government to life. Costas Couvaras was a Greek who had studied in the United States on scholarships and had now returned to serve with the OSS (the American branch of the AMM). Free of British (SOE) supervision, Couvaras expresses views that seem to underlie much of what Mulgan was feeling.

> May 25, 1944
>
> These days I am following the deliberations of the National Council more or less regularly. It is an inspiration to attend these sessions, and to see and hear the delegates talk about the problems of their country. One gets the feeling that he is following history in the making. This assembly, which is composed of intellectuals, farmers, workers, priests, and soldiers—all of them resistance fighters—might prove very important in the history of Greece. Greek history books refer to the Troezone Assembly of the Greek Revolution of Independence; in the future they might also refer to the National Council of Koryshades. My only criticism of this assembly so far is that it has not come out with any important declaration on the right of the small nations [like Greece] to be independent and on their desire to avoid interference in their internal affairs by friend or foe. I was talking about this to one of the leaders yesterday, and it seems they are reluctant to come out with such highfalutin phrases because they do not want to offend England, at least not as long as the war is on.[17]

Then on 1 June:

> The Greeks that go to Cairo are not representative of the majority of the people here [. . .] they are either former army officers or

---

17   Costa G. Couvaras, OSS, 'With the Central Committee of EAM'. n.d. web.stanford. edu/~ichriss/Couvaras.htm, 33–34. Date of access 29 May 2020.

professional men who feel bitter about the changes that have taken place among the majority of the population and mostly among the lower classes. These changes do not favor the middle class or the army caste. Against the latter a great part of the population feels a certain bitterness because army officers did very little to take leadership against the enemies of the country. [. . .] The EAM is not all communist, but is far to the left of the old political parties of the country. These parties seem to be totally dead, as far as most of the people that I have talked to are concerned, along with the monarchy.[18]

18   Ibid., 40–41.

CHAPTER 5

EAM-ELAS in Crisis

At Karpenisi General [Sarafis] in tears &
threatening resign. Surrealist dinner [. . .] talked
to Tsamakos till midnight, slightly assuaged.

—Mulgan's diary, 2 May 1944

1944 was the year things began to fall apart for EAM. Given its achievements in improving infrastructure and welfare for most ordinary people in Greece—acknowledged even by its harshest critics like Woodhouse[1]—this was a tragic blow.

Historians of EAM are divided as to what caused the rapid decline of this by now well-embedded revolutionary programme. Much of it, of course, had to do with the British drive to dismantle it, but some of the causes were also internal. The movement's rapid expansion meant there was often little time to consolidate policy, and that decisions taken at PEEA HQ were insufficiently implemented in the field or at meetings abroad where major decisions were taken. Two crucial events of the year were to hasten EAM's downfall. In both, Mulgan would play a small part.

---

1   The achievements of EAM-ELAS's organisations throughout the country, Woodhouse acknowledges, 'had given [Greece] things that it had never known before. Communications in the mountains, by wireless, courier, and telephone, have never been so good before or since; even motor roads were mended and used by EAM/ELAS. [. . .] Schools, local government, law-courts and public utilities, which the war had ended, worked again. Theatres, factories, parliamentary assemblies began for the first time. Communal life was organised in place of the traditional individualism of the Greek peasant' (1948, 146–47).

The Psarros murder

In the late stage of the resistance, soon after PEEA was formed, an event of huge significance would change the course of EAM-ELAS's history and development. Characteristically, Mulgan refers to it (in *Report on Experience)* only in general terms, without names or context. Its implications, however, were to affect him directly.

This was the murder by an ELAS partisan, on April 17, of Colonel Dimitrios Psarros, leader of the third largest guerrilla band, 5/42-EKKA. The passage in *Report on Experience* comes within the context of Mulgan's post-liberation work compensating victims, for which the Psarros case was to give him much trouble.[2] But in his book he felt able only to make a statement about the horror and ambiguities that result from civil war:

> Some of those who had survived the Gestapo and the Security Police had killed each other in the civil war. One of the best of these, who had dodged and fought the Germans from underground for two years was taken prisoner by the Communists and killed on a lonely piece of road by the village of Kiffisokhori, above Levadhia. The post-mortem report, when they brought his body back, described him as having been shot through the eye at fifteen feet, but I suppose in fact he was struck down by a power that is wider and more savage and more long-lasting. (RE 176–77)

The details here would have come from first-hand reports as the event occurred right next to Mulgan's mission station in Fourna. To a certain extent 5/42-EKKA was a rival band to ELAS; unlike EAM-ELAS, it was given unqualified support from beginning to end by the British. But Psarros represented the less right-wing faction of his band, one willing to collaborate with ELAS in the national interest. Indeed, Psarros had expressed himself willing to join PEEA, and made many visits to ELAS HQ near Viniani, one day's trek away from Fourna. (EKKA's stronghold further south, in

2   This will be further explored in Chapter 8.

the district of Fokida, was also close, bordering along the Spercheios valley with Mulgan's Area 3.) Mulgan would almost certainly have known Psarros fairly well and was not the only one within the PEEA community to be horrified by his unexpected murder.[3] What is noteworthy about the description, however, is the stark contrast in the last sentence between the ghastly detail (shot through the eye at fifteen feet) and the Mulganesque qualification, taking us out to its broadest implications. In the concluding antithetical clause, he encourages us not to remain with the violence but to look at the bigger picture, to remember that the incident is part of 'a power that is wider and more savage and more long-lasting'— namely, the revolutionary struggle.

Dimitrios Psarros had been active in the resistance from the start. Along with Ioannis Tsigantes, his close friend and brother-in-law, he was sent to Athens by the first British intelligence teams in Cairo in August 1942, to see what progress could be made in organising resistance bands. After Tsigantes was killed the following January by the Italian occupiers, Psarros stayed on in Athens. But later, along with his friend Stefanos Sarafis, he managed to organise the 5/42 fighting regiment as the military arm of EKKA, based in his native district of Fokida in southern Roumeli. Both men were career officers and of what could be called a Popular Front or Eurosocialist persuasion: republican, left of centre and tolerant of communism. Another close friend of both men, with similar background and politics, who had begun with EKKA but ended up as an ELAS stalwart, was Bakirtzis. Sarafis would also soon join EAM-ELAS— as its military Commander-in-Chief.[4] These moves didn't appear to

---

3   For a full description of the history of the 5/42 regiment, the fighting wing of EKKA, as well as the conflicts between 5/42 and ELAS, see Mamarelis 2014. The details of Psarros's murder by Zoulas are dealt with on pages 192–207 of Mamarelis. BLO John Ponder, who interacted with Mulgan on many occasions at this time, gives a first-hand account of his own attempt to mediate between EKKA and ELAS (1997, 120–26).

4   Sarafis was persuaded to join ELAS after his capture by the band but subsequent (and to some surprisingly sudden) conversion, based on an understanding of its strength and impressive organisation. For a full description, see Eudes 1972, 54–55. According to what Edmonds heard, the conversion occurred after a night-long discussion in Athens with the communist philosopher Dimitrios Glinos (Edmonds 1998, 101). Edmonds's description of his dealings with Sarafis at this early stage depicts him as speaking good French and 'faltering English',

destroy the friendship between the three men, and Psarros remained sympathetic to much of what EAM-ELAS was doing. Like Sarafis, Psarros became increasingly worried, even tormented, by the right-wing elements within his own 5/42 force, which were to trigger his eventual death.

The Psarros story has been told in detail in the excellent book by Argyrios Mamarelis, *The Rise and Fall of the 5/42 Regiment of Evzones* (2014), based on his PhD thesis for the London School of Economics. Mamarelis records the band's gradual split between, on the one hand, Psarros and his political supporter Georgios Kartalis, who struggled to maintain its national character, and, on the other, the extreme pro-royalist and anti-communist faction under Efthymios Dedousis. The band's origin in a specific geographical area gave it a cohesion of common loyalty which initially held it together despite political differences. But as the war progressed these differences became impossible to reconcile. Defying Psarros, Dedousis and several other officers began increasingly to provoke ELAS. In retaliation and attempting to incorporate 5/42 into its forces, ELAS had succeeded in disbanding the group on two previous occasions—in May and June 1943—before the tragedy of 17 April 1944. By this time tensions between the much smaller 5/42, fully supported by the British, and the by now huge ELAS, facing considerable opposition from the British, had reached a climax. As Mamarelis tells it, the last battle took place near the village of Klima in Fokida, resulting in the third and final disbanding of the 5/42 force. Psarros did not participate in the battle but was confronted soon after by a band of ELAS partisans, and in the heat of a fierce argument, although all had been given strict instructions that he must not be harmed, Efthymios Zoulas of ELAS shot Psarros at close range.[5] Another 66 5/42 officers and *andartes* were killed in the

---

someone 'respected by most of his countrymen to the extent of being something of a national hero' (64).

5   Mamarelis discusses the allegation that EAM-ELAS's Siantos had covertly authorised the shooting by Zoulas, which Siantos never ceased to deny, but writes that he is unable to find convincing proof (2014, 144).

conflict.[6] Writing of himself as always in the third person, Sarafis records the reaction at ELAS HQ as follows:

> Colonel Psarros's death came as a grave blow not only to Colonels Bakirjis and Sarafis, who had been friends of his for over twenty-five years, but to all the members of the Political Committee [of PEEA], especially Svolos, Tsirimokos and Siantos. (Stefanos Sarafis 1980, 280)

Psarros had been under impossible pressure. He had told Bakirtzis that he would come to negotiate joining PEEA, which he clearly wanted to do. But his condition was that ELAS cease threatening 5/42 militarily. Sarafis had agreed to this, on ELAS's condition, however, that Psarros hand over for court-martialling those right-wing members (Dedousis, Kapetsonis and Psiloyiannis) who were exacerbating the tensions. Psarros agreed to court-martial the three, but by this time the Dedousis faction was more or less a law unto itself.[7] Some historians have blamed Psarros for failing to take a political stand against his internal rebels in good time. Others have noted the impossibility of his dilemma given a fundamental loyalty to his band. Psarros was also under pressure from his British supporters. As we have seen, after the Plaka armistice two months previously, a private meeting took place between Woodhouse and the two EKKA leaders, at which Psarros and Kartalis were persuaded not to participate in PEEA (Stefanos Sarafis 1980, 282).

The Psarros murder not only cut deep into Mulgan's political allegiances and military responsibilities, but also touched on his close personal friendship with Kostas Tsamakos. Tsamakos, we remember, was the ELAS officer singled out for special mention in *Report on Experience*, where Mulgan wrote of his 'great friendship'

---

6   Numbers vary between accounts. According to David Close (1995, 113), 350 EKKA fighters were attacked by a much larger ELAS force and around 175 were killed.

7   After the disbanding of EKKA, according to Sarafis, 'One section of it under Kapetsonis and Dedousis crossed over to Patras where it amalgamated with the Security Battalions. Later on these forces, in company with German troops, made repeated landings at Nafpaktos and eventually established themselves there permanently and continued to harass our [ELAS] forces' (1980, 280).

with the Greek and his promise to 'adorn' his reminiscences with his photo (RE 146.) As it happened, however, the man who shot Psarros, Efthymios Zoulas, belonged to Tsamakos's 13th Division.[8]

Zoulas had in fact been something of a thorn in the side for Pat Wingate, Mulgan's close friend and collaborator in the mission. Wingate's extended post-operational report to General Headquarters Middle East makes interesting reading alongside Mulgan's diary for the way it fills in details common to the activities of both. Wingate's record of their dealings with ELAS demonstrates an overall sympathy for the band. He had participated in the planning for the destruction of the Asopos viaduct in May–June '43 and was critical of some of the SOE team's impatience with Aris and his band, feeling that too much was expected of them, given their lack of arms and training in guerrilla warfare.[9] But he became increasingly impatient with ELAS's Major Efhyimios Zoulas and his failure to co-operate on joint ventures.[10] Zoulas seems to have been a particularly tough character with no time for British interference.

Mulgan's diary in the days immediately following the assassination reveals an atmosphere of intense anxiety. The next day, 18 April, he received 'mail from Viniani', SOE HQ in the mountains, and visitors from 'Paliokastro' (Palaiokastro), ELAS's 13th Division HQ, each no doubt giving their own versions of the event. On April 19 he set off with his interpreter Paul Contomichalos

---

8   Originally, when Mulgan first arrived, Tsamakos was leader of the 16th Division (Regiments 51, 52 and 54). Then with the restructuring of military command at the formation of PEEA in March 1944, the 16th Division became a Brigade (Regiments 52 and 54) that was attached to the 13th Division, of which Tsamakos was made commander (Stefanos Sarafis 1980, 186 and 274).

9   In his late-1944 report describing the failed deployment of Aris and his band on the Asopos operation, Wingate wrote: 'Having seen there [sic] from various directions, I now think that with the weapons available the chances of an Andarte attack [on the Germans guarding the viaduct] there succeeding were remote. I think also that they might have been tried out first on an easier target a short way north. From later observation, chances of success would have been quite good and might have done a lot to give them confidence' (Major P.J.F. Wingate, 'Report on Events in Greece: Roumeli & Thessaly [N° 3 Area] May 1943 to November 1944'. TNA HS 5/636, section headed May 1943).

10 For example, in October 1944 Wingate records that when he and Tim Foley attempted to induce Zoulas and his 36th Regiment to shoot at retreating Germans on the road near Dhelfinon, Zoulas 'lived up to his previous performance and backed out at the last minute' (TNA HS 5/636).

to carry out some pre-planned harassing operations on the railway line near Djoba. The first night, in Smokovo, he records getting 'No sleep at all', though whether from anxiety about Psarros, the forthcoming operations or perhaps the bed bugs is unclear. The next day the railway line demolition job seems to have been reasonably successful.[11] The following day, the 21st, he set off again feeling 'tired' and with a 'bad conscience for Djoba'—reprisals, as Sarafis records, were soon to follow.[12] Back in Fourna the next morning he sets off again early, on foot, for Tsamakos's HQ in Paliokastro, struggling to make the trek in two and a half hours, 'afflicted with internal restlessness'. As on other occasions, it seems, he had come to talk things through with Tsamakos, who functioned as something of a mentor, certainly a political ally. The next day he records having regained some 'mental and physical peace'. But the diary continues to detail turmoil and unresolved conflict between ELAS leaders and SOE command. The 24 April entry reads: 'Some writing and many signals. Corp with 7 ELAS chiefs went through. Arrived runner from Viniani. Political news is again ugly. Chris [Woodhouse] said to be on way out'. The next day visitors (including New Zealander Arthur Edmonds) again 'pile in' at Fourna, 'Chris now not going out'. The AMM was clearly applying significant pressure to keep Woodhouse in his post despite strong opposition from EAM-ELAS. (A year earlier, EAM-ELAS had made a formal request to get Chris Woodhouse and Tom Barnes 'replaced and removed from Greece' on account of their lack of impartiality [Stefanos Sarafis 1980, 135].) The following day, 26 April, after collecting everything from the recent dispatch on the dropping ground, the diary records, they sit round and have 'Dinner all together when tried to discuss effect of Chris'.

The Psarros murder had further intensified Woodhouse's antagonism to EAM-ELAS, which from now on became a driving force in British policy. The context is explained further by researcher

---

11   This is recorded by Pat Wingate, section headed April 1944 (TNA HS 5/636).

12   Sarafis records passing through what he spells as 'Tzomba' a week or so later and finding the village empty after the villagers had fled following the arrival of the Germans (1980, 290).

Alan Ogden, himself no ELAS sympathiser.[13] Tensions between the BMM commander and the dominant guerrilla group had been festering for months: Woodhouse himself records that EAM-ELAS regarded him as an 'enem[y]' (1948, 213). Ogden writes:

> The second occasion when EAM formally asked for Woodhouse's removal was in May 1944. When he returned to Viniani from a tour of his Missions, he found that ELAS had launched a campaign to force his superiors to remove him from the command of the AMM: 'The blame for all the internal conflicts in Greece had been officially ascribed to me,' Woodhouse signalled to Lieutenant Colonel Hammond and he considered himself suspended from all duties until Cairo decided on his position. Woodhouse was soon re-confirmed in his command, and EAM-ELAS did not press the matter further. (2012, 98)[14]

Aside from his own disagreement with Woodhouse's position, there may have been another reason for Mulgan's restlessness and sleeplessness at this point, which had to do with the degree of responsibility he felt for his own involvement in the conflict between ELAS and 5/42. In March, Cairo had asked the BLOs in Roumeli whether there was anything to be concerned about in the reported tensions between the two bands. Mulgan replied that 'The EKKA/ELAS trouble is apparently not serious. I expect it to blow over' (TNA PRO HS 5/355; Mamarelis 2014, 284–85). As Mamarelis records, Hammond shared this view of Mulgan's, reasoning that a clash was unlikely, in his opinion because 'ELAS would fear the onus of a second civil war'.[15] The leading BLO in the EKKA area was a straight-talking South African named Geoffrey Gordon-Creed (called 'Major Geoff' by the Greeks), who had played a leading role

13   Ogden's conclusion to all these difficulties is that 'it is hard to imagine anyone other than Woodhouse who could have prevailed over adversity and Greek fickleness so successfully' (2012, 104).

14   Ogden gives May as the month of Woodhouse's resignation then reinstatement by Cairo, but Mulgan's diary makes it clear that it was late April.

15   Hammond records inviting Bakirtzis (President of PEEA at the time) to tea and getting a pledge that 'no trouble was brewing between EKKA and ELAS' (1983, 135).

in the destruction of the Asopos viaduct the previous year.[16] He too did not anticipate further fighting between the two bands. Gordon-Creed seems to have sensed, like Mulgan and others in the area, that EKKA was a lost cause,[17] clung to, without reason, by the British. In early April 1944, Gordon-Creed signalled Cairo the following question: 'enlighten me, has the EKKA great political influence in Cairo [i.e. with the British-backed government-in-exile]? I think it must have otherwise we should have left it [*sic*] fade out long ago' (Mamarelis 2014, 284, 288). Gordon-Creed favoured accepting ELAS dominance in the area and confessed to Hammond on 11 April that he was 'bored stiff with the whole outfit [5/42/EKKA] [. . .] I know perfectly well that at least 50% of them will join Ralis [*sic*] [i.e. the Security Battalions supported by the collaborationist government in Athens] in the hope of getting a chance to avenge themselves should the ELAS disperse them' (Mamarelis 2014, 288–89). His scepticism is endorsed by Sarafis, who reports the BLO asking Zoulas: 'Why do you put up with EKKA? Why not disband them and be done with it?' (1980, 275). He could not have guessed how fateful his suggestion was to prove. Gordon-Creed would soon be removed from Greece on account of this scepticism.[18] There is no question, therefore, of Mulgan bearing responsibility for Psarros's death. But he might well have felt that, with his influence with the ELAS 'chiefs', he could have done more to calm the waters. Tsamakos's involvement, as well, would have added to the burden of responsibility. As Sarafis explains, on 7 April Zoulas's 36th Infantry Regiment (of Tsamakos's 13th Division) had been ordered,

16   Gordon-Creed had been dropped into Greece in March 1943 to lead Operation Washing, the demolition of the Asopos viaduct, which took place a few months later. New Zealander Don Stott also had a leading role in this operation, along with Pat Wingate and Arthur Edmonds (indirectly). For Tom Barnes's record of Edmonds's description of the venture, see Barnes 2015, 234–40.

17   'Doc Moyers', a US army doctor who appears frequently in Mulgan's diary, expressed his opinion (in his own diary for 10 Feb. 1944) that Psarros 'could not command a band of 10 *andartes*, let alone a regiment' (Mazower 2001, 304).

18   Hammond describes Gordon-Creed becoming 'impatient and tactless' in his dealings with EKKA. He was summoned to Viniani and 'after some probing' by Woodhouse, when he admitted unwillingness to co-operate with EKKA in future operations, he was sent out of Greece (1983, 134–35).

presumably by Tsamakos himself, to reinforce ELAS's 5th Brigade in the Klima area for an attack on 5/42-EKKA. This followed the failure of the latter to meet an ultimatum to release detained ELAS hostages and return stolen stores and equipment (Stefanos Sarafis 1980, 278–79). Throughout intense negotiations between Sarafis and Bakirtzis for ELAS and Psarros for EKKA, the three of them friends for over 25 years, Psarros indicated that he was losing control of the right-wing faction of his band represented by Dedousis and Kapetsonis.

The murder had a disastrous effect on the reputation of EAM-ELAS. It has been argued, in fact, that it represented the turning point in Britain's attitude to the band, which had previously been a preparedness to turn a blind eye to its politics. But this was different. Psarros was the leader of their own chosen group, and his murder registered almost as treasonous. EKKA was resentfully known among ELAS guerrillas as 'the golden resistance' for its lucrative backing (Mamarelis 2014, 268). None of this did much to motivate the band, or (despite concerted efforts by Woodhouse) to unite it with EDES against ELAS, and it achieved little as a fighting force. Its annihilation, however, remained an ugly stain on the reputation of EAM-ELAS in the months (indeed years) ahead.

Historian Solon Grigoriadis describes the tragic timing of Psarros's death. He writes:

> The day Psarros fell in the ravine at Klima, an aeroplane was waiting at the airport abandoned by the Germans at Almyros [near Volos] to take the representatives of PEEA to [Lebanon]. The moment had arrived for the beginning of the decisive hammering out of an agreement for national unity and the representatives of the left had to leave under the weight of Psarros's body. (III, 48)

His dates should be read metaphorically rather than strictly historically; according to Sarafis, the PEEA delegation, comprising seven men (with Sarafis as military adviser),[19] did not set out for

---

19   The other six were: Professor Svolos, President of the Political Committee of PEEA; Askoutsis

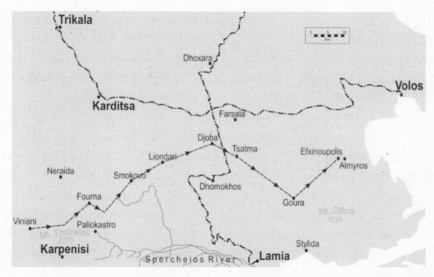

Route taken by the EAM delegates on their way to Lebanon, setting off from the airstrip at Almyros, where departure facilitated by Mulgan.

Lebanon for another week or so. Their journey seems initially to have involved passing through Mulgan's station at Fourna: Mulgan records 'Corp with 7 Elas chiefs went through' on 24 April. Then in early May, again according to Sarafis, their departure was delayed but finally facilitated by Mulgan himself from Goura, close to the airstrip at Almyros (1980, 292–93).[20]

Mulgan, it seems, had been hard at work attempting to mend fences between ELAS and the SOE mission. On May 1 he records

and Angelopoulos, PEEA Committee Secretaries; Porfyroyenis and Stratis representing EAM; and Petros Rousos representing KKE.

20   Sarafis too, in our estimation, is jumping the gun here with his dates. He records meeting Mulgan at Goura near the airstrip on 28–29 April (1980, 282–83) to arrange the seven delegates' departure for the Lebanon Conference. Mulgan's diary, however, records that between 24 April and 1 May he had determined on taking a 'holiday' from travelling to cope with stress and anxiety, and indeed, as is shown in the diary, it was only on 2 May that he set off again—when he joined the EAM-ELAS-PEEA group, first in Karpenisi. Sarafis writes that the conference was 'scheduled to begin on 11 May' (304); Grigoriadis, however, names the 14th as the initially proposed starting date. (It was in fact postponed on account of Papandreou having a fever.) In the end the conference began on 17 May (Sarafis says it opened on the 15th [308]). Writing his diary daily, Mulgan's dates are almost certainly more reliable. Marion Sarafis, who oversaw its translation after his death, records that Sarafis wrote his book 'immediately after demobilization [at the beginning of 1945] [and, as he put it] "with fire, in the ardour of the moment"' (1980a, xiv).

in his diary that he has 'Received thanking letters from Tsamakos re assassination'. With Tsamakos as mediator, he has clearly been offering encouragement to EAM-ELAS to continue collaboration. The next day he heads south with Paul, to PEEA HQ at Koryschades, near Karpenisi. There, he records:

> At Karpenisi General [Sarafis] in tears & threatening resign. Surrealist dinner with Colonel [probably Bakirtzis], general & [Dick?], talked to Tsamakos till midnight, slightly assuaged.

His mediation may have been successful as the diary begins the next day: 'More cheerful morning, left one o'clock'. But again, on 14 May, by which time the seven-man delegation was in Lebanon, he writes:

> Rode alone to Paliokastro, lovely on hills and Heroiko [his treasured horse] happy, here found TSAMAKOS in tearful retirement. Dread over all, & relations friendly tho' undercurrent of malaise.

(It's striking the way these tough middle-aged officers were able to share their emotions with Mulgan: this is clearly part of the intimacy he was to refer to.) He seems to have spent the night in Paliokastro, as he records an 'Angry night with fleas & bed bugs.' Sarafis's description of the delegates' four-day journey to the airstrip at Almyros is much more upbeat, detailing the high morale in the ELAS-supporting villages they rode through (1980, 289–92). Mulgan, however, had picked up on the anxiety and sense of vulnerability among the delegates, a mood that was to dominate during their time at the conference.

The Lebanon Conference (17–20 May 1944)

After the two planes finally took off with the delegates, they landed first in southern Italy, from where Sarafis, leaving the others to follow him later to Lebanon, flew to Cairo for 'urgent' talks with GHQ Middle East (Stefanos Sarafis 1980, 295). In Cairo, he had a meeting with the newly appointed Prime Minister of the Greek government-in-exile, Georgios Papandreou, which gave him a foretaste of what was to come. Papandreou, who was appointed by the British Ambassador to the Greek government-in-exile, Reginald Leeper (and was also backed by the king), was attempting to form a 'government of national unity'. This attempt, Sarafis understood, would mean a severe challenge to the influence and integrity of EAM-ELAS, in spite of its dominance in Greece. Papandreou made it clear that what was demanded was the disbanding of ELAS as a fighting force. Sarafis protested that the already-existing ELAS army of 30,000 fighters[21] was a ready defence for Greece's protection, and could well be expanded to include other bands, warning Papandreou that 'he shouldn't be perpetually thinking about the danger of Communism or his judgement would be impaired' (300). But the ideological polarisation was becoming hard set, with EAM-ELAS pitted against the combined opposition of the British (i.e. Churchill's 'agent', Ambassador Leeper, who controlled the Greek government-in-exile under Papandreou),[22] the Greek king, the Security Battalions,[23] EDES, and the remnants of EKKA.

In his 1948 book *Apple of Discord*, Woodhouse reveals another reason why Sarafis, as military commander of ELAS, would have been on the defensive. As he records, it was around this time that EAM-ELAS became aware that the British authorities, under pressure from Papandreou, were considering a plan to withdraw the AMM altogether from Greece and that Churchill should denounce EAM-ELAS publicly as an 'enemy of the Allied cause', a plan

---

21 Woodhouse gives the number of ELAS fighters at the time as 40,000 (1948, 195).

22 John O. Iatrides describes the way the British Ambassador, Leeper, 'coached' Papandreou throughout the conference, adding that 'Every delegate, but especially those on the Left, knew only too well who had been the real sponsor of the conference and on whose authority Papandreou ultimately spoke' (1972, 64).

23 These right-wing units were soon to be joined by others such as 'X', the Sacred Squadron and the Mountain Brigade, the last two comprising units formed in the Middle East after the purge of those involved in the mutiny. X, significantly, was represented at the Lebanon Conference by General Vendiris, who brought with him a verification signed by, among others, Don Stott (Hamodrakas 2016, 20).

which, he writes, 'amounted to a declaration of war upon ELAS'. Eighteen months later the KKE press printed the texts of several telegrams exchanged between the British authorities and the AMM (Woodhouse 1948, 194–95). This plan was eventually rejected, not least (although he doesn't say this here) by Woodhouse himself, who argued that such a plan would only strengthen ELAS's hand. All that was needed, he wrote to Cairo, was to 'Give EAM-ELAS a little more rope with which to pull their weight and in the end they will hang themselves'.[24] As it turned out, Woodhouse's cynical prediction would eventually be played out to his satisfaction—in the short term, at least. Papandreou is sometimes referred to in Greek circles as the Trojan horse which infiltrated destruction into the left-wing cause. On the face of it he stood for a liberal programme. He had been leader of the Democratic Socialist Party and now entered the scene promising social justice, equality and free elections, even a free plebiscite to decide on the fate of the king, the very king who had endorsed his appointment as Prime Minister. Beneath this, as Sarafis knew well, lurked a fanatical anti-communist. But in all he claimed to stand for, Papandreou looked and sounded so close to EAM and PEEA's own programme that he was able to pre-empt most of their claims in Lebanon.

The differing accounts of what happened in those three days of the Lebanon Conference provide one of the best pictures of just how polarised the two sides had become. It was in Lebanon, as Marion Sarafis confirms, that the EAM movement began to unravel.[25] In

24   Mamarelis cites at length from a signal Woodhouse sent to Cairo (now available in the archives at Kew: PRO HS 5/223) on 6 May 1944, in which he warned against the withdrawal of the AMM from Greece and declaration of war on ELAS, urging that this would have 'precisely the opposite [desired effect]. Please see my Nov and Dec appreciation which I consider proved by events. Especially conclusion "Give EAM-ELAS a little more rope with which to pull their weight and in the end they will hang themselves". [. . .] maintenance Allied Mission despite Present [sic] difficulties offers resistance to Huns and encourages self destruction of EAM-ELAS. Way to beat EAM-ELAS is send as many troops as possible and then more and NOT repeat NOT withdraw from Greece' (Mamareilis 2014, 292). Another unnamed BLO from the area, whom Mamarelis is almost certainly correct to assume is Hammond, reiterated this view on 11 May: 'Only hope of discrediting EAM is to give them enough rope to hang themselves' (Mamarelis 2014, 293).

25   She writes that 'Though [the previous conference at] Plaka had been a defeat, Lebanon is usually regarded as EAM's first fatal slip and it certainly seems that, from this time, the

addition to the fallout from the Psarros murder, mutinies had broken out the previous month amongst the Greek armed forces in Egypt,[26] and EAM was blamed for inciting the rebellions. Soon after the formation of PEEA and in solidarity with its programme, first the Greek army in Egypt and then the Greek navy had risen up against right-wing and royalist elements in their ranks and demanded the resignation of the government-in-exile. The rebellions were put down by British military authorities and more than 2,000 mutineers were confined to internment camps. Prime Minister Tsouderos resigned, as did his successor Sofoklis Venizelos, to be replaced by Papandreou. At the conference, EAM denounced and disclaimed responsibility for these mutinies; subsequent evidence proves that this was indeed the case. But there is little doubt that the success of the EAM movement, symbolised by PEEA, had encouraged the rebels in their demands. Parenthetically it's worth noting that soon after Lebanon, New Zealand Prime Minister Peter Fraser was taking an interest in these rebellions. He had recently travelled to the Middle East, where he met Papandreou as well as the king— whom he seems to have had little time for. Subsequently, Fraser broke the customary unwillingness of the dominion to challenge British war policy by writing to London urging that the best way of 'solidifying the Greek people' was to commute the death sentence of the mutineers (Brown 2019, 132). Unlike the other New Zealand BLOs in Greece who were anti-EAM, Mulgan would certainly have agreed with Fraser. A year later he was to point out to J.V. Wilson, with half-concealed indignation, the 'curious irony' of the fact that

---

leadership progressively lost its grip on events' (1980a, lxix).

26   As Artemis Cooper explains in *Cairo in the War 1939–1945*, the First and Second Greek Brigades comprised volunteers and conscripts from the Greek community in Egypt, troops evacuated after the fall of Crete, and refugees. Although the majority favoured a liberal government, many in the forces, particularly the Egyptian Greeks, were socialists and communists. There had already been two mutinies amongst these forces, first in Syria in 1942 and then in July 1943, when purges of left-wing elements had taken place (Cooper 1989, 288–300). As historians have documented, the mutinies in the Greek army originated from the Anti-Fascist Military Organisation (ASO) initiated by a member of the Communist Party, Yannis Salas, in October 1941. Initially, Salas had turned for support exclusively to unranked soldiers, inspired by Lenin's model from 1916. In the spring of 1944, the ASO spread to the Greek navy and the Greek air force as well.

some Greek agents who had escaped arrest or death while serving the British in the early stage of the resistance (1941–42) became 'leaders of the mutiny in the Greek army and are now imprisoned [by the British] in the Sudan.'[27]

There was, therefore, a great deal of static in the air around the table at Lebanon. One of the most impassioned speeches came from Georgios Kartalis, who had remained close to Psarros throughout the history of EKKA. According to Panayiotis Kanellopoulos, who was representing the government-in-exile, Kartalis held forth for two hours in denunciation of ELAS, in particular of Sarafis as its military commander, to the intense discomfort of the latter (2012, 91). Sarafis rallied, however, and replied at equal length, with a detailed account of ELAS's military achievements between November '42 and May '44, followed by a long catalogue of the weaknesses and betrayals of EDES (Stefanos Sarafis 1980, 314–17).[28] But by this time, with careful manoeuvring by Papandreou,[29] the group was on the back foot and at the end of the conference all seven EAM delegates agreed to sign the Lebanon Charter, conceding a great deal more than they had intended in joining a government of national unity. In spite of their overwhelming support in the country, they were given only six ministerial posts out of 20, and these of minor importance. These posts were later refused, but in August, after some modifications and endless haggling, finally agreed to.[30] Four months later, at the

---

27   ATL, J.V. Wilson Papers, MS-Papers-6875-2, 1.

28   As Couvaras reports on 28 May, back in Koryschades, at meetings of the PEEA Council, the leaders were to struggle in debate to hold on to the basic principles of the movement:

> PEEA Vice-Premier Bakirdjis made an important speech yesterday at the last session of the National Council. Among other things, he said that the minimum demands of the PEEA, in order to agree to participate in the new Greek government, are as follows: (1) King George should not return to Greece before a plebiscite takes place; (2) EAM and the Communist party should be represented in the government in proportion to their strengths; and (3) the ELAS army should be strengthened and its character as a people's army retained. (n.d., 39)

29   For Papandreou's denunciation of the guerrilla resistance in the Greek mountains, see his speech at the conference in Lebanon on 17 May 1944 (Papandreou 1963, II, 61–68).

30   For a description of the negotiations between the Papandreou government and the PEEA government in the summer of 1944, from his point of view, see Woodhouse 1948, 192–99. It should also be remembered, as Haritopoulos records (2003, 577–78), that the Russian delegation which had visited the mountains in late July had put pressure on PEEA and ELAS to compromise.

conference in Caserta in Italy, the EAM-PEEA delegates would be
similarly manoeuvred into signing a document which subordinated
all the resistance forces to the command of Britain's General Scobie.
As German historian Heinz Richter argues, 'Until the bitter end
the Greek Left tried to avoid civil war as is proved by its constant
readiness to compromise which came close to self-abnegation' (1980,
86).

Following the Lebanon stand-off from the Greek mountains,
Mulgan recorded tersely in his diary: 'Papandreou provides hell acct
[account] of Elas from safe distance of Lebanon.'[31] It's clear from this
what he thought of Papandreou's betrayal of the Greek resistance.
For the British, however, Lebanon represented what Woodhouse
describes as a resounding success:

> Agreement on a coalition was achieved by battering the delegates
> of PEEA, EAM, ELAS and the KKE into a mental daze in which
> they were hardly responsible for their actions. (1948, 191)

Vindictive triumphalism of this sort would inevitably backfire.
Before long, the sense of injustice in the EAM-ELAS movement,
among both leaders and rank and file, would lead to an irreconcilable
stand-off.

The crisis rumbled on through the summer. Svolos and his
colleagues stayed on in Cairo after Lebanon and didn't return to
PEEA HQ until mid July. When they did, the reaction at PEEA was
one of fury at the concessions granted. A diary entry of Mulgan's
after 23 July records:

> Politics in vague crisis still with H.M.G. [His Majesty's
> Government of Britain] backing Papandreou, our boys denouncing
> all & sundry but think uneasy tolerance may continue.

---

31   Diary entry at end of week beginning Monday 15 May. For a full description of Papandreou's
      'hell account' of EAM-ELAS at Lebanon, see Iatrides 1972, 62–64, which includes the
      citation of Papandreou's resolve to 'dissolve ELAS myself, with the help of the British [. . .]
      After liberation' (63).

Torn between 'our boys' and the government he was supposed to be representing, Mulgan would have felt the heat from both quarters. A tolerance, desired on both sides, would eventually become impossible: the British authorities were tightening the noose gradually and carefully.

A great deal has been written about the downfall of EAM-ELAS, with most agreeing that there were internal as well as external factors. One important internal factor was that the movement failed to produce the right leader at this crucial time—that Greece, as some have put it, lacked a Tito. Aris was an outstanding partisan leader; Sarafis was a highly respected commander of the ELAS forces; Karagiorgis possessed all the intellectual gifts and commitment needed. But the first two lacked the political maturity to lead a nationwide movement and the last, perhaps, the military energy. Zachariadis, who returned from internment in Germany to take over leadership of the KKE after liberation, turned out to be a deeply divisive figure who, most commentators agree, made several fatal mistakes.

But there is no doubt that external factors were becoming near insuperable. At the very time the 25 Greek delegates were battling it out around the table in Lebanon, the big powers were setting things up behind the scenes. On May 18, Churchill wrote a long message to Roosevelt saying that the Soviets 'have today told us they accept the broad principle that they take the lead in the Romanian business and give us the lead in Greece' (Barker 1980, 24). The American State Department was not happy with the idea of carving the Balkans up into 'spheres of influence' but by late June, after further pressure from Churchill warning against the way 'EAM would work a reign of terror', Roosevelt agreed (Barker 1980, 25).

The eventual arrival of Papandreou's new so-called 'Government of Unity' in Athens on October 18, immediately after the German withdrawal, was hardly a moment of celebration for the predominantly (some say 85–90 percent) anti-monarchist population of Greece,[32]

---

32   These figures are from an unnamed questioner at the London School of Economics conference on 12–13 May 1978 (Marion Sarafis 1980b, 75).

who were having serious misgivings about what lay ahead. Richard Clogg, one of the most well informed and balanced historians from the British point of view, describes the return as follows:

> thanks to the high-level horse-trading between Churchill and Stalin, a dramatic change had been wrought, within the space of a few months, in the fortunes of the Greek government-in-exile. An insignificant and demoralized exile government, which the British government had despised and kept in deliberate ignorance of many aspects of British policy towards Greece, and one which commanded little loyalty either inside or outside the country, had been transformed from a rump of squabbling politicians into a national government that was to enjoy, if only briefly, the illusion that it was a government that was truly representative of the people of Greece. (2000, 164–65)

It is hardly surprising that at the festivities to celebrate liberation in Lamia in late October, Mulgan appears to have been less than enthusiastic. With British regiments under Colonel Lord Jellicoe marching in in triumph, Chris Woodhouse delivering speeches and British war correspondents pouring in to trumpet a British victory,[33] his diary for 20 October records 'Self feeling to hell with it all.'[34] These seven words, scribbled and barely legible, concentrate a year of accumulated fury and despair that would increase still further in the months ahead.

33 Edmonds, as head of the AMM by this time, rode in to Lamia on horseback on 23 October alongside Sarafis and Aris for formal celebrations. Recording the event many decades later, he noted wryly the way the BBC was covering the liberation of the city, claiming that British troops were driving the Germans out before them, whereas in fact they arrived two days after the Germans had left (1998, 236). ELAS had entered the city well before this (on 18– 19 October) (Stefanos Sarafis 1980, 462). As with the reporting of the destruction of the Gorgopotamos viaduct, the BBC was airbrushing Aris and ELAS out, refusing them any credit for successful operations. (For Gorgopotamos, Aris and the BBC, see Eudes 1972, 22.)

34 The same diary entry, as far as it is legible, also records 'much disgusted' and 'Arrived 3 war correspondents.' In reaction, it seems, he found an American flag to hoist up beside the Union Jack at the Mission HQ (Day 1977, 44).

CHAPTER 6

Taking Sides

At this stage, our focus on Mulgan's political position begins to centre increasingly on his disagreement with the policies of 'the old man of Downing Street'. As he was well aware, there were numerous dissenting voices within Britain itself. But as victory grew closer, and encouraged by adulation for his vital role in its achievement, Churchill felt free to ignore advice from those on the ground and was given free rein to push ahead with his agenda. He was of that imperial military caste that had dominated the British ruling class for centuries. Imperialism, as Tariq Ali puts it, was his 'true religion':

> Empire so dominated Churchill's political thought that no adventure was too risky, no crime too costly, no war unnecessary, if British possessions, global hegemony and trade interests were at stake. (2022, 9)

This obsession had driven and would drive Churchill's political career, from his time as Secretary of State for War in 1919–21 when he sent in the notorious Black and Tans to fight the Republicans in the Irish War of Independence, to his time as Prime Minister in the 1950s when horrendous atrocities were committed under colonial rule in Kenya (11,000 rebelling Mau Mau were killed to prolong British rule for a few more years). Given Mulgan's long-standing and passionate opposition to imperialism, he was bound to rebel openly against Churchill's plans for Greece, sooner or later.

The post-operational report

At the end of his time as an SOE agent Mulgan wrote an extended report of the sort required by all BLOs, describing what he considered the achievements of his Mission in Area 3.[1] The single-spaced, eight-page typed document followed protocol in detailing organisation of the Mission stations, personnel, military situation, stores and supply, operations (described by the month), plans for and outcomes of the Noah's Ark operations (harassing the retreating Germans), and then a final summary. Out of the factual details emerges an attitude to the undertaking that, though worded with extreme caution, strongly indicates his allegiances.

He begins with a short description of the ELAS forces in his area. Praising their good record of fighting against the Italians, he compares the often-strained relations between ELAS and the AMM in other areas in Greece with those in his own, attributing these good relations to the character and sympathy of the Division Commander Kostas Tsamakos. No mention is made of his own sympathy for ELAS, and throughout he deflects attention away from any personal achievements. Full praise is given to the way, throughout the winter of 1943–44, neither he nor any of the AMM officers or NGOs 'met anything but the greatest friendliness and hospitality from both Andartes and civilians' (1). He expresses none of the usual complaints about ELAS: no fear of being 'bumped off'

---

1   O'Sullivan gives the date of the report as 1 November 1944, which is probably the date on which it was distributed to the BLOs. The date on the report itself is 26 February 1945, which seems to have been the date Mulgan completed it (TNA HS 5/634).

(Foot 2010, 14), no talk of being hindered or deserted, of jealousy and suspicion at ELAS HQ—although he would have known such slurs would have chimed well with Cairo expectations. He concludes the Introduction by calling out ELAS detractors, demanding a different understanding:

> I would like to place this [the unequivocal friendliness of both *andartes* and civilians] on record since I am aware that other members of the Mission had less favourable experiences elsewhere in GREECE. It is also worthy of note that East THESSALY remained one of the few parts of GREECE in which no charge was ever made to members of the Mission for mules or guides or for lodging and food when travelling. (1)

Andartes and civilians, he stresses, were unified under a 'national' EAM-ELAS banner in his area. (He had made the same point in his earlier—1 August—response to the questionnaire, subtly challenging any assumption that ELAS was not a dominant nationally-supported movement.)

Most of his criticism is reserved, with quiet insistence, for the failure of British authorities to supply ammunition to ELAS from the time operations against the Germans began, in April '44.[2] Although the ban was partially lifted in August, its effect throughout the spring and summer was considerable. ELAS *andartes* in his area had adequate arms, on the whole, because of what they had confiscated from the Italians. But under pressure from the Foreign Office, SOE refused to supply them with ammunition after the Psarros murder, and Mulgan details the consequences in his report:

> A difficult situation was created by the ban on arms and

---

2   This is one of the main theses of Stefanos Sarafis's book *ELAS*, where he argues that:

> while ELAS put all the resources it had at the service of the Allied struggle, the British constantly made difficulties for ELAS. Instead of supplying it with the equipment it needed to organise itself more efficiently and assist the Allied struggle, they were careful to provide only a bare minimum of aid to ensure that, when the fighting ended at liberation, ELAS would be exhausted and without ammunition, and so unable to fulfil its duty towards the people; in other words, in no position to oppose the British plans. (1980, 234)

ammunition to ELAS laid down in April, since at that time we
had begun sabotage operations in the area and the Andartes
argued, with some justice, that it was unreasonable to invite
GERMAN retaliation in this way without at least a guarantee
that ammunition would be forthcoming if they were attacked. (3)

The severity of the German reprisals is listed with calm detachment:
12 hostages from Lamia shot at the scene of a railway sabotage and
17 hanged in Dhokala, 40 villages between Lamia and Karpenisi
destroyed in August and over 100 civilians killed.

> This system of reprisal, together with the difficult political
> situation and the ban on arms and ammunition to ELAS during
> May and June hampered our work [and meant that we could not]
> give to the Andartes of ELAS that support which would have
> ensured their complete cooperation. (3)

Any lack of co-operation, is his implication, was not the fault of the
andartes. There was a deeper cause for this understanding: Mulgan's
empathy with the local population concerning the tragic implications
of these acts. It was all very well, he knew, to urge bravado when it
was someone else's family and home that would be murdered and
destroyed. (He was to make this point with some asperity in *Report
on Experience*: 'If you meet in later days men who pride themselves
on partisan exploits, question them a little more closely on the
matter of reprisals' [162–63].) He would also have been well aware,
as Pat Wingate records in his own report for June 1944, that in the
German attacks on Kaitsa, Spercheias and other EAM-supporting
villages in their area that month, British-backed collaborationist
forces had been used: 'Moroccan [mercenary forces employed by the
Germans] and Rallis troops [the Security Battalions] were employed
on this drive' (TNA HS 5/636).

A fascinating detail given by Dionysis Haritopoulos in his
impressively documented 800-page study of Aris within the context
of ELAS strategy throws further light on Mulgan's anger about

the activities of these Rallis forces. On 26 August, Haritopoulos records, citing from the Contemporary Social History Archives, John Mulgan, 'as official representative of the AMM in Greece', sent a written message to the Security Battalions, whom he calls 'the collaborators with the occupying forces', in which he wrote (in not incorrect but slightly unidiomatic Greek):

> This is to inform you, on behalf of the AMM, which is working with the ELAS andartes, that no protection will be given to those who continue to help the Germans. Your only salvation is to abandon the Germans now, and to surrender your arms under the following conditions: We are in a position to promise you that you will stay alive [tha zisete], but those who continue to fight against Greece and its allies have no hope of surviving. (Haritopoulos 2003, 579)

An almost identical threat was repeated by Sarafis on September 3 (Haritopoulos 2003, 579), which tells us two important things: first, that Mulgan had taken upon himself, at least unofficially, the task of directing policy now that Woodhouse had (from June) stepped down as commander; and second, that Mulgan's identification of the aims of the AMM with those of ELAS, at a time when Cairo was attempting to enforce a directly opposing strategy, was quite deliberate.[3] Mulgan and Sarafis were clearly still working in close collaboration. As a result of their joint directive, 1,000 members of the Security Battalions in Agrinion and 650 in Nafpaktos surrendered their weapons and returned unharmed to their homes (Haritopoulos 2003, 579). As the Security Battalions disbanded over the coming months, however, large numbers of their forces, instead of being prosecuted as traitors, were taken into the Greek army.

To Cairo, in his report, Mulgan continued to promote a generally positive picture of the ELAS forces. They did well, he wrote, in

---

3   It might be objected that having recently spoken at length with Barker-Benfield, who was less hostile to ELAS than most in Cairo, at least so it at first appeared, Mulgan had gained a new confidence to insist on the joint collaboration with ELAS. Barker-Benfield's motives may not have been entirely straightforward (Woodhouse 2002, 96).

small groups. He would have known what subsequent historical analysis has made clear, that the combined SOE-*andartes* forces throughout the country were indeed inflicting serious losses on the Germans.[4] On a large scale, of course, their forces 'had no military value', particularly in defence, when opposing a determined German drive (8): their military contribution, when measured against the success of regular warfare, was small. However, Mulgan's criteria are different. Never losing sight of the fact that his work was in guerrilla warfare, he carried with him the lessons of Tom Wintringham in the UK and Spain, Orde Wingate in Ethiopia, and, possibly, Tim Foley with the Provisional IRA in Ireland, and measured success not according to enemy casualties, but by the numbers of enemy forces deployed to counteract their operations. These he lists in his report in careful detail: for example, 'in the 66 kilometres of railway lines between LAMIA and DHOMOKHOS where the line was particularly vulnerable a total of 1000 Germans were employed' on garrison duty. These guards were increased as their guerrilla operations continued, he writes, until, in the last phase of the German withdrawal, four extra battalions were brought in to guard the line. Similarly on the road, after a series of ELAS ambushes in May and June, the Germans were forced to station garrisons on the high ground, deploying two battalions with artillery to drive back the Greeks (2). During the last fortnight of the German withdrawal, the concentration of German forces on the road and railway was such that all Mulgan and his troops could do was conduct quick hit-and-run operations (6).

Unlike those of other BLOs, Mulgan's descriptions of his work

---

4   In a report of 27 June 1945, Julian Dolbey recorded that the total casualties inflicted by
      SOE (with *andartes*) on Germans in Greece was 20,050, and on 'other enemy troops' 14,650.
      Information, he records, was collected through daily signals 'by over 600 British and 3,000
      Greek observers' (BHA 259, 7). For more evidence from the British point of view on the
      important role ELAS played in the resistance, see also reports sent every three months by
      Lord Selborne (head of SOE in London) to the Prime Minister about the thousands of deaths
      SOE was inflicting on German troops, where it becomes obvious that such damage could not
      have been caused by small numbers of SOE agents without significant help from the *andartes*
      (TNA, PREM 3/408/1). From the Greek side, see the *Inventory of War Events of the Greek
      Nation* 1989 (published by the Directory of Military History), 148–61, which details battles
      against the enemy by Greek resistance groups; also Stefanos Sarafis 1980 *passim*.

with the *andartes* are always in terms of the assistance he gave them, rather than the commands. This was a conscious policy. As he puts it in the report, 'it was thought better in principle that Andarte officers should retain nominal command and responsibility for operations, particularly those that might entail reprisals' (4)— where, presumably, *andarte* officers would be in a better position to estimate the degree of risk to their own people. This is not to say that without the BLOs the Greeks would have done the job themselves, since 'so many good reasons can be found in GREECE for doing nothing' (8), Mulgan comments wryly. But essential to the trust and cooperation was the sense that they all shared the same conditions. Mulgan understood Greek *filotimo*: if he showed he was going along anyway, he was bound to be supported.

The last paragraph of his report, which reads as follows, is not as simple as it looks:

> I feel that we were fortunate in having a more or less non-political area to work in. It may well be that this area was left as a cloak to cover the misdeeds of ELAS elsewhere. We did find, however, that where A.M.M. personnel provided direction and incentive, there was seldom any difficulty in persuading ELAS Andartes to undertake operations against the GERMANS. It was possible to attach to ourselves groups of Andartes and particular officers with whom we worked closely and to get from them a greater loyalty than they showed to their politicians. (8)

That his area was used by ELAS as a cloak to hide their misdeeds elsewhere was a comment made by several others as they watched Mulgan's success with ELAS and sought an explanation. Hammond writes: 'At this time [spring '44], ELAS GHQ always pointed to Mulgan's area as the one in which ELAS co-operation was freely given, because Mulgan treated ELAS properly. It was a regular gambit of ELAS to have one such model area, but Mulgan deserved his luck' (1983, 141).[5] It was also a common move on Mulgan's part

5   Hammond made the same point to Paul Day in 1965: 'The policy of ELAS was definitely

to deflect attention from himself by semi-endorsing ('It may well be that . . .') these sour-grapes views, then to refute them. But what are we to make of his comment that his area was 'non-political'? Nothing could have been further from the truth. Did he mean that as it was ELAS territory, almost exclusively, there was no political friction of the sort found in other areas? Or was he perhaps attempting to downplay his own political engagement by calling the group he did so well with 'non-political'? Finally, when we read his conclusion, that he got from ELAS guerrillas 'a greater loyalty than they showed to their politicians', he can't mean the EAM-ELAS-PEEA political leaders, unrecognised in Cairo. The phrase, surely, calls for another interpretation, a clue to which is given in the policy expressed by Sarafis, that his aim was to establish guerrilla forces free from loyalty to the politicians put in office by the British.[6] For the ELAS *andartes,* at least at the end of Mulgan's time with them, 'politicians' meant the Papandreou government that would ride roughshod over everything they had fought for. But the imputation is discreet, easy to miss.

The 'effect of Chris' (Woodhouse)

In sharing EAM-ELAS's mistrust of the Papandreou government and its politicians, Mulgan was at odds with the policy being enforced more rigidly than ever by now from Cairo. Chief among its enforcers was Woodhouse, and by this time, it now seems fairly clear to us, the relationship between the two men was far from comfortable. We should not be misled by Woodhouse's high praise of Mulgan after his death. He wrote to Gabrielle that 'No other officer in the whole country—and I say this after long experience—had so much

to favour one BLO . . . (I had been so favoured in Macedonia) and it made it more difficult for such a Liaison Officer to view ELAS as suspiciously as the other officers did' (Day 1968, 53–54).

6   According to Bill Jordan, Sarafis told Myers this around mid 1943, before he joined ELAS (1969, 94). This view is reinforced by Mark Mazower, who has analysed the way the successive (official) Greek governments at this time had lost control of the state apparatus, especially the judiciary—'the extraordinary weakness of an unpopular political elite, which was unable to organize itself and was challenged by the proven and successful rival EAM/ELAS, which had become in terms of Greek politics the organization par excellence' (2000, 12).

success in persuading the ELAS guerrillas in carrying his plans into action' (LJB 311), deftly side-stepping his own deep mistrust of ELAS. Woodhouse had spent some time with Mulgan in the last six or so months of the occupation, and Mulgan's diary entries subtly indicate the tensions. In late April, when Mulgan recorded sitting around with the group in the Mission station (*andartes*, Ian Neville and others) 'try[ing] to discuss effect of Chris', at a time when ELAS was demanding Woodhouse's removal, things were clearly not going well. Then when he returned several months later, Mulgan writes (on 25 September): 'Chris arrived in afternoon. He talked at length, I listened.' Mulgan was clearly holding his peace with some difficulty. He would, however, have revealed enough of what he thought about ELAS for it to be conveyed by Woodhouse to Cairo. Three weeks later, on October 13, the diary records: 'Home by dark to find offensive telegram from Cairo'—at a time when Mulgan was daily laying his life on the line in the Noah's Ark operations. The criticism from Cairo, which does not seem to have survived, was almost certainly political rather than military. Much later, in his autobiography *Something Ventured*, Woodhouse gives his own description of his time with Mulgan at this point:

> During the last days of the occupation in Greece, I had spent some days on operations with John Mulgan, a former Rhodes Scholar [*sic*] from New Zealand. By night we blew up the railway line, by day we mortared the halted trains, being bombarded in turn by the angry Germans. In the intervals we discussed the postwar world which was now so imminent. 'I suppose it's time to start doing something serious', Mulgan remarked one day. I was puzzled at first. Had we been doing nothing serious for the last five years? I intended to ask him what he meant, but I missed the opportunity. (1982, 103)

Wouldn't this have been Mulgan's way of saying that what concerned him was not the victory of the Allies but rather the broader political implications of what they'd been doing—not the 'form' of the struggle (war or peace), as Lenin put it, but its 'content', the rights of national sovereignty against the scramble for economic territory ('the division of the world') among the major imperial powers (Lenin 2010, 91). Such a 'division' of Greece was occupying Churchill and Stalin at this very time,[7] and Mulgan would have been reflecting on it all as he prepared to write up *Report on Experience*. Woodhouse was first and last a diplomat, a master of 'bluff'—as he confessed to his close friend Tom Barnes when the latter asked him how he managed to keep his temper with the Elasites.[8] But his allegiances were clear; when he gave up the command in February 1945, Woodhouse recommended the fanatically anti-ELAS Barnes to replace him. Mulgan's allegiances, Woodhouse would have become aware, were very different.

As liberation approached, Woodhouse had the complete confidence of the policy makers in Cairo (and ultimately, the Foreign Office). Mulgan did not enjoy this same confidence. Around this time an undated list, based on recommendations by Woodhouse,[9] was drawn up by SOE evaluating the officers who had operated under Woodhouse's command. There are five categories in this list. The first is of sixteen men 'TO BE RETAINED FOR OVERT SOE WORK OF THE "DISTRICT COMMISSIONS" TYPE'. Included are two New Zealanders: Tom Barnes, who is categorised as 'Excellent for SOE work of overt type, but may not wish to remain',

---

7   Citing from FO records at the time, Elisabeth Barker (head of Balkan Region, Political Wartime Executive, 1942–45) gives the following account of Churchill's notorious deal with Stalin in the meeting at the Kremlin on 9 October 1944:

Churchill [. . .] said that he was not worrying very much about Romania. That was very much a Russian affair. But Greece was different. Britain, he said, must be the leading Mediterranean power and he hoped Stalin would let him have the first say about Greece in the same way as Stalin about Romania. He then produced what he called a 'naughty document' showing the relative interests of the Soviet Union and 'the others' as 90 to 10 in Romania, and 10 to 90 in Greece, with less extreme figures for Bulgaria, Hungary and Yugoslavia. (Barker 1980, 27–28)

8   Barnes records a conversation with Woodhouse in which he describes the trouble he's having with Aris. He tells Woodhouse: 'I'm no good at diplomacy. Not like you', to which Woodhouse replied: 'Sometimes you just have to bluff, Tom [. . .] and hope it works out' (Barnes 2015, 286).

9   'The following attempt to divide the BLOs in Greece into various categories applicable to post-hostilities conditions is made as a result of discussions with Colonel Woodhouse' (TNA HS 5/363).

and Arthur Edmonds, described as someone who 'Could succeed Woodhouse or Hammond as Commander'.[10] On the second list are three names recommended for 'SOE WORK OF SUBVERT TYPE'. The third list of those 'SUITABLE FOR EMPLOYMENT IN OFFICE WORK OF SOE TYPE' also has three names. List number four, those 'SUITABLE FOR EMPLOYMENT ON SOE OPS OF MILITANT CHARACTER ELSEWHERE' has 21 names. The fifth and final list, giving names of those least desirable for future SOE work, refers to 'OFFICERS WHO SHOULD BE OUT-POSTED FROM SOE'. Nine men are listed here. One is Rufus Sheppard, the left-wing sympathiser Mulgan had joined in the mountains on his arrival in Greece. Sheppard, it is stated, 'has too trusting a character to be really satisfactory at SOE work, and has been throughout hoodwinked by EAM/ELAS'.[11] With him on this list is Mulgan, categorised as 'suitable for Regimental duty or civilian employment' (TNA HS 5/363).

The reasons why Woodhouse recommended Mulgan be 'out-posted' are not given, but it seems clear to us that they are related to his similar tendency to be 'too trusting' of EAM-ELAS. Woodhouse's inclination was in the opposite direction.[12] Arthur

10   Indeed, as already mentioned and as Edmonds himself records, 'In the later stages of the occupation I became acting Senior British Officer of the Allied Military Mission to Greece' (1998, iii).

11   By the time of his death at the end of that year, Sheppard was working with an American organisation in Athens. According to Allied reports Sheppard was killed by a booby trap planted by ELAS in Athens during the *Dekemvriana* (Myers 1985, 165n; Mace and Grehan 2012, 250). He had been transferred to UNRRA (Greek Mission) 'with effect from the beginning of Nov. 44 [. . .] at Force 133's request' [KCLMA Dobrski GB0099, 30] and appointed chief intelligence officer in the organisation by the Americans. Sheppard would probably have felt more comfortable working with the Americans, who at the time were critical of British policy in Greece. At the time of his death, several reports of foul play circulated in Athens. Known as 'Hills' by the Greeks, Sheppard was suspected of being a victim of the British Intelligence Service, as were two other British ELAS sympathisers (Kailas 2005, 431–32). Marion Sarafis (1990, 132) records that Sheppard was killed 'under controversial circumstances.' Further evidence is needed to support these claims.

12   Woodhouse's opposition to the left-wing partisans has been well documented. In a book on the Greek resistance, the eminent German historian Heinz Richter assesses Woodhouse's role in Greece, including detailed comments on how Woodhouse continued for several years after the war to deny that he knew about Zervas's dealings with the German General in Epirus, Hubert Lanz. Eventually Woodhouse reversed his claims (Richter 2009, 113–16). See also correspondence between Woodhouse and Lars Bærentzen and George Alexander in KCLMA, GB 99, 5/5, where Richter's comments are validated. For a Greek interpretation of

Edmonds, publishing many years later when he was free to detail his relationship with Sarafis, gives a small but telling example of what he calls Chris's 'heavy-handed' method of dealing with the Elasites. Woodhouse, knowing he himself wouldn't get very far in asking anything of ELAS, asked Edmonds after a meeting to obtain an order promised by Sarafis,

> saying the only way I'd get it was by staying at Sarafis's GHQ, until it was put in my hands. I tried this method but when I saw the incredulous expression on Sarafis's face I quickly decided that in this case at least, trust was the better course. Sarafis said that he would send the order to my HQ before 7 p.m., which was the time Chris required it. I left his office and when I returned to my HQ at 7 p.m. I found the order had been delivered. (Edmonds 1998, 238)[13]

O'Sullivan assesses Mulgan's outposting as follows:

> In the context of Woodhouse's esteem for Mulgan as an outstanding soldier and officer, and his earlier recommendation for a Military Cross, this can only be taken, surely, as an astute guess that Mulgan, whatever refinement one might put on it, was pretty much 'burned out'. (LJB 313–14)

Given the political conditions, we would argue, another interpretation seems plausible: that having toed the British line with discretion for several years, Mulgan was becoming less inclined to remain silent, and had been expressing his opposition in too many quarters, even to Woodhouse himself. In the event, Woodhouse's suggestion was only partly followed, as Mulgan's later work in Athens for the Liquidation Fund put him among those on the third list (as suitable for SOE office work). He would still have been regarded as a reliable

Woodhouse's role, see Hajis 1980, 71.

13   Edmonds also felt comfortable enough by this time to protest about the way the BBC was reporting that the Allied troops had landed in Greece 'to liberate the country, whereas in reality, they were occupying Greece on the heels of the Germans' (1998, 235).

representative of British interests, at least as far as obligations to the Greek people were concerned. It was to be proved, thereafter, that to remove him from direct military service was not necessarily to remove him from political engagement.

Ta Dekemvriana (3 December 1944–11 January 1945)

The 'greater loyalty' Mulgan got from the ELAS *andartes* could not have been anything but reciprocal, and Mulgan's sympathies for the EAM-ELAS movement would endure until the last. The two ventures outside official duties he made towards the end of his life were to visit Greeks who had made a loyal or heroic contribution to the Greek resistance. (By this time his Greek was fluent enough for him to relate directly to local people without an interpreter.)[14] After the Germans evacuated in mid October he was posted back to Cairo, flying out from Tatoi (a small airport in the north of Athens) on November 8. From the Egyptian capital, however, his thoughts kept returning to the tragedy he had left behind. In Roumeli thousands of villagers were now homeless, with the prospect of winter ahead. An official report that summer had documented that overall in Greece 879 villages had been totally and 460 partially destroyed (Mazower 2001, 183), mostly by the method of sprinkling flammable dust which was then ignited by gunshot. Thousands of civilians had been rounded up and shot or burned alive—in Kalavrita, Distomo, Hortiatis, Kommeno, Vianos, Kandanos and Kontomari, to name only some of the villages. And on evacuation, employing their scorched-earth policy, the Germans had made every attempt to cause as much human and material devastation as possible. Another source of anxiety for Mulgan would have been the hardening of British policy towards EAM-ELAS, which was to

14   He claims with characteristic modesty that when he landed in Greece he had little knowledge of the modern Greek language apart from a few lessons at the Mount Carmel camp in Palestine (RE 137). In an official British army record made a year later, however, he is classified as being fluent in French and Greek (TNA HS 9/1073/3), and certainly by a few months later, at his new post in Athens, he was confident to conduct formal interviews without the aid of an interpreter (as he seems to acknowledge in a letter to Gabrielle [AGM 290]). The intervening year had clearly brought about an intensive initiation into Greek culture.

reach a tragic climax in December.

Immediately after the evacuation of the Germans, from mid October onwards, the British started bringing in more troops, to the jubilant welcome of the Greeks, many of whom had little idea of what was in store for them. Smaller Allied units had already started arriving in early summer (the British RSR units and the American Operation Group [OGs] who served with Mulgan), and by November 1944 there was an army of around 24,000 British troops in Greece. By January 1945 it would double to around 50,000, and by March nearly double again—to a massive force of 80,000,[15] larger even than the Germans' occupying force. Between the months of February and April 1945, Greece had been transformed into what Heinz Richter calls '*de facto* a British protectorate' (1985, 165). As part of this drive, Churchill's fast-evolving plan was to eradicate ELAS altogether, calculating that if there was to be armed conflict it should be in Athens, given ELAS's invincibility in the mountains.

On December 1, the six EAM ministers who had agreed to join the hoped-for government of national unity resigned in protest against the head of the British forces in Greece, Roland Scobie's, insistence that ELAS disband by the 10th of the month. A peaceful demonstration was announced by EAM for the 3rd, defying a government ban. The outcome of what turned out to be a massive gathering of Greek supporters in Syntagma Square was a fatal turning point—a brutal assault by the police, who opened fire on unarmed demonstrators, killing 28 and leaving 148 wounded. The police fired without provocation, as verified by many eyewitnesses (for example, McNeill 1947, 137–40; Edmonds 1998, 245), even by British personnel who in other respects were critical of EAM-ELAS (Byford-Jones 1946, 138 ff.; Clive n.d., 161). We also learn from Chris Woodhouse that Angelos Evert, head of the British-supported Athens police, confessed to him in 1958 that he had been ordered to disperse the crowd, if necessary with the use of arms, by Papandreou himself (2002, 127). Immediately afterwards, Churchill

---

15   See the American report by the commanding officer Charles F. Edson of OSS, in Clogg 2002, 191.

gave the notorious order to Scobie: '*Do not [. . .] hesitate to act as if you were in a conquered city where a local rebellion is in progress*' (Churchill 1953, 289). The December fighting began the evening of the 3rd, immediately after the violence in Syntagma Square. The reserve (mostly civilian) fighters of EAM, initially in small groups, responded to police violence by attacking police stations. They then proceeded to carry out summary executions of those thought to be collaborators (Close 1995, 141). As in several other countries in Europe, the end of Axis occupation produced a collapse into anarchy, with retributive punishments meted out for wartime activities on a large scale and the basic premises of civil behaviour destroyed by totalitarian government and total war. In France, as Tony Judt records, of the approximately 10,000 summary executions carried out after the fall of the Vichy government, most occurred during the following weeks. And in Italy, most of the 12–15,000 shootings for fascist or collaborationist activities occurred before or during the weeks of liberation (2000, 301).

Meanwhile, units of the *andartes*' forces from the mountains, operating on a limited scale in outlying districts, were blocked by British troops on the northern outskirts of the city. Papandreou's government forces, joined by the British army on the 5th, began to set up blockades, eventually employing 350 tanks and more than 120 planes to strafe city areas known to be strongholds of the left. (According to Haralambidis, over 1,650 air sorties from Italy brought in troops, ammunition and supplies to the British-backed combatants [2014, 188].) Over the following days the Greek Minister of Defence ordered the deployment of the Greek military, which by now comprised only those individuals who supported an anti-communist cause and included members of the notorious Security Battalions, some of whom had been successfully disbanded by Mulgan and Sarafis just three months earlier.[16] ELAS was now

16   O'Connor describes the Security Battalions as 'numbering about 20,000 in 1944 [. . .] made up of local fascists, convicts, sympathetic prisoners-of-war and forcibly impressed conscripts under the command of the Germans' (2018, 264). It is important to remember, however, that the conflict between the left and the police forces had been whipped up by the Germans during the occupation. As Mark Mazower records, in the early stages of the occupation, under the Italians, the Greek police had helped the resistance, with many taking to the mountains.

at war with the British army, which only a few months earlier had been supplying it with (admittedly limited amounts of) arms and ammunition. It is deeply ironic, as André Gerolymatos notes, that the British were obliged from now on to follow the German policy of 'rais[ing] the spectre of communism to rally the forces of the Right against the andartes' (1992, 337).

By early January the ELAS forces, whose hand grenades and sniper fire were no match for British tanks and RAF Spitfires, were defeated and forced to accept a humiliating truce. Casualties on both sides ran into several thousands.[17] Tens of thousands of civilian EAM-ELAS sympathisers fled the capital and, according to the official KKE account, the *Lefki Vivlos* (White Book), within a short space of time 50,000 Greek combatants who had been taken prisoner and held in North Africa were prohibited from returning to Greece for fear they would join left-wing forces (1945a, 93–94). A stark indication of how far apart the two sides had become in outlook, what we have called the parallel universes they inhabited, can be seen in the account of the armistice signing on 11 January given by Brigadier Hugh Mainwaring, deputising for Scobie:

> Scobie was utterly fed up with their [EAM-ELAS's] double-dealing and shiftiness and refused to see them. I was strictly no-nonsense with the EAM delegates and although I knew they wanted to smoke I told them: 'When people are conducting a truce there will be no smoking.' I was letting them know they were naughty boys. When earlier I had dealt with Sarafis I had thought he was an absolute four-letter word shifty man. Zevgos, the wordy school-

But after September 1943 and the takeover of the police by the SS, Greek collaborators were encouraged to set up anti-communist militias against the resistance, 'indiscriminately killing civilians to dissuade them from supporting EAM [. . .] and many serving Gendarmes were deliberately dismissed from their units to force them to enrol in the new Security Battalions' (1997, 131).

17 Close (1995, 140–41) gives the official British casualty figures: 210 British, 3,480 right-wing Greeks and 2–3,000 Elasites; overall deaths, 17,000. The unaccounted-for 11,000, most commentators agree, includes many ELAS-supporting civilians as well as Athenian civilians caught in the crossfire. Many mass graves were found in ELAS neighbourhoods, which had been under relentless strafing and tank fire (Haralambidis 2014, 303–11).

master zealot, did most of the talking, frequently digressing into floods of ideology. (Maule 1975, 265–66)

Compare this view of Sarafis with that of Angelos Angelopoulos, the Professor of Economics who was one of the founders of PEEA, who described ELAS's Commander-in-Chief in terms of 'his high ethical quality, his knowledge, his exceptional organizational skills, his objectivity and modesty, and his enormous contribution to the resistance struggle' (1994, 222). There was clearly no way the two sides, the one punishing the 'naughty boys' and the other 'digressing' into the ideological causes of their movement, could find a common language.[18] Woodhouse's noose was tightening exactly as he had predicted and hoped. But its outcome, as he himself would have conceded, was to be worse than he could have imagined.

Mulgan arrived back in Athens a couple of days after the January armistice, and one can guess his reaction to this stand-off.[19] Writing *Report on Experience* while still under oath of allegiance to the British, he repeats the British directives as if their iteration might somehow convince someone (us? himself?): 'We were fighting Germans, or trying to, or at least keeping that in front of us as a reason for being there. [...] We are here to fight Germans and have no politics.' The following sentence, however, uses parenthesis, a rhetorical question and a modal verb ('may have been') to interrogate the first: '(Was this true or a lie? It was true when said personally, but in its wider applications may have been falsified by events)' (RE 171–72). As the *Dekemvriana* escalated out of control, in private correspondence and in defiance of censorship Mulgan began letting down his guard

18   The American Ambassador in Athens, Lincoln MacVeagh, wrote to Roosevelt on 8 December:
'. . . at bottom, the handling of this freedom-loving country (which has never yet taken dictation quietly) as if it were composed of nations under the British Raj, is what is the trouble, and Mr. Churchill's recent prohibition against the Greeks attempting a political solution at this time, if a blunder, is only the latest of a long line of blunders during the entire course of this present war.' (Iatrides 1972, 196)

19   *Ta Dekemvriana* continues to arouse debate both within and outside Greece. For a 2014–15 series of responses published in the British *Guardian,* see theguardian.com/world/2014/nov/30/athens-1944-britains-dirty-secret?CMP=Share_iOSApp_Other and theguardian.com/media/2015/mar/28/readers-editor-on-athens-44-british-army?CMP=Share_iOSApp_Other. Date of access 20 Feb. 2022.

and speaking in increasingly strident terms, laying much of the blame for the hostilities on Churchill. On December 15 he wrote to Gabrielle: 'Those who have seen him recently say that he's very old and tired and dogmatic, not any longer able to listen to opinion and argument' (Day 1968, 68). Then a few days later, again to Gabrielle: 'Things in Greece seem to become daily more tragic' with slaughter on both sides—by the hard-line Athenian communists (in contrast to those he'd worked with in Thessaly) and by the British. The latter, he wrote, had been 'consistently wrong [. . .] since the beginning in trying to influence Greek politics and Churchill's light-hearted idea that you can brush away a large resistance movement just by landing a few troops shows how wrongly-advised great men can be' (AGM 283).

It has often been argued that had Churchill agreed to the replacement of Papandreou as Prime Minister by Themistoklis Sofoulis at this time, a suggestion backed by all Greek political parties, including EAM, then a more mutually acceptable compromise with ELAS over demobilisation and much else would have been achieved (Marion Sarafis 1980b, 88; Sfikas 2004, 76–77). Many in the EAM movement, Tsamakos among them, shared Sofoulis's mistrust of some of the practices and policies of KKE but simultaneous willingness to work with them to counter the elements of the extreme right which were taking over in the country.[20] But Churchill, 'wrongly advised' or (more likely) refusing all advice, was in no mood for compromise, despite protest at home and abroad.

In New Zealand, a parliamentary debate, supported by public opinion, expressed dismay at what was happening in Athens, and trade unions were appalled. Prime Minister Peter Fraser reassured the New Zealand public that no troops had taken or would take part in attacks in Athens.[21] Among related documents in the Hocken Collections at the University of Otago is a pamphlet from

20   In a book published the same year as *Report on Experience,* the American William Hardy McNeill describes Churchill's refusal to accept the resignation of Papandreou and the appointment of the more left-tolerant Sofoulis after December as a 'fateful decision' based on 'ignoran[ce] of the opposition that the King aroused among his subjects' (1947, 144).

21   For a well-documented summary of the reaction to *Ta Dekemviana* in New Zealand, see Brown 2019, 233–49.

the General News Service in London which was circulated with a Preface by CPNZ activist and editor of *The People's Voice* Sid Scott. The trenchant attack on British policy is headed 'The Greeks have not Been Heard'. The struggle is not ended, predicted Scott on 9 January:

> It is a crime that British soldiers who have gone back to Greece should be ordered to shoot down people who have assisted New Zealanders to escape, even to starving themselves. I feel sure that every New Zealander who fought in Greece will be behind me in this statement [. . .] let every man and woman in New Zealand say firmly: HANDS OFF GREECE! (Scott 1945, 4)

It was this public outcry which was soon to lead J.V. Wilson to consider Mulgan the appropriate person to ask (on behalf of the Minister of External Affairs, Alister McIntosh) for an unofficial insider's report on Greece.

A great deal of outrage was also expressed within Britain itself, where many, not only those on the left, came out in protest. Writing in the weekly *Tribune* at the end of December, George Orwell called it a 'crime' to have interfered in Greek politics, and the following month accused the Tories of hypocrisy in their criticism of Soviet intervention in Poland and the Baltic countries while all the while 'defending our own coercion of Greece' (1970, 349, 368–69).[22] At the Labour Party conference from 11 to 15 December Ernest Bevin, minister of labour in the coalition government, attempted to defend Churchill's policy but was rebutted by Labour MP Nye Bevan, who pointed out that only three bodies had come out in support of his policy: fascist Spain, fascist Portugal and the majority of Tories in the House of Commons (Sakkas 2012, 29).[23] Even *The Times* came out with fierce criticism written by its reporters

---

22   Orwell wrote weekly articles under the title 'As I Please' in the left-wing weekly the *Tribune*, which he edited.

23   See also Haralambidis 2014, 207–10, for further details, including how Bevan attacked Churchill in the House with the charge that the British had entered Greece as liberators but were staying on as tyrants. For further details of the British reaction to the December events, see Mihiotis 2005, 270–71.

in Athens, insisting on December 9 that EAM was not a gang of communists and bandits, as Churchill had stated in the House on the previous day, but a wide organisation which embraced 'the whole range of opinion from centre to extreme left'. On December 14 another leading article argued that the national provisional government in Greece should be headed by someone accepted by the underground resistance movement, 'which has kept the flame of nationhood alight under enemy occupation, privation and terror' (Sakkas 2012, 33). These articles caused fury in the Foreign Office, with permanent undersecretary Alexander Cadogan recommending that their authors be tied up and thrown into the Thames (34). In response to this barrage of criticism, Churchill flew to Athens on Christmas Eve and met with EAM leaders, to whom he pledged that the king would not return until a favourable plebiscite had been held.[24] Refusing to be bullied, *The Times* continued with its critical reports, writing on 1 January '45 about the shame felt in Britain at 'the knowledge that British troops have been engaged in house-to-house fighting in a working-class suburb of Athens' (35). Contrary to the Soviet press, under strict control of Stalin's promise not to offend the British, the American press was equally if not more critical of British policy. As Heinz Richter records, in the *New York Times* for 11 January, eleven out of twelve US reporters complained of having their negative views suppressed (1997, 36n40). Historians have also drawn attention to solid evidence that EAM-ELAS Kapetans had met earlier, in November, and agreed *not* to seize power after the German withdrawal (Mazower 2001, 302). Mazower also makes the important point that the object of ELAS aggression was not so much the British as the Greek collaborationist forces, 'the collaborators who they believed were returning to power and deliberately provoking them under British protection' (370).

In the months ahead, tensions between the two sides would increase still further, in spite of many attempts at conciliation by EAM leader Giorgis Siantos. Soon, things were to turn significantly

---

24   This pledge was to be compromised in 1946 when the plebiscite was postponed and preceded by national elections, from which KKE abstained, making a favourable vote for the return of the king a foregone conclusion.

worse for the left. The Varkiza Agreement (signed on 12 February '45), where ELAS agreed to surrender its arms, did little to encourage trust on either side. Seminal points of the Agreement (that a plebiscite to decide on the king's return would be held within the year, and that participation in political and military institutions would be guaranteed to EAM-ELAS, who would retain all civil and political liberties) were soon violated by the governments of Plastiras (who replaced Papandreou) then Voulgaris. Freedom of individual expression was restricted, left-wing newspapers were suppressed, amnesty for political crimes was not granted, and the plebiscite to decide about the monarchy, scheduled to take place before the general elections, was cancelled in London in September. In Britain, despite the shift to a Labour government in mid 1945, Foreign Office mistrust of the Greek left continued. A pertinent example of this concerned the hardly radical Nikos Kazantzakis, author of *Zorba the Greek*, who in 1946 was expelled from Cambridge by the British Council for expressing reservations about British policy in Greece.[25]

The resulting stand-off saw Greece now enter into full-scale civil war, which was to last nearly four years, with thousands killed on both sides. From 1947 the British in Greece were replaced by the Americans who, by 1949, had forced the remaining communists into exile in countries of the Eastern bloc. The forces of the left, the *Dimokratikos Stratos* (Republican/Democratic Army), which fought mainly with light armaments against air attack and napalm bombs, was no match for the American-supplied 'Greek National Army':

---

25   Kazantzakis was expelled for having broken his promise, in the view of the British Council, not to get involved in British politics. In a meeting with Labour Minister of State, Hector McNeill, at the Foreign Office, in late 1946, Kazantzakis expressed the view that the only solution to the Greek problem was the formation of a broad-based government (under a leader like Sofoulis, whom he supported), which would include KKE. When asked his opinion about the strength of communism in Greece at the time, he replied that it represented at least 30 percent of the population, contradicting the minister's report that it was not more than 5 percent. In the interview Kazantzakis gave to Vasos Georgiou in Paris on December 16, immediately after his expulsion, he accused the British government of supporting 'neo fascism' in Greece. Kazantzakis has himself sometimes been accused of fascism, at least when he visited Spain in 1936 and interviewed Franco. But before his 1946 visit to Britain, he had written an open letter to the newspaper *Eleftheria* claiming that British-dominated control in Greece had been taken over by traitors and informers and that those who had fought for liberty had been imprisoned and exiled. The details of this incident are described in Georgios Romeos 2019, 137–46.

its defeat was ruthless and inevitable. Looking back, historians have described *Ta Dekemvriana* as a key moment in the early stage of the Cold War. As Roderick Beaton writes in his recent *Greece: Biography of a Modern Nation*, polarisation was to dominate the nation's history for decades to come:

> After March 1946, there were only two political positions left. Either you were a communist or you were not. If you were not, you must be for the king. [...] Thousands will suffer violence, torture or death, through being identified with one side or the other, regardless of what they actually thought or believed. Under conditions of blatant intimidation, the long-promised and long-delayed referendum on the monarchy was held on 1st of September [1946], overseen by a government in which monarchists held all the power. The result was a foregone conclusion. Before the month was out, King George II, now aged fifty-six, and as it would turn out with only half a year to live, duly returned to Greece from his second period of exile. He came not as the saviour of his people, and with no prospect, and seemingly with no intention, of uniting them. This unloved, unbending and ultimately egotistical figure was accepted back on his throne as the lesser of two very considerable evils. (2019, 298–99)

* * *

By this time Mulgan's anger at what he regarded as British imperialist aggression in Greece was giving urgency to his long-held desire to join the New Zealand forces. He had been waiting for some time.[26] On December 28 he wrote to Gabrielle from Cairo:

26   He was scheduled to join them in April, on the very day he died. Mulgan's application for transfer on his return to Cairo on 8 November 1944 was supported by a strong recommendation from the then head of SOE in Cairo, Brigadier K.V.B. Barker-Benfield, who concluded, perhaps somewhat ambiguously: 'I hereby certify that the above transfer does not originate in any cause effecting [*sic*] the honour, character or professional efficiency of Major Mulgan' (TNA HS 9/1073/3). (Mulgan is referred to here as Major although by this time he had become Lt. Col.; the system of promoting an officer was based on serving needs and the official verification by HQ was usually delayed. In Mulgan's case he had been Lt. Col. since 12 April 1944 but the verification came through only on 16 November [TNA HS 9/1073/3].)

> Well, I have still not had an answer from the NZ army so feeling that I couldn't wait indefinitely here, I've agreed to go back to Athens and help our own people there. I more or less laid it down [to his British commanders] as a condition that I wouldn't take part in fighting against the Elas forces—I have too many friends and something unfortunately of a reputation as a friend among them. (AGM 285)

The civil war rapidly developing around him was a cause for serious concern, though it would be hardly fair, he continued to Gabrielle, to blame the ordinary British soldier:

> The trouble with all civil war seems to be that as it goes on and casualties occur both sides get more bitter and that will probably start happening now with the British soldiers in Greece who began without any feelings in the matter at all and indeed thought it was all rather a joke. (AGM 286)

But after five years serving with the British, it is clear he can no longer identify as a British soldier himself. When he says he must return to Athens to 'help our own people there', it's fairly clear he means the ELAS fighters and their families, who desperately needed economic support.

He expressed greater ambivalence, however, over support for the hard-line (KKE-controlled) sector in the EAM-ELAS movement that was determined to fight it out until the bitter end. On the one hand, as we have seen, he would write to his parents on January 13 that instead of waiting for the right form of government to look after them, it was time the 'common' or 'little' people 'got up and helped themselves' (AGM 287). For all his gentle demeanour and sensibilities, Mulgan understood that revolutionary struggle sometimes necessitated violence. He was no pacifist, as many stories of his courage, even foolhardiness in battle, testify.[27] But on the other

---

27   See, for example, the description by Al Borgman of Mulgan's 'savage' bravery in the attack at Kaitsa (LJB 300). The sabotages he oversaw in Lamia, he acknowledged with 'sober satisfaction', had been responsible for the death of 300 Germans (LJB 315). A moving passage

hand, like most witnessing the escalating brutality around him, he recoiled in horror at the bloodshed. In a letter of 5 December '44, as the *Dekemvriana* descended into chaos, with summary executions of collaborators, he wrote:

> The communists, of course, are bloody. I've seen enough of them at close quarters not to have a thorough distrust of their methods. They have no ethics but only what they dignify by the name of realism and are quite unscrupulous in twisting facts and people and in using a situation like this for their own ends. Also they do quite a lot of killing. (AGM 282–83)

But in the book he had begun to write, Mulgan showed he was no opponent of pragmatism in class warfare. He was also adept, as part of a censorship-evading tactic, at the rhetorical stratagem of oppositional balance ('it is true that . . . however'), as a way of softening his own views. As on repeated occasions in *Report on Experience*, British (Foreign Office) views are stated in his letters yet contradicted by the arguments that come before or after, or both, as in this instance:

> I'm afraid people will grow impatient and ask why these Greeks and Belgians and others can't behave sensibly. It's hard from outside to imagine what they went through, not only in physical suffering but in humiliation from the Germans and their associates. [. . .] Meanwhile the mass of the people—and I should guess it's the same all over Europe—want peace, food and quiet, and in politics some sort of democratic liberation with honesty of government. You can't blame them for wanting to punish those who worked with the Germans, but reprisal seems to lead to reprisal. (AGM 282–83)

Significantly, in this same letter Mulgan tells his parents about the imminent visit home of Bill Jordan, a fellow SOE operative and

---

in *Report on Experience* expresses Mulgan's view of military courage as always a matter of solidarity with those around you (RE 120–21).

fanatical anti-communist who, as O'Sullivan puts it, was convinced
that John 'was simply soft on commies' (LJB 283). Jordan is, he
tells them, 'An interesting chap whom you'll like' (AGM 282). To
Gabrielle two weeks later, however, he has a discreetly different
message: 'He's a nice chap, quite crazy and very self-opinionated.
We differ on Greek matters' (284).[28]

By this time Mulgan's views 'on Greek matters' included zero
tolerance for foreign intervention. Telling the Greeks to 'behave
sensibly' was ludicrous in the face of the conditions they were
enduring. For one thing, this was a country, as he would put
it in *Report on Experience*, with 'a tradition and cadence that ran
back through centuries of Turkish slavery', where young children
necessarily grew up with politics as their alphabet. In opting to join
the New Zealand forces, Mulgan was siding, after over a decade,
with his original 'own people', with the nation which he hoped
understood and sympathised with these circumstances. But before
this could happen, he would have the opportunity to help those he
most immediately identified with, the victims of one war who were
now fighting another, in both cases with an ideological agenda close
to his heart.

---

28   Jordan's anti-communism is usually attributed to the fact that he witnessed the shooting of
     fellow New Zealander Arthur Hubbard by ELAS partisans. In an account given a year later
     in the New Zealand *Evening Post*, 7 October 1944, entitled 'Shot By Greeks: An Officer's
     Death', Jordan is recorded as saying that Hubbard was shot when he came out of Jordan's
     headquarters (where he was helping with communications) 'for the purpose of investigating
     the noise which the party of Greeks made when attacking the point' (paperspast.natlib.govt.
     nz/newspapers/EP19441007.2.85). Jordan describes Hubbard's death in detail in his book
     25 years later (1969, 164–75). The ELAS version, however, is very different. According to
     Kapetan Lambros, who was also there, the Greeks went to investigate shooting from inside a
     house in Triklino and surrounded the house, forcing the inhabitants to come out. Hubbard,
     pistol in hand, shot at them, and they replied, shooting Hubbard in the process. Inside the
     house, Lambros continues, they had been drinking heavily (Bekios-Lambros 1976, 606
     ff.). Richard Clogg records the findings of the subsequent Court of Inquiry, 'on which the
     Mission [SOE] was represented', as was ELAS, which 'determined that the shooting had been
     accidental' (2002, 218n13). Hammond records that the ELAS officer was found 'guilty of
     negligence, but [. . .] the shooting was accidental and not deliberate. The finding was accepted
     by us and by ELAS' (1983, 142).

With ELAS officers. From left: Lieut.-Col. Ioannis Papathanasiou, Commander of ELAS 4th Regiment, Major John Mulgan, Col. Konstantinos Tsamakos, Commander of ELAS 16th Division, and Major Philip Worrall, BLO (Courtesy of Simon Worrall)

Stefanos Sarafis (Commander-in-Chief of ELAS) and Mulgan on a reconnaissance operation (Spyros Meletzis)

Mulgan on his horse Heroiko

Stefanos Sarafis (left) with Aris Velouhiotis

Aris Velouhiotis (Spyros Meletzis)

ELAS *andartes* on demolition operations in Thessaly (Spyros Meletzis)

Women carrying supplies to ELAS *andartes* (Spyros Meletzis)

Paul Contomichalos, Mulgan's
interpreter (left) with Mulgan

Dimitrios Psarros,
Commander of EKKA-5/42

Chris Woodhouse,
Commander of the BMM
and AMM in mainland
Greece (Spyros Meletzis)

Arthur Edmonds,
New Zealand officer
in the BMM

Tom Barnes (on right) with Napoleon Zervas (second from left),
Commander of EDES forces (courtesy of Katherine Barnes)

Rufus Sheppard
('Hills'), British Officer
in the BMM

Main representatives of PEEA. From left: Kostas Gavriilidis, Stamatis Hatzibeis, Angelos Angelopoulos, Manolis Mantakas, Giorgios Siantos, Petros Kokkalis, Alexandros Svolos, Bishop Ioakeim of Kozani, Evripidis Bakirtzis, Ilias Tsirimokos, Nikos Askoutsis (Spyros Meletzis)

Evripidis Bakirtzis, Vice President of PEEA, speaking at PEEA HQ in Koryschades (Spyros Meletzis)

PEEA: Women voting for the first time in Greece (Spyros Meletzis)

PEEA: A people's court (Spyros Meletzis)

The EAM-ELAS delegation en route to the landing strip to leave for the Lebanon Conference in late April 1944, their departure facilitated by Mulgan. (From left) Petros Rousos (for KKE), Alexandros Svolos (President of PEEA) and Stefanos Sarafis (Commander-in-Chief of ELAS). (Spyros Meletzis)

Liberation, Lamia around 20 October 1944. (From right) Ilias Tsirimokos (of EAM and PEEA), Aris, Takis Fitsios (of KKE & PEEA). (Spyros Meletzis)

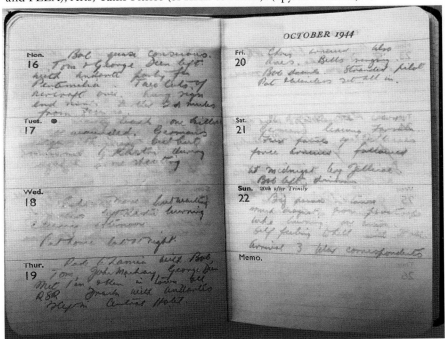

John Mulgan's Diary

'Christine' (Krystyna Gustava Skarbek) in Palestine, 1942

Julian Dolbey
(Count Julian Dobrski), SOE
Secret Intelligence, 1942

British (of the 5th Scottish Parachute Battalion) fighting EAM-ELAS in Athens during *Ta Dekemvriana*, December 1944

Crowd gathered for demonstration in Athens organised by EAM, 3 December 1944
(Spyros Meletzis)

III | From Athens to Cairo

CHAPTER 7

Report on Experience

I destroyed I'm afraid more than there is here
—Mulgan to Gabrielle, 15 March 1945 (RE 30)

Report on Experience, completed in the crucial few months immediately preceding his death and published posthumously in 1947, is one of the most intimate expressions of Mulgan's politics. It is, however, no ordinary confessional text. Rather, it sets out a range of topics, from the very general (the politico-economic roots of war) to the very specific (anecdotes from his time with the Greek villagers and *andartes*) in a manner that often seems evasive and remote, as if Mulgan is reluctant to say too much, is watching his back at every step. This is hardly surprising. 'Anything written in that period about clandestine operations', it has been noted recently, 'is almost bound to have elisions and evasions. The Official Secrets Act still hung invisibly over [the] typewriter' (Ascherson 2020, 27). In admitting to Gabrielle that he's 'destroyed I'm afraid more than there is here', Mulgan seems to be suggesting some form of restraint, although he wasn't of course at liberty to say what or why. This evasiveness or sense of things withheld leaves much open to interpretation. In the Foreword to the new edition of the book in 2010, for example, the British war historian M.R.D. Foot (who was commissioned to write the early official history of SOE in north-west Europe) writes about Mulgan's time with what he calls 'the communist-run half-bandit groups with which he tried to work' and concludes that Mulgan 'was quite lucky not to be unobtrusively bumped off by the communists' (2010, 12, 14). This assessment misses both the substance and the tone of Mulgan's text: if it has one core thesis amidst all the qualifications, it is his bond with the left-wing *andartes* with whom he lived, as he records, 'in complete friendliness' (RE 146).[1] The assumption that members of the AMM were at risk from the Greek *andartes* is demonstrably wide of the mark.[2] Mulgan's unique success with the ELAS guerrillas, for which he was well recognised, derived precisely from his mistrust of such misconceptions, his capacity for empathy with these mostly rural people, as well as his almost unique sympathy among SOE operatives for their left-wing programme.[3] A more nuanced, though carefully general, conclusion is drawn in the Preface to the same edition by John's son Richard, who writes 'how, in the war against fascism, individuals of humanity and honesty faced up to the terrible dilemmas that governments and political movements so blithely imposed upon them' (Richard Mulgan 2010, 10). Regardless of these different interpretations, it is clear that *Report on Experience* is a text which deserves a much closer reading from a political perspective than it has so far received.

We cannot claim to be more impartial than M.R.D. Foot about EAM-ELAS or in our interpretation of Mulgan's relations with them. But in reading from a different historico-political perspective, we notice other kinds of evidence in and behind Mulgan's narrative. Reading *Report on Experience* today, what strikes us is the way the text

---

1   In his frequently cited *SOE: An Outline History of the Special Operations Executive 1940–1946*, Foot makes passing reference to Mulgan's *Report on Experience* in order to comment on how 'appalled' Mulgan was 'at the way two men who were hardbitten enough could dominate the life of a hill village' (2008, 290). Mulgan's view of village organisation, as we have seen, was considerably more sympathetic than Foot suggests.

2   Even Nicholas Hammond, one of the BLOs most suspicious of EAM-ELAS to overlap with Mulgan in the Pindus mountains, would insist to his GHQ throughout the occupation that 'the danger of ELAS liquidating us was small' (1983, 110). If anyone was at risk from ELAS it might have been Woodhouse, who admits that he was regarded as their 'enemy'. But he too never suggested such a thing and moved freely among them.

3   Richard Clogg writes that 'the great majority of SOE's operatives in the field, as in SOE Cairo and London, shared the common assumption that communism was a "bad thing", and that the establishment of a communist regime in postwar Greece would be seriously damaging to British interests' (2000, 67).

seems to say then un-say what its author is thinking, the way it covers its tracks, veers off in a safer direction just as it seems to be close to revealing something. James McNeish puts his finger on it when he writes of the 'contained' or 'oblique' quality of the writing in the *Report*. We get the sense, he observes, that Mulgan 'is not quite levelling with us' (2003, 245). This is exactly right. Crucial in understanding this evasiveness is an awareness of the timing of the book's composition in the closing months of the war, just as Mulgan was preparing to leave the British army and join the New Zealand division. This proposed shift seems to have given him an even greater sense of distance from British policy. But you can't miss the caution, Mulgan's awareness that his military commanders held very different political opinions, and that his own were considered unwelcome if not dangerous. A close comparison with Woodhouse's *Apple of Discord*, a book with a similar theme written almost contemporaneously, provides a useful perspective, outlining the military and, most importantly, political context within which Mulgan was operating—and against which he was increasingly rebelling, at least internally. To read Mulgan's text beside Woodhouse's, as we shall see, is to understand just how much Mulgan had to hide.

The rhetoric of evasion

In writing about British military objectives in the immediate aftermath of *Ta Dekemvriana* and against the background escalation of Cold War paranoia, Mulgan had to choose his words extremely carefully, both to protect his own position and if he was to have any hope of publication. In some ways these restrictions would not have presented too great a challenge. His habitual writing style had always been terse and understated, described by Mulgan himself as 'Hemingwayesque' (AGM 147), or by C.K. Stead and others as the product of an Auden-inflected rebellion against Georgian romanticism (Stead 2013, 164). At moments of greatest expressiveness, especially when describing the village people and their resistance fighters, he can use this restraint to great effect. For example, he writes: 'Partisan warfare is puny in its standards and puny in results, but you get somehow a disproportionate satisfaction from it' (RE 159). This is hardly a romantic description, but the key word, 'satisfaction', shines through all the stronger for these qualifications. Or again, he writes that there was 'some quality in these people' that made you 'proud to know them and more proud if you felt that they liked you' (153). 'Some quality' is vague yet powerful, encouraging readers to flesh out the causes and effects of this pride in their own minds. But when it comes to more directly political matters, this expressiveness is held carefully in check. *Report on Experience* is a text that requires of its reader a constant alertness to the twists and turns in tone and nuance. And in some cases, we find, the evasions can be as revealing as the disclosures.

If we are tempted to read the narrative restraint as a personal trait of Mulgan's, a mere diffidence of character, the frame of the text as a whole should alert us to another story. As with *Man Alone*, *Report on Experience* returns repeatedly to the Spanish Civil War and the struggle against fascism, as if this political conflict were the template for all subsequent wars. (The index to this short book lists twelve references to Spain, Madrid and Franco.) What is striking, however, is the absence of explicit comparison between the clearly similar aims of the left-wing guerrillas in Spain from 1936 to 1939 and those of EAM-ELAS in Greece at the time Mulgan is writing. It's as if Spain stands in for the unmentionable situation in Greece. Occasionally it becomes fairly clear that Mulgan is writing about ELAS but without naming them, as in the following important passage from Chapter 6:

> There is probably a lot to be said for having an army whose individuals have a private and passionate feeling about the war and who, because of this, do not mind at all what happens to themselves personally. But armies of this kind are more rare than is commonly believed. They flare up in some cause, usually lost, and die, and soldiering takes on again the cool precision of the Illyrian legions. This kind of army is more often found in defence

than in attack. It fights on its home ground when the issues are desperate, as before Madrid in 1936. There would have been an army, several armies of this kind, in England in 1940 if the Germans had arrived. I believe there was an army of this kind in Russia for the first bitter winter of their war and probably for as long as the Germans stayed in Russia. This kind of army is clearly very difficult to deal with and professional soldiers are apt to regard the whole proceeding as unmilitary, which indeed it is. [. . .] The French who fought at Valmy were an army of [. . . this] bitter, desperate kind, fighting for their revolution in their own country. (118–19)

For all its references to Spain, England, Russia and France, this description fits the ELAS *andartes* exactly. The Greek guerrillas were fighting their own 'revolution' on 'home ground', more 'in defence than in attack', 'desperate' and (in the eyes of Mulgan's British colleagues, and indeed of himself at times) 'unmilitary'. Mulgan's account of the *andartes* differs from those of fellow SOE fighters like Woodhouse, who are rarely prepared to see beyond their scruffy appearance, less hierarchical discipline and unwillingness to engage in open combat. In spite of frustrations, Mulgan understood these as necessary features of irregular warfare. In the post-war era such tactics would be used by guerrilla fighters against the Americans in Vietnam and the Soviets in Afghanistan. Michael Hardt and Antonio Negri describe these strategies in terms very similar to Mulgan's:

> guerrilla forces cannot survive without the support of the population and a superior knowledge of the social and physical terrain. Guerrilla attacks often rely on unpredictability: any member of the population could be a guerrilla fighter and the attack can come from anywhere with unknown means. Guerrillas thus force the dominant military power to live in a state of perpetual paranoia. (2004, 52)

Whenever complaint was made about the ineffectiveness of the ELAS army, Mulgan was quick to retort, in both official reports as well as in *Report on Experience*, that their tactics clearly induced this kind of paranoia in the occupying forces, and that the Germans were obliged to maintain a huge army in Greece as a result. In the face of the 'private and passionate' commitment of his fellow fighters in the mountains, the 'cool precision' of fascist-imperialist wars led by Franco or Hitler (or the ironically dismissed army of Napoleon, which 'went over Europe [and] knew it was good'), comes down in Mulgan's text on the side of an 'evil' (119), against which everything else needs to be judged. It seems clear that Mulgan wants to reassert, against the tide of opinion from the Foreign Office, that such 'unmilitary' practices as those of the *andartes* must not be so peremptorily dismissed. And yet the tone is guarded and assertions are qualified. In saying here, for example, that 'professional soldiers are apt to regard' this kind of (guerrilla) warfare 'as unmilitary, *which indeed it is*', he keeps 'military' cover at the very moment of challenging its assumptions. Such nuances are easy to miss.

Mulgan also regularly employs the syntactic manoeuvre of following an assertion with a subordinate clause or contrasting conjunction (But, Yet, However . . .). This is particularly apparent in the second chapter, dedicated to the English. Mulgan's opposition to the direction of British policy in Greece is one of the major themes of the book, yet it is the one subject he needs to be most cautious about expressing.

> The English are a very great people, and this author for one is proud to have been with them during this war. They have virtues of patience and sanity in time of crisis, and they always win the last battle. But they cut things rather fine in 1940, and another time it might be preferable to win some battles before the last or perhaps prevent the war from starting at all. (56–57)

(Readers of the 'Behind the Cables' columns will remember Mulgan and Cox's angry denunciations around 1936–37 of Britain's failure

to show solidarity with the Spanish Republican cause, as well as
Popular Front attempts to unite Europe against fascism.) We should
not be misled by the inflations of the assertion ('very great people',
'proud to have served', 'virtues of . . .'), or by the nonchalance of the
subordinate clause ('might be preferable', 'or perhaps'). Again on the
next page: 'This England is a fine country, or was, or will be again.
But in those [immediately pre-war] years she gave no comfort to her
lovers' (58). It is only under cover of such inflations that the criticism
in the contrasting clause may be slipped in. A literary comparison
that comes to mind here is the famous poem by Andrew Marvell
where an ardent man makes a playful attempt to persuade his 'coy
mistress' to cease resisting his advances as time is running out on
them. 'The grave's a fine and private place,' he urges, 'But none I
think do there embrace' (Marvell 1967, 76). Mulgan had to exercise
caution with his irony, but the impact is there all the same. Like
other servicemen attempting to publish at this time, he had had
plenty of practice in writing under wartime censorship. Still, he
sometimes overstepped the mark and his publisher chose to exclude
the chapter on English colonels, where perhaps the most outrageous
example of this stylistic tic occurs. There he'd described one colonel
(identified by O'Sullivan as S.F. Saville) as 'one of the most charming
individuals that I met in army life [. . .] it only took about a fortnight
for it to become apparent that he was, roughly speaking, ga-ga' (RE
107). It helps here to recall that 'charm' tended to make Mulgan
uneasy. In his writings on early experiences in Oxford, he admits
that he 'laboured under the disadvantage of a Colonial belief that
equated—not always incorrectly—personal charm with insincerity'
(2011b, 33). There was clearly a great deal of ambivalence and defence
in Mulgan's attitude to the English, or at least to the English ruling
classes, and critics are right to draw attention to a long confrontation
with the internal voice of the liberal Anglophile (his father?) evident
in *Man Alone*. But we need to listen carefully to catch its inflections
here, which accumulate only gradually.

Report on Experience begins in the past, starting with New
Zealand between the wars, with the Depression cited as the

determining event, overshadowing everything like 'a grey and ghastly visitor to the house' (44). Within the socio-economic analysis initiated by the Depression, which Mulgan sustains throughout the book, the contrast between the lives of those in 'the smooth suburban gardens' of Remuera in Auckland and those of the workers further out of town shows up a rift destabilising this seemingly egalitarian society. Did we hear, he asks rhetorically, 'the voice of a people that has recognized an injustice, that has perceived the possibility of disorganization in its midst?' (47). His own positive answer to this question is left vaguely hanging, to be picked up from time to time in later chapters with references to Lenin, Trotsky, Marx or British socialists like Tom Wintringham, quotations from whom function as a discreet chorus. 'Certainly, comrade, *c'est la guerre capitaliste*': Lenin's words are quoted at the end of the following chapter. But in the next breath Mulgan edges away to seemingly safer ground by posing another rhetorical question, as if in challenge to these 'comrades':

> And suppose again, comrades, that the capitalists do make the war, and that it becomes under their hands a different kind of war, that turns against them, and in which they themselves have to struggle to survive as human beings, let alone as capitalists? Have you considered the answer to that one, comrade, or deliberated on your actions in that event? (61)

These questions read like a piece out of Auden and Isherwood's *On the Frontier* where the arrogant industrialist, Valerian, meets his just deserts in the chaos of revolution and civil war resulting from a capitalist-incited war with a neighbouring country. Although cast in the form of a challenge to communist comrades (what have you got to say to *that*?), Mulgan's theatrically posited question hints at the justification for a 'different kind of war', a class war that would see the war-mongering capitalists themselves struggling to survive.[4] But

---

4   This suggestion can be interpreted as an echo of some of his 'railing' outbursts immediately before the war. For example: 'At times I've looked forward with a sort of gloomy pleasure to the destruction of this country and its selfish intolerant ruling classes' (AGM 133), cited in Chapter 1.

to duck the too explicit, he finishes the chapter with a safer voice, that of jovial barracks resignation: 'It may not be *la guerre capitaliste*, comrade, but it's a war all right' (61).

Mulgan's handling of this very personal narrative can be uneven to say the least. Peter Whiteford notes the way Mulgan sometimes switches from a first-person address to the rather clumsy and old-fashioned description of himself as 'the author', which the editors of the 1947 edition amended to 'I'. It is worth noting, Whiteford comments, 'that at certain moments in this narrative this typically direct writer chose to distance himself from his material in these rather uncomfortable circumlocutions' (2010, 25). Whiteford wisely restores the original wording. Another distancing strategy involves switching, sometimes puzzlingly abruptly, to a narrative mode whereby opinions of others are given in either direct or indirect dialogue form, as in the jovial barracks example above. In some ways this method is reminiscent of the practice of 'doing voices' employed by T.S. Eliot in *The Waste Land*. As a device it has the effect of masking Mulgan's own opinions, allowing him to steer clear of open statement on sensitive topics.

Examples occur throughout. As mentioned, parallels are suggested (though never stated) frequently between the Greek resistance and other national resistance movements of recent times, not just (on page 56) to 'Madrid and Barcelona', but to 'Shanghai and Chungking', two Chinese cities that suffered appalling losses after fierce resistance to Japanese invasion. Significantly, there is another name at the end of this list which was deleted by OUP for the first edition: 'and Warsaw'. This could perhaps be interpreted as a reference to the aerial bombing of Warsaw by the German Luftwaffe during the siege of Warsaw in 1939. But the more likely reference is to the Polish resistance Mulgan's readers in the mid to late 1940s would have had vividly in mind: the ill-fated Warsaw Uprising against German occupation by the Polish underground resistance in the summer of 1944. Through his numerous friendships with Poles in Greece and Cairo, Mulgan would have shared their despair at the razing of Warsaw in reprisal

for the resistance, and along with it, probably, their resentment at
what has been regarded by historians (as well as by Polish resistance
fighters at the time like Krystyna Skarbek) as the betrayal of the
country by the Allies.[5] For Mulgan to refer to Warsaw at this
hypersensitive moment of relations among the Allies was clearly
regarded as too provocative by the editors at OUP, in spite of the fact
that he had attempted to slip this implication in discreetly through
the use of the 'voices' method:

> [. . .] the pride of a people that had watched in silence, strangled
> and hushed by their leaders, the endurance of Madrid and
> Barcelona, Shanghai and Chungking, and Warsaw, and could
> now share as veterans in their own right the same communion of
> suffering. This, at least, was the comment of an American in 1940
> who added, talking in his remote and friendly way [. . . etc.] (56)

On other occasions Mulgan uses the voices tactic even more
directly, not with reported speech, as in the above Warsaw reference,
but by reproducing an imagined dialogue between different players
on the scene. A notable example is the parody of British military
etiquette. Unlike Evelyn Waugh, who satirises the vacuity of army
protocol with humorous affection in his *Sword of Honour* trilogy,
Mulgan, always the pragmatist, felt only impatience with the
incompetence. The imagined dialogue comes in the paragraph after
that beginning 'This England is a fine country [. . .]':

---

5   For Skarbek, see Masson 1975 and Mulley 2012 *passim*. History has judged the British
     handling of Poland, especially that by SOE during the Warsaw Uprising, in the harshest
     terms. On 6 August 1944 Polish General Bor signalled the following outcry from the heart
     of the Uprising: 'We begin the sixth day of the battle of Warsaw . . . I state solemnly that
     Warsaw in fighting does not receive assistance from the allies in the same way as Poland
     did not receive it in 1939. Our alliance with Great Britain has resulted only in bringing her
     our assistance in 1940 in repelling the German attack against the British Isles, in fighting
     in Norway, in Africa, in Italy and on the Western Front' (Harrison 2000, 1087). Garlinski
     (1969, 223) describes how at the end of March 1945, the Polish Home Army commander,
     Leopoldi Okulicki, who had been hiding underground since the failure of the Uprising, but
     revealed himself when invited to London for talks with the Soviets, was instead arrested in
     Warsaw and flown, along with a dozen or so other underground leaders, to the Lubianka
     prison in Moscow, where he was murdered in December 1946.

The years and events rolled faster towards the close. Talking with journalists, the bloodshot-eyed and cynical, in dark Johnsonian taverns, fresh back from Europe, from *Anschluss*, partition, nationalist *risorgimento*—like talking to explorers sunburnt from darkest Africa in the darker eighties. Plotting with mild detached interest the arrows of penetration on the map, intelligence officer for the democracies. You have the staff plan, sir? No, not actually the plan. The command have not yet entrusted me with their plan. We can be sure, nevertheless, that it will be a good one when it is finally handed out to the order groups at the conference to which I am daily expecting to be summoned. A plan which, I should judge, relies on enticing the enemy forward, allowing him a good deal of ground on which to waste his substance, deceiving him as to our real allies by removing all weapons from those who rashly try to engage him now. (58–59)

This complex paragraph pulls in several different directions. The presumed context is immediately pre-war Britain, or perhaps more specifically Northern Ireland, where Mulgan had served for two years from 1940 to 1942, although the satire on the colonels in the British army with whom Mulgan came into conflict in North Africa could also be at issue. The self-importance of the colonel here (being 'entrusted' with a plan, 'summoned' to a conference, etc.) thinly disguises muddled ignorance. For all the arrows on the map, this ironically titled 'intelligence officer for the democracies' has clearly no clue as to an overall direction. And then what are we to make of the last sentence here, outlining the British intention to deceive the enemy (presumably the Germans) 'as to our real allies' by 'removing all weapons from those who rashly try to engage him now'? Who are these falsely presumed 'real allies'? Anyone familiar with the Greek situation at this very time (late '44 to early '45) will immediately think of another interpretation—that these so-called allies, EAM-ELAS, are in fact quite the reverse, and that the Allies' aim was to remove all weapons from them. The strategy of 'enticing the enemy forward, allowing him a good deal of ground on which to waste his substance' could on the one hand be read as a fairly precise description of the British handling of the German troops in Greece. (The British were in no hurry to get rid of the Germans in 1944 as their presence delayed the slow march south of the Soviets.) On the other hand, however, it is also strongly suggestive of that other 'enemy' in Greece, the 'communists' of EAM-ELAS. Allowing the enemy 'a good deal of ground on which to waste his substance' echoes Woodhouse's recommendation to Cairo that ELAS be given more rope with which to hang themselves. But it is impossible to pinpoint Mulgan's exact reference here, given the rapid switches in time frame throughout the paragraph, with references to *Anschluss* (the German annexation of Austria in March 1938), nationalist *risorgimento* (the nineteenth-century movement for Italian unification), and to sunburnt explorers 'from darkest Africa in the darker [eighteen] eighties.' Perhaps most evasively of all, in the second and third sentences (and elsewhere)[6] Mulgan omits a subject altogether ('Talking . . .', 'Plotting . . .'), in effect giving us only a sentence fragment. *Who* is doing the talking and plotting? It is impossible to say. The voices (colonel, subordinate, journalists) provide a pastiche behind which Mulgan's own views can shelter. The next paragraph restores the predominant frame by returning to the Spanish frontier in 1938 as the archetypal battleground between left and right. It is less a matter of the specific historical context, in other words, and more to do with the underlying ideologies at stake.

Representing communism

After the first two background chapters on New Zealand and England, Chapter 3 moves to a narrative of the present which, strikingly, seemed to require first and foremost for Mulgan an assessment of the place of communism in the current war. But by the end of 1944 this was not a theme to be espoused openly, and Mulgan's solution is to treat it at length but via an array of distancing

---

6   Another example: 'Paris again, then, the day before the war, Paris and the Gare de l'Est, watching the quiet lonely soldier [. . .]' (RE 59–60).

strategies. His muffling of the subject here has led many readers astray. M.R.D. Foot, for example, reads the book as illustrating cynical scorn after loss of faith in communism, that Mulgan was one of the first 'to perceive that it was not after all the harbinger of Paradise on Earth most of them had supposed, but a despotism like any other' (2010, 14–15). Mulgan's position on communism was far more complex than this, although the evidence is often veiled.

His first tactic is to confront the force of the dreaded spectre, 'communism', by splintering it, arguing that there is not one but 'many kinds of Communism' (RE 66). From his present perspective, the pre-war version he followed in Oxford was a tame and cosy affair, 'a parlour game as we played it' (68)—rather different, he imagines, from what went on at the time in the mining and industrial areas in the north and west of Britain. Many comrades from that time have 'reformed' now (66) (which could mean 'regrouped', perhaps, as much as 'mended their ways') and shown a willingness to admit to mistakes—unlike, significantly, the fascist supporters of the time, who have continued to adhere rigidly to their principles. This is not to say, he adds, that like all religions, communism did not have its own 'defects of rigidity and dogma', some of which seemed 'fairly ridiculous' now (67). And the newspaper image of a smiling Stalin shaking hands with Ribbentrop in August 1939 was a serious challenge to them all. It was inevitable, he continues, that the early idealistic version of communism should give way to realism as the capitalist war of 1940 gave way to the anti-fascist war of 1941 (68). By 'continental standards', those that Mulgan encountered in conversation with Theodor Adorno or his German friend Otto, British communism, with its Left Book Club debates, was a pretty 'soft' affair (68).

But in Greece he encountered something he could relate to directly, something more practical—as he explains it towards the end of the book in a passage quoted in an earlier chapter here:

> under the duress of war, we were subjected to rather more searching tests in matters of politics. The Communists we met in

Greece were not working on any yellow-backed, Left-Book-Club manual. They were practical fellows and inclined to argue by results—pragmatists, I suppose you might call them. They were the cause of concern to us and something of a readjustment in our political thinking. (166)

As so often with the use of the first-person plural, 'our' political thinking here can only mean Mulgan's own. The 'readjustment' resulting from his response to Greek communism would eventually outweigh the element of 'concern', which caution obliged him to mention, although 'concern' could also be a sly suggestion of 'engagement' here.

There is no talk in Chapter 1 of a New Zealand version of communism, though 'Socialism' is mentioned in passing as existing (at least in the estimation of some) for a brief period before the war (48). Charles Brasch described the dilemma for the New Zealand ideologue of Mulgan's generation as 'not between Capitalism and Communism [but] between individualism and communism' (LJB 69). But this, if it ever had been, was no longer Mulgan's position. Looking back, he was having his doubts about New Zealand individualism, as he expressed it in an important letter to his parents on 25 April (Anzac Day) 1944. His diary around this time indicates that he was following political changes in Britain with some optimism, noting the way 'Midpoint Labour wins West Derbyshire from hereditary Conservative Alderman Price v Devonshires'—a reference to the Labour victory in the West Derbyshire by-elections.[7] Mulgan wrote to his parents:

I feel that England must be very interesting now, politically, from all the news I get. N.Z. by contrast will probably be swinging back the other way to a regime of individualism. Are the views we

7   Mulgan's diary in the memo for the week ending 20 February. In the by-elections on 17 February the Labour candidate, Charles Frederick White, defeated Conservative candidate William Cavendish, Marquis of Hartington and elder son of Edward Cavendish, 10th Duke of Devonshire. Defeats such as these were a sign of things to come in Britain in the immediately post-war period.

get here of N.Z. distorted? The huge & record sums being spent on racing for example. Will N.Z. remain after this war and in spite of its fine tale of work & service still a rather selfish playtime country? (AGM 273)

Within the context of European modes of thought, for him it was not so much a matter of deciding *between* individualism on the one hand and communism/anti-capitalism on the other. Rather, it was a matter of how individualism may be integrated into a broader, more radical left-wing approach. This was what he called 'practical' communism or socialism: the two terms were often used interchangeably—as they were by the Popular Front, which could accommodate communist (especially economic) theory, when necessary, but focused more on what could be achieved through both individual and group action. The Greeks of EAM-ELAS were working according to this same combination. 'All Greeks are individualists and intensely interested in their own possessions', he writes. For this reason, 'Some element of Communism might be made suitable to Greece, but it would have to be of a very cooperative and democratic nature to last' (RE 166–67). Back in Chapter 3, these bearded Greek communists, 'remote from the theories of those pre-war days', are described as 'belong[ing] to a later and more serious passage of experience' (69). Once again, he omits the pronoun, eliding the question of *whose* experience is at issue. But whose could it be but his own?

It would be wrong, however, to assume that practicality excludes ideology in Mulgan's vocabulary. He doesn't of course explain this here, but he would have known that these 'practical' Greek communists who 'argue[d] by results' had in fact a solid base of theory to draw on. In the early stages of the EAM movement, before PEEA was formed, each area had its '*politikos*' to advise on principles: serious theoretical debate was an important part of the movement. Several of the leading political advisers had studied at the Workers University in Moscow—among them Dimitrios Partsalidis, Yannis Zevgos and Kostas Karagiorgis, all of whom Mulgan seems to have known. Their frame of reference was clearly indebted to Lenin, who is referred to here (page 166) and at several other points in Mulgan's text. Among theorists of communism Lenin is known as the pragmatist, the interpreter of Marxist theory for practical application to specific socio-economic conditions. The activities of what Mulgan's fellow fighters called 'Mulgan and Co', men of action, may be interpreted as exemplars of materialist revolutionaries, individuals confronting an uncertain future, submitting to the material conditions of history without concern for individual will or consciousness. Subjective will, Lenin argues, is too easily co-opted by hegemonic power; imperialism, itself the inevitable product of capitalism, is its end product. In his discussion of revolution in *What is to be Done?* (1901), Lenin emphasises that the struggle must be organised by people who are professionally engaged in revolutionary activity, with a strong leadership and discipline. And given the underlying divisions in the social order, conflict is to be embraced, if not welcomed. An awareness of this would have made Mulgan more tolerant of the KKE influence in EAM. But the text that seems to have informed *Report on Experience* most deeply is Lenin's *Imperialism: The Highest Stage of Capitalism*, which was a popular read in left-wing circles in the 1930s. At one point in his comparison of different world economies, Mulgan writes that Lenin 'devoted a few words to Spain'—to its peasant economy, which is superficially like that of Greece (RE 166). *Imperialism* is the only text of Lenin's (as far as we have been able to detect) which makes reference to Spain. At another point, Mulgan quotes directly from this book.[8] For Mulgan to be citing from it in this way suggests either that he was carrying a copy of it with him from the mountains to Athens, or

---

8   Passing references to the Spanish economy come on pages 72, 78, 89, 90 and 140 of Lenin's *Imperialism* (2010). The direct quotation from Lenin comes (in RE 169) where Mulgan refers to facts, 'which, as Lenin remarked, are stubborn things.' In the first chapter of his book Lenin writes:

   Today, monopoly [capitalism] has become a fact. The economists are writing mountains of books in which they describe the diverse manifestations of monopoly, and continue to declare in chorus that 'Marxism is refuted.' But facts are stubborn things, as the English proverb says, and they have to be reckoned with, whether we like it or not. (Lenin 2010, 18–19)

   We will return to this comment, part of which is quoted by Mulgan in RE 169, in Chapter 11.

that he was carrying it in his head. Either way, it was clearly a very familiar text. Its central thesis concerning the way wars are driven by monopoly capitalist-imperialist aggression had by this time become the mainstay of Mulgan's political and emotional position.

In his book *The Theory of the Partisan* (1963) the political theorist Carl Schmitt argues that Lenin must be regarded as the first and paradigmatic theorist of guerrilla warfare:

> For Lenin, the partisan war belongs to the realm of the methods of civil war and is concerned, like all others, with a purely tactical or strategic question relating to the concrete situation. Partisan war is, as Lenin says, 'an unavoidable form of combat,' one to be employed without dogmatism or preconceived principles just like other means and methods—legal or illegal, peaceful or violent, regular or irregular—depending on the particular situation. The purpose is the communist revolution in all countries of the world; whatever serves this purpose is good and just. (2004, 34–35)

In this process, according to Lenin, the directing theorist (such as the *politikos* of EAM)[9] has a vital role to play.

Mulgan may have read Lenin's 1906 essay on *Der Partisanenkampf* (translated as 'Guerrilla Warfare'). In light of Lenin's insistence on the combination of the 'purely tactical or strategic question relating to the concrete situation' and the fundamental role of guiding ideologues, it is interesting to hear Mulgan's account of the Greek communists' meetings he attended and his thoughts on the role there of ideology:

> They were experts in mass-meetings, coiners of slogans, which sometimes contradicted each other but were always temporarily effective. Early attempts at argument, misquotings, denials of

---

9   The most important men here included Konstantinos Despotopoulos, Giannis Ioannidis, Kostas Karagiorgis, Dimitris Partsalidis, Petros Rousos, Giorgis Siantos, Andreas Tzimas, Markos Vafiadis and Gianniis Zevgos. (Of these, Mulgan mentions Karagiorgis, Partsalidis and Siantos in his report to J.V. Wilson.) Some of these men served as *politikoi* with the fighting bands; others were political leaders in either KKE or EAM.

something which we ourselves might have seen and have known
to be true, soon persuaded us that we were working outside our
charter and probably beyond our depth. (RE 170)

This comment is revealing on two levels. Firstly, for all Mulgan's
observation of what his fellow SOE operatives would have regarded as
communist failings (contradictory slogans, misquotations, counterfactual denials), what mattered was that these ideological strategies
'were always temporarily effective.' Ideology must be at the service of
practical results. Secondly, it reveals an impressive lack of arrogance
in the acknowledgement that he and the other Liaison Officers had
no business intervening in these meetings, that their only right was
to seek the *andartes'* permission to fight Germans on the railway
lines. Reading the history of SOE operatives in Greece, it's clear
that with very few exceptions Mulgan stood alone in his view that
they were operating under false pretences—that they were in control
of things, that this was *their* business. Colonial assumptions that
the command was theirs, he implies, put them 'probably beyond
[their] depth' from the start. Events were to prove, with disastrous
consequences, how right he was.

Mulgan makes clear that the freedom he was fighting for was not
only to do with 'democracy or the Four Freedoms' as defined by the
Allies: Roosevelt's freedom of speech and religion and from want
and fear (113).[10] Throughout his text, at times almost imperceptibly,
he voices resistance to British ideals of freedom employed to justify,
as in Greece, the suppression of others' national objectives. Since the
publication of the unexpurgated edition of *Report on Experience* in
2010, attention has naturally been paid to Chapter 5, the one dealing
with Mulgan's 'trouble with lieutenant-colonels',[11] considered too
sensitive for publication in 1947. Behind this trouble lay Mulgan's

10   Later Mulgan rejects another (fifth) 'Freedom' added by Herbert Hoover to Roosevelt's list:
      that to 'accumulate property' and that of 'private enterprise' (196, 196n181).

11   This phrase occurs in a paragraph at the end of Chapter 4 which was deleted during revisions.
      The final three sentences read: 'And in the end when one did come to real war [after training],
      one found one's time taken up with absurd and almost personal problems. At least that was
      my experience. My own function in the army seemed to be, at one period, to have trouble
      with lieutenant-colonels' (RE 89n64).

exasperation with the way the British army was dependent on what he called the assumptions of the 'self-selected' (54), with their 'peculiarly maddening form of confidence' (80) in their right to rule. This complaint, as we shall see, was shared by many Americans in the Allied Military Mission. Costas Couvaras, for example, notes in July 1944 that 'even the Communists' wanted the US to come on side as 'they feel that American interest helps in weakening the British grip on Greek affairs' (n.d., 76). In resisting Britain's imperialist motives in Greece, and in their perception of the ideological and ethical indefensibility of British policy, men like Mulgan and Couvaras were ahead of their time. An overall assessment by Mark Mazower summarises the recent consensus of international scholarship on the issue. Acknowledging that the question of who bore responsibility for the *Dekemvriana*, which led to civil war, was to become 'one of the most bitterly contested issues of modern Greek history' (2001, 363), Mazower does not doubt who that was, given Churchill's 'imperious contempt' for the ELAS guerrillas and his authorisation to General Scobie to 'use such force . . . as may be required to crush ELAS' (365). EAM's aims, Mazower argues throughout *Inside Hitler's Greece*, were primarily social rather than political—a new style of egalitarian politics. He concludes:

> Like many other radical guerrilla organisations of the war and immediate postwar years—the Huk in the Philippines, the partisans in Italy, the FLN in Algeria all offer striking parallels— ELAS was essentially fighting not for communism, but for what it called a dual war of liberation—for national liberation against an external oppressor, and for internal social reform. (315)

During the long winter nights in the mountains from September 1943 onwards, Mulgan had ample opportunity to discuss these different kinds of communism, socialism and republicanism with his fellow fighters in Thessaly and north Roumeli. There would have been theoretical debates, but many of them—like Sarafis, Tsamakos or Bakirtzis, all career officers—also had long practical experience in political revolt. Taking a stand against the royalist dictatorship of Metaxas in the 1930s, these men had lost their posts in the army. Their talk would have acquainted Mulgan at first hand with the way the tactics of opposition in Greece were necessarily practical. Although (as we have seen) Mulgan got sick of 'Venizelos and Pangalos and Metaxas as subjects for debate' (167), he came to understand a good deal about why Greek communists, like those in other dictator countries of Europe, 'had an organization that was already underground and habituated to working in the dark' (168), as well as why the concept of truth-telling was not as simple a matter as others might assume. 'They had heard too many lies themselves,' he writes, 'to be overstrict in matters of propaganda' (168–69). This understanding set Mulgan starkly apart from his commanding officer.

Contra(dicting) Woodhouse

The writing of SOE's history was to be carefully controlled from London—by the Foreign Office, in the final analysis. Given the sensitivity of the subject, the fact that so many of the communications were 'Top Secret', it is not surprising that the British government commissioned its own historians. It is interesting therefore to read what happened to the first attempt to give an account of SOE activities in mainland Greece, that of Eddie Myers, head of the British Military Mission there in the period immediately before Mulgan's arrival. As recounted in Chapter 2, Myers was a practical military operative who worked collaboratively with ELAS in 1942–43. In the summer of '43 he had agreed to the *andartes*' request to accompany their representatives to Cairo for talks with the government-in-exile and British authorities. Making no secret of the strength of anti-monarchist views in Greece, Myers caused fury in the Egyptian and English capitals and was promptly removed from his post. When in 1945 Myers tried to publish his version of what happened, as Mark Mazower records in an essay entitled 'The Cold War and the Appropriation of Memory: Greece After Liberation', his first typescript, submitted to the Foreign Office for vetting, was 'lost'. When he tried again two years later, the Foreign Office reaction was to solicit a different version from Chris Woodhouse, who 'was given special facilities in the Foreign Office library for the purposes of doing so', although this assistance was to be kept secret. Myers' manuscript, it seems, was blocked and only appeared (with the title *Greek Entanglement*) in 1955 in expurgated form; it had to wait until 1985 to be issued in a fuller version. Meanwhile Woodhouse's *Apple of Discord* (1948), as Mazower puts it, 'quickly became regarded as an authoritative analysis of wartime British policy' (1995, 281–82). Published only a year after Mulgan's account, Woodhouse's version is heavily coloured by Cold War attitudes and, although his later writings on Greece were somewhat more balanced in the assessment of EAM-ELAS, his approach to the left-wing resistance was always in stark contrast to Mulgan's.

Christopher Montague Woodhouse, fifth Baron Terrington, DSO, OBE (1917–2001), was to become Conservative MP for Oxford, 1959–66 and 1970–74. Educated at Winchester and Oxford, where he took a double first in classics, Woodhouse was sent into Greece at age 24 with impressive skills: high intelligence, knowledge of the language and history of the country and an exceptional resourcefulness and courage. In many ways he was like Mulgan: in addition to their academic excellence, both were known for their physical stamina in the mountains as well as their leadership skills. (There is no doubt that had he survived, Mulgan would have attained high office in some field.) Perhaps there was even an element of competition between the two. In the 2010 edition of *Report on Experience*, Peter Whiteford quotes from a letter Woodhouse wrote to John's father Alan Mulgan in June 1947, some time after reading Mulgan's manuscript. (It seems Woodhouse was given the manuscript for vetting, as many others were.)[12] In the letter Woodhouse says that he has 'many times tried to put into writing my own feelings about Greece' but that 'John has made the task harder by doing it almost perfectly himself' (Whiteford 2010, 24). This may

12   Whiteford traces the trajectory of the MS after its submission to OUP, describing how it was passed through the War Office at one point. As we will see later, it was also carefully scrutinised by Julian Dolbey of SOE, who may have had a hand in some revisions.

be somewhat disingenuous. Ever the 'diplomat', as Barnes called him, Woodhouse lavished praise on Mulgan both before and after his death, but also recommended he be 'outposted' from SOE—in effect removed from contact with ELAS. Reading Woodhouse's immediately succeeding account, you sometimes get the sense that he's composing a counterargument to Mulgan's, correcting what he saw as Mulgan's naïve and (a favourite adjective) 'hoodwinked' views of the left-wing movement in Greece.

Mulgan's discomfort with Woodhouse stemmed from a fundamental mistrust of ruling-class British airs of entitlement, which cut deep into his early post-colonial sensibilities as a New Zealander. The opening two chapters of *Report on Experience*, on New Zealand then England, follow a biographical trajectory but at the same time set up this post-colonial confrontation. On page 86 he describes the response of fellow New Zealanders fighting in the desert, who 'tried hard to hide the aversion that overcomes them whenever they meet an English officer, but you can always see how they feel.' There was clearly an element of projection in this response. On the next pages he continues: 'Something, at least, was wrong with the British Army [. . .] The young gentlemen of England do their best, of course. They always do their best, particularly in wartime. In peacetime, the young gentlemen can be average hell' (RE 87). (The lash of the last word here, like the 'ga-ga' in the earlier example about the charming colonel, pulls the rug out abruptly from under the pseudo-gesture of admiration.) Later, in the mountains, he seems to have heard comments from Woodhouse that made him squirm. Woodhouse describes Psarros in *Apple of Discord* as 'the only guerrilla commander who was what the British Army calls an officer and a gentleman' (1948, 85). Mulgan's fine-tuned reaction can be sensed in passages such as the following, which describes the Italians from the Pinerolo division who had recently surrendered, in particular those from

the Duke of Aosta's cavalry, a rare fighting force that had ridden its splendid horses and burned villages on the Thessaly plain for over a year. They were beautifully dressed. An English officer of aristocratic tendencies remarked, 'How nice to deal with real soldiers again.' They had at least the uniforms. (RE 130)

This lovely piece of sustained irony may well have been aimed at Woodhouse, fifth Baron Terrington, although Woodhouse wasn't alone in this attitude.[13] But Mulgan's opposition to these class-based assessments of the guerrillas was political as much as national. In their official histories of SOE, both Woodhouse and (later) Foot argue that the role of the SOE operative had nothing to do with politics,[14] as if each agent were sent in as a blank slate and simply fought the enemy. Richard Clogg, however, cites from a minute by Alexander Cadogan of the Foreign Office in April 1943, to which Charles Hambro, head of SOE, agreed, that 'S.O.E.'s operatives would now be instructed to say that "while they don't mix in politics, they knew that H.M.G. support the King and his Government"' (1975, 175). Experience was to demonstrate, and recent scholarship has emphasised,[15] that blank slates are an illusory phenomenon—especially, we might add, when it came to the independent-minded New Zealanders serving with SOE.

Mulgan's narrative throughout *Report on Experience* is discreetly attentive to communism, concluding with the Popular Front-style recommendation that 'Some element of Communism might

13   Nicholas Hammond questioned the view (expressed by Barker-Benfield) that EAM-ELAS 'would behave like gentlemen' in the post-liberation period (Hammond 1983, 177).

14   Woodhouse writes about the SOE officers: '[what] they were really sent to Greece to do [. . .] had nothing to do with politics [. . .] no one wants to read about such things any more' (1948, 99); Foot expresses this in a way that suggests some recognition of this myth of political objectivity:

> The training staff [of SOE agents] took the line, almost always, that agents were sent abroad to perform strictly military tasks, and must take neither part nor even interest in domestic politics at all. Hardly ever were they given even the most rudimentary political training; they were forced back on their own common sense, and on such innate political judgement as they might possess [. . .] They were therefore liable to be clay in the hands of seasoned agents of the Comintern or of other well-established Continental political parties. (2008, 188)

Mulgan, as we have seen, puts forward this claim for their apolitical mission only to challenge it (RE 172).

15   For an analysis of the way attention needs to be directed towards the political (as opposed to the exclusively military) role and operations of SOE, see Wylie 2007b, 109–29.

be made suitable to Greece, but it would have to be of a very cooperative and democratic nature to last' (167). In counterpoint to this, Mulgan's personal 'evil' is set as the fascist imperialism which, like Napoleon, 'went over Europe' and 'knew it was good' (119). By contrast, Woodhouse's *Apple of Discord* laid the groundwork for the thesis that Greece was in the grip of a very different evil, a deliberate and devious Soviet-communist plot. To support this argument, he constructs a theory of three 'acts', the three stages of what was not a resistance to Axis powers but rather, from start to finish, a civil war in Greece, a struggle by KKE to gain 'absolute power' in the country. Many historians would echo this narrative in the decades to come.

As tensions increased between EAM-ELAS and the British, each side accused the other of conspiracy and lies. The official British view was, as Woodhouse put it, that 'the mass of ELAS was only pretending to fight [. . .] the Germans' (1948, 199). Mulgan wasn't the only one from SOE to disagree with this allegation. In 1954 Bickham Sweet-Escott, who had been Chief of Staff at SOE HQ in London (and later in Cairo), dismissed the then 'fashionable' opinion that the Greek resistance was of little or no value to the Allied war effort (1954, 30). Mulgan didn't hesitate to comment on the haphazard military skills and organisation of the left-wing guerrillas. But he never doubted the sincerity or significance of their contribution and would have winced at words like 'rabble' or 'buffoons' that Woodhouse used to describe them (1948, 199 and 184). A passage towards the end of Chapter 8 in *Report on Experience* takes on a combative tone, as if in reply to Woodhouse:

> It would be untrue to say that in all the attacks and depredations which had been conducted by the Germans, our *andartes* had offered no resistance or defence, but the resistance was of a formal kind [. . .] They never surrendered or compromised, and as a result the Germans kept five divisions guarding Greece all through the war. The Greek people paid a terrible and disproportionate price for this resistance. When people speak slightingly of Greeks and

of their waywardness and foolishness in fighting each other, there
is some point in remembering these things. (146–47)

The German strategy, as Voglis and Nioutsikos remind us, was to
encircle and evacuate villages in order to send their inhabitants
into German-occupied cities and deprive the partisans of food and
recruits (2017, 330). It failed, as Mulgan reports, because of the utter
solidarity between villagers and partisans:

> Their [the Germans'] purpose was clear in all this burning. They
> wanted to break the resistance movement by starving out the
> mountains, and also by showing the people that their *andartes*
> were worthless and offered them no protection. In a more complex
> civilization this might have succeeded. But the villagers, once they
> understood what was happening, hid their stores of grain and
> flocks in the hills and waited until the enemy had gone, and then
> moved back again into the ruins of their houses. What hatred
> they felt continued to be concentrated on the Germans who had
> burned their houses. Towards their own fighting men who had
> brought this on them they felt perhaps apathy and showed despair,
> but never hostility. (147)

The second myth instigated by Woodhouse from this time was that
the sole purpose of those directing the *andartes* was to gain political
power in order to unite Greece with the Soviet Union. He writes:

> For three years they [the KKE] had worked faithfully for a Soviet
> policy in the Balkans, alternately by armed violence and diplomatic
> intrigue. Their purpose had been to achieve the Sovietisation of
> Greece by attaining political power themselves. (1948, 234)

This 'intrigue' involved using a policy of 'political infiltration under
the guise of co-operation' (183), in order that Greece be absorbed
into a Soviet Federation of the Balkans. Woodhouse's account of this
crucial period in the mid 1940s, in many ways balanced and well

informed, at times gives way to expressions which reveal an intense animus. For example, we are told that what the EAM-ELAS-KKE leaders had in common was a 'ruthlessness, lust for power, and a sense of conspiratorial security' (65) and that their military methods were similar to those of the Gestapo and the SS (63). This animus is all the more striking in view of Woodhouse's professed respect for 'facts', which he keeps insisting on (57, 60), but which obliged him to acknowledge considerable evidence to the contrary—for example, that most members of ELAS were *not* communists, that EAM tried repeatedly to form coalitions with other resistance groups or like-minded political parties, that EAM-ELAS proved its sincerity by *not* invading Athens immediately after German withdrawal, at a time when it had vastly superior forces, and finally and most pertinently that the Red Army was *not* and never had been interested in building up communism in Greece.[16] In spite of all this, Woodhouse asserts that those who didn't mistrust EAM-ELAS had been 'fooled', were 'simpletons and buffoons' (184)—Mulgan, presumably, among them.[17]

For all his philhellenism, Woodhouse's attitude to the majority of the modern Greek population was dismissive. His conspiracy theory of EAM-ELAS plans was dependent upon a particular view of the Greek character.

> A Greek peasant [. . .] will vote Communist because he has been told that Russian planes will then come and sow his fields from

16   Woodhouse himself acknowledges this when elaborating on the Soviet position in *The Struggle for Greece* 28 years later. Describing the arrival in the mountains (in Mulgan's area) of the Soviet Military Mission under Colonel Popov, on the night of 27–28 July 1944, he explains that Popov's message to EAM-ELAS was that there would be 'no material help from the Soviet Union, and that EAM must make its peace with the British' (2002, 92). See also Grigoriadis 2011, III, 333.

17   As late as 2008 (his book was first published in 1984 and revised twice, in 1999 and 2008), M.R.D. Foot still echoes the counterfactual argument that EAM-ELAS were victims of Soviet-communist control, attempting 'to seize state power in the teeth of whatever wishes the bulk of the Greek people might have' (2008, 290)—in obvious contradiction to the fact that 'the bulk of the Greek people' had demonstrated their independence in the most radical way possible, by voting for a newly formed alternative government in the mountains which championed an outcome that left Greece free to establish its own political policies independent of foreign control, British or Soviet.

the air so that he need never work again [. . .] His only objection to
Metaxas was based on a law restricting goats in the interests of re-
afforestation. His wit is quick but his judgment is weak [. . .] This
huge majority [of EAM-ELAS supporters], having in common
only a terrible ignorance of its direction, its dangers, its personal
stakes, was divided up and blindly led by the minorities who did
know where they were going. (1948, 57)

To these charges Mulgan would likely have replied, as he did in
Report on Experience, that he personally would 'back the shrewd
sagacity of a Greek mountain peasant to smell out most falsehoods',
propaganda or otherwise (173). Whereas Mulgan observes that
many of the ELAS fighters he lived amongst were 'clever men,
speakers of many languages, well-travelled' (RE 170),[18] Woodhouse's
assumption throughout *Apple of Discord* is that the 'huge majority'
of ELAS supporters were 'terribly ignor[ant]', 'belonging to another
century and another continent' (from 'western civilization') (55–57).
On this basis, he argues, the non-communists in ELAS were mere
'sticks' for the communist match to ignite (65), an 'obedient rank
and file' (64), 'fly' to the KKE's 'spider' (69). Here his perspective is
most warped, for, as most subsequent analysis has emphasised, both
inside and outside Greece, one of the extraordinary achievements
of the EAM movement was to have united the hearts and minds
of the vast majority of the Greek people in their opposition to both
an occupying army and a foreign-controlled royalist government-in-
exile. Woodhouse's aim throughout *Apple of Discord* is to celebrate
the way Greece was 'rescued' from communism. Mulgan's view of
what Greece needed to be rescued from sits in direct opposition to
this. Woodhouse expresses incredulity at the gullibility of the Greek
people. Their patriotic opposition to the Axis powers is easy to
understand, he writes, but

What cannot be seen so easily is why, if EAM/ELAS was only

---

18   Mulgan's view is endorsed by Mazower, who writes that 'many leading ELAS kapetans were
indeed educated men with radical views' (2001, 301).

a cover for the KKE, the non-Communists who joined it for
patriotic reasons remained in it when its true character gradually
became revealed. (66)

He may have voiced this incomprehension of EAM's 'true character',
why the Greeks continued to hold faith with it, on that day back in
September when Mulgan recorded in his diary that 'Chris arrived in
afternoon. He talked at length, I listened.' There would have been
no use explaining.

Towards the end of *Report on Experience* Mulgan reveals, in no
uncertain terms, his impatience with the British-supported Greek
government-in-exile, as well as those (by implication including and
in particular Woodhouse)[19] who were responsible for implementing
its policies:

> People make jokes about the Greeks and I know that much
> bitterness came afterwards, as is inevitable with civil war, but few
> of those whom I heard criticizing them are competent to judge. I
> would take comments, and I know the villagers of Kaitsa would
> take them, from Londoners or Czechs or front-line soldiers in
> the campaign of the last winter of the war, but not from anyone
> else and not from exiled governments living abroad in comfort.
> (163–64)

This is fighting stuff to be writing between late 1944 and early 1945, a
direct challenge to Allied military policy, and the censors would have
taken note as the manuscript passed through their hands on its way
to New Zealand. But its sentiment lies at the heart of Mulgan's text:
sympathy with those who had endured the consequences of conflict
at first hand (Londoners during the Blitz, the Czechs under violent
Nazi occupation, front-line soldiers in the worst battle conditions),
and, ultimately, identification with the people around him (in Kaitsa
and many other EAM-supported villages) whose daily endurance

---

19   Woodhouse had been appointed representative of the guerrillas in the mountains, at the end
      of 1943, by Tsouderos, then Prime Minister-in-exile (Grigoriadis 2011, III, 8).

testified to their fidelity to their principles. It is on this question of principles that Mulgan and Woodhouse are probably most at odds. According to the latter, in perhaps the most outrageous statement of his book, 'The KKE had a policy but no principles; the British authorities had principles but no policy' (219). Woodhouse is at least honest enough to admit to his failure to understand the Greeks when he writes at the end of *Apple of Discord* that 'It is impossible to share the life of the Greek people without [having] a sense of something radically preposterous' about them (284). He makes another point, however, which Mulgan would have understood, though perhaps in a rather different sense, that 'the unreasoning sentimentality of Anglo-Greek friendship' has often done Greece more harm than good (286). Perhaps philhellenic expectations, in Woodhouse's own case, had been the prelude to such disillusioned disdain. Mulgan's feelings contain none of this backward-looking romanticism but rather emerged from participation in a common historical moment and a shared underlying ideology.[20] As he refrained from explaining to Woodhouse in their time together on sabotage missions, it was ideology, not nationalism, that was at stake. He felt sufficiently free in *Report on Experience,* however, to make this distinction in relation to Churchill's limitations:

> In the end [of the immediately pre-war period] Fascism, the idea, broke on nothing except old-fashioned nationalism, first in England, then in Russia. You never found Churchill worrying about one ideology or another in June 1940, only about Germans and English. (RE 115)

Mulgan had complete sympathy with the need to defend one's national territory, but his ultimate sympathies, his text suggests, were ideological and international.

* * *

20   Woodhouse, according to Clogg, 'believed that the best antidote to romantic notions about EAM was personal experience of the organization' (2000, 140). Mulgan's unromantic and sustained sympathy for EAM-ELAS was to challenge this assumption.

But for all the reader's sense of a strong though half-concealed left-wing agenda throughout *Report on Experience*, the final pages of the book present as much of a puzzle as a conclusion. Whiteford notes (RE 187n174) that the title 'Chapter Twelve' was added by the OUP editors (there was no heading or number in the typescript), so it is possible that Mulgan did not intend this as a conclusion. It does, however, take up the question of 'the world after the war', which 'We spent a lot of time during the war talking about' (187). Once again, the inclusive 'we' is ambiguous. Is he referring to discussions with the Greek comrades? Or does he mean the other BLOs?[21] At first it seems his interlocutors were Greeks, those with a radical political project whose demands might not be met by the hegemonic forces to come:

> I know that they will require some persuasion before they abandon
> what they ask for, and it is just as well to bear these things in mind
> when alternative programmes are being offered or civil discipline
> is being called in to enforce the discussion. (187)

The voice here seems to be that of Mulgan warning the Anglo-Greek authorities to handle EAM-ELAS claims with prudence in the post-liberation period.

But as the chapter progresses, the emphasis gradually shifts to an English frame of reference. The phrase 'In a future English world' (190) sets the context for what develops into a programme for post-war society to which his assumed readers could relate. Disingenuously disclaiming any intention to offer a political programme ('Politics are better left to the earnest professionals' [191]), Mulgan nonetheless proceeds to lay out some guidelines for the implementation of the freedoms he considers basic, and once

---

21 In the few pages Woodhouse dedicates to the BLOs as participants in the resistance, apart from stating that what they were sent to do 'had nothing to do with politics', he notes it as inevitable that their 'unconscious sympathies' should have guided their actions. Perhaps with Mulgan in mind, he writes that 'it was sometimes not clear, even to [the BLO] himself, what he meant by the word "we": since it could refer equally, and sometimes did so indiscriminately, to the guerrillas and himself collectively, or to his own authorities [in Cairo] and himself collectively' (1948, 99–100).

again the recommendations, though couched in general terms, are specific. The Spanish Civil War is drawn on to demonstrate the importance of the freedom to be with 'the people that you care about' (193): the Basques fought best, he has heard, when living close to their wives and families. Once again, Mulgan seems to be anticipating the pleasure of returning to quiet domesticity. On the next page, being with 'the people that we care about' is repeated as a 'basic liberty' (194), in contrast to the kind of individual liberty offered by a platform like John Stuart Mill's, which according to Mulgan could result in 'The liberty of the Birmingham small arms manufacturers to sell Hitler fifty million pounds' worth of arms in 1934' (194)—Hoover's fifth ('economic') liberty (to accumulate property and engage in private enterprise), he calls it a few paragraphs later. This sort of capitalist liberty, he repeats, is one 'we can do very well without' (196).

In the last three pages Mulgan's gaze is forward, towards the days ahead and the potential for change. Past experience has shown that 'Few Englishmen are revolutionary in their instincts': 'We may sometimes [. . .] have wished that they were more so' (197). But the experience of war has made them 'more dogmatic and sombre' in their demands, so that

> if there were no alternative, no way of breaking down the oblivion of those who govern them, I feel that they might now choose more desperate courses. The afflictions of England were matters not only of economics but also of understanding. The most deadly part of human life, the sorrow that Karl Marx felt like a scourge, was this oblivion that clouds the understanding of the well-possessed. (197–98)

If this wishful prediction of revolution in England sounds extreme, it's worth remembering what George Orwell, one of the twentieth century's most noted prognosticators, wrote in his 1941 book *The Lion and the Unicorn: Socialism and the English Genius*:

It is only by revolution that the native genius of the English
people can be set free. Revolution does not mean red flags and
street fighting, it means a fundamental shift of power. Whether
it happens with or without bloodshed is largely an accident of
time and place. Nor does it mean the dictatorship of a single class.
[. . .] What is wanted is a conscious open revolt by ordinary people
against inefficiency, class privilege and the rule of the old. (1971,
108)

The frame of reference is strikingly similar to that in which Cox
and Mulgan were writing a few years earlier in 'Behind the Cables'.
Orwell was of course correct in his prediction of imminent change
in Britain: the landslide victory of the Labour Party in the general
election of mid 1945, a few months after Mulgan's death, was to
result in some of the most radical political changes in Britain's
modern history.

So, at the very end we have returned full circle to the class
divisions that Mulgan's book opened with, and a hint that the British
may resort to 'more desperate courses' to resolve these divisions. And
it is here that Mulgan posits his rather extraordinary concluding
paradox: that 'For ourselves, we have been the gainers from this war'
(199). Within the context of the political aspirations just outlined,
the 'gain' here would seem to be the promise of a new egalitarian
society. But Mulgan finishes with the general explanation that
exposure to so much death has led to an acute appreciation for the
living and a new sense of promise. 'We are not likely to find time
lying heavy on our hands', he concludes, 'in an immediate future
of armed peace and tentative experiment' (200). 'Armed peace' is
a phrase usually used for the period of 36 years after the Congress
of Berlin and before World War 1, when peace was maintained in
spite or because of the build-up of arms in Europe. It could also be
a prediction of the Cold War he sensed approaching. But it may also
refer to an implied commitment to a future political experiment.
The ambivalence is left unresolved.

When James McNeish writes of the 'contained' or 'oblique'

quality of the writing in *Report on Experience*, he speculates that perhaps Mulgan has been 'numbed' or emotionally 'amputated' by his experiences in the mountains (2003, 245).[22] This may have been the case. But Mulgan would also have known that much of his text would not have got past the censors if he had expressed his opinions more openly. During his late-September tête-à-tête in the mountains with Woodhouse, he had had to let the British commander do all the talking. Now, in his textual reply to Woodhouse's soon-to-appear officially sanctioned version, he could voice some opposition, but needed all the same to remain carefully (semi-)inscrutable.

22 It has also been suggested that this quality of inscrutability was part of Mulgan's character. In the Foreword to the first (1947) edition of *Report on Experience*, Mulgan's New Zealand friend Jack Bennett writes that 'even his most intimate friends found much in his nature that was secret and impenetrable, if not deliberately concealed' (Bennett 1947, v).

CHAPTER 8

The Liquidation Fund

*It will be years before Greece is
anything like normal again*

—Mulgan to Gabrielle, 21 March 1945
(AGM 294)

On arriving in Cairo in November 1944, Mulgan was asked by the officer in charge of SOE secret intelligence, Julian Dolbey, to return to Athens after Christmas to administer the Liquidation Fund, set up to compensate Greeks who had helped the British during the occupation. Mulgan was killing time, waiting for transfer to the New Zealand forces, but was reluctant to accept the post on account of a sense of unease about which side he'd be on in the country, about 'a job done that makes me ill-inclined to revisit it', he told Gabrielle (Day 1977, 46). In the end he agreed, on condition that he take no part in fighting against ELAS forces. (He would have been well aware by November of plans for British military intervention.) It was at least an opportunity to help the Greeks. The office for the Liquidation Fund had been established in the centre of Athens that month under the command of L.E.D. (Larry) O'Toole, with the assistance of Michael Ward. Mulgan was to work there from 15 January to 19 April 1945—until only a few days, that is, before his death.

These were dark times to be in Athens. Political tensions in the immediate aftermath of *Ta Dekemvriana* showed no sign of easing and martial law had been imposed. The sheer scale of suffering and destruction would have been deeply shocking. Malnutrition bordered on starvation for large numbers of the population, around one third of whom were suffering from malaria; communications systems had been almost completely destroyed; and the currency was 'in the throes of one of the wildest inflations of modern times' (Sweet-Escott 1954, 96). On a literal level as well, evenings in the capital were shrouded in darkness as, in an attempt to curb violent clashes, the British, who had control of the city, including the Electricity Department, had imposed a curfew. Mulgan noted in a characteristic sardonic aside, however, that the privileged class who lived around Kolonaki Square seemed to be doing all right. His description of life in the city is evocative and politically charged:

> When I came back to Greece, alone and not very willingly, in January of the New Year, the last year of the war, Athens was dark and silent. A cold curfew closed down on the city with sunset. Stray shots broke the quiet of the long, dark, winter hours. In the streets were sad-faced men and women, still hungry and no longer happy. English soldiers moved with guns ready, as if in a hostile land. [. . .] you might ask yourself, being still of an inquiring nature, if this was the free Greece which we had toasted in rare, comfortable hours a year before. I don't know what we had expected then or what kind of mask we had thought the revolution might wear, but certainly not this antithesis of our dreams. [. . .] As the lights came on again in Athens, in well-to-do apartments, we heard many stories of Communist savagery. It wasn't so easy to extend sympathy to those who had lived comfortably under the Germans and were prepared to live the same way under any regime that would let them alone. (RE 175–77)

Mention of 'the free Greece which we had toasted' and 'revolution' here sprinkles the political message cautiously enough, and as always identities and details of groups are kept deliberately vague. In referring to 'Communist savagery', the charge is a reported one, coming (via its adjacent position) from those members of the Athens bourgeoisie who have colluded, directly or indirectly, with the enemy and come off unscathed. Mulgan's description is echoed five decades later by Mark Mazower, who from his own research into Greek and German sources writes of the way the Athenian bourgeoisie, 'From their expensive flats in Kolonaki round the shops of Lykavettos', were the first to spread horror stories about Communist atrocities and even believed that ELAS was planning an assault on their district (2001, 347, 371).

It is worth pausing for a moment to consider these reports of communist atrocities, that have continued to dominate many accounts of these events to this day. Much of the animus seems to be the result of the criteria applied to the activities of regular warfare, which sanctions mass killing by certain established means, as opposed to those of irregular or guerrilla warfare, which may resort to any method available. There was outrage at the fact that, during the *Dekemvriana*, much of the attack came from men or women in plain clothes, and that women delivered hand grenades to their fellow fighters hidden in shopping baskets or even in their underwear. Against such methods, British tanks quickly set up a grotesquely uneven battle,[1] but the sentiment continued that ELAS fighters were 'shifty', 'ungentlemanly' or 'double-dealing'. The most serious limitation of guerrilla warfare, as Eric Hobsbawm points out, is that it cannot win until it becomes regular warfare, capable of meeting its enemy on their strongest ground, which is invariably the capital city (1977, 169). Stories of ELAS fighters laying blankets on the streets in an attempt to tangle the treads of British tanks, for example, give some idea of such unpreparedness (Haralambidis 2014, 231). This was a lesson learnt, with tragic consequences, by the fighters in the Warsaw Uprising which Mulgan referred to. In addition, as Orwell pointed out, the fact that the tale is left to be

---

1   Brigadier Alan Block, 'the victor of Piraeus', was sent to the western city of Patras and on 9 January sent an order to ELAS that they had 48 hours to get out 'or accept the consequences'. Block records that Hawkesworth (who had replaced Scobie as Commander) told him to repeat what he had done in Piraeus. Block told the brigade commanders: 'If any house causes you trouble put a tank in and blow it to bits!' (Maule 1975, 263).

told by the victors has meant that many of the so-called atrocities have been challenged only recently, decades after the events, with the availability of documentary evidence rather than rumour. An example here is the new evidence brought forward to challenge reports of the mutilation of bodies of right-wing Athenians executed by ELAS in the suburb of Peristeri outside Athens.[2] But appalling acts of violence, the inevitable product of civil war, were committed on both sides. A notorious example of ELAS violence, in response to the British dispatch of some 8,000 left-wing sympathisers to concentration camps in the Sudan (Woodhouse 1948, 224; Stefanos Sarafis 1980, 520n1), is the capture of several thousand hostages considered traitors, some of them British and others middle-class Athenians. Taken on a 'long march' north, many died before reaching Volos, where survivors were rescued by the Red Cross. These abductions, as Mazower records, 'destroyed much of the moral credibility which EAM/ELAS had enjoyed in the eyes of the world until then' (2001, 372).

These few months after *Ta Dekemvriana* would have been heartbreaking for Mulgan to witness, as he did, at first hand. The occupying British, roaming the streets with guns at the ready, seemed to him an appalling outcome of the radical struggle for change in the country. Some of the common British soldiers clearly felt extremely uneasy about their role. Floyd Spencer, reporting for the Americans, reveals that during the *Dekemvriana* some British soldiers, feeling 'ashamed of what they considered British duplicity', had disobeyed orders and refused to fight their former allies (1952, 75). Peter Glass of the Black Watch regiment recorded with unease

2   Evidence held in the General State as well as the Court Archives from a gravedigger at Peristeri reveals that many of the 485 bodies buried there at this time had been brought from other areas in Athens, some from hospitals (Haralambidis 2014, 299 and 299 n569). See also Richter (1985, 29), who cites from a book by Colin Wright, a member of the British intervention forces, who wrote in a letter of 13 March 1945 about the way EAM investigations into the atrocity stories were revealing them to be 'pure moonshine. Some frightful tricks have been perpetrated, it is alleged, by the Right against the Left. People who have died from natural causes have been exhumed, noses and ears cut off, eyes removed and genitals interfered with, and corpses shown as ELAS atrocities'. Richter also cites here from sworn evidence from a member of the former Security Battalions who confessed to carrying out these mutilations on bodies which were then thrown into graves in Peristeri, where they were examined by the investigative team under Walter Citrine, sent in by the British.

how civilians caught on the street during curfew were shot on sight; it's been estimated that at least 500 died in this way (Haralambidis 2014, 310). A few of the occupiers relished the opportunity to put down the Reds. One of these was Henry Maule, also of the Black Watch, whose book title would be enough to raise the hair on the back of the neck of most Greeks today: *Scobie: Hero of Greece* (1975). But many, it seems, simply had little idea of what they were doing. One warrant officer wrote: 'Mr Churchill and his speech bucked us no end, we know now what we are fighting for and against, it is obviously a Hun element behind all this trouble' (Vulliamy and Smith 2014).

Paradoxically, by this time the 'Hun element' was not Britain's enemy but its ally. Soon to be overseen by Sir Charles Wickham, the 'British Police Mission' was working to integrate the Security Battalions (the Third Reich's 'Special Constabulary') into the new Greek police force. Wickham had from 1922 been the first Inspector General of the Royal Ulster Constabulary, conceived not as a regular police force but as a counter-insurgency unit, applying what Irish historian Tim Pat Coogan calls 'the narrative of empire' in Northern Ireland, 'and, of course, they applied it [over the next few years] to Greece. That same combination of concentration camps, putting the murder gangs in uniform, and calling it the police' (Vulliamy and Smith 2014). Security Battalion members who had collaborated with the Germans were taking charge on the streets. Writing *Report on Experience* with Lenin in mind at this time, Mulgan may have been reminded of the celebrated Chapter 8 of *Imperialism*, where Lenin details the 'parasitism' of imperialist capitalism and cites the British economist J.A. Hobson, who pointed out (in 1902) that

> Most of the fighting by which we have won our Indian Empire has been done by natives; in India, as more recently in Egypt, great standing armies are placed under British commanders. (Lenin 2010 [1916], 129)

Particularly distressing to Mulgan at this time was the irrevocable split occurring not only between left and right but within the left itself. The trigger for this was the Varkiza Agreement of February 12, when the requisitioning of its arms placed EAM-ELAS at a crucial crossroads. One branch of the movement favoured compromise with the British; another, led by Aris, was appalled by this 'betrayal'. Sarafis himself was torn. Haritopoulos describes the dilemma over the disbanding of ELAS as follows:

> When Sarafis asked Aris to come and sign the decree, Aris refused. The General [Sarafis] was instantly in a dilemma: 'There's no way I'm going to sign for the dissolution of an army which you created' [he told Aris]. The General [then] weighed up the situation more dispassionately. The same day he returned with a different view [and finally] signed with a heavy heart. (2003, 671)

Complicating the mix was the role of the KKE, which agreed with Aris's refusal of a compromise but did not approve of his independent politics. Aris's reaction was to set up a 'new ELAS' with a specifically anti-imperialist agenda—what was called Metopo Ethnikis Anexatisias: National Independence Front (MEA). Now denounced by the KKE and pursued as a war criminal by the British, Aris took to the mountains again, but by this time thousands of Elasites, exhausted by years of conflict, were returning quietly to their homes. By June, Aris and his faithful band were attempting to flee the country, but were eventually trapped north of Trikala. This uncompromising ideologue, by now regarded by many as the devil incarnate, committed suicide (or was murdered) along with his second in command, Tzavellas. Meanwhile, the National Defence forces, backed by the British and increasingly reinforced by members of the Security Battalions and other right-wing elements, dominated the streets of Athens. In his description of the 'cold curfew closed down on the city' and the 'stray shots' that broke its silence, Mulgan evokes the horrors of the White Terror to come.

Describing his work for the Liquidation Fund in *Report on Experience,* Mulgan writes that he had before him 'the melancholy task of trying to find and compensate those people who had been killed or crippled fighting for us during the occupation. [. . .] to help those who had directly belonged to us and had fought and worked with us' (RE 176). It seems to have been a question, again, of who this 'us' stands for, as the uneasy repetition of the word suggests. Was it the British authorities he was serving, or the ELAS partisans? By this time, as was clear to everyone, it could not be assumed that the Elasites '*directly* belonged to' the British—far from it. Some SOE operatives like himself *had* 'fought with' the ELAS partisans. But in the main, in the minds of the British, those who *had* 'worked with' SOE were the EDES bands (and, to a limited extent, before April '44, EKKA). The category of those most 'directly' helping the British, he well knew, could even apply to those associated with fascist groups such as the Security Battalions.[3] To these, he makes abundantly clear elsewhere, he felt no sense of allegiance whatsoever. The question of exactly who was most eligible for compensation was to become a moot point, one on which he was not always in agreement with his boss in Cairo, Julian Dolbey.

American allies

Evidence suggests that the British offer of compensation to Greek agents and informers was prompted less by gratitude than by the intention to single out Greek Anglophiles who might be useful in the future. Greece stood at one of the most politically sensitive points of communication in the Empire, and the retention of British interests in Greece was vital for maintaining control over the routes linking Britain with Iraqi petroleum, with the Suez Canal and India, with China and the Pacific. Julian Dolbey was to be a key figure in promoting these interests in post-war Greece.

---

3   For British tolerance of members of the Security Battalions (who had now joined the 'National Army') as a counterweight to EAM/ELAS, see Richter 1997, 208n56 and Mazower 2001, 328–31 and 353. Immediately after the war, Woodhouse conceded that 'The British authorities were at least morally, if not juridically, at fault' in failing to insist on the punishment of the leaders of the Security Battalions, 'men whom they had already formally stigmatised as traitors'. This failure, he writes, 'is one of the worst sores to be presented for inspection, and one whose accumulated poison has not grown less deadly' (1948, 98).

Britain's objectives had been picked up early on by the Americans in the area serving with OSS.[4] In a bid to counter British dominance, the Americans had appointed Lincoln MacVeagh as US Ambassador to the Greek and Yugoslav governments-in-exile in Cairo in September 1943. MacVeagh did not mince his words in his report to Roosevelt in February 1944:

> British policy [. . .] is essentially today what it has always been [. . .] It is directed primarily at the preservation of the Empire connections and sea routes to India [. . .] it all shapes up to finding where Britain can secure the firmest vantage ground for the preservation of a stake in the Balkans—obviating total control of Southeastern Europe by any other great power. It is very far from a policy aimed at the reconstruction of the occupied countries as free and independent states. (Iatrides 1980, 454)

Earlier, in disagreement with the British move to cut off supplies of arms to EAM-ELAS, whom most Americans regarded as crucial to the country's future self-determination, members of OSS continued to support them (Jones 2007, 102). By June 1945, two months after Mulgan's death, tensions between British and US political and military positions over Britain's policies in Greece had increased to such an extent that the Americans even considered themselves under threat. The head of OSS Secret Intelligence in liberated Athens, Captain Charles Edson, observed that the British were so 'fed up' with their ally's attempt to distance themselves from Britain's policies that the Americans were being 'subject to a certain amount of calculated though concealed obstruction [. . .] It is my present feeling that our field missions are likely to encounter increasing difficulties and possibly actual danger' (Jones 2007, 104). Although Roosevelt himself, following the Teheran Conference in late 1943,

4   Jones (2007, 101–5) gives a balanced description of the anti-British sentiment of the Americans towards the end of the war. He cites from an American summary of British policy which stated that the British had 'consistently supported rightist elements and opposed Greek moderate and leftist elements'. EAM, it estimated, was no more than about 20 percent communist, and 'appears to represent an actual majority of Greek opinion [. . .] it is primarily concerned with achieving a liberated and independent Greece' (103).

continued to support Churchill's policy to reassure the Greek king that the monarchy would be restored after liberation, the US State Department regarded British policies in Greece with considerable suspicion.[5]

It is probably no accident that most of Mulgan's friendships in Greece and Cairo at this time were with American servicemen and journalists.[6] An interesting incident involving Mulgan and the Americans at policy level during the war is recorded by Richard Clogg in a detailed essay entitled 'Distant Cousins: SOE and OSS at Odds over Greece'. The Research and Analysis branch of OSS in Cairo, Clogg records, appointed academics to report back on the situation at first hand. One of these was the head of the branch, Moses Hadas, Professor of Classics at Columbia University, who was, according to Clogg,

> a man of forthright opinions as far as Greece was concerned. When he went into Greece in the summer of 1944, [Nicholas] Hammond had arranged for him to join the New Zealand British Liaison Officer John Mulgan, 'the most enterprising of our commanders' [Hammond 1983, 160] but this did little to allay his deep suspicion of the direction being taken by British policy in Greece. (2000, 135)

This shouldn't surprise us. Mulgan's opinions of the situation were necessarily less 'forthright' than Hadas's, given his position. He was adept, as we have seen, at getting on with the job in hand and

---

5   An account of what was happening in Greece, prepared by the American scholar Floyd Spencer (for the Library of Congress: European Affairs Division) and covering the years 1940–50, records that Churchill's memoirs present 'a best-foot-forward account' of British policy but show 'little inner understanding of the Greek country or people' (Spencer 1952, 9).

6   From his time in the mountains Mulgan had maintained close association with several Americans in Greece. See, for example, the descriptions of Mulgan by the American medical serviceman Al Borgman of their time together in the mountains, where Borgman expressed his admiration for Mulgan's 'complete emotional stability' (LJB 299–300, 317). Back in Cairo at the end of 1944, as O'Sullivan records, he chose to spend Christmas with Americans, 'a people whose company he increasingly liked [. . . and] had become good friends with several, especially Ernest Ramsaur, a naval lieutenant he had met in Greece in the first days of liberation' (323–24). In Athens in January 1945 Mulgan shared a flat with the American war correspondent George Weller (AGM 287).

keeping quiet about his opinions. But we can imagine what he said to Hadas: many of his own views, to be expressed more directly in the coming months, were very close if not identical to those of the American. It is highly likely, too, that Hadas was drawing on Mulgan's opinions in his subsequent attack on British policies, although he would have protected the identity of his informant. In a report to OSS marked 'Secret' on 'Observations on Greek Affairs in Cairo', submitted in September 1944 but not published for nearly 60 years, Hadas describes the resentment among Greeks, liberals and conservatives alike, about 'British interference in Greek political affairs' and the subsequent 'intolerable diminution of Greek sovereignty'. Some clandestine publications, he records, warned that 'a German occupation must not be changed for a British one'. The British, a former professor of physics in Athens told Hadas, 'were proving treacherous friends' (Clogg 2002, 178–79). Hadas's view of Chris Woodhouse as 'perfectly sincere, cultivated, and competent, but [. . .] incapable of appreciating Greek problems in their totality' could have come straight from Mulgan, syntax and all. Woodhouse's 'political and social temperament', Hadas asserted after taking extensive soundings, rendered him 'incapable of forming true judgements of the Greek political situation' (Clogg 2002, 183). Hadas also emphasised in a report of the previous week that what he was talking about was official policy rather than the views of those on the ground, where 'disapproval of British policy was unanimous among both British and Americans'. He goes as far as to name British Colonel O'Toole of SOE Cairo, regarded as the 'best informed man on Greek matters'. O'Toole, whose family had lived on Cephalonia since the nineteenth century and who spoke perfect Greek, is said to have 'deplored the policy of H[is] M[ajesty's] G[overnment] even more than I [Hadas] did' and blamed it on the Foreign Office (Clogg 2002, 176–77). He was selected to head the Liquidation Fund office immediately before Mulgan, but lasted only a short while there.[7]

7   Michael Ward, always careful to observe the Official Secrets Act, gives no reason for O'Toole's departure, simply noting that 'In January 1945 Larry O'Toole was posted to Germany, being succeeded in command by Major John Mulgan [. . .] In May [*sic*] he [Mulgan] died suddenly

American attitudes, of course, would change significantly from 1947 onwards, when the American Mission for Aid to Greece, providing military as well as economic assistance, took over from the British and supported the right-wing Greek government which eventually defeated the Republican/Democratic Army of the left. For this reason, accounts by mainstream British historians like Woodhouse (and even Clogg) tend, with some justification, to end with a 'told-you-so' adoption of the moral high ground.[8] But during the months before Mulgan's death, British paranoia towards those attempting to undermine its policies was at an all-time high.[9] It was within this climate that Mulgan was given the near-impossible task of deciding who deserved compensation for having helped the British cause.

In the Athens office

Who, then, was Julian Dolbey, the man who was to play such an important role in the final months and weeks of Mulgan's life? Dolbey was an adopted surname. After the war he reverted to his Polish birth name, with accumulated awards: Count Julian Dobrski, MC, OBE (1901–1968). As General Staff Officer 1 of Force 133 (SOE) in Cairo and Commanding Officer of operations in the Aegean,[10]

while on a visit to Cairo and I assumed command of the unit in his place' (Ward 1992, 222–23).

8   Clogg in fact singles out Hadas as his target in the concluding lines of his essay on 'Distant Cousins: SOE and OSS at Odds over Greece':

The irony inherent in the somewhat sanctimonious attitudes adopted by the Americans in 1943 and 1944 vis-à-vis the British entanglement in Greece when contrasted with the way in which they themselves became mired in Greek affairs in 1947 and subsequently, after London had yielded its traditional hegemony in Greece to Washington, calls for no emphasis. After all, Moses Hadas as late as the summer of 1944 had been arguing that 'of all the Allied powers America alone seems disinterested [sic] in the internal political concerns of Greece.' (2000, 143)

9   Another influential Greek in Cairo whom Hadas talked to 'characterised British behaviour as like that of a man in a panic. Their arrests of persons in Cairo and Alexandria for security reasons, with no charges preferred, their too patent control over every move of the Greek Government, their distortions of news for press releases, and their extremely severe censorship contributed to such an interpretation' (Hadas, Clogg 2002, 178–79).

10   For the purposes of secrecy SOE from a certain time on was referred to as Force 133, which involved SOE Greece, Bulgaria and Romania. Force 399 involved SOE Yugoslavia, Albania

Dolbey oversaw every facet of Mulgan's activities, both in Athens and in Cairo, and visited the Greek capital regularly.[11] Despite the significance of his role in the war from 1943 and beyond, he remains a shadowy figure, almost certainly because of his highly sensitive position in Cairo at this time as head of undercover operations in the Balkans, what he called the 'Subversive Sections' of SOE.[12] Details beyond a *Times* obituary (Tillotson 2011, 134) and a few general anecdotal accounts are hard to come by[13] and his name rarely appears in any of the by now very numerous histories of SOE.[14]

The son of a Polish count and an Italian mother, Dolbey took British citizenship shortly before the war, recording himself in January 1941 as Director of Lyons Silk Ltd.[15] Brought up in France, he was distinguished by his fluency in many European languages as well as his wide experience of war. With his Polish roots, Dolbey had good reason to be anti-communist, particularly after the Red Army invaded Poland on 12 January 1945, followed by the Soviet annexation of the country, tacitly accepted by Roosevelt and Churchill at the Yalta Conference in early February. For the hundreds of thousands

and Hungary (and later Czechoslovakia and Poland).

11　See the two memoranda by Dolbey of February and March 1945 (Dobrski 30). A small part of Folio 30 was made available to us after permission from Richard Mulgan, to whom we extend thanks.

12　Personal report for December 1943. TNA Dobrski HS 9/437/4, 2.

13　Christopher Woods describes Dolbey's early life, that he was born in Italy of mixed Polish and Italian parentage and served in the Italian army for two years before moving to England in 1928, where shortly before the war he took up British citizenship. In October 1941 he was sent to Malta and in June of the next year was made head of the Italian section of SOE in Cairo (2006, 93). With his knowledge of the Italian language, he was selected to take part in George Jellicoe's operation (named 'Rodel') to Rhodos on 9 September 1943 in the attempt to rally the Italian forces against the Germans. On this mission he broke his leg in the parachute drop but displayed 'remarkable stoicism [... and] insisted on seeing Admiral Cambioni before having his injury tended' (Mortimer 2013, 74). Educated at the university in Lyon, Dolbey had a fluent command of many languages. Lorna Almonds Windmill describes him as six feet tall with a slim but strong build and speaking 'perfect BBC wireless announcer English' with a very slight accent (2008, 68). He visited Greece several times after the liberation and according to existing documents had a thorough knowledge of the country and of those Greeks who had collaborated with the British. His wife, Countessa Niki Dobrska, helped arrange the Dobrski files in the Liddell Hart Archives at King's College, many of which are still not in the public domain.

14　A recent detailed study by Jeffrey Bines, *Poland's S.O.E.: A British Perspective* (2018), which makes use of newly released archival material, makes no reference to Dolbey/Dobrski.

15　Personal report on Count Julian Augustus Dobrski. TNA Dobrski HS 9/437/4, 2.

of self-exiled Poles, many of them forming divisions and brigades on the side of the Allies, communism represented an immediate and terrifying threat. Many members of the massive Polish force, the Polish Home Army (Armia Krajowa), provided the main source of intelligence to the British from Central and Eastern Europe (as detailed on the website 'Polish Contribution').[16] His anti-communist sentiments made Dolbey a strong advocate of British control in the Balkans, on account of which he was given a key role in developing future trade links there.

From the time of his appointment to the Athens office, Mulgan was in more or less daily contact with Dolbey; after only six days, on 21 January, he referred in one letter to the 'already large amount of correspondence that seems to flow between us'.[17] Many of these letters have yet to be declassified,[18] but from the little evidence available, relations between the two, although initially cordial and always carefully measured in tone, seem to have become increasingly strained. Dolbey was Mulgan's commanding officer in Force 133, although his equal in rank, and Mulgan was always careful to maintain etiquette. But Mulgan's views on who deserved compensation, as well as on future British interests in Greece, seem to have created tensions, of which he could give only subtle indication. On January 28 the two appear to have differed in their opinion of ELAS, as we find Mulgan insisting to Dolbey, as he had done and would continue to do to others, that 'It may be true, as Churchill said, that ELAS never did any fighting against the Germans, but certainly the latter found it necessary, or thought fit to kill a great many Greeks in reprisal for doubtless imaginary offences' (Dobrski, 34). The edgy tone of this remark is revealing. Calling the *andartes*' activities against the Germans 'doubtless

---

16   Since the early 1930s, the Poles had excelled in intelligence, their code breakers hot on the heels of the German code makers' early version of the Enigma machine. Just before the outbreak of war, the Polish Cipher Bureau shared its Enigma-decryption techniques and equipment with French and British intelligence. They were later excluded from working at Bletchley Park.

17   Mulgan to Dolbey, 21 Jan. 1945. KCLMA Dobrski GB 0099 (hereafter cited as Dobrski), 34.

18   Even today, researchers are given access to only a very limited number of these documents.

imaginary' indicates that Mulgan's irony is beginning to lose its subtlety.

As he grew more critical of British policy and less inclined to hide his views, Mulgan began to expose himself to censure from above—as he was increasingly aware. On February 2 he began a letter to Gabrielle from Athens: 'I started to write to you four days ago in a brief spell of leisure in my office and then found my comments on the political scene were such that I would probably be arrested if I put the letter in the post and so destroyed it.' (We remember at this point how much he said he destroyed—more than what he left in—of *Report on Experience*.) Still seething, however, he returned later in this letter to descriptions of the suffering of the Greeks: though 'Outwardly, the situation is quiet—it ought to be with all these British soldiers here.' He concluded: 'I think I better lay off this subject' (AGM 290). He did permit himself a mild complaint about the arrogant behaviour of British soldiers on the streets of Athens in the earlier letter to Dolbey on January 21, where he wrote that he had 'developed an odd sympathy towards GREEKMIL[19] in their attitude towards us [the British] [. . .] I can understand their feelings towards our officers who continue to lead the irregular life rather beyond its term' (Dobrski 34). (In plain language this reads: what business do British officers have acting like overlords in the city, amidst such suffering?) By this time, British intentions to restore the monarchy, as well as activities in support of right-wing militias, were a daily reality. As anti-ELAS sentiment mounted among his colleagues, Mulgan was becoming increasingly isolated and angry, but could only vaguely express this, mainly in letters home. In a letter around this time held in military archives in New Zealand, he wrote that 'The British [. . .] won't admit that there might be any good people in these left movements and I'm likely to get arrested for even suggesting such a thing' (Brown 2011, 104).[20] Anxiety about this threat, we sense, was no joking matter.

19   'Odd' because it would not have been natural for Mulgan to feel sympathy for the Greek National Army at the time, which included many right-wing elements.

20   Extract from a letter to his parents given by Alan Mulgan to J.V. Wilson in January 1945 (no date given here).

Judging from the few letters available in the correspondence with Dolbey, it seems it became increasingly clear to Mulgan that the Liquidation Fund had less to do with compensation to war victims than it had to do with the rewarding and selection of Anglophile Greeks—for positions in departments of trade, banking, mining, aviation, electricity, etc.—to further British industrial and financial interests in the post-war period. The extent to which the Greek palace kowtowed to the British in these arrangements is indicated in a letter of 23 April 1945 from Princess Frederica to Lord Killean, British Ambassador in Cairo, expressing views that would have warmed the heart of Cecil Rhodes himself.[21] Her husband, Crown Prince Paul, she wrote, was of the opinion that Greece 'should try for admission in some form or other to the British Commonwealth of Nations' (Evans 1972, 340).

The detailed information Mulgan needed to gather in his work for the Fund required close investigation and involved dispatching colleagues to various places throughout the country to interview those who might possess knowledge about the work of each petitioner.[22] Helping him in the office on Amerikis Street in Athens were several others appointed by Dolbey: Michael Ward (of SOE), Aristotelis Protopappas (a British Officer in the Intelligence Corps),[23] Kostas Benakis (who would go on to do extensive business with Dolbey in trading silk),[24] Erikos Moazzo and Zoi Tsiminaki, along with a few interpreters and assistants.[25] Tsiminaki and Moazzo were particularly

---

21   In *Imperialism*, Lenin cites a comment by Rhodes in 1895 after the latter had attended a meeting of the angry unemployed in the East End of London:

        My cherished idea is a solution for the social problem, *i.e.,* in order to save the 40,000,000 inhabitants of the United Kingdom from a bloody civil war, we colonial statesmen must acquire new lands to settle the surplus population, to provide new markets for the goods produced by them in the factories and mines. The Empire, as I have always said, is a bread and butter question. If you want to avoid civil war, you must become imperialists. (Lenin 2010, 97)

22   See letters from Mulgan to Dolbey 25 Jan. 1945 and Dolbey to Mulgan 6 Feb. and 21 Feb. 1945 in Dobrski 34.

23   Protopappas remained in British employ in Greece. On 19 November 1945 he is recorded as working for the Allied Screening Commission of Force 133 (BHA 259, 1–2).

24   Dobrski 31–32.

25   The office for the Liquidation Fund had been employing some of these agents since November 1944, before Mulgan took over its command the following January. Michael Ward gives

useful, having been directly involved in undercover operations from early on in the war in the famous Apollo missions. In this capacity Tsiminaki in particular worked closely with Yannis Peltekis,[26] a Greek agent of the British Intelligence Service, who would figure prominently in Anglo-Greek relations after the liberation.

Known by his code names 'Apollo' or 'Yvonne', Peltekis had been one of the leading agents of British Intelligence from early on in Athens and Piraeus, having successfully accomplished large sabotage missions given these same code names. The Apollo organisation, reputed to number over 600 agents at one point, attracted unusual praise from the British. Lord Selborne, Minister for Economic Warfare with overall responsibility for SOE, wrote in late 1944 that Apollo had 'a splendid record', having 'sunk or damaged 26 major vessels from 7000 tons downwards and many smaller craft in the last 14 months, and provided much intelligence on German sea traffic in the Aegean enabling sea and air strikes to be made with marked success' (Clogg 2000, 62–63).[27] Peltekis's reputation, however, was challenged on several occasions from different quarters. Richard Clogg details one incident, illustrative of what he calls the 'perpetual warfare between the Foreign Office and SOE', when Peltekis was accused by members of the Greek government-in-exile and the British Embassy in Cairo of being a supporter of EAM, to which he was supplying large quantities of sovereigns. Churchill himself weighed in on this rumour and demanded to know who in SOE was guilty of this 'neglect or perversion of his duties'. 'Nobody', he

details of the atmosphere and activities of the office before, during and then after Mulgan's time there, when Ward took over from Mulgan as head of the office (1992, 208–9).

26 As Ward records, Tsiminaki 'had been one of Yannis Peltekis's trusted collaborators in the Apollo group in Athens and had escaped with him to the Middle East when its security was threatened in the summer of 1943' (1992, 181). Some of Mulgan's time in the office, as well as outside it, was spent with Tsiminaki. According to O'Sullivan and others, Tsiminaki was Peltekis's mistress (LJB 324), but given some indications of their daily contact (Day 1977, 50), and the affectionate letter Mulgan wrote to be sent to her on the night he died, she may have been sleeping with Mulgan as well, though Michael Ward, in the office with them, doubted this (LJB 333). Whatever her feelings or motives, Tsiminaki remained close to Peltekis: over the coming years, Dolbey's letters to Peltekis were always sent to Tsiminakis's address.

27 Sweet-Escott, citing from an official paper at that time still on the secret list, gives much higher figures: Peltekis, it is claimed there, 'sank or damaged no less than 250 vessels of about 68,000 tons in all' (1954, 23).

thundered, 'ever gets punished for doing these kind [sic] of things' (Clogg 2000, 61–63). A military court of inquiry was convened and Peltekis, with the help of Julian Dolbey it seems,[28] was not only cleared of all charges of assisting EAM but awarded a Distinguished Service Order and granted the honorary rank of Lieutenant Colonel (BHA 259, 1–2). His politics were said to be of a liberal, left-leaning persuasion, although, as Clogg reveals, there is some uncertainty about this. The report of the committee of inquiry, Clogg records, 'is known to survive but is not available for consultation' (2000, 63, 176n6). Whatever details are given in that report, Peltekis went on to deny categorically being a member of EAM-ELAS[29] and has since continued to attract the highest praise from British commentators such as Woodhouse.[30] Significantly, and certainly exceptionally, Peltekis is recorded by Woodhouse as having 'enjoyed the confidence of British officials in Athens after the liberation of Greece', especially when he became Minister of Mercantile Marine in the last unelected Greek government under Sofoulis (between 22 November 1945 and 4 April 1946) (Woodhouse 1948, 37). Like that of Benakis, Peltekis's close association with Dolbey continued for several years after the war, as can be seen from the extensive correspondence between the two (held in the Benaki Historical Archives in Athens) concerning business and security matters.[31]

There is another side to the Peltekis story, however. Inside Greek

28   Sweet-Escott describes the allegations and inquiry. He writes of the business in the SOE offices in Cairo around spring 1944 that 'most of it was done by Julian Dobrski, who had several difficult matters to handle. Of these the most important and by far the most unpleasant was the Apollo inquiry' (1965, 221).

29   A later statement made by Peltekis asserted that neither he nor Zoi Tsiminaki (with whom he was in a relationship) were members of EAM-ELAS. This confessional document exists both in the original and in translation from the French with the title 'Analysis tis Katalixeos tou Pelteki ypo tou Idiou'—see DIS, Athens, Peltekis, 953, 3 and 4. For the inquiry into Peltekis's activities, see also Ward 1992, 181.

30   See, for example, Woodhouse in *Apple of Discord*, where he refers to Peltekis as the 'most brilliant' and 'most spectacularly successful' of the Greek agents serving in the British Intelligence Service (1948, 35 and 36). Thirty years later Woodhouse was repeating the same praise: 'There were intelligence and sabotage networks in the towns, among which that of Peltekis (Apollo) was one of the most brilliantly successful in any capital city of occupied Europe' (2002, 107).

31   See documents listed under 'Peltekis' in BHA 259, 1–2, 6, 7 and 9.

sources record allegations against Peltekis from the start in relation to his untrustworthiness with money. Interesting testimony is given by the woman who later married Charalampos Koutsoyiannopoulos (who replaced Bakirtzis as head of the Prometheus network). Mairi Parianou acknowledges Peltakis's success as saboteur but details his sly (πονηρός) dealings.[32] He was, she records, a well-known gambler (2007, 36).

Mulgan's view of his undoubtedly brave colleague seems to have been less than enthusiastic and he would have had his reasons. If Peltekis was left leaning as Woodhouse claimed, it was a leftism which was deeply suspicious of EAM-ELAS and almost certainly fanatically anti-communist. Far from supporting EAM, as the Foreign Office and Churchill feared, the Apollo group was in fact informing against the organisation. Clogg reveals that in a rare accessible memo, it is clear Apollo was reporting on the 'systematic murder of officers by EAM' (Clogg 1981, 105). Clogg also records how 'During the winter of 1943–1944 rumours began to circulate in Cairo that Peltekis was some kind of double agent' (1981, 103). This claim can be neither proved nor disproved until the report of the three-man committee of inquiry is finally released. In addition, Theodoros Sampatakakis has explored how, around the time of the Lebanon Conference (May '44), Peltekis was manoeuvring to have himself installed as Papandreou's adviser, with much encouragement from the latter (2006, 266).[33] To further these ambitions, it seems, he was reporting to Cairo not only to denigrate EAM but also to fan ill-founded rumours about aggressive Soviet and Yugoslav intentions in Greece. This can be seen from the following report of 24 June, 1944, which can only be interpreted as either shockingly misinformed, coming as it did from someone in Secret Intelligence, or else deliberately distorted:

32 After working closely with Koutsoyiannopoulos, Parianou was captured and transported to a concentration camp in Austria. According to her, Peltekis appropriated £2,000 given to the Prometheus group by the British to bribe a jailer to have Koutsoyiannopoulos released from German detention. As it turned out, £5,000 had already been given for this purpose (Parianou 2007, 35–36).

33 After some to-ing and fro-ing, SOE eventually intervened to block the position (Sampatakakis 2006, 266).

Communist party, badly manoeuvred, has been exceedingly provoking, and being conscious [of] their unique force as organised Party of country, have decided [to] endeavour [to] impose proletariat dictatorship. The Party reject Lebanon Agreement which they qualify as compromise at any price. [. . .] Politbureau prepares urgently Soviet plans to lay hands on Greece. Orders given to reinforce communist ring around E.A.M. Influential E.A.M. followers who are not communists are either killed or threatened. [. . .] New situation due to TITO becoming in effect protector of E.A.M. Every important decision including LEBANON/Cairo conference directed by TITO. LEITMOTIV of Mountain's [PEEA's] policy is to prevent any Greek political action hindering TITO as sole defender [of the] BALKAN peoples. [. . .] TITO works to dismember my country by complete destruction [of] Anglo-Greek relations. Greek communists are little men with 1917 mentality. (TNA HS 5/547)[34]

Working with him, Mulgan became aware of the ways Peltekis played up to British prejudices to secure for himself a stake in future British interests in the country. On 22 March 1945 we find him losing patience with Peltekis's constant efforts at self-promotion with the British. He writes to Dolbey:

APOLLO has asked again for a special certificate to be issued to his own people. He tells me that he feels strongly about the grouping of YVONNE persons with others from lesser organisations and the overall issuing of Certificates of Service and letters of Commendation to all concerned. What he would like would be a special certificate which describes shortly the work of YVONNE. He would also like a letter detailing the achievements of YVONNE to be sent by General PAGET to the Greek Government. I am, as you can guess, a little tired of all this. Much as I like and admire APOLLO the continued pressure to recognise and differentiate

---

34   The report was sent on 11 July. It was written originally in French, then sent in English translation.

YVONNE from the others doesn't make life easier here. I feel
that SOELIQ have made a very considerable differentiation in
monetary awards [to Peltekis's group], the Education Trust, etc.
The letter from PAGET might, I suppose, be obtained. Your
answer about the certificate I think I know in advance but you
will probably have APOLLO on your hands again over this matter
when you return at the end of April. (Dobrski 34)[35]

Once again Mulgan was right. The British would indeed have
Peltekis 'on their hands' for a long time to come—with their initial
consent, although it seems that in time he was to become something
of a handful.[36] As always, the issue for Mulgan was that he was not
happy to play ball in this game. 'Much as I like and admire APOLLO
. . .' puts his opposition under careful wraps via his characteristic
syntactic move. But the main thrust of his point is that Peltekis has
already had more than his share and is being a pest. Others in the
office like Captain C.J. Harris (real name Gogas), who was jostling
for position in British circles with an eye to the future, got similar
short shrift from Mulgan.[37]

35 Dolbey obliged Peltekis with a letter of fulsome praise addressed to the Greek War Ministry
on 29 June 1945 in which he details the achievements of Apollo missions during the
occupation (boats and trains destroyed, Germans killed [100], etc.), and recommends him
for 'immediate promotion' (BHA 259, 1–2).

36 Peltekis's access to large amounts of gold sovereigns was to endorse what Mulgan had
predicted when he wrote that 'The comrades accused us of trying to corrupt the country with
"yellow fever" and they may have been right' (RE 151). (Sweet-Escott [1954, 96n2] records
that 'According to the *Bank of Athens Review* for December 1951, two million sovereigns
were brought into Greece by the Allies and the Axis during the occupation.') 'Secret' British
Embassy correspondence after the war reveals that the British were following the way Peltekis
had been investing heavily on the gold market in Athens. D. Patrick Reilly of the Embassy
writes to W.G. Hayter at the Foreign Office in London on 20 February 1948:

    It is notorious that Peltekis did make a very great deal of money during the occupation
    through his control of large sums in gold sent in by Force 133, but I do not think that
    anybody with any real knowledge of the matter maintains that he embezzled any of the
    sovereigns he received. What he apparently did was to speculate on the gold market on
    which he made large profits. His present financial reputation is frankly not good. He is
    believed to have used his position as Minister of Merchant Marine in 1945–46 to obtain
    ships which he has registered under the Panama flag. He was very recently prosecuted for
    bringing into Greece from Egypt a considerable sum in gold which was discovered by the
    Customs. His defence was that it was no crime to bring gold into Greece, but only to export
    it and he was acquitted. (TNA FO 1093/450)

37 See letters between Mulgan and Dolbey which detail Harris's attempts to obtain compensation

The petitioners

In his work for the Liquidation Fund Mulgan acquired something of a reputation for excessive caution, which seems to have had to do with his suspicion of claims from those whose loyalty was predominantly to the future interests of the British.[38] There is evidence of a dispute between Mulgan and a Greek agent for the British named Spyros Kotsis, whose claims for reimbursement for intelligence work were rejected by Mulgan. The case, which involved several high-profile figures, deserves closer attention.

Kotsis, who describes himself as 'a simple policeman' (TNA HS 5/636, 8), later wrote to Churchill himself to complain about his treatment. In a detailed nine-page letter he singles out two SOE officers as the source of his resentment. One was Mulgan and the other was 'Major O'Toole', the same Larry O'Toole who had railed against British policy to the American Moses Hadas and from whom Mulgan took command of the Liquidation Fund office. Previously, while in Smyrna at the end of 1943, O'Toole had refused to be impressed by Kotsis's sketches, maps and evidence of signals with MO4 (SOE) authorities. According to Kotsis, as he wrote to Churchill, O'Toole suggested Kotsis show all his evidence to the intelligence branch (SIS), who would exploit it to 'gain prestige', which his own branch (SOE) was not interested in. Feeling 'greatly insulted' by O'Toole, Kotsis continued to press his case in Cairo, where he was praised, sent on to another office, then finally told to wait until after the war. Attempting to curry favour with Churchill, he made a point of attacking EAM.[39]

If O'Toole had 'insulted' Kotsis, his treatment by Mulgan was

---

as well as get his Automatic Telephone and Electric Company up and running in Greece. Mulgan tried repeatedly to have him removed from the office. Dolbey, again, was taking Harris's side. Mulgan finally told Dolbey (in a letter of 3 March 1945) that he'd prefer it if in future the matter were dealt with by Cairo rather than his office (Dobrski 30).

38   Dolbey chides Mulgan on 28 February for his 'second Scottish nature' (Dobrski 34).

39   Kotsis had given, he wrote to Churchill, a 'true picture of the situation in Greece [in early 1944] and of the communist campaign carried on by EAM of which the responsibles [sic] in Cairo [in SOE] had altogether different views' (TNA HS 5/636, 4–5). Writing in April 1945, Kotsis would of course have known of the hostilities between SOE and the FO over EAM-ELAS, as well as Churchill's opposition to the band.

considered by the Greek as nothing short of scurrilous. Vincent O'Sullivan cites the conversation between the two, in which Mulgan, 'with a characteristic movement of his head', according to Kotsis, indicated that he thought Kotsis's documents were probably forged, and what's more, that Kotsis may well have been collaborating with the Germans (LJB 329). Kotsis's letter, parts of which have been redacted, ends by listing fourteen witnesses to verify his story, most of them from the right in Greek circles.[40]

O'Sullivan records that Mulgan's suspicions about the veracity of Kotsis's claims were later confirmed; Martyn Brown comments briefly on the implication of Don Stott in this case (Kotsis was keen to accuse SOE of the collaboration of one of its agents with the Germans).[41] There is another twist, however, to the story. A recent publication by André Gerolymatos reveals that Kotsis *was* employed early on by an important agent attached to the British Secret Intelligence Service named Ioannis Tsigantes, head (along with other high-ranking Greek officers) of a right-wing group in Athens calling itself Midas 614.[42] (Kotsis mentions Tsigantes and

40 In Cairo in November 1944 Kotsis was given a hearing by 'a Lt. Colonel whose name I do not recollect' (an unusual omission in a document with careful records of everything) in the offices of Force 133. This individual heard his evidence and 'answered that in a few days he was leaving for Athens and would arrange this matter' (TNA HS 5/636, 6). This could well have been Dolbey, head of the Intelligence section of Force 133, whose traces are rarely visible. Of the fourteen names listed as witnesses at the end of his document, the thirteenth has been redacted. Did Dolbey argue Kotsis's case with O'Toole and get the kind of answer that made clear O'Toole's (like Mulgan's) opposition to types like Kotsis who were part of the right-wing Midas group?

41 For further comments on the case of Kotsis, see also O'Sullivan, LJB 329 and Brown 2011, 101–2. Both cite extracts from Kotsis's letter to Churchill which, according to Brown (101) 'was apparently never sent, but was analysed by SOE'.

42 Gerolymatos 2016, 73. In an earlier publication Gerolymatos gives further details of Kotsis's involvement in early resistance activities. It is worth noting, however, that the source of his information is Kotsis's own book, *Midas 614* (Athens, 1976) (Gerolymatos 1992, 266–67). Woodhouse records that Tsigantes 'certainly had little sympathy with the left. Although he had taken an anti-monarchist course by participating in the 1935 revolution, he had in 1942 sufficiently made his peace with the King of the Hellenes, or at least with his Government, to be sent on an official mission to occupied Athens with their approval' (1948, 37). Kotsis himself stated, at a conference held at the London School of Economics in May 1978, that he 'arrived in Greece in July 1942 with the Tsigantes mission from the Middle East—12 people, though only 6 survived. I am in a position to have direct knowledge of the Don Stott affair since I was in charge of the mission for quite some time, after Tsigantes' murder' (Marion Sarafis 1980b, 103). Hagen Fleischer, who was also at the 1978 conference, challenged the veracity of a number of Kotsis's points. Mamarelis concurs that Midas 614 'was organised by

Midas in his letter.) This group had set off from Lebanon and arrived in Athens in August 1942 with significant financial backing (12,000 sovereigns) from the British, with the aim of forming resistance bands to be sent to the mountains. Early in the occupation, according to Gerolymatos, Kotsis had indeed been given the mission to investigate which of the viaducts was suitable for destruction.[43] In his report Kotsis recommended the Gorgopotamos viaduct, giving details of its structure which were forwarded to Cairo by Tsigantes. His instructions, according to this account, were used for the preparation of the first high-profile sabotage mission to Greece in November 1942, the Harling mission. In light of this information, the rejection of Kotsis's application can perhaps be interpreted as mistrust by Mulgan not so much of the veracity of Kotsis's version of the story but rather of those serving with Midas 614. Despite its significant British support and some preparatory resistance in Athens in the few months of its operation, the Midas group disbanded soon after Tsigantes was killed in a shoot-out with the occupying Italian forces in January 1943; the group never got to the mountains. Clogg records that Tsigantes had been sent into Greece in 1942 to further the ambitions (deemed 'a complete farce' by a leading SOE functionary) of 'quite mythical Royalist organisations' such as the Six Colonels, who turned out to be less interested in resistance than in 'plotting global strategy from Athens' (2000, 156–57).

Mulgan ended up having quite a lot of trouble over the Midas group. We hear him complaining to Dolbey on February 24 that 'Midas is a mess to start with' as he attempts in his work for the Fund to disentangle who assisted SOE, who is rather the exclusive responsibility of the British, and (underlying this) who in his mind was a worthy recipient of compensation. Mulgan stood up to Dolbey in the case of claims for compensation from the EKKA group, whose leader Psarros, as we have seen, was murdered by an ELAS partisan. Although Mulgan shared the shock of many ELAS fighters at this

---

"the Anglo-Greek committee", a joint effort between the British secret services in Cairo and members of the Greek government-in-exile', all of whom were hostile to the left (2014, 90).

43   Initially the plan had been to demolish the Karyon bridge, north of Lamia, but this idea was soon abandoned.

brutal act against a fellow guerrilla, he was not prepared to submit to unjustified pressure from EKKA claimants. Dolbey disagreed: his argument ran as follows in his communication to Mulgan of 1 February:

> a) No claims of guerrilla organisations are recognised by SOELIQ [SOE Liquidation Fund]. But EKKA, although technically an Antartes organisation, was for all practical purposes an artificial organisation created and sponsored by us [. . .]
>
> b) The case of the widow of PSAROS comes under the same condition as given in above para (a). Again, however, we should take into consideration the fact that PSAROS was working almost under our direct orders, that his widow is a well known person in ATHENS, and her sister, Mrs. TSIGANTES, whose husband was killed by the ITALIANS whilst leader of our THURGOLAND [Midas 614] Mission, received a pension of £1050.[44]

Mulgan's reply was measured in tone but nonetheless determined in its opposition to those whose distinction was, as he put it, that they were a 'friend of ENGLAND':

> SOELIQ (MED) [Middle East Division] have laid down that no claims will be recognised from ANTARTE organisations, but only from agents of SOE, or personnel definitely hired by SOE agents. I do not think we can therefore admit any EKKA claims in this category without exposing ourselves to a flood of similar claims from other political and resistance organisations. [. . .] The question of a pension to PSAROS' widow is surely a matter for the GREEK Governor, if it is felt that he died as a friend of ENGLAND, for a present from the BRITISH Government through the Embassy; but certainly not a matter for Force 133. (TNA HS 5/575)

44   Mulgan also probably knew about earlier generosity to the family. On the agenda for the 11th meeting of the Anglo-Greek committee of 30 March 1943 at the office of the Minister of State was the item: 'special grant to the daughter of the late Lieutenant Colonel Tsigantes as a mark of appreciation of her father's service' (TNA HS 5/338).

As far as EKKA's claim for compensation for the maintenance of their wireless set was concerned, Mulgan had reviewed past funding and noted: 'I see that we allowed ZERVAS 200 sovereigns per month on his budget for expenses in connection with the ATHENS set.' With EAM-ELAS, however, Mulgan remembers that the policy was otherwise: 'I think EAM maintained W/T set "NIKO" without funds from us and regarded it as being there for their own convenience'. Anyway, he concludes, it seems that the 'Intelligence' transmitted by the EKKA set was not 'of any value; and I do not think we should admit any claim for it'.

For all his sympathy for Psarros personally, Mulgan was not prepared to let EKKA get preferential treatment because of its 'friendship' with England. The 5/42-EKKA group, Mulgan well knew, had been overtaken by fanatical right-wing and pro-monarchist elements, some of whom had joined the Security Battalions which were at this time (as Geoffrey Gordon-Creed had predicted) taking violent revenge on left-wing resistance fighters. If no compensation was to be awarded to claims from *andartes* from any band, he was not going to see British-backed EKKA made an exception of. Mamarelis and Brown cite this case as evidence that 'Mulgan and Dolbey's disagreement showed that EKKA had not simply been a British stooge' (Brown 2011, 101; Mamarelis 2014, 273–74). But the emphasis should probably be placed elsewhere. Although neither Mulgan nor Dolbey disputed the fact that EKKA had been, as Dolbey put it, 'an artificial organisation created and sponsored by us' and that 'PSAROS was working almost under our direct orders', they disagreed over the extent to which this should qualify it for special compensation. Dolbey seems to have shared the predominant British view of Psarros as an exception, someone they could communicate with, on the same wavelength (Woodhouse's 'the only guerrilla commander who was what the British Army calls an officer and a gentleman' [1948, 85]). Mulgan, we sense, was chafing under such prejudices. We can imagine, too, his not being particularly moved by the fact that the claim for the wireless set had been sent in by Kartalis, Psarros's right-hand man, an 'ex-minister and well known politician', as Dolbey put it. Similarly, Dolbey's 'strong plea' on behalf of Psarros's widow would not have cut much ice. Like Tsigantes's sister, Dolbey urged, Mme Psarros was 'a well known person in Athens'. Mulgan more likely had in mind that Colonel Christodoulos Tsigantes, the other (older) brother, was head of the Sacred Squadron, the band loyal to the Papandreou government which was at this time absorbed under the Allied High Command and soon to merge with the National Army which would oppose the left in the civil war. The original aim of the Psarros-Tsigantes/Midas group, as was well known, had been to unite resistance groups to act as a 'counterweight' to ELAS (Grigoriadis 2011, I, 271–72).[45] Mulgan's resistance to Dolbey's urgings is all the more striking given that, as we have seen, his own actions may have unwittingly contributed to Psarros's death.

In late February Mulgan is still responding to Dolbey's criticism of some of Mulgan's recommendations to do with the Midas group. The tone is conciliatory, perhaps forbearing; his letter begins:

> Your temperate and, I fear well-merited reproach, reached me by our first mail after a snowbound period. I shall try and explain more or less what I think has occurred, realising it must be something more than a nuisance to you if you can't have full confidence in the recommendations that come from here. (24 Feb. 1945. Dobrski 34)

What were the issues this time? Dolbey, in his similarly conciliatory letter of 'reproach' of 21 February,[46] complained that Mulgan wasn't giving enough detail on those of the British-backed Midas group who deserved compensation, and that he'd been slapdash, submitting two separate lists with different recommendations for the same

45 As Mamarelis records, Psarros was originally 'attached to the SIS [British Secret Intelligence Service]-Tsigantes network' (2014, 103).

46 Dolbey concludes with these conciliatory words: 'I hope you will not take all this as a grouse. All the more so as I quite realise that we have often impressed upon you the necessity to speed up liquidation. I only hope that if similar mistakes are occurring on our side you will not fail to point them out to me in order that I may try as much as possible to put matters right' (Dolbey to Mulgan, 21 Feb. 1945 [Dobrski 34]).

person. These lists need careful attention, Dolbey insists, because London intends to compile a 'White List' from this information, 'to cover all Greeks who may be usefully employed by British interests'. Therefore, he continues, 'the fact that a man is at present in employment is no reason why he should not be recommended as suitable for employment by a British firm at a later date'. To assess these claims, he continues, 'we must submit to SOELIQ as many facts as can be gathered either in Athens or in Cairo' (Dolbey to Mulgan, 21 Feb. 1945 [Dobrski 34]).

The issues for Mulgan, however, would have been different—to do, again, with what he calls the 'mess' (in other words, the complex and often troubling political implications) of the Midas operations. His reply to Dolbey continues:

> I sent this lot of record sheets off to you because they're all of little importance and are all recommended for something less than a certificate of service. The main debts of the MIDAS group I have devoted some time to and don't think I will have to alter my last recommendation to you contained in my Adv/133/104/MIDAS of the 21st Feb, 1945. (24 Feb. 1945 [Dobrski 34])

Paul Day reports that the reproach concerned 'stories told by Greeks about their activities which the B.L.Os now in Cairo were unable to substantiate' (1977, 47). But Mulgan's resistance to allocating grants to Midas people is more likely to have been politically motivated. The underlying gist of his argument here, as indicated again in the syntax, goes as follows: *Yes*, apologies for having failed to add anything to these lists of (actually pretty unimportant) Midas claims. *But* I'm not prepared to change my mind about the important issues concerning Midas (such as compensation to Psarros's widow). Blaming it on his own 'impetuosity' can be read as a disingenuous deflection from what was in fact his political instinct. Dolbey, in his letter, has dropped the dark warning that 'in the case of secret operations the onus is almost entirely upon you'. Mulgan promises to 'investigate further'.

Significantly, on March 28 Mulgan doesn't hesitate to express his views to Dolbey on the so-called 'SHEPPARD affair'. Rufus Sheppard, the British academic whom Mulgan was first sent in to join and who later incurred the mistrust of Woodhouse for his faith in EAM-ELAS, had been transferred out of Force 133 to the United Nations Relief and Rehabilitation Administration (UNRRA), where he was appointed chief intelligence officer by the Americans. He was killed soon after, during the *Dekemvriana*, reportedly by a mine laid in Athens by ELAS.[47] The Sheppard 'affair' involved a Greek-American reporter, Constantine Poulos, who was working as a translator for UNRRA and was accused of whipping up further anti-British sympathies in an article in the American press based on documents found on Sheppard at his death. These appear to have been receipts for payments to EAM. As a result of this Poulos was dismissed from UNRRA. Mulgan regarded this affair, followed closely by both the Foreign Office and the Americans, as 'scandalous' (Dobrski 34). On 3 March we find him telling Dolbey that Poulos, with the help of Grigory Popov, had escaped to Bulgaria with the receipts and that he (Mulgan) was attempting to recover them (Dobrski 30). Mulgan, one imagines, was rushing to Sheppard's defence. The British Embassy later cleared Sheppard on the grounds that these were legitimate payments made when he had been earlier employed by SOE.[48]

A related but less personal issue arose around the same time in connection with articles published in the Greek newspaper *I Vradini* which mentioned British agent David Pawson[49] and were considered sufficiently compromising to Britain's reputation for Churchill to order the British military in to close the paper down (Brown 2011, 102–3). In contrast to Dolbey's concern about the *I Vradini* articles,

47   See Chapter 6, note 11.

48   For further details on an anti-British article written by Drew Pearson that seems to underlie this affair, see Clogg 2000, 116–17.

49   Clogg writes: 'One of SOE's key operatives before the occupation in Greece, and subsequently in Izmir, until his capture by the Germans during the ill-fated British attempt to take the Dodecanese in the wake of the Italian armistice in September 1943, was David Pawson. He had lived in Greece since 1933 as an employee of the British-owned Electric Power and Traction Company and had an extensive and useful range of contacts' (1981, 107).

however, Mulgan seems to have been comparatively laid back about the inevitability of press allegations of this sort, with which he probably had a degree of sympathy. On 10 April he writes to Dolbey: 'I am afraid that you may have thought that we have been treating light-heartedly the question of newspaper publications.' But as he sees it, he continues, 'These "I Vradini" articles are only symptoms, notable for their lack of security, of what is appearing daily in the papers. The political situation has deteriorated sharply with the recent successful Right Wing attack on the PLASTIRAS Government. I am afraid that newspapers will continue to be filled with recriminations' (Dobrski 34).

Amidst all these political allegations, some large sums were being distributed by the Liquidation Fund. The total amount distributed, according to one estimate, was around £100,000 (LJB 325), equivalent to around £28 million in today's currency. The documents in the archives contain no lists of names signed by Mulgan. Detailed lists of hundreds of Greek names had been endorsed by Dolbey, but there is no indication as to whether these were compiled by Mulgan (TNA HS 5/363; also BHA 259, 1–2). In any event, the final decision on compensation, in cases where sums exceeding 25 sovereigns were recommended to Cairo, was made by Dolbey and Barker-Benfield, commanding officer of Force 133.[50] A document of 23 August 1945, four months after Mulgan's death, indicates that Peltekis and his associates were being handsomely rewarded: 3,003 gold ingots, to cover 'bonus payments due for H. [Eriko] Moazzo 1,200, I. Mavromatis 1,000, J. Skoulas 750 and 126,860 to balance Dr [Drachmas] to your [Peltekis's] personal account' (BHA 259, 1–2). These were huge sums for the time; many of these individuals were to continue their prominence among the affluent

50   See, for instance, relevant references in the two memoranda by Dolbey (13–16 Feb. and 12–17 Mar. 1945, in Dobrski 30), which include the following: 'the Liq officer [i.e. Mulgan] has been given authority by SOELIQ to settle claims up to £25'; 'It is, however, necessary that Cairo should be immediately informed in all cases where an assessment is altered by the Liq officer'; by 17 March 'About 800 claims were assessed in Athens'; 'Should any agent apply to Adv Force 133 (Liq) no payment will be made until Cairo has been consulted and has given its agreement'. See also Paul Day (1977, 47) for some references to undercover groups to which the Fund was distributed.

middle classes in post-war Athens. Along with them Zervas, for all his debts and unreliability, was rewarded with the post of Minister of Public Order in February 1947, as a member of the Maximos government, a move that resulted, as Sweet-Escott records, in a series of large-scale arrests and deportations into exile of known left-wing sympathisers (1954, 73; Voglis 2002, 61). Zervas's political career was soon cut short, however, after revelations at Nuremberg—at the 'Trial of the Southeastern Generals'—of his wartime contacts with the Wehrmacht occupiers (Mazower 1995, 277).

One last petitioner who did get a sympathetic hearing from Mulgan, so much so that he was given a star role in *Report on Experience*, was Georgios Fafoutis. As his term ran out in the office, Mulgan requested leave from Dolbey to make a trip to Evoia (Euboea) in mid April to 'fix up FAFOUTIS for whom I have a considerable affection'.[51] Fafoutis is the unnamed 'old man' referred to in *Report on Experience* simply as 'Janni', 'instance of individual greatness' (RE 181, 177)—cited to counterbalance the frustrations of dealing with some other Greeks who were proving very tiresome. 'Considerable affection' and 'greatness' were not words that came easily to Mulgan, so it's worth looking a little more closely at this man's profile.

He's hardly romanticised, but this 'one-eyed pirate' (RE 185) had provided valuable assistance to the Allied cause in the early stages of the occupation. From his village on the remote south-east coast of Evoia, Fafoutis carried out several rescue operations of stranded Allied troops and arranged their safe passage, first by caïque from Evoia to Smyrna and then on to Syria or Lebanon. When the call came, Fafoutis would make the 215-kilometre trek to Athens through mountain passes and enemy-controlled terrain to fetch the men. He did this thirteen times, in his estimation, before he was captured in December 1943 and taken to the notorious Averoff prison where, as Mulgan described it to Gabrielle, 'the Germans among other refinements hanged him by one arm and leg for eighteen hours while they beat him so that his left arm is still more or less paralysed' (AGM 299).

---

51   Mulgan to Dolbey, 28 Mar. 1945 (Dobrski 34).

On one of the first operations he undertook, in March 1942, he recounted to Mulgan, Fafoutis was asked to help collect some explosives ('magnetic charges like turtles' [RE 181]) parachuted onto Evoia, then take them on to Athens. His contact was a nameless 'friend that had come from Cairo' (180–81) after hearing of him as a trustworthy patriot. In these operations, he said, 'there are no names here', only 'friends' (183). These same explosives, Fafoutis continued, were used to blow up enemy ships: 'you will have read all about it,' Fafoutis told Mulgan, 'how they sank two large steamers with them in the Piraeus' (181). Mulgan would indeed have known about these early sabotages of German ships in June and July 1942, which disrupted the supply line to the Axis Africa Corps. In a recent book titled *Sabotage in Greece during the Second World War* (2018) Bernard O'Connor identifies these two steamers as the German SS *Plouton*, headed for Libya, and the requisitioned Greek SS *Ardena* carrying German troops between Piraeus and the Dodecanese and Crete (117).[52] After this Fafoutis was approached frequently by this 'friend' who lived in Athens: 'you will know his name so I do not need to tell it to you,' Mulgan records Fafoutis telling him (182).

In the early stages of the resistance several Greek agents were operating out of Athens with help from the British (Section D, set up by the SIS) in Cairo. One of the earliest, the group with which Fafoutis was collaborating, it turns out, was Prometheus or 333, initially under the command of Evripidis Bakirtzis, the 'Red Colonel' whose activities with ELAS and then in PEEA we have detailed in Chapter 4.[53] From mid April 1941, the SIS had provided Bakirtzis with a radio transmitter and explosives in order to maintain contact with occupied Greece and carry out possible sabotages.[54] Reports to

---

52   In fact, it seems that the 'limpet' mines (Fafoutis's 'turtles') failed to go off on several occasions because (as confirmed by agent Ian Pirie), out-of-date fuses had been used. But they were soon replaced by 'other methods' and the two steamers were successfully damaged and put out of action for a time (O'Connor 2018, 117).

53   According to Woodhouse, Bakirtzis 'left Greece clandestinely in the summer of 1942, stating his intention to "make contact with Moscow"' (1971, 348n1). He was, however, persuaded by the British to return to Greece.

54   A report by Peltekis in the Kew archives (TNA HS 5/547) records that 'the most successful of our sabotage and resistance organisations in the ATHENS area was laid on for us during the winter of 1940–41 by Colonel BAKIRDZIS, D.S.O. This officer is now Vice-

another agent working with Prometheus from Cairo, Ian Pirie, relay Prometheus's description of the drop onto Evoia on the night of 2–3 March 1942 that Fafoutis described to Mulgan, when much was lost but two 'limpet' mines were found. These reports to Cairo fill in many of the gaps in Fafoutis's narrative.

This drop onto south-east Evoia was in fact of considerable historical significance as it was the first attempt at an air sortie to Greece, the method which would become standard practice over the following two and a half years. It was not entirely successful, as Prometheus records, because of lack of light due to a total eclipse of the moon: one bale was dropped on a lignite mine at Aliveri, 30 kilometres away, half of the four bales collected were in bad condition, and 'The greatest part of the dropped material fell into the hands of the Italians' (TNA HS 7/151, 176–77). Bakirtzis, Pirie's report notes, was doubtful about whether such drops could continue. But the agent who would soon replace him as 'Prometheus II', Charalampos Koutsoyiannopoulos, was more optimistic, and wrote to Pirie that

> although this dropping proved unsuccessful as such, it was instrumental in proving how it is very well possible to supply groups on the ground from the air, provided the signals on the ground are well recognised by experienced pilots who should effect dropping from the lowest possible altitude, with a perfect system of parachutes and packing.
>
> It was then that the formation of Andartes (Guerilla) bands came first to the surface and could be considered as realisable. (TNA HS 7/151, 178)

Fafoutis and Mulgan would no doubt have talked about the Prometheus group when Fafoutis showed up in the Athens office that day. Both Bakirtzis and Koutsoyiannopoulos were Venizelist

President of the Political Committee in the mountains of Greece of which he was for a short time President. From the late summer of 1941 till early in 1943, the day-to-day management of this organisation was in the hands of Colonel BAKIRDZIS' deputy, Colonel KOUTSOGIANNOPOULOS of the Royal Hellenic Navy.'

officers who had fallen out of favour after participating in the abortive coup in 1935 against the pro-monarchist government. After long service in the resistance, Bakirtzis suffered the fate of many on the left after the war and was sent into exile on the island of Fournoi Korseon, southwest of Samos, where he died, possibly committing suicide, in 1947. Fafoutis's 'friend from Cairo', however, seems to have been neither of these men who were running Prometheus but rather one Elias Deyiannis, a doctor in 'British hospital 63' serving in Prometheus (TNA HS 8/516, 8915).[55] Mulgan naturally avoids names in his book, but describes in detail how the nature of information sharing he had with Fafoutis needed to be conducted in a tavern where the two could sit over a drink and talk more freely than in the office.

Although Fafoutis comes across in Mulgan's narrative as something of a lone maverick, he was in fact a recognised agent who went under the codename Kapetan Barba Petros, or Dimos.[56] He was recruited in 1941 by Pawson and/or Pirie, who, according to his personal file, contacted him, probably after he began assisting Allied soldiers to evacuate soon after the occupation (TNA HS 8/516, 8929). Born in 1890, Fafoutis had eight children and was, it seems, a man of some property on Evoia. Subsequently, it also appears, for all his links with the Red Colonel, he came into conflict with ELAS forces on the island, known to be an ELAS stronghold,[57] although whether this was because he had (according to one report) set up a rival 'nationalist' band is unclear.[58] During his visit to Fafoutis's

55   O'Connor records a request from Koutsoyiannopoulos in December 1941 for arms to be delivered to the monastery near Kymi on Evoia (mentioned by Fafoutis to Mulgan), and that Koutsoyiannopoulos was assisted by Deyiannis and two others (2018, 95, 41).

56   He is elsewhere listed in a Force 133 group called 'BARBARITY' (HS 5/341, 2).

57   As happened in the central mainland mountains of Greece, when the Italians surrendered on Evoia in 1943, local resistance fighters seized their weapons and formed strong ELAS units (more than 2,500 volunteers came forward). Subsequently, heavy fighting took place on the island against both the Germans and the Security Battalions. 'I Evoia sto B' Pangosmio Polemo, 1940–1944'. 2014. eviaportal.gr/eyboia-pagkosmios-polemos-1940-1944/. Date of access 17 Jan. 2020. Evoia was also the home and seat of resistance of one of Greece's most heroic women agents, Lela Karagianni, who began operations in May 1941 and died in Haidari prison where she was executed by firing squad in September 1944.

58   The Fafoutis file (of some 90 pages) also contains a report from early 1945 by Major A.N. Paton, who seems to have regarded some of Fafoutis's stories as 'far-fetched'. One version of

village on Evoia, Mulgan met and talked with his friend's mother, now in her nineties. As for Fafoutis himself, Mulgan told Gabrielle, 'He poor fellow is still in hospital in Athens' (AGM 299). As an agent for the Prometheus group, which had rescued many Allies (including New Zealanders), and one who had withstood torture without betraying his comrades, Fafoutis would naturally have attracted Mulgan's sympathy. After Mulgan's death, he was to lose his benefactor, however, and indeed to have got on the wrong side of Allied authorities. As Brown records, in August 1945 Fafoutis wrote to both Peter Fraser and the Australian Prime Minister asking for financial assistance for further medical treatment. Fraser replied the following April saying Fafoutis's case had been investigated by the Allied Screening Commission, which concluded that he had already received 'appropriate recompense' (2019, 191). But for Mulgan, Fafoutis was 'a man [. . .] among smaller men' (RE 177), one who had shown resourcefulness and indifference to his own safety in exceptionally dangerous circumstances. If Mulgan was a soft touch for this Odyssean narrator, there were deep reasons for his affection.

* * *

Compensation work entailed getting to know a large number of people in the immediately post-liberation scene and as a result becoming deeply involved in Anglo-Greek politics of the time. Mulgan gives very little away, as was proper in his position, but incidental anecdotes occasionally reveal something of what he may have been thinking. One day in March, the New Zealander Tom Barnes, whom he didn't know personally but would have known about because of Barnes's close involvement with Zervas and EDES, came into the office on Amerikis Street. Barnes records their meeting as follows:

> the story is that in September 1943 Fafoutis persuaded Smyrna to request Cairo's permission to issue a wireless transmitter and 500 sovereigns 'for the creation of a nationalist group in Evoia'. This venture failed and resulted in a feud with ELAS who, 'regarding him as a landed proprietor, had earmarked him and his property for special attention'. Paton concludes: 'I am persuaded that Fafoutis earned his own retribution by deliberately encouraging civil war with ELAS' (TNA HS 8/516, 8907).

Back in Athens I called in to see John Mulgan at Advanced Force 133. I had heard about him constantly from Chris [Woodhouse] and Nick Hammond—he was one of the best liaison officers, hugely successful at getting ELAS to go on ops—but as he had been in Thessaly I had never met him. Now we made up for it.

'Cairo are screaming for you, Tom,' he said with an engaging grin.

'Really?' I said. 'Why?'

'Beats me,' he said. 'But you'd better get cracking.'

They met for lunch the next day, but there is no record of what was exchanged between them. Barnes simply notes that after the lunch 'Old Zed saw me in the street as he passed in his car and took me back to his house' (Barnes 2015, 374–75). He was still associating closely with Zervas, although the latter was no longer in good favour with the British on account of his debts and probable dealings with the Germans.[59] But Mulgan, in his usual friendly but knowing way, seems to have assumed that pro-British EDES operatives like Barnes would be more than welcome in Anglo-Greek circles in Cairo as they planned their next moves.

59   Barnes cites from a letter from Woodhouse of 2 February 1945, which warned Barnes to 'feel your way carefully' in relation to Zervas, who is 'still regarded with suspicion and even contempt within our own HQ'. Commenting on the letter, Barnes wrote of how Woodhouse 'would always understand, even if no one else did. Why I loved Zervas (even if what Chris said about his dealings with the Germans was true, which I doubted)' (2015, 370–71).

CHAPTER 9

The Wilson Report

The British are at present trying to give it
[Greece] the status of a second grade colony

—Mulgan to J.V. Wilson, 20 April, 1945

Back in Cairo himself, a month after his meeting with Barnes, Mulgan would have known that his own political sympathies made him far less welcome with the British authorities. He would not have been expecting, however, that these sympathies be put to the immediate test. His plan was to wind up the last details of the Liquidation Fund reports with Dolbey and then transfer to the New Zealand forces, right away from Greek affairs and the British army. But when he arrived on April 19, he was surprised to find waiting for him a letter from the Department of External Affairs in Wellington, requesting his views on the Greek situation. The letter, he noted in a reply the next day to its sender, J.V. Wilson, had taken over two months to reach him—'by what vagary of international air-lines I cannot guess'.[1]

What lay behind this request? The Australian-based historian Martyn Brown, who has researched the New Zealand–Greek wartime connection in depth, has detailed the considerable misgivings Peter Fraser and the Labour government were expressing

---

1   Mulgan to Wilson, 20 Apr. 1945 (ATL, J.V. Wilson Papers. MS-Papers- 6875-2). All further references to the Mulgan–Wilson correspondence at this time, and to Mulgan's report, are from this source.

to London about Britain's handling of the Greek situation. In May, Fraser had felt indignant enough to tell Anthony Eden that supporting the establishment of unpopular European monarchies in the newly liberated countries (Greece, Yugoslavia and Italy) was 'a mistake of the first magnitude' (Brown 2011, 98). And then on 22 December, with union protests and outraged press reactions fuelling the response to the news of British (and some New Zealand) soldiers firing on Greeks in the streets of Athens, exacerbated by Churchill's statement in the Commons that the commonwealth dominions had been consulted over military action in Greece, Fraser sent London a carefully worded telegram of protest:

> The special circumstance that New Zealanders fought in Greece and formed a particularly close attachment to the Greek people renders especially repugnant the adoption of forcible measures against the population. I know that similar feelings are also entertained by the British Government and people. (Brown 2019, 245)[2]

Brown adds that

> Churchill responded to Fraser two days after the latter sent his telegram of protest. He did not answer the essential question about the monarchy (not even the possibility of a plebiscite was considered) but related developments around the issue of appointing a Regent. Churchill was pursuing the standard British diplomatic practice of not 'consulting' with the Dominions [. . .] Frustrated that Churchill's answer did not address the issues raised, Wellington considered other options to gain intelligence about the situation in Greece. (2011, 99)

2   Fraser to Secretary of State for Dominion Affairs, London, 20 Dec. 1944. Alister McIntosh of External Affairs in Wellington, on whose behalf J.V. Wilson was soon to ask Mulgan for his views, wrote to a colleague in Moscow the next day that 'The situation is a most unfortunate one, and we appear to be well offside in the view of all radicals in all countries. Trade Union circles here have not been behindhand with their criticism, and we receive a number of telegrams every day or so' (Brown 2019, 245). For a short summary of the New Zealand reaction, see Brown 2011, 97–99.

General Bernard Freyberg (who had led the New Zealand Expeditionary Force in the Battle of Crete, the North African campaign and the Italian campaign) was apparently proposed by Wilson as a source of intelligence but ruled out on the grounds that he was an officer of Field Marshal Alexander, who had been directing the British operations in Athens (Brown 2011, 99) and therefore hardly in a position to offer an independent opinion. It was at this point that Mulgan was proposed.

Letting down his guard

Although this was to be an official intelligence report to the New Zealand government, Mulgan's friendship with Wilson meant it would go through personal mediation. He had met Joseph Wilson several times before the war, first in Oxford and then, in September 1936, as a young New Zealand delegate to the meeting of the League of Nations in Geneva. A career diplomat based in Geneva at the time, Wilson was with him at the briefing in London for the New Zealand contingent and seems to have been on the same wavelength. In Geneva the two spent 'a good deal of' time together (AGM 109). A generation older than Mulgan (he had fought, with distinction, in WW1), Wilson seems to have shared the scepticism of many in the Labour Party about the impartiality of Britain's interests in the region. In a memo of 29 December 1944 to his boss in the Department of External Affairs, Alister McIntosh, Wilson made the astute observation that Britain 'will use force not against those whom she dislikes on ideological grounds but against those who interfere with [her] objectives' (Brown 2019, 248). In replying to Wilson's request, Mulgan seems to have assumed a sympathetic ear from his friend, who would have listened with a very different perspective from those in the Rustum Buildings who had received his previous reports to HQ. He hastened the next day to send a long letter to Wilson explaining the delayed receipt of the request, and promising to send a short summary of what he'd observed in Greece within the next couple of days.

In the event, his account was not a short summary but rather four and a half single-spaced typed pages (around 4,000 words) of considerable detail. Addressed to the New Zealand Department of External Affairs on 22 April, three days before his death, this account is by far the most candid expression of Mulgan's political views at the time.

In the 20 April letter Mulgan confesses to ignorance about the situation in other parts of Greece (Macedonia, the Peloponnese, the islands). The report itself, however, reveals a nuanced and deeply informed knowledge of the historical and political background of central mainland Greece; for its time, it constitutes a rare Anglophone assessment of past conditions and ideological complexities in the area. There is no idealising here, but rather a plain-speaking insider's view of the choices the Greeks had before them. Probably because of his quiet practicality and preparedness to keep his head down, Mulgan had managed to stay on in the mountains without being peremptorily removed, as several of his predecessors critical of British policy (Gordon-Creed, Sheppard, O'Toole) had been over the past year or so. Now at liberty to report with greater candour, he describes the radical political experiment which took place around him from the point of view of someone who assumed that social revolution was not only possible but necessary.

The report begins with a description of Greece's 'bare peasant economy' and lack of industry (and hence of a proletariat), presenting an economic challenge the Greeks are ill prepared to face 'if the Communists come to power' (1). But the political will for national independence is there, with all its bravado; with a few drinks in them, Mulgan comments, the partisans are apt to start talking about 'marching an army into Sofia' to take on the Bulgarians (1), who like so many other nations are always ready to undermine Greece's national sovereignty. But nationalism aside, it is communism once again which is Mulgan's topic: its trials, its failures and its promise. The myth of the Moscow peril is dismissed by him as scornfully here as it was nine years previously. He had seen how, immediately after the liberation, Stalin ordered the Bulgarian troops to retreat from

Greece back to Sofia. And EAM-ELAS commanders had known for some time that Stalin was offering them no encouragement to rebel against the Allies. A few ignorant Greeks, he writes, especially the middle classes in Athens, were inclined to suspect that the British were preparing (with the help of the Greeks) 'to fight the Russians' if and when they arrived on the northern borders (1). Most, however, did not buy into this myth. He doesn't mention this in the report, but in the questionnaire back in August he had responded to the question about Greek attitudes to Russia and communism by reminding his commanders in Cairo that the affiliation with Russia had a long-term historical basis in Greece, given Russia's support for the Greek revolution against the Turks the previous century.

When it comes to partisan leaders, Mulgan again represents a contrast to other BLOs by not dismissing the EAM movement as a whole on the basis of reports of individual brutality. It was 'the communist ARES VELOUCHIOTIS', he writes, who organised 'the first [resistance] band to take to the hills' (1). In describing Aris to the New Zealand Ministry, Mulgan doesn't shy away from Aris's brutality, or at least the rumours of it. But he had met Aris himself on numerous occasions and sums him up with a genuine respect: 'He afterwards achieved something of a reputation as a killer—of Greeks, not Germans—but is by his early history a fine natural guerrila [*sic*] leader' who couldn't be bought off with sovereigns or got friendly with over a drink, as you could with other 'non-political' partisan leaders. Clever and taciturn, Aris stood, in Mulgan's eyes, for that 'good standard type of Balkan communist' (2), the ideologue who was attempting to shape Greece in a different direction long term. Using Eudes's terms here to flesh out Mulgan's description, we might say that Aris represented the 'peasant' faction of EAM, as opposed to the Stalin-influenced members in the Central Committee who had spent time in Moscow. This 'other type of Greek communist', described by Mulgan in the next paragraph, would also have crossed paths with him in the mountains on many occasions. The three names he mentions here, Siantos, 'Pantselides' (i.e., Partsalidis) and 'Karageorgos' (Karagiorgis), were all influential in Thessaly and Roumeli in Mulgan's time.[3] Unlike Aris, he explains, these men were highly educated[4] and well travelled, and didn't circulate with a belt full of knives and pistols. They were, perhaps, rather like Mulgan himself, although they were only 'superficially friendly' to this 'British' officer and were 'in practice undeviating' in their ideological aims (2). Mulgan may, like Tsamakos, have found these hard-line communist comrades somewhat 'μυστήριους' (strange or inscrutable) types (Haritopoulos 2003, 356). But he would have understood them and, unlike Woodhouse, had no need to bluff in his friendship with them. Mulgan would also have understood their reticence in relation to the British, given what he describes as the British 'attempt to dissociate E.L.A.S. from its political control' (3). After October 1943, he records, 'relations between the British and E.L.A.S. were at best uneasy and most of the time very bad' (3). Mulgan was, of course, an exception to this, though he doesn't say he regarded himself as such.

Napoleon Zervas, leader of the rival band EDES, is, however, given short shrift in the report. Although like Aris he could be described as 'a good natural guerilla leader', 'the type of cheerful scoundrel that it pays to employ in war-time', the payment in his case was literal: 'He has not been empoverished [*sic*] by the war' (2). His table manners are better than Aris's, 'which tends to endear him to British officers.' But the overall assessment is damning, as it became in time by Zervas's own British supporters. It was 'a mistake', Mulgan concludes, for the British 'to lean heavily upon him or build him up as the leader of a non-communist resistance movement' (2). Zervas was, at the time of the report's writing, in Athens with a clean-shaven face and running 'a political office—policy unknown' (2). Mulgan may have heard about these unknown policies from Barnes at lunch that day, when the conversation is likely to have turned to Old Zed's

---

3   The first two, Siantos and Partsalidis, along with Tsirimokos, represented EAM in meetings with the Greek government after the *Dekemvriana* and the surrender of EAM-ELAS, signing the Varkiza Agreement in Athens on 12 February 1945.

4   Although Aris was not uneducated: born in 1905, he had attended the Averophia Agricultural Middle School in Larissa and worked for a time as a teacher. In 1928 he was a journalist on the paper *Rizospastis*.

loss of British support after reports of his dealings with General von Lanz in Yannina (Barnes 2015, 365). Barnes was to remain loyal to the last, but Mulgan, as always, was deeply suspicious of anyone in it for material gain.[5]

Like Greek commentators on the left, Mulgan repeats in the report that of the around 50,000 ELAS partisans, only a small percentage (around 1,000) were originally communists, though many more had since joined the party. Their organisation, especially after the formation of PEEA (although even at this late stage he doesn't name the organisation), which had its own police and secret police, 'kept everyone in line quite effectively' (3). You could dismiss the movement, if that was your politics, he argues, 'but you could not deny its efficiency. So large a movement could not depend entirely on terrorism' (3). Here, Mulgan is laying his cards on the table, as denunciation of EAM-ELAS, in both Greece and abroad, was at this time dependent on the 'terrorist' label to justify its suppression. Its support, he continues, varied in different regions, and he proceeds to give details of the particular geopolitical conditions in the Peloponnese (conservative and royalist), Macedonia (complicated by anti-Slav sentiment, in spite of links with Tito and Bulgarian communism) and Athens (where it flourished among the dock workers in Piraeus). But in his area EAM-ELAS 'was very much a popular movement, shared in and believed in by a majority of the people' (3).

When it comes to the December events, Mulgan speaks in terms of civil war rather than British intervention, following the British policy of putting those Greeks they supported in the front line of battle against ELAS:

> When I left Greece in November 1944, E.A.M-E.L.A.S. were in control of all Greece except a small circle round the Grande-Bretagne hotel in Athens where the Papandreou government was functioning. On the whole they were behaving very well but it

5   For details on how Zervas's financial dealings were known at the time and a source of embarrassment to the British, see Brown 2011, 105–6.

was quite clear that they were not going to surrender their control peacefully. When the civil war started on 6 December 44, the E.L.A.S. partisans began very cheerfully to fight the Athens police and the right-wing Sacred squadron whom they regarded as their natural enemies. They were hurt and many of them, I think, reluctant at first to fight the English. After a week or two, however, with the bitterness that belongs to all civil wars, they had developed a fair degree of hatred for British soldiers and some of them probably retain it now. (4)

From a popular movement dominating the country, EAM-ELAS had been outmanoeuvred by superior military forces in the capital and forced to choose between surrender or a return to guerrilla tactics. A period of superficial calm prevailed after the nominal surrender, he writes, but Mulgan could see that civil war was inevitable.

As he moves to a conclusion, Mulgan shifts from descriptive to predictive and sometimes advisory mode. In retrospect, he states, 'There is a good argument for saying that the British should have supported them [EAM-ELAS] from the beginning, and probably fewer people would have been killed if the British had done this' (4). But this could not have been achieved without consequences: 'it would be unrealistic to do this in the name of democracy' (4) (note that he writes 'would be' rather than 'would have been'). He takes this one step further:

> There is very little to be said for the professional right-wing politicians who are now forming successive governments in Greece. They are without understanding of the problem that they face and without responsibility in facing it. They are all very old men and go back to a different era when revolutions were planned in coffee-houses and carried out without bloodshed. (5)

A new era may require something much more radical—even, he was prepared to concede, if it meant dispensing with elections, at least in the meantime. For all the 'socialistic' elements in the movement, which had dominated early on, which Mulgan himself preferred, and which he predicted (over-optimistically) would prevail eventually, the movement had been forced to take a hard-line approach in response to developments. If elections were to be held, EAM would probably do badly, he predicted correctly, because of the now prevailing fear of its bitter determination. Elections (under British control) would result in more of the same (British-supported anti-EAM sentiment) for a while, but voters will eventually 'go left again' in accordance with those elements of EAM-ELAS that brought it to national dominance in the first place (5). In the longer term, as he saw it, 'Greece will be anti-monarchist and I am afraid anti-British, or at least against those British who have been concerned with their present politics' (5). He could never have predicted how much longer this would take, that it was only with the ousting of the colonels, or even the fall of the Berlin Wall, that criticism of the British handling of Greece would become mainstream in historical accounts, both inside and outside the country.

The last paragraph of the report, in which he most radically distances himself from these 'present politics', contains his most candid and personal statement:

> The Communist party in Greece has a good future, with or without Russian support, because it has a good organisation and discipline and knows where it is going. If I were a young man in Greece now, I would be tempted to join it with the idea of trying to ameliorate it from within (5)

—by helping, among other things, to eliminate the elements of 'village thug[gery]' which compromise it. In this conclusion, Mulgan raises the tone and opens the topic out to the future, in much the same way he does at the end of *Report on Experience*. Joining the party would have the double advantage, he continues, of staving off 'despair with its antithesis on the right' as well as allowing one to be part of something which is 'likely to come to power sooner or later' anyway (5). In any event, he concludes, the 'brave new world' ahead needs a clean sweep—with the help of an ameliorated communist movement, particularly one willing to collaborate with 'left-wing liberals'. For all this brave talk, however, part of him must have feared that what he calls the 'good' 'top men' in the EAM movement (5) (he would have had in mind Tsamakos, Sarafis, Svolos, Bakirtzis) were likely to be in for a very rough time ahead.

In this report to Wilson, in other words, the British are held to account on a range of different levels, above all for their failure to understand the will of the Greek people. But the main thrust of Mulgan's oppositional stance comes in the 20 April letter to Wilson, sent two days before he dispatched the report. Whereas the report focuses in some detail on describing the situation in Greece, the letter concentrates on the British handling of the situation. With his knowledge of the recent New Zealand opposition to Britain's role in the *Dekemvriana*, Mulgan clearly feels free to make no bones about the fact that, as he sees it, the British are trying to give Greece 'the status of a second grade colony.' What Greece needs, he writes, is a 'period of quarantine under the potential military government of a remote and disinterested nation' (which Britain most certainly was not). Did he have New Zealand as an ideal candidate at the back of his mind?

> You have probably heard from other sources [he tells Wilson] of the great friendship that has grown up in the war between Greeks and New Zealanders. This seems to have arisen partly through circumstances and partly through a natural affinity of the countries, geographical and otherwise. Also I think that the Greeks recognise in New Zealanders all the qualities that they admire in the English and know at the same time that New Zealand is a small country that is not going to interfere in their politics, so that the friendship can be disinterested as it can't be with the English.

Yes, he repeats, the Greek resistance, at least against the Germans (though not against the Italians), was pretty much a 'farce' in military terms.[6] But, he continues, the Greeks have suffered from the Germans 'as if their resistance had been paying heavy dividends.' This, he concludes 'has always made me personally a little humble in judging them and a little sceptical of wholesale condemnation.' (The tight-lipped repetition of 'a little' here only serves to enforce the scepticism.) Condemnation of ELAS was of course by now official policy at SOE Headquarters.

The report's recommendations were hardly firebrand stuff, far less radical than some in EAM would have proposed. Mulgan wasn't recommending outright revolution, only pointing out (in characteristic moderate tones) its not undesirable likelihood, given present conditions. Was he irresponsible to do this, or at best naïve? Was this another example of the mutiny he had staged at the end of his time in the regular army? He had got away with it then, but now, as a member of a clandestine operation, things were different. Mulgan knew he was on dangerous ground: he had confessed as much to his family. But we sense the personal need to come clean after so many months of silence, to speak out about his 'noble and regrettably intimate acquaintance with EAM-ELAS' and to write things down in plain terms, without prevarication—in the name of 'history' as he sees it. What he has to say may be out of date, he apologises to Wilson in the letter, 'but since we make history daily it's only just that we should make archives at the same time.' It is as if he feels that his viewpoint is to a certain extent unique, or at least specific to a unique experience, and that given his addressee,

6   In the report itself Mulgan repeats what he had said to Dolbey on 28 January, that 'It would be untrue to say, as Churchill in fact did say, that E.L.A.S. did no fighting against the Germans, but they did very little' (3)—although, he writes, they did a considerable amount against the Italians. He gives an astute assessment of the reasons for this. First, on an individual level the partisans were terrified of the Germans (and he would have had the reprisals in mind here). Second, the movement had got too large to control militarily. And finally, from the end of 1943 onwards it was clear to the EAM directorate that the Germans would soon be defeated, so that what mattered was Greece's future in a post-war era (3–4). He also repeats the point made in *Report on Experience* that although the Greek partisan movement may not have been of great military worth, 'The Germans acted nevertheless as if E.L.A.S. was a major enemy and made clearing drives and burned villages all over Greece'. In his estimation, around 1,000 villages were destroyed and 50,000 Greeks killed or starved to death under German occupation (4). The constant need to insist on these points indicates what Mulgan was up against.

he can express his views less obliquely, without too many layers of ambiguity. All the same, in the short cover letter that went off with the report (on 22 April) Mulgan warns Wilson that although he estimates that 'Little secrecy is infringed by anything I've written here', still he'll leave it to Wilson to restrict its circulation as he thinks best, 'since as an army officer I'm not officially free to write or express my views without censorship.' The risk, though, must have seemed worth taking.

Passage through the censors

As it left Mulgan's hands, the bulky report to the New Zealand government would have been of considerable interest to the British, attempting to keep their colonial allies onside at this sensitive time. That he wasn't 'officially free to write or express [his] views without censorship' was something of an understatement. He would have been well aware of the heavy censorship to which all correspondence was subjected. Detailing the activities of MI5 in Cairo, Ben Macintyre describes how it was well known in the city that journalists' reports had to be vetted by three consecutive officers before being dispatched (2010, 13–14, 85–87).[7] The correspondence of Force 133 officers would have been even more stringently vetted. But as he prepared to transfer to the New Zealand division in a post-war climate, the necessity for caution may not have worried Mulgan quite so much.

The first to be informed of his revelations was almost certainly Julian Dolbey. Dolbey's view of Mulgan seems to have shifted gradually between November '44 and April '45. We have the reference he wrote for Mulgan on 15 November, in which he recommends him in very high terms in support of Mulgan's request for transfer to the New Zealand forces. Assessing Mulgan's time in Greece, Dolbey writes:

> Since the beginning of the year 1944 he has been Area Comd
> [Commander] in ROUMELI and has done extremely well during

---

7   See also Cooper 1989, 183.

all the operations. He is thought of very highly by his brother officers. His promotion to Lt Col whilst he was Area Comd is at present under consideration by SO(M).

If and when he is transferred to the Far East with the New Zealand forces, as seems likely, Dolbey concludes, 'In view of his capability, efficiency and experience gained in GREECE his services would no doubt be of use to SOE, FAR EAST, if required' (TNA HS 9/1073/3). He would at least be 'of use' outside Greece.

But if Dolbey, like Woodhouse earlier, had undergone a change of heart, there is no direct evidence of this; the little declassified correspondence available maintains formal cordiality. However, Mulgan's behaviour after his last meeting with Dolbey on the night of the 25th seemed to a couple of people he met to be uncharacteristically tense. Before he went in to Dolbey's office in Garden City (HQ of Force 133) some time around 6.30–7.00 pm, Mulgan chatted with Major Wilfred Angus from the office, who later reported only that Mulgan confirmed he would visit NZHQ at Maadi the following morning in connection with his transfer.[8] Immediately after the meeting with Dolbey, as reported by Edmonds to Vincent O'Sullivan in later years, 'as he left Garden City John ran into the genial Arthur Edmonds. They went briefly to a bar where John struck his old colleague as a touch subdued' (LJB 335–36). Back at the Continental Hotel, as his friend Christine Atherton recorded at the inquest, unlike on the preceding evenings he 'seemed very restless and worried', though he brushed off her concern (ATL, 7906–40). 'All the time he was in my room,' she recorded in an earlier statement, 'he did not appear to be his normal self.'[9] Had Dolbey given Mulgan a dressing down, or an ultimatum, over what was in all likelihood his intercepted report to Wilson? The request from Wilson had arrived puzzlingly late, no doubt after

8   Report of G.A. Murray to the Assistant Provost Marshall, 6 May 1945, 3 (ATL MS-Papers-7906-40). In his statement of 27 April, Angus said that Mulgan 'has at no time indicated that he was ill or depressed, on the contrary he looked an extremely well built and fit man' (ATL MS-Papers-7906-40).

9   Christine Atherton, statement of 29 Apr. 1945 TNA FO 841/524.

careful scrutiny in various quarters; the intelligence bureau would have been on the alert.[10] The completed report would not have done anything to reassure British authorities, further compromising as it did their already tarnished reputation in relation to the handling of the Greek situation. But after his final meeting with Mulgan, Julian Dolbey—whatever he had said—did what he had to do and remained silent.

Twenty years after the war, Paul Day wrote to Dolbey (now calling himself Colonel Dobrski and living in Switzerland) to get his views of Mulgan for inclusion in the biography he was writing for Twayne Publishers in New York. Dolbey's reply emphasised the absence, to the last, of 'any sign of a worried or deranged mind. Quite the contrary', he said. Further on he repeats this: 'The strongest argument against suicide is John's normal, sensible and sane behaviour during the period December 1944 to April 1945. At no time in these four months did he give even an indication of being worried and not in full control of himself'. The only time he noticed anything strange, he records, was with Mulgan's unwillingness to reveal why he was initially reluctant to return to Greece to serve in the office for the Liquidation Fund (Dolbey to Day, 3 April 1964. [Dobrski 34]). (Mulgan was clearly unwilling to share his sympathy for EAM-ELAS with his commander.) He gives no indication of any disagreement between the two on the night of April 25. From time to time, especially at the beginning, Dolbey had expressed reservations about the official verdict on the cause of Mulgan's death, although this has been interpreted as an attempt to deflect attention away from suicide to protect the family in New Zealand, as requested in the suicide letter to Dolbey found by Mulgan's bed.[11]

This retrospective (two-decades-old) assessment of Mulgan's

---

10   In the last months of his life Mulgan was almost certainly kept under observation by the Security Service. In March 1944, John Senter was head of SOE Security Section in Cairo and warned James Klugmann, under suspicion for his left-wing views, that 'the organization [SOE] was reviewing carefully all cases where an officer's political sympathies might be so extreme as to create a situation of divided loyalty' (Bailey 2007, 82).

11   The full letter is reproduced in Appendix B here. Paul Day records: 'It appears that Dolbey attempted to go some way to acquiescing in Mulgan's request to hush up his suicide' (1977, 52).

character makes a point of emphasising the New Zealander's 'objectivity'. Dolbey repeats the idea, in fact, three times. His first impression of Mulgan was, he writes, 'of a very objective man, experienced above his years, and gifted with a sound and balanced judgement of people and situations'. When he renewed acquaintance with him in Cairo, Dolbey continues, he chose Mulgan as 'by far the best officer for the job' of heading the Liquidation Fund office in Athens. The reason for this, he says, is that 'Too many of our BLO's who had now come out of Greece lacked the objectivity and judgement required to investigate the record of the Greeks who had worked for our missions'. The BLOs, as he would have known only too well, developed an unfortunate tendency to take sides with one or other political group. But not Mulgan: 'What attracted me most to John Mulgan in those days was his unusually objective approach to any problem. He seemed to analyze carefully in his mind every possible fact and aspect of any question being discussed before reaching conclusions of his own in a curiously detached, almost clinical, way' (Dobrski 34).

The comment tells us more, perhaps, about the relationship between the two men than about Mulgan himself. This 'curious detachment' was perhaps Mulgan's strategy for survival in employment which promoted a politics he had come to deplore. By now he was certainly being far from objective in communications to those he trusted, or else those he knew might share his views (Gabrielle, J.V. Wilson, Hadas, etc.). It's hard to believe, though, that Dolbey had had no indication of Mulgan's clear preference for the Greek left. And given Dolbey's enduring fidelity to British interests, he must surely have shared Woodhouse's view that Mulgan, like Rufus Sheppard, had been thoroughly 'hoodwinked' by EAM-ELAS. Mulgan could survive in the system provided he kept his opinions to himself and remained 'objective'. But in the Wilson report he had let down his guard. With so much emphasis on Mulgan's impartiality in the long letter to Day, then, was it perhaps a matter rather of Mulgan's now-revealed *partiality* that was at issue? There's a sense about it of the gentleman protesting too much. As head of

SOE Intelligence, Dolbey's profession allowed him no licence for the expression of political opinions, his own or anyone else's. It was his job to maintain policy and paste over opposition from within.

In the years that followed, Dolbey continued to hover over information about Mulgan's last months. When Oxford University Press was considering issues of security and possible libel in relation to the publication in 1947 of *Report on Experience*, the Press's representative Geoffrey Cumberlege contacted Dolbey. In the letter to Paul Day in April 1964 Dolbey writes: 'I assume that your wife [Gabrielle Mulgan, now Gabrielle Day] is aware that in 1946 I had several meetings with Mr. Cumberlege of the Oxford University Press in connection with the editing of "Report on Experience"' (Dobrski 34/4).[12] His interventions, over 'several meetings', may or may not have included excisions apart from the offending 'Colonel episode'.[13] Dolbey would perhaps have been less concerned about the passages (restored in the 2010 edition) criticising officers Mulgan had served under in the regular army. But he would certainly have wanted to scrutinise what Mulgan said about the operations of SOE (Force 133) and the Liquidation Fund office (Advanced Force 133). Others consulted, as Peter Whiteford records, include Chris Woodhouse and the War Office (Mulgan 2010, 24, 21–22).[14]

Further on in the 1964 letter to Day, Dolbey gives his reply to

12   Dolbey continues: 'My memory of events was fresher then than now and I was therefore possibly in a position to give him better detailed information, as well as some papers and documents. But no doubt you have already been in contact with him' (Dobrski 34/4). In his 'Introduction: The Textual History' to the book, Whiteford makes use of important correspondence relating to the publication of *Report on Experience* held in the Alexander Turnbull Library (MS-Papers-7906-50). Significantly, correspondence with Dolbey is not recorded here. Whiteford simply notes that 'Cumberlege proposed showing it [the MS] to Colonel Dolbey (although there is no evidence whether he did so or not)' (2010, 22). Dolbey would probably have kept evidence of his involvement out of the archives at the time. It was only after a couple of decades that he felt able to reveal his hand in the publication.

13   One excision that suggests Dolbey's hand occurs in relation to the 'old man' (Fafoutis) Mulgan accompanied out of the 'military office' (i.e., the Liquidation Fund office) whose story Mulgan wanted to hear 'because that was the work I was doing then' (RE 178, 178n169). This last phrase identifies Mulgan with Adv. Force 133 work, which the (by then disbanded) SOE would have wanted to avoid.

14   Whiteford also records that General Freyberg had been consulted and had advised against publication of the criticism of the colonels. He notes that it was probably Dan Davin, who had served under Freyberg and was now working for the Press, who had suggested seeking Freyberg's advice (2010, 22n11).

Day's question about his impression of Mulgan's character as follows:

> For additional information, please see the foreword of Mr. Jack
> Bennett to 'Report on Experience'. I fully agree with every word
> of it. All the more so as I was given a chance by the Oxford Press
> to comment on the draft before publication. (Dobrski 34)

Does this mean he also intervened in Bennett's Foreword? He seems
to suggest as much. As guardian of the Mulgan story, his reach
seems to have been extensive. Bennett's Foreword to the first edition,
not reprinted in the 2010 edition, maintains a careful discretion,
simply stating that Mulgan was 'typical of all that was honest and
uncompromising in an uneasy generation' and that he had 'more
fellow-feeling than most of us for the intransigent and the rebel'
(Bennett 1947, vi, vii).

* * *

One last question seems necessary at this point, concerning
the trip Mulgan made in the last few days of his life to see Paul
Contomichalos, the Egyptian Greek who had served as his interpreter
in the mountains. Did this have anything to do with his 'regrettably
intimate acquaintance' with or 'fellow-feeling' for EAM-ELAS?

Contomichalos was the son of an established Greek trader and,
like many of the Greeks in Egypt and elsewhere in the Middle East,
had volunteered to join the Allied army.[15] Arthur Edmonds describes
how in August 1943 his own interpreter, George Karadjopoulos,
taking advantage of the rapid growth in SOE support for all three
bands (ELAS, EDES and EKKA), went to Athens from Roumeli
to recruit other young men like himself who had attended private

---

15 The Greek population in Egypt in the 1930s numbered approximately 150,000—see
Nefeloudis 1981, II, 236–38; also the census of 1937 in Soulogiannis 2009. Most Egyptian
Greeks had enlisted to form (along with military evacuees from Greece) the two Greek
brigades. Units of these brigades had taken part in battles in the desert and the 1st Brigade
had fought at El Alamein. But after the spate of left-wing rebellions in their forces from spring
1943 onwards, mentioned in an earlier chapter, these brigades were disbanded by the British
and replaced by a brigade of nearly 4,000 right-wing privates and officers.

schools in Athens or had a bilingual background. Contomichalos, who told Paul Day in a letter of 1965 that he arrived in the mountains from Athens in August immediately before Mulgan (ATL MS-Papers-7906-42), was probably recruited with this group.

Most of the interpreters for BLOs serving with the partisans were volunteers, and there is some evidence that the *andarte* band they joined was a matter of political choice. Polarisation between EDES and ELAS was by now deeply entrenched in this area,[16] and those agreeing to serve in ELAS areas like Mulgan's would have done so with open eyes. Nicholas Hammond recounts the story of one interpreter sent in to work with ELAS who had to be rescued from his post after expressing opposition to the band's policies (1983, 137).

In existing lists of interpreters in the archives, Contomichalos's name does not appear with those on the payroll of the British. This may mean he was recruited outside normal procedures, although a number of interpreters were not registered officially by the British administration in order to prevent future claims for compensation (Hammond 1983, 137).

It is known that the Mission required interpreters to accompany BLOs for verification during negotiations with the *andartes*. Mulgan and Contomichalos travelled together extensively from village to village throughout the following year: 'to Paliokastro [HQ of ELAS's 13th Division] with Paul' is a frequent refrain in Mulgan's diary. Contomichalos's admiration for Mulgan, his 'even tempered' and 'gentle' manner, his stamina, comes across in everything he writes to Day. 'John Mulgan loved his job,' he writes, 'and was, I believe, one of the most popular Allied officers in this region.' But not a trace of reference is made to the politics the two were clearly involved in. This caution suggests that he was still under oath. Large numbers of Egyptian Greeks who volunteered were known to be of left-wing

16   Edmonds's testimony from August 1943 is characteristic:

I was amused to learn that Zervas had asked the Brigadier [Myers] to replace me because I was 'anti-EDES'. It seemed that Greek passions were so stirred by political viewpoints that it was considered impossible, even for a member of the British Military Mission, to remain disinterested and 'neutral' and because I was not anxious to see EDES outnumber ELAS in my area, EDES considered me to be against them and probably a communist. (1998, 132)

sympathies, and Mulgan's trip to visit his friend in Alexandria could well have been prompted by concern for his well-being at this time of harsh right-wing retribution. But as with so much about the last months of Mulgan's life, these conjectures have yet to be verified.

CHAPTER 10

Who was Christine Atherton?

> *[SOE] [a]gents had to accept one another*
> *without the usual background of information as*
> *to country of origin, family or past experiences.*
> *All the usual small exchanges which go to the*
> *gradual building up of a relationship were*
> *eschewed, so that friendship, desire and even*
> *love under these hothouse conditions blossomed*
> *rapidly, and as quickly faded and died.*
>
> —Masson 1975, 130–31

At this point, in the last days of Mulgan's life, gaps in the story loom large. A key witness at the legal investigations into his death on April 26, 1945, and the recipient of one of the three letters found in the room with his body, was a woman calling herself Christine Atherton. We have been unable to find any trace of this name in the archives, although she was clearly something more than a private Cairene citizen. Given this lack of information, conjecture necessarily becomes part of the narrative. Who was she, what was her connection with Mulgan, and what was she doing in Cairo? Without documentation, we can only hypothesise as to her identity and role as we explore the social atmosphere amongst the agents of irregular warfare in the city Mulgan was briefly immersed in before his death. It was an atmosphere rife with gossip and intrigue, but also shrouded in considerable secrecy.

When Mulgan came to Cairo from the Greek mountains back

in November 1944, an American naval officer introduced him to a Polish 'widow' named Christine Atherton.[1] There is no record of how often they met before Mulgan returned to Greece in January; perhaps it was only a few times. But on his return to Cairo from the Athens office the following April, the contact was renewed. Atherton records in her testimony that they spent the evenings of 19–22 April together before he left for the two-day trip to Alexandria (to see Contomichalos). Then, on the night he died, as his biographers have recorded, they had a few drinks in her room at the Continental Hotel, where they were both staying, before he left at 9.15 pm.[2] After the initial inquiry in late April and the inquest in September 1945 there is no record of her anywhere: no description, no photo, and no reliable indication of what happened to her. In her statement four days after Mulgan's death she signs herself as 'C. Atherton'. But in her affidavit at the inquest in September, her name appears as Gustava Krystyna Atheston (with an 's') (TNA HS 9/1073/3). 'Gustava', in Polish nomenclature, is the genitive form of a husband's first name (Gustav).

It appears likely that Atherton was working at the time for SOE. Julian Dolbey knew quite a lot about her, although this could perhaps be explained by their shared participation in Polish circles

1   Atherton's evidence at the inquest in September 1945, where she was sworn in as 'Gustava Krystyna Atheston [*sic*], widow, Continental Hotel, Cairo' (ATL 7906-40). The American naval officer may have been Ernest Ramsaur, whom O'Sullivan mentions as being close to Mulgan at the time (LJB 324).

2   The evidence of Christine Atherton about Mulgan's last hours, both in her affidavit of 29 April ('Report on Evidence to the Assistant Provost Marshall, Special Investigation Branch, 17 Area, Cairo'—henceforth referred to as 'Report') (TNA FO 841/524) and at the September inquest (ATL MS-Papers-7906-40), ran as follows. When she met him in the corridor of the Continental around 8 pm on 25 April, they went to her room where they had drinks (two double whiskies); he drank his own and half of hers and had a sandwich. On previous evenings (19–22 April) he had 'seemed to be quite normal and glad to have left Greece. He spoke about joining the New Zealand army in Italy. He did not seem depressed or worried' (Inquest). But on the night of the 25th he seemed, she said, 'very restless and worried'. Then they were joined by a third unidentified man, either a 'mutual friend' (Inquest) or a friend of Atherton's (Report), and the three of them either went to his room (Inquest) or stayed in her room (Report), where they had another drink. At 9.15 Mulgan excused himself to leave and according to Atherton asked the friend on three or four occasions to 'Look after her', which she thought strange. Before leaving the room, as reported at the inquest, Atherton reminded him of the arranged meeting the next day at 4.00 pm with the Polish corporal who had served under him in Greece and who was very fond of him, to which Mulgan replied 'Oh marvellous I would love to see the boy' (Inquest).

in Cairo. In his 1964 letter to Dolbey, Paul Day asked whether they would ever solve the 'mystery' of Mulgan's death, to which Dolbey replied: 'We never will. What is certain is that the answer is not to be found in Mrs. Atherton's liaison or in other feminine adventures' (Dobrski 34). Categorically ruling out Atherton's involvement, even though the question had not been directed at 'feminine adventures', seems rather odd.[3] But no details are given in her evidence at the September inquest as to where Atherton was working. All that is recorded is that on April 23 (the day he was leaving for Alexandria) she called on Mulgan in his room 'at about 7.30 am before going to work'. To have been resident, as she claims, at the Continental Hotel for at least two years,[4] although this may well have been on and off, she must have been earning a good salary, or had her expenses paid, as the Continental was one of the most expensive hotels in Cairo. The mystery of her name may be a clue to her identity as SOE agent. As 'C.' Atherton in April, she could well have been circulating under an alias in the still operational organisation. By September, the month of the inquest, SOE operatives had been demobilised, which could explain her reversion to her original Polish forenames.

Dolbey's claims about Atherton may need to be treated with circumspection. His 1964 letter also informs Day that he 'heard [. . .] that she was pregnant and the mistress of John. What is certain is that no child was born'. This rumour seems to have been backed up by a suspicion of Arthur Edmonds 'sometime later', presumably after Mulgan's death, that she was 'looking "dreadful", when there was talk of an abortion'.[5] Dolbey's other assertion, that Atherton 'is now [in 1964] wedded to a Mr. Michael Ward, who in 1944/45 also worked at our Adv. Force 133 Hqs. in Athens', is incorrect, although

---

3   Dolbey may have been attempting to counter the claim by Sergeant G.A. Murray (of the Cairo Military Police), who was first on the scene in Mulgan's room and found the two letters to Atherton and Tsiminaki, that 'The evidence in hand would suggest that he [Mulgan] was very much attached to his female friends, and preferred suicide rather than sever his associations with them'. Report to the Assistant Provost Marshall, 6 May 1945 (ATL MS-Papers-7906-40).

4   She begins her testimony at the inquest on 13 September: 'I have lived at the Continental Hotel since April, 1943'.

5   Reported by Edmonds to O'Sullivan (LJB 335).

he does admit that he's 'not at all certain' about this (Dobrski 34).[6] This secrecy (or fudging) of information about her could perhaps be explained if Atherton was indeed working for SOE intelligence, or another British undercover organisation.

Mulgan had a special affection for Poles.[7] In the letter to Day, Dolbey praises the way Mulgan managed 'to get over 100 Poles to desert the German Army and formed with them a most efficient guerrilla unit'. We know too of Mulgan's 'great grief' when most of the Poles left the mountains to join the Polish corps in Italy: 'I felt as if I were losing many friends,' he wrote in his diary on 30 July 1944. Mulgan was also sensitive to the Polish predicament. Just before he was dropped into Greece he wrote to his mother:

> I've been living very much lately among men who are refugees from Europe, homeless and countryless, and can feel the power in them now as the turn of the war comes and they get ready to go back and rebuild again. It's going to be a long struggle, not only the war but afterwards, in reconstruction and putting the world together again [. . .] There's a bitter but abiding satisfaction in associating oneself to this outlook on life, to the concept of Europe in our day. (AGM 265)

As the months progressed, Poles like Christine would have been increasingly anxious about what they saw as the Soviet threat, and after the Yalta Conference of February 1945, where the Allies agreed amongst themselves that Poland would be taken by the Soviets, the

---

6   As he explains in his own book, Ward married a Greek woman named Avra, whom he met in November 1944 in Athens and married in 1947 (his book is dedicated to her) (Ward 1992, 201–2, 263). Ward preceded and then replaced Mulgan in the office in Athens; he returned to live in Greece after the war. Dolbey also recommended in this same letter of 3 April 1964 that John's son Richard might want to meet Peltekis (or Tsiminaki, Moazzo or Benakis) if he was going to Greece on his honeymoon that year, and that one of them might be able to put him in touch with Ward.

7   This affection seems to have predated his time in Greece. O'Sullivan records that back in 1936, representing New Zealand at the League of Nations meeting in Geneva, Mulgan is known to have 'carried on with a Polish woman' whom he described to his parents as 'a young Polish countess (so called)' and learned a romantic phrase in Polish, which he used when writing to another female friend (Jean Alison) in London (LJB 170–71).

rebuilding of their country took on a very different aspect from what they had been fighting for. In describing the 'ruined' state of Greece after the German withdrawal, Mulgan noted in *Report on Experience* that 'Only Poland, perhaps, had suffered greater privation' (RE 175); Poland lost around one fifth of its population (approximately six million people) in the war. Mulgan was probably sensitive to the way the Polish resistance (culminating in the Warsaw Uprising) had been handled by the Allies and would have known a great deal about Polish despair at their current predicament.

It is at this point that some speculation as to Atherton's identity is difficult to resist. By striking coincidence, extraordinary at the least, there was an equally mysterious compatriot and near namesake in Cairo at the time, also staying at the Continental and calling herself a widow—one whose identity and activities have recently attracted considerable attention. Krystyna Gustava Skarbek, who circulated under many aliases,[8] was a highly attractive undercover agent who had fled Warsaw for London after the German invasion of Poland. The daughter of an impoverished Polish count and a Jewish mother, she had a glamorous but unstable upbringing and was now looking to serve her country. The Secret Service in London took her on and in the early 1940s she performed several daring operations across Europe, mainly in Warsaw, Budapest and France. One of the most well-known was her single-handed rescue from a German detention camp in mid 1944 of three resistance fighters serving with the Marquis, including the leading SOE agent Francis Cammaerts ('Roger') as well as Xan Fielding, shortly before they were due to be executed. There are now two excellent biographies of Skarbek, one by Madeleine Masson in 1975 that makes use of statements from many who knew Christine (as she was usually called), and one in 2012 by Clare Mulley, which adds details from newly released archival material. As both biographers record, Skarbek was constantly on the move, but between October 1944 and the end of 1945 was coming

---

8   Some of these were Christine Granville, Christine Gettlich (after her first husband), Christine Gizycki (after her second), Olga Paloski and Jacqueline ['Pauline'] Armand.

and going regularly from Cairo (Masson 1975, 224),[9] which meant she could well have overlapped there with Mulgan, who was in the city from 8 November 1944 until 14 January 1945, and then from 19 to 25 April 1945. While in Cairo Skarbek stayed frequently at the Continental Hotel. Her biographers have not been able to pinpoint her movements around winter 1944–45 with complete precision: a key principle of agent practice is of course to cover your tracks. It is known, however, that she met a Major Michael Dunford (who was to reappear again in her story as a rejected lover) at the Continental Hotel in October 1944 (Masson 1975, 224). Then, from December 27, Skarbek was in Italy, hoping to be dispatched to Poland as part of the Hudson mission. Her role in this mission was cancelled and she returned to Cairo,[10] by which time she was employed by SOE. There is also evidence that she was in close contact with Dolbey, both at this time and later.[11]

9   Mulley records (2012, 172) that in early April 1944 Skarbek was supported by the new head of the Balkans section of SOE in Cairo, Bickham Sweet-Escott. In May she was sent to the SOE base in Algeria for training in preparation for being dropped into the south of France (under the alias Pauline Armand)—where she was to perform several successful missions with the well-known agent Francis Cammaerts. After France, then a couple of months in London, then Bari in Italy, waiting for the abortive Polish mission, on 21 November she was granted an honorary commission in the Women's Auxiliary Air Force (WAAF) at the rank of Flight Officer and offered employment in Cairo in the Movement Section of GHQ, MEF (Multilateral Force), which dealt with displaced persons. She remained in this employment until demobilised in May 1945 (Masson 1975, 224; Mulley 2012, 277 and 281). This meant, according to Mulley, that for a short while she was 'now on a tax-free salary of £511.12.0 per annum, well above the national average and at the high end of the scale for a female agent' (2012, 270). On this salary, presumably, she could afford to reside at the Continental at the time she overlapped with Mulgan in Cairo. Patrick Howarth, who knew her well, records that 'Being largely undomesticated, she found it easier to live in a hotel or a boarding-house than in a flat' (1980, 48). Economic security was short-lived, however. After the war Skarbek was kept on by 'the firm' (SOE, Force 133) on half pay until the end of 1945, after which time she constantly struggled to support herself with short-term employment. After the war, many of the men in SOE apparently viewed her as, 'for want of a better word, "scatty", and were quite looking forward to dropping her' (Mulley 2012, 285).

10   An undated fragment of a report on Skarbek ('GIZYCKA') in her file in the Kew archives states that after the aborted operation to Poland, she 'returned to CAIRO where she has been ever since' (TNA HS 9/612).

11   See Dobrski Papers (Dobrski 21/6) where Dolbey recommends Skarbek for a mission to Hungary in March 1944 (it never came off). In November 1945, he reports that she is back in the UK (Dobrski 32). In this same file there is a two-page reference, unsigned but almost certainly by Dolbey in November or December 1945, written for 'Krystina Gizycka (alias Christine Granville)', which details at length her assistance to the British war effort, seemingly to help her obtain a British passport. Masson records that in London after the

The main observation made about Skarbek by those who knew her at the time had to do with her reserve. As Masson records, 'Christine had made friends in many spheres but her friends, like her life, were compartmented and she never committed the error of mixing them together. Nor did she ever talk of her own mysterious activities. She was a very private person' (1975, xxv). She was 'fanatically secretive', she continues, 'an embroiderer' who 'had to cover her tracks' (xxxiii). Within what many have described as the hothouse conditions of wartime Cairo, secret agents tended to form relationships with little or no reference to nationality or past, so that affairs often began and ended quickly. 'Nobody was more adept than Christine,' Masson argues, 'in giving only that which she wished to give'—with the result that 'a whole area of her life has been shadowed by a question mark' (131). Others were to put it that in playing the roles of different aliases, she seemed to inhabit a fictional world. Naval intelligence officer Ian Fleming, who probably had a brief affair with her after the war, portrayed her as Vesper Lynd in *Casino Royale*. 'She literally shines with all the qualities and splendours of a fictitious character', he wrote (Mulley 2012, 342). This surface allure gave the impression she had much to hide. The British agent Xan Fielding, whom she had rescued in France and then later saw frequently in Cairo, wrote a book about her in 1954 entitled *Hide and Seek: The Story of a War-Time Agent*.

While no direct evidence exists of meetings between Mulgan and Skarbek (as opposed to 'Atherton'), we can trace a number of connections between the two based on common acquaintances. Michael Ward (whom Dolbey mistakenly told Paul Day had married Atherton) records in his book that he had 'a mild and innocuous friendship' with Skarbek when they were both working for SOE in Cairo in the summer of '44. Along with her long-term lover and compatriot Andrzej Kowerski ('Andrew Kennedy'), Ward writes,

war 'Julian Dobski [*sic*], who was in touch with all the Poles in London as he had been with them in Cairo, was worried about Christine [Skarbek], and tried, time and again, to find her congenial occupation. He was unsuccessful'. Masson goes on to record that on arriving at Dolbey's flat in Park Street one day, a mutual friend, Pussi Deakin (wife of Sir Frederick Deakin), was asked by Dolbey to try and 'Find out what she really wants to do with her life' as she appeared to be 'just drifting' (1975, 235).

'Christine Granville (whose real name was Krystyna Skarbek)' had carried out several hazardous missions in Nazi-occupied Poland but was by this time 'in disfavour with the Polish Army intelligence for working for SOE instead of the Poles'. After being trained as a wireless operator, he continues, she left Cairo to be dropped into France in early July '44 (Ward 1992, 182). Ward later recounted that he found her approaches rather too strong for his liking (Mulley 2012, 137). She had, as Masson records, a 'wide choice of admirers' in Cairo (1975, xxxix). Female promiscuity was still regarded with far less indulgence than male; later, people used phrases such as 'very free with her favours' and 'a loose cannon' to describe her (Mulley 2012, 277, 290). Ward makes little reference to Mulgan in his book, although the two men were together for months in the Liquidation Fund office in Athens and his name appears frequently in Mulgan's reports to Dolbey. His reference to Mulgan's death in April is strikingly cautious.[12] Clare Mulley was in communication with Ward in Athens, but as she recounts in a 2013 talk at the National Army Museum in London, Ward died before she had finished her research (Mulley 2013).

Based on evidence given at the inquires after Mulgan's death, another speculation can be made here. As mentioned, on the night he died, Mulgan had gone to Christine's room at the Continental around 8.00 pm. There they were soon joined by an unidentified man whom Mulgan told several times to 'take care of' Christine—which she found odd (though he was leaving to join the New Zealand forces the next morning and would probably not see her again). Then in the letter addressed to 'Christine Atherton', written immediately afterwards and found in his kit in his room, he wrote: 'Make Bill look after you, or some one equally good'.[13] There was one 'Bill' at the time in Cairo who was close to Christine Skarbek and whom Mulgan is bound to have known. This was Bill Stanley Moss, who like Mulgan had fought at El Alamein and then been recruited around the same time into SOE. Moss and his fiancé

---

12   Ward 1992, 222–23, cited earlier in Chapter 8, footnote 7.
13   Evidence from Atherton at inquest, ATL, 7906-40.

Zofia Tarnowska were prominent in Cairo circles at the time. Like Skarbek, Zofia was a Polish aristocrat who had fled the Nazis. Described by Mulley as 'a society beauty who loved huge house parties' (2012, 139), she was now working for the Cairo branch of the Polish Red Cross, which she had founded. Moss, by this time, had something of a hero's status on account of his abduction in Crete of General Heinrich Kreipe (with Patrick Leigh Fermor and a group of *andartes*), recounted in his book *Ill Met by Moonlight* (1950). Moss would have been an obvious person to 'take care of' the unattached and somewhat self-destructive Skarbek. Writing of her after her death, Moss called Christine 'without a doubt [. . .] the greatest secret agent to have operated for the Allies in either World Wars' (1956, 17–18), which seems hard to credit but is typical of the kind of adulation she evoked in some people. He was quick to add, however, that he 'would never become involved with Christine. It would be like buying a Hispano-Suiza [a very fast car]' (Mulley 2012, 167).[14] Although Moss was now based in Britain and was soon to leave for further SOE operations in the Far East, he had returned to Cairo in late March for a month's leave and for his wedding to Tarnowska on April 26, the day after the meeting at the Continental (Ogden 2014, 314).[15] Such was the closeness to Skarbek that Moss and Tarnowska named their first child Krystyna after her (Mulley 2012, 307). After Skarbek's murder by an obsessive lover in London in June 1952, Moss connected with Christine's long-time partner Andrzej Kowerski/Kennedy and the two achieved a certain fame through their investigation into what had happened to the reserves of the Nazi Reichsbank.[16] The status of 'adventurer' was sometimes hard for these war heroes to throw off—as it was for Christine too, it seems. Moss published four articles about her after her death, entitled

---

14   Contemporary descriptions of Skarbek, by both men and women, invariably vacillate between admiration for her daring and wariness of her sexual freedom. Moss wrote that 'her attractiveness lay in "a blend of vivacity, flirtatiousness, charm and sheer personality . . . like a searchlight" which when she chose "could blind anyone in its beam"' (Mulley 2012, 167).

15   For some descriptions of Skarbek's social activities in Cairo around April 1945, mostly involving the Tarnowska–Moss wedding, see Mulley 2012, 280.

16   See W. Stanley Moss, *Gold is Where You Hide It* (1956), where Moss describes his post-war adventures with Kennedy.

'Christine the Brave' (in *Picture Post* for September–October 1952). He also wrote a biography of her, which, however, Kowerski did not approve for publication; the whereabouts of the manuscript is apparently unknown (Mulley 2012, 395n15).[17]

In her book *Cairo in the War 1939–1945* (1989), Artemis Cooper paints a graphic picture of the parties held by Moss, Leigh Fermor, Xan Fielding, and Tarnowska and other Poles, sometimes (Mulley records) attended by Skarbek. The most riotous were those the previous winter, where on one occasion a flaming sofa was thrown out the window and on another some of Zofia's Polish friends shot out all the light bulbs (Cooper 1989, 287). For Mulgan, the Poles he knew at the time were 'a little crazy' as a result, he assumed, of everything that had happened to them. They fixated on the 'idea of Poland', he wrote, as all that was left to them (RE 156). In wartime Cairo, in moments of respite from the risks they undertook in the field, identities and cover stories amongst these secret agents were changing fast. But it is difficult to believe that there were two Polish Krystyna Gustavas in the orbit of SOE, both calling themselves a 'widow' (though both of Skarbek's husbands were still very much alive),[18] both connected with Dolbey, and both living at the

17   Another possible connection between Mulgan and Skarbek would have been through Patrick Howarth (1916–2004). Howarth read English at Oxford in the mid 1930s and may well have met Mulgan there. After this he moved to Poland, where he edited a political quarterly. In wartime, when Guy Tamplin was appointed to the Balkan section of SOE in 1942, Howarth replaced him as head of the Polish section in Cairo. In this post he played a dominant role in the SOE employment of Skarbek and Kowerski. He is also credited by Masson with responsibility for sending to Greece Poles who had deserted from the German army, presumably some of the same Poles Mulgan trained in the mountains and became fond of. Howarth was particularly close to Skarbek, who apparently guided him in the intricacies of Polish politics. He was the one who arranged for her to be trained as a wireless operator (Masson 1975, 137). Mulley records that Howarth was one of the small group of men, most of them ex-lovers, who became the 'Panel to Protect the Memory of Christine Granville' soon after her death in 1952 (2012, xviii, 338). It is not recorded whether Howarth was also a lover, though a fulsome reference he wrote for her, for a drop into Hungary, led one of its readers to suspect that Christine had 'obviously worked overtime' on him (Mulley 2012, 171). Howarth's book *Undercover: The Men and Women of the Special Operations Executive* (1980, reprinted in 2000) makes frequent reference to Skarbek.

18   Skarbek had married Gustav Gettlich in 1930 and Jerzy Gizycki in 1938. She met her long-time partner Kowerski/Kennedy soon after this. Mulley describes the 'curious work of fiction' that constituted the British naturalisation certificate Skarbek was finally granted in November 1946, where her date of birth was 'seven years shy of the truth' and her marital status listed as 'widow' (2012, 292).

Continental Hotel around the same time. It is recorded, too, that Skarbek had had numerous abortions or miscarriages, at least eight according to one later lover (Mulley 2012, 354–55). Although it may seem unlikely that Atherton's identity as Skarbek would not have been known to an SOE officer like Edmonds, it is possible that her identity and cover story were kept secret by SOE as part of a wider military cover-up. Nina Crawshaw, wife of SOE Polish expert Guy Tamplin, told Masson that although she herself worked in SOE HQ in the Rustum Buildings in Cairo, she never once saw Christine Skarbek there—possibly, she suspected, 'for security reasons'. Like others, Crawshaw noted that Skarbek was 'exceedingly reserved' and secretive (Masson 1975, xxix).

Skarbek's biographers emphasise the role played by Andrzej Kowerski and Francis Cammaerts (both of SOE and both her lover at different times) in their perhaps not entirely altruistic determination to prevent media speculation and sensationalism after her death. (They had all, of course, signed the Official Secrets Act.) Some of her friends (such as Vera Atkins of SOE and Zofia Tarnowska Moss) complained of a 'whitewash' after Masson's biography appeared (Mulley 2012, 339); Mulley's version, for its part, tends to err on the side of tragic heroism. Although Skarbek's heroic status has predominated in recent years, there can be no doubt that in addition to her spectacular acts of bravery she was also involved in some pretty seedy operations. Mulley records in her talk at the National Army Museum that Skarbek didn't like to shoot people but had, she adds (with the suggestion of its future usefulness) 'excelled' in 'a course in silent killing' (Mulley 2013).[19] More telling is the revelation of a Polish friend close to Skarbek after the war, Anna Czyzewska. In a recording reproduced in a 2011 film available on YouTube, she describes how Christine later suffered badly from nerves, and attributes this to the horrors of some of her work as an undercover agent. She comments: 'It was a terrible job. Can you imagine how it feels to have to kill someone with whom you have just been intimate?'

---

19   The course included using a knife, a rope and, apparently Skarbek's preferred method, your hands. She was, Mulley adds, Britain's most highly trained female agent (Mulley 2013).

Of course, she adds, Christine was a well-trained agent and rarely talked about what she had done.[20] Behind the glamorous, sanitised reputation we occasionally catch hints like these of something more sinister.

Mulgan's biographers have described the affair with Atherton (very briefly) in sentimental terms, based on the statement she made at the inquest, that she 'was very fond of him and he was also fond of me' (TNA FO 841/524).[21] But there's every reason to believe that if Atherton was Skarbek/Granville, then Mulgan was far from being her exclusive lover at the time. He was after all in Cairo for only five nights after his return from Athens, and (apart from Andrzej) names such as Michael Dunford, George Michailov (a Serbian pilot) and Henry Threlfall (Binney 2002, 105–6) appear in the records of acknowledged liaisons Skarbek had at this time.[22] Mulgan's relationship with her, in other words, would almost certainly have been very private and fleeting.

After Stalin's attack on Poland on 12 January 1945, Skarbek and her Polish colleagues were 'dumbfounded and bitterly resentful' at the failure of the Allies to support Poland at the Yalta Conference the following month (Mulley 2012, 275). As it became clearer that the war was ending, Skarbek's services as daring agent were no longer in demand, and she had little appetite or training for office work. In one of the few letters from her that survives, dated 25 March 1945, she petitions 'Perks Kochany', a term of endearment for Harold Perkins, head of SOE's Central Europe section, who had played a dominant role in British-Polish collaboration: 'For God's sake, do not strike my name from the firm [SOE]' (Mulley 2012, 278). By this time, she would have given up all hope of returning to Soviet-administered Poland, where her anti-communist sympathies were

20   'Krystyna Skarbek/Christine Granville'. 2011. youtube.com/watch?v=UeKH4N-YIE8. Date of access 29 Dec. 2019.

21   McNeish adds spice to his account by calling Atherton 'a merry widow living at the Continental' (2003, 257).

22   Clare Mulley, in an email to us on 10 January 2017, wrote that although she had not come across the name 'Atherton' in her research, 'It is tempting to imagine it was the same Krystyna'. Her own work revealed to her, she continues, that 'not all of Krystyna's Cairo romances are clarified'. Our thanks to Clare Mulley for this communication.

well known. After her murder in a London hotel in 1952, Scotland Yard conducted a criminal investigation into the possibility of a political assassination, on the grounds that she might have been thought by the Soviets to know too much about the Polish anti-communist underground. MI5, however, concluded that it appeared to be a crime of passion (Mulley 2012, 339–40).

Paradoxically, perhaps the most convincing evidence as to the possibility that Atherton was Skarbek is the *lack* of evidence in relation to her. If she had been an ordinary wartime acquaintance, the inquiry or inquest would surely have recorded more information about her. Mulgan's biographies offer no insight, with a complete absence of reference to Atherton's past or future, except (much later) the single comment from Edmonds and the mistaken conjecture from Dolbey, both of which could be examples of SOE official secrecy. Why, we wonder, was this blanket of silence thrown over her, given that so many potential witnesses were available, the third person in the hotel room being an obvious one? Brown notes that among the glaring omissions in the investigations into Mulgan's death is the fact that no one interviewed or even recorded the name of this third person in the room (2014, 138–39). The most likely (or at least one reasonable) answer is that 'the firm' would not have revealed anything about either Christine or this man in order to avoid blowing their cover. Like Leigh Fermor, Bill Stanley Moss had a large reward out on his head by the Germans for his kidnapping of General Kreipe (Ogden 2014, 309–10). Given the high profile of both Skarbek and Moss as British agents at this time, every effort would have been made to conceal their identities. The security risks, let alone the scandal, would have been considerable if it became known that Skarbek was associated with Mulgan immediately before his mysterious death. As Brown points out, despite repeated attempts to dismiss it, there is still considerable ambiguity surrounding Mulgan's death. This has been fed by a wide range of theories, some more and some less conspiratorial. We'll explore a few of these, within their political context, in the next chapter.

An even darker conjecture, one that hangs over this whole tragic episode, is that 'Atherton'/Skarbek was indeed somehow involved in Mulgan's death. Skarbek's famed daring and cool, her excellence in the art of 'silent killing'—possibly assisted by Dolbey's research into and development of lethal poisons, explored in the next chapter—as well as her expertise as a gatherer and keeper of secret information, all make this at least possible. The evidence for Mulgan's death by an overdose of morphine, as we shall see, is contradictory at best. From the start of her time in Cairo, Krystyna Skarbek had played an important role in providing 'a good deal of valuable information' for the British (Mulley, 2012, 154), to which her numerous liaisons gave her access. There seems little doubt, in other words, that along with the brave adventuring went a function as a honey trap. Mulgan, as we have seen, would have aroused increasing suspicion in the Rustum Buildings in relation to his opposition to British policy and its paranoia about communism at this time. Given the exceptional sensitivity of the information and opinions he had just sent to the New Zealand Ministry of External Affairs, it is not out of the question that his every move was under close observation. We may never know whether this observation was assisted by 'Christine Atherton'. Further research, when more documents are one day declassified or discovered, may perhaps be more successful in either proving or disproving this hypothesis.

CHAPTER 11

Posthumous Fragments: Facts and Fictions

'In war-time,' I said, 'Truth is so precious that she should always be attended by a bodyguard of lies.'

—Winston Churchill, 30 November 1943
(Churchill 1951, 383)

The news of Mulgan's death was received with shock and disbelief, both in New Zealand and in Egypt. Was it possible that a man who seemed so healthy in body and mind to all around him, who had enormous opportunities opening out before him, should take his own life? Could someone of his integrity have left a suicide letter full of lies?

New Zealanders who knew him best refused to believe it.[1] Finding the verdict 'quite fantastic', his father campaigned to initiate a full inquiry (Brown 2011, 107–9), based on a suspicion that the Greek communists were behind it. (Mulgan himself, if he ever feared for his life, had pointed in the opposite direction; service with ELAS, he wrote to Dolbey, may be regarded as a 'liability', leaving agents like himself vulnerable to attack from the right.)[2] His Auckland

---

1 Paul Day and Vincent O'Sullivan have given detailed accounts of the debates surrounding the mystery of Mulgan's death. Martyn Brown, more recently, has added further details.

2 In a letter to Dolbey of 5 March 1945, Mulgan emphasises the threat from the right in post-occupation Greece: 'there seems, in fact, to be a danger that Force 133 may be regarded as the force which supported ELAS during the occupation and that service with it may be a

University College friend Jean Alison, whom he'd continued to see in London, didn't believe it 'for a moment' on the grounds that John had 'a core of hard egotism that wouldn't be likely [. . .] to destroy itself wilfully' (Ross 2019a, 18). Mulgan seemed to endorse this at the beginning of the war when he wrote to his parents, in relation to post-war work at the Press, that 'there will be work to do after the war and I have a very strong survival complex' (AGM 159). In *Dance of the Peacocks* James McNeish records the response of the expat circle, most of whom knew Mulgan well (Cox, Bertram, Milner, Davin, Bennett), that after liberation, 'None of them had yet accepted that John Mulgan had committed suicide' (2003, 282). 'Accepted', of course, carries ambiguity: does it mean 'believed', or rather that none of them were able to absorb the shock of it? In any event, the phrase certainly suggests that a suicide was unexpected. The response in Egypt from those who had seen him recently was similar. Tom Barnes wrote that 'It seemed impossible to believe. [. . .] He had seemed perfectly OK when I saw him last' (Barnes 2015, 380).[3] Brigadier J.M. Mitchell, who had driven Mulgan from the airport to his hotel on his return to Cairo six days before, confirmed that 'he certainly did not appear to be a chap who had anything to worry him unduly. He was very chatty and easy to get on with, seemed to be pleased to be back in Cairo, and was looking forward to transferring to 2nd N.Z.E.F. within the next

liability' (Dobrski 34). Clogg records a case of an SOE agent who in early 1944 had shot a Greek-American SIS agent, 'who had made no secret of his pro-ELAS [. . .] sympathies' (1981, 106; see also 358n11). Mulgan would have been aware of such risks from the start.

3   Brown records (2011, 108) a comment in a letter from Barnes to Gabrielle, about 'how well Mulgan had looked the day before his death' (this was reported by Alan Mulgan to Peter Fraser, 21 Aug. 1945, ATL McIntosh Papers MS-Papers 6759-044). Barnes was probably instrumental in encouraging Alan Mulgan to follow up the idea that the Greek communists might have killed his son. There are several reasons to believe that this was extremely unlikely. Barnes gives no evidence for his claim that 'Communists had murdered several people in Cairo' (Brown 2011, 109). As we have seen, and as Barnes's 'Report on Observations in Greece' shows, he had a clear bias against EAM-ELAS and the communists (ANZ, C.E. Barnes, 'Observations in Greece'). Unless the British secret services had decided to turn a blind eye, the murder of a British officer by communists in Cairo would not have been passed over lightly. Outside the military inquiry, there were no investigations by the British authorities into Mulgan's death. The way the Court of Inquiry was conducted suggests that the SIS and SOE were keen to close the case less for their own sake than to the legal satisfaction of the New Zealand government.

two weeks' (LJB 334). In a statement on April 27, Major Angus, who had known Mulgan from July 1943 when the latter first joined SOE, described how he had chatted with him for about an hour on the night he died, before he went in to see Dolbey. Mulgan, he testified, 'has at no time indicated that he was ill or depressed, on the contrary he looked an extremely well built and fit man' (ATL MS-Papers-7906-40, para. 17). The only person who appeared to find a suicide verdict credible, at least initially, was his Egyptian-Greek interpreter in Thessaly, Paul Contomichalos, who had spent a couple of days with him in Alexandria just a few days before he died. In August 1946 Contomichalos replied to Eric Curtis, who had served with Mulgan in the mountains and was attempting to gather evidence that Mulgan died 'on active service', in order to help get Mulgan's widow and son a pension—as 'They have not been adequately provided for'. Contomichalos agreed to support the petition:

> I don't remember the exact date of John's death, but I know I saw him very few days before in Alex. He had lunch at home and we also went to the beach once or twice and one night he joined us at a dancing. I cannot say he was very gay during those meetings and I remember thinking to myself, after I had heard of his death, that probably he had committed suicide. I was not told of it at the time.
>
> It struck me as rather odd that I was not called to give evidence at the inquest but the whole thing was conducted in a most mysterious way. It is over a year now it all happened and I must say details are not any more very clear infront [*sic*] of me but I distinctly recall that I was most amazed at the way the whole thing was being hushed up. I remember I asked for his wife's address but was told that I could not have it for the time being.
>
> It is my firm belief that John did not kill himself 'whilst the balance of his mind was disturbed'. As I said, I saw him just before his death and he kept telling me how fed up one gets after some time of repeated disappointments and I know very well how disappointed he was with the way his work was criticised. Anyone

else would have taken the matter lightly but John was much too conscientious for that and he really took it to heart. I honestly believe that this is what drove him to his end.[4]

Significantly, however, twenty years later Contomichalos had reached a different conclusion. In reply to Paul Day in March 1965, after expressing high regard for Mulgan's strength and modesty, Contomichalos wrote:

> His death in Cairo and the way he died was and remains to this day a big mystery to me and although there were rumours at the time that it was suicide I who had seen him and talked to him just a few days before could not believe it. May be [*sic*] you could give me some more information on this? (ATL MS-Papers-7906-42)

What had occured in the meantime to make him change his mind? The suicide letter left for Julian Dolbey (reproduced in Appendix A here) has divided its readers. On the one hand it seems irrefutable in its sometimes authentic tones: the self-effacing comment about how if he's achieved anything in his 'short and not very productive life' it's to have lived 'in friendship with a lot of different and differing Greeks', the quote from the classics (Seneca), etc. And a graphological analysis of the typewriter used to type the letter reveals that it's the same machine, or at least the same brand of machine, that Mulgan used to write to J.V. Wilson.[5] To counter this, a sceptic could point to the sophistication and skill of SIS forgery units in Cairo at the time, and the fact that the secret services would have had access to the typewriter while Mulgan was in Alexandria, or even posthumously, to write the letter. It would have been easy for experts to forge Mulgan's self-deprecatory style and expressions of affection for the Greeks, of which there are plenty of examples in his letters home. But above all, the letter makes preposterously false

4   Our thanks to Nicolas and Gerassimos Contomichalos for making this letter available to us.

5   The graphologist we are referring to here is Ioannis G. Dosis, a professional forensic consultant for the Athenian courts, former Brigadier and head of the Greek Police Forensic Office. The ten-page report (in Greek) is dated 27 January 2017.

claims: that he had for years been suffering from throat cancer, that he had attempted unsuccessfully to treat it, that he couldn't face being a burden on his family, that he didn't want an army pension as his wife was 'adequately insured', all of which sound completely out of character. So, although most have relied on the letter as proof of suicide, many still reiterate Paul Day's view that it is a 'thoroughly puzzling document' (1977, 52).[6]

Medical and scientific evidence did not help to clarify the situation. Little attention has been paid to a routine psychological examination Mulgan had been given on November 24, when he came out of the mountains. The results of the examination (reproduced in Appendix B here), performed and written up by Dr (Major) A. Kennedy, insist that 'on his return, [Mulgan] showed no signs whatever of strain although quite a high proportion of officers who served in his area exhibited signs of anxiety.' He continued: 'While episodes of mild depression are not uncommon in men of his intellectual level, there was no evidence in Col. MULGAN's case at the time that he had ever suffered from such an attack and no evidence whatever that he was likely to entertain the idea of suicide.'

Legal investigations followed. On May 6, a 27-paragraph report on evidence to 'The Assistant Provost Marshall', signed by Sergeant G.A. Murray of the Special Investigation Branch of the Cairo Military Police, laid out what was discovered in Mulgan's room at the Continental and records details of statements made by Angus, Dolbey and Atherton (ATL MS-Papers-7906-40). Following a post-mortem on the body, which Murray had found 'still warm' at 7.15 pm on April 26, a forensic report of 20 June contradicted an initial statement that 'the deceased poisoned himself', stating that only 'traces of either Morphine or Hiroine [sic] were found in the entrails' (TNA HS 9/1073/3).[7] This uncertainty about the amount

6   Paul Day, who as Gabrielle's second husband would have had opportunity to talk things through at length with her, began by calling Mulgan's death an 'insoluble mystery', but over the years reverted to the officially accepted view—see Brown 2014, 131.

7   Dolbey testified to the Court of Inquiry on August 18, on the basis of all the evidence produced, that 'No traces of either poison or morphia were found in the glasses, tubes, boxes or other receptacles found in the deceased's room' (ATL 7906-40; also TNA, HS 9/1073/3). A sample of blood was sent to the chemist after the autopsy (TNA HS 9/1073/3), but no results were reported.

of morphine in Mulgan's system, complicated by the fact that he was taking small doses of morphine for malaria, was never fully resolved (Brown 2014, 140). Later in the year the 'Inquest at his Britannic Majesty's Court for Egypt at Cairo', concluding in September, came up with what Brigadier Bill Stevens of Maadi Camp told Alister McIntosh in Wellington was 'some conflict of medical opinion', though it 'appears that the case must be considered as closed' (ATL 8612-091). Stevens in fact told McIntosh on September 27 that 'the evidence is by no means conclusive but I don't know how much is to be gained by pursuing it further' (Ross 2019a, 18). Since then, biographers have usually repeated the verdict delivered at the coronial inquest on September 26, that 'the cause of death was poisoning by an overdose of morphia taken intentionally by the deceased while the balance of his mind was disturbed' (TNA FO 841/524).[8] James Bertram, Vincent O'Sullivan and James McNeish have tended towards a 'writerly' explanation of mental disturbance, that Mulgan's suicide was due to a profound sensitivity to the hopelessness of the human condition in 'some final revelation of the treachery of the heart from the Greek debacle' (Day 1977, 53–54). Whether despair led to a mental imbalance, however, seems more difficult to verify.[9]

After Mulgan's death, the two SOE representatives who stood guard over his reputation, lavish in their praise, were Woodhouse and Julian Dolbey. Dolbey's challenge to the suicide verdict at the first hearing has been explained as stemming from his attempt to fulfil

8   Another challenge to the verdict of a morphine overdose has been offered by Ken Ross (2019b), who argues that Mulgan may have committed suicide as a result of the debilitating effects of falciparum malaria, an extreme and cerebral form of the disease. However, it seems difficult to reconcile the accounts of the mental and physical well-being displayed by Mulgan in his final weeks with descriptions of the symptoms of this disease (fever, chills, sweats, vomiting, leading to delirium and coma).

9   An approach that seems to us more plausible was suggested by Dean Parker in the *New Zealand Political Review* in 1998. Parker compares Mulgan with fellow New Zealand Marxist Gordon Watson, who was killed on April 17, 1945, during the Allied invasion of Italy. Watson was a victim, Parker argues, of the Allied deal to repress partisan revolutionary forces in Italy and Greece. Mulgan, he speculates, may have committed suicide 'by lethal injection' out of despair or guilt at having provided information to SOE (during his time in the Athens office) about his left-wing Greek friends, whom he knew would be persecuted (Parker 1998). Parker underestimates, however, the extent of Mulgan's left-wing commitment to the end.

Mulgan's request in the suicide letter to conceal the cause of death from his family. But it also might be contended that given SOE's overall control of the first inquiry and confiscation of all documents in Mulgan's room, Dolbey's challenge to the suicide verdict to an extent deflected suspicion away from an assassination charge.[10] (If SOE was fabricating the suicide verdict, in other words, why was its head of investigations challenging it?) In stating his view at the hearing in August that there was not enough evidence to support the suicide verdict, Dolbey testified:

> I find that his death is due to causes not yet ascertained, that he was not on duty at the time of his death, and that he is to blame for the circumstances which immediately preceded his death. (ATL 7906–40)

What does Dolbey have in mind here? Why this defensiveness? For those of a conspiratorial bent, there is plenty to go on. In light of more recent information about special operations activities during the war, by both SOE and SIS, Dolbey's knowledge of and involvement in methods of doing away with enemy elements (possibly internal as well as external) may be relevant. In a document of January 1944, Dolbey asked Major Kennedy, doctor and poisons expert,[11] about 'the use of drugs for poisoning, as narcotics, and to induce sickness'. The document, which contains minutes of a meeting with Kennedy, states clearly what Dolbey had in mind:

> He inquires 'on the principle that we can take as agreed (that when murder is attempted it must not fail, once the position is made clear a specially selected officer in specially selected country

---

10   Martyn Brown argues that Dolbey's disagreement with the suicide verdict 'would show that at least he was out of [i.e. not part of] any joint concerted effort' at a British cover-up (2014, 142). To this it could be countered that Dolbey's specialisation was in fact in the very field of subtle and sophisticated bluff and cover-up operations.

11   This was the same Major Kennedy who had conducted the psychological examination of Mulgan when he returned to Cairo the previous November. Significantly, it was also he who was called to identify Mulgan's body when it was taken to the 15th Scottish General Hospital on the morning of 27 April (ATL 7906-40).

sections should be told what drugs are available, what they are intended for, and how they are to be used. [...] Two systems are available, injection and by absorption. The poison to be eaten [...] putting into wine, soup, etc. The best way is possibly to disguise them in articles such as chocolate, quinine pills, etc. Poisons are available which have immediate effect and which have effect with a delayed action of as much as 24 hours or more. In the latter group poisons are available which show every sign of death due to normal disease. [...] The only other way to administer them is in some medicine [...] medicine which soldiers have to take daily or weekly, such as quinine, anti-malaria preparations, etc [...]' (Dobrski 21/5)

Dolbey had been given the massively responsible task of planning and organising British interests in the Balkans after the withdrawal of German troops from Greece, and was passionately committed to an anti-communist programme.[12] His suggestions for what should be done circulated to other departments and to his superiors.[13] He also continued to be part of the think tank preparing the ground for a 'solid basis' of support for the Papandreou government (KCLMA, GB 0099, 21/3). In short, Dolbey shared the concern stated in an earlier report (22 April 1944) by Brigadier Barker-Benfield, his chief commander, that 'If no occupation of Greece is contemplated at the time of German withdrawal, ELAS will be left in complete control of the whole country' (BHA 259, 6). (For a brief period that summer, as mentioned earlier, Barker-Benfield was advocating support for ELAS as a matter of expediency—an approach, however, which was

---

12 In another document in the King's College archives, Dolbey is revealed to be working in early 1944 towards establishing a secret espionage office in Hungary with Krystyna Gizycka, alias Krystyna Skarbek, the Polish expatriate who, as described in the previous chapter, had been employed as a British agent in several posts (see Dobrski 21/6, [Mar. 22 1944, Apr. 14 1944] and Dobrski 32, [Nov. 1–Dec. 7 1945]). In her biography of George, 2nd Earl Jellicoe, who participated with Dolbey in a mission to Rhodes in September 1943, Lorna Almonds Windmill (herself an ex-army officer and civil servant) describes Dolbey as 'a secret Agent of the Special Operations Executive (SOE), the tough dirty tricks branch of the secret services' (Windmill 2008, 67). For the fears of SOE secretary Hermione, Countess of Ranfurly, in relation to '"security and double-crossing" within SOE [Cairo]', see Clogg 2000, 128–29.

13 Dobrski 31, 23 and 34.

soon overruled.) Dolbey visited Athens more than once after the liberation, knew every detail about the Greek economy and Greek agents for the British, and from March 1945 was head of planning in HQ Force 133 (BHA 259, F9). We needn't necessarily follow Brown in arguing that in light of hard evidence to the contrary, the suicide verdict must be accepted. But Brown is right that all avenues of investigation seem to be closed. All that can be said at this stage is that the *lack* of direct evidence seems most telling. Relevant here is Contomichalos's 1946 statement about the 'most mysterious' way in which the inquest was conducted ('I was most amazed at the way the whole thing was being hushed up'). Today, anyone attempting to consult the Dolbey files (including the full Mulgan–Dolbey correspondence) at the Liddell Hart Centre for Military Archives, King's College London, will be told, as we were, that 'the Dobrski files 27–30 are currently closed due to personal-sensitive information and are therefore not available for viewing'.[14] This correspondence covers the crucial period from 27 June 1944 to 21 April 1945. Contomichalos's statement that he 'kn[e]w very well how disappointed he [Mulgan] was with the way his work [for SOE] was criticised' seems to be behind this.

Stranger than fiction

Fiction writers have flocked to this time and place in history to explore the fertile interchange between fact and fiction, history and rumour. Trilogies and tetralogies have proliferated to give space to the atmosphere: Lawrence Durrell's *Alexandria Quartet*, Olivia Manning's *Balkan Trilogy* and *Levant Trilogy*, Evelyn Waugh's *Sword of Honour* trilogy, and, in Greek literature, Stratis Tsirkas's *Drifting Cities*.

Part of the attraction is clearly the vacuum created by the

---

14   Email to the authors of 12 March 2018 from the archives assistant—although Richard Mulgan had kindly given his consent for us to consult these documents. The main problem confronting any researcher in this sensitive field is that even those files made available have been carefully weeded out: paginated manuscripts indicate many missing pages (see, for example, MS of Aug. 1944 which is classified 'Most Secret' in Dobrski 14). In some cases folios have been classified as closed 'indefinitely'.

shortage of (historical) facts, which imagination rushes to fill. An article by Duncan Stuart on the 'Origins and Vicissitudes of the SOE Archive' (2006) records how the secret services during the war, SOE in particular, were founded on the avoidance of written records. Douglas Dodds-Parker wrote in his book *Setting Europe Ablaze*: 'From 1940 it had been said "the less the paper, the more the action"; that by the normal rules of a Secret Service, nothing would ever be written by us or about us' (Stuart 2006, 218). In the event, however, a lot of paper was shuffled around: Stuart, himself working in the SOE archive, estimates that in April 1946 there were 30 tons of paper comprising 66,000 files (223–24). But by this time the mammoth task of weeding out was well under way. It began early in 1942, when Cairo was clouded for days by smoke and ash as the services set fire to sensitive material in anticipation of Rommel's (fortunately averted) capture of the city. Then, between 1945 and 1950, 'at least 87%' of the files were destroyed in London (228); in late 1949 'something like 100 tons of material was destroyed' (225). Official 'weeders' have been busy ever since, in a process fiction writers have found fascinating. Michael Ondaatje's recent novel *Warlight* (2018) tells the story of Nathaniel, whose mother was involved in clandestine work with the partisans in Yugoslavia and who, after her mysterious murder, gets himself employed in the 1950s in the secret service archives in the attempt to trace her activities. His mother, it seems, has done 'unspeakable' things for her country and the novel attempts the task of finding words to articulate the disguises, pseudonyms and subterfuge used to protect wartime interests—of detecting the 'grains of sand', as the novel puts it, which might give evidence of a story. 'Anything questionable,' Nathaniel discovers, 'was burned or shredded under myriad hands. So revisionist histories began' (Ondaatje 2018, 133). Stuart writes:

> It would be interesting to hear more from surviving SOE veterans about the attitude which prevailed in the Service towards keeping records of highly sensitive operations (e.g. assassinations). Again,

there is a marked absence in the archive of documents on these.
Were they never created? Or were they carefully destroyed? If so,
when? (2006, 219)

But the window of opportunity, as he notes, closes by the year.

These revisionist histories have been greatly interested in the way
myth, rumour or fiction may prove valuable in piecing together the vast
array of information that constitutes an historical account. Nowhere
would this be more the case than in the history of a secret organisation,
where the webs of 'lies' are essential, as Churchill put it, as a bodyguard
for truth. In his study of British intelligence entitled *Empire of Secrets*
(2013), Calder Walton cites David Petrie, wartime Director General
of MI5, telling Foreign Secretary Anthony Eden that if the 'full story'
of World War 2 could ever be told, 'it could perhaps claim acceptance
as truth mainly on the grounds that it seems stranger than fiction'
(Walton 2013, 30). If it is not to be read as science fiction or fantasy,
historical fiction must be believable: it must strive for verisimilitude.
So when history itself exceeds verisimilitude, fiction may take on the
role of representing the truth of wartime conditions using different
kinds of evidence: subjective experience, hearsay, the half said. Cairo
at this time, as Artemis Cooper has demonstrated at length, was a
hotbed of intrigue fuelled by intelligence networks. Walton in fact
argues that wartime intelligence effectively began in Cairo: 'before
either MI5 or SIS had begun to envisage the idea of strategic deception,
it was being pioneered by a small, crack intelligence outfit attached to
the Cairo-based staff of the British commander in the Middle East,
General Archibald Wavell' (2013, 39). (During the war, he records,
Section B1a of MI5 was employing the astonishing number of 120
double-cross agents [43].) It was within this context that SIS made
use of writers such as Malcolm Muggeridge, Graham Greene and Ian
Fleming. One famous double agent codenamed Garbo was credited
by his MI5 handler as having an 'imagination [. . .] worthy of Milton'
(Walton 2013, 44). Operations such as Mincemeat, Torch or Fortitude
(the D-Day landings) have remained within the popular imagination
as evidence of the power of creative fictionalising for wartime strategy.

Mulgan himself, who during his time with SOE inhabited this world of inference and the not-fully-articulated, was interested in the deceptions to which 'transparent facts' may give rise. We can see this in a fascinating passage towards the end of *Report on Experience* which we have dipped into earlier but which deserves closer attention. The context is his assessment of 'a form and technique of political organization' which he has encountered in Greece, but which is 'probably not peculiar' to the country, where attitudes to truth are very different from those in the liberal environment he grew up in. Having by the start of the war suffered under at least a decade of fascism, the Greeks 'had heard too many lies themselves to be overstrict in matters of propaganda' (RE 168–69) and Mulgan, with his historical perspective and internationalist sympathies, questions the validity of his own inherited values, refusing the easy denunciations of most of his fellow BLOs in relation to communist propaganda.

> The armies of Communism have a tougher and stricter discipline than the Wehrmacht. In Lenin's day, the party had room in it for discussion and argument. If differences became too acute and on too serious a matter, the party might split, but for the most part it was evolutionary and tentative.[15] It was feeling its way and trying to look for facts, which, as Lenin remarked, are stubborn things. There is no longer any need for nonsense of this kind. The Communists we knew were organized to take and hold power and to get orders and to carry them out. They would accept any recruits that were prepared to accept their discipline and any ideas or slogans that fitted the needs of the moment.
>
> We had been brought up, I suppose, in some kind of liberal atmosphere, however incomplete. What education we had tended to make us sceptical of assertion and lovers of facts that could be proved. I don't know whether the Germans first sanctioned a

---

15   Marxist historian Eric Hobsbawm makes this same point in an essay on 'The Dialogue on Marxism' published in *Revolutionaries*: 'until the first great split within the Marxist movements during and after the first world war and the October revolution, it was accepted that a constant process of debate was normal within the social democratic parties' (1977, 111).

completely amoral basis for propaganda, or whether it goes back
to Northcliffe [newspaper magnate and Director of Propaganda
in Lloyd George's government in 1918], or is really as old as the
history of men. In our time, and in the armies that have been
fighting on our side, men have had still to be a little careful of
their facts. Deliberate distortion has been dangerous. Even over-
optimism and painting of the lily has been liable to censure. There
has been a nice salt feeling among the united nations that we
would take our facts even if they were unpleasant.

No similar happy scruple, no inhibitions from an outdated form
of education, hampered our comrades in the hills. They were clever
men, speakers of many languages, well-travelled, and they looked
on men and their emotions as something pliable to be moulded.
They were experts in mass-meetings, coiners of slogans, which
sometimes contradicted each other but were always temporarily
effective. Early attempts at argument, misquotings, denials of
something which we ourselves might have seen and have known
to be true, soon persuaded us that we were working outside our
charter and probably beyond our depth. (RE 169–70)

As so often in this slippery text, contradictory readings could
be made of this passage. Surely, one might think, this is a defence
of a Western ('united nations') reverence for facts and mistrust of
slogans or propaganda which violate this code? In claiming that early
communism's search for facts was 'nonsense', Mulgan is surely being
ironic at the expense of the Greek communists? And isn't the 'happy
scruple' to favour 'facts' an ironic jab at those who would *refute* it?
It's as if Mulgan is offering readers the opportunity to hold on to
standard liberal views if they so wish. But the underlying trajectory
of the passage, written at a time when he felt that the future needed
radically rethinking, seems to be leading stealthily in the other
direction, towards a critique of the liberal values he was raised in
and respect for the political pragmatism of his communist comrades
('always temporarily effective'). Lenin's 1916 comment about the

stubbornness of facts (in his *Imperialism*)[16] belongs to an earlier phase of communism, before the war, when his Greek comrades had time to sit around and tease out different interpretations from these stubborn facts. Those days are gone. All that matters now is the interpretation that works, including propaganda if need be. British culture, dominated by magnates of the popular press like Northcliffe, had nothing to congratulate itself on when it came to unbiased reporting and control of public opinion. The comment about liberalism (and its blind faith in facts) being an 'outdated form of education', therefore, could be read quite straightforwardly, without irony. To readers who may jump to the conclusion that mistrust of facts is symptomatic of a backward culture, Mulgan hastens to inform them that these Greeks were clever, well-educated and well-travelled men who knew what they were doing. The 'happy' scruple and 'nice' salt feeling (of the Western observer) are epithets Mulgan used often to distance himself ironically from others' complacency and prejudice.[17]

George Orwell had raised this same issue to do with historical facts or truth in one of his 'As I Please' articles in 1944. On the basis of his experience in the Spanish Civil War, Orwell pondered the way that while up until World War 1, 'the major events recorded in the history books probably happened', in the present climate 'No such thing would be possible' (1970, 109). The new power of media manipulation, it is suggested, has meant that history now 'is written by the winners' (110), who grab control of the narrative. If Franco wins in Spain, he contends,

> the history of the war will consist quite largely of 'facts' which
> millions of people now living know to be lies. One of these 'facts',
> for instance, is that there was a considerable Russian army in

16   For earlier uses of the proverb (by Alain-René Lesage, Tobias Smollett and John Adams), see quoteinvestigator.com/2010/06/18/facts-stubborn/. Date of access 22 Dec. 2021.

17   Perhaps the starkest example comes amidst his enumeration of atrocities under German occupation, concluding with the comment, 'Happy days, I guess, all over Europe' (RE 162). Another example is a confession to Gabrielle on 1 April 1945, that he no longer has 'any of the nice clear-cut theories in which I used to specialise when you knew me' (AGM 296).

Spain. There exists the most abundant evidence that there was no such army. Yet if Franco remains in power, and if Fascism in general survives, that Russian army will go into the history books and future schoolchildren will believe in it. So for practical purposes the lie will have become the truth. (110)

The parallels with the victors' (Anglo-American) narratives about Soviet intentions in post-war Greece are striking. As if fully aware of this danger, Mulgan has laid himself open to a Greek education, to a revision of the idea of the transparency of facts and a new respect for Greek shrewdness. He had been re-educated, that is, to understand that not only are facts stubborn and unyielding of their truth, they are also manipulable in the hands of stronger forces, on both sides.

SOE: History and anti-history

Joining SOE and signing the Official Secrets Act meant taking an oath not only of political neutrality but of lifelong confidentiality, meaning that most veterans held off publication of their SOE histories until the 1980s, and even then, guarded their views carefully. Mulgan's *Report on Experience* was a rare exception to this for reasons which are not entirely clear but probably had to do with its seeming compliance with official views on the resistance in Greece and evasion of open challenge to British policy at the end of the war—at least after it had passed through various stages of vetting and editing. As we have seen in the case of Myers, the accounts of other operatives rarely had a smooth passage to publication. For those of explicit left-wing sympathies, the attempt was near impossible.

An important example here is the case of Frank Thompson, whose experience as SOE agent to the communist partisans in Bulgaria remained the subject of investigation for his brother, the eminent historian E.P. Thompson, for many decades after the war. (His conclusions were only published posthumously, in 1997.) Frank Thompson had been an undergraduate at Oxford in the late 1930s in the same highly politicised climate as Mulgan, who was nine years older. Under the influence of his close friend Iris Murdoch, Frank Thompson had joined the Communist Party before volunteering for the British army and serving first in the Middle East and then on the Greek desk of SOE in Cairo in autumn 1943, immediately after Mulgan's departure for Greece. A gifted classicist with fluency in the Slavic languages of eastern Europe, Thompson was an avid admirer of the Greek resistance effort and had set his sights on underground work in Greece.[18] In the event, he was parachuted into Serbia in early 1944 to cross into Bulgaria, where he was killed by the collaborationist forces of the Bulgarian State Gendarmerie a few months later.

E.P. Thompson cites from a letter Churchill sent on 6 April 1944 to the British Ambassador in Algiers saying, 'I suppose you realise that we are weeding out remorselessly every single known Communist from all our secret organisations'. Then in a minute the following week he is quoted as saying: 'We are purging all our secret establishments of Communists because we know they owe no allegiance to us or our cause and will always betray secrets to the Soviet, even while we are working together' (E.P. Thompson 1997, 95). Although 'purging' could be read to mean 'sacking rather than liquidating Communists', as Frank's biographer Peter Conradi suggests (2013, 357), E.P. Thompson reads it more literally, with a sinister edge. E.P. Thompson's research, like our own, was considerably hampered by the refusal of access to vital documents. He writes: 'The papers of SOE remain closed to research, and such papers of the Foreign and War Offices as have been released have been carefully weeded by anti-historians.'[19] In spite of the difficulties E.P. Thompson encountered, he provides persuasive evidence that his brother was deliberately left to his fate with little intervention from SOE. Details of Frank's arrest

18 On the eve of the Sicilian landings in mid 1943, in which he was soon to participate, Frank wrote to Iris Murdoch: 'I want to talk to you about Greeks, because they are staunch anti-fascists, because they are simply among the best people I have met' (E.P. Thompson 1997, 53).

19 E.P. Thompson writes that an associate of Frank's, Sargeant Scott, 'has been prevented from publishing his own account [of their crossing into Bulgaria] by a marvellous British anti-historical device known as the Official Secrets Act' (1997, 33).

on May 31 by Bulgarian government troops and his sentence by
a mock trial of the puppet administration (which at the time was
attempting to switch allegiance to the Allies) left little doubt in
E.P.'s mind that his brother's execution six days later took place
after 'some gesture or signal' from the British administration
'offered them some license. Somebody winked' (97–98).[20] Within
the Cold War climate that had overtaken policy, British aid to
Bulgarian partisans 'was defined, by silence, as a non-event, an
unhappening' (E.P. Thompson 1997, 43). In other words, London
refused to reveal that it had attempted to take part in the Bulgarian
resistance, in this way concealing that it had originally endorsed
Frank Thompson's mission.[21]

We have referred many times to the way Churchill and the
Foreign Office's attitude to the communist resistance and to left-
wing ideologues in the armed forces began to harden from spring
1944 onwards. In a minute of February 1944 Churchill had
attacked Brigadier Myers, head of SOE in the Greek mountains
until his sudden removal in October 1943, as 'the chief man who
reared the cockatrice brute of E.A.M.-E.L.A.S.', and then, two
months later, telegraphed the Ambassador to the exiled Greek
government, Archibald Leeper: 'we are to be completely firm with
all this nonsense and pull the Greeks up with a jerk, if necessary
using force' (Auty and Clogg 1975, 180; Evans 1972, 283). There
were, therefore, precedents for rebukes and removal of sympathisers
with EAM-ELAS well before Mulgan's involvement with them; he
had slipped through to the mountains, we think, on one of SOE's
final surges of support for the left-wing *andartes*.

Frank Thompson's story makes instructive reading within the
context of Mulgan's experiences. Like Mulgan, he was of left to far-
left sympathies but described himself as a democrat, someone who

---

20   For details of the trial and its various interpretations, see Conradi 2013, 339–40.

21   In their 1947 edition of Frank's letters and diary, T.J. and E.P. Thompson only hint in passing
      at this silence. Unlike the Bulgarian government, they write, which has given 'generous
      recognition' to the role played by the British in the resistance, 'In contrast to this, official
      sources in this country have scarcely acknowledged even the existence of any Bulgarian
      resistance movement' (182).

'cares more than anything for democratic freedom' (E.P. Thompson 1997, 99). Both shared the atmosphere of 'radical populist euphoria of 1944', a belief in the possibility of 'a new communal ethic' in Europe after the war, which was itself a product of the optimism fashioned during the years of the Popular Front (E.P. Thompson, in Conradi 2013, 269). For both, a broad sympathy for many communist beliefs included (in the immediate context) the perception of the Communist Party as (as E.P. Thompson puts it) 'the universal organiser of resistance, with a discipline tough enough to withstand [the] incredibly rigorous persecution' of the Axis forces (1997, 57). For both, men like Geoffrey Garratt served as a model for an anti-imperialist critique which was all too often stifled by ruling-class interests in Britain. Garratt's *Mussolini's Roman Empire* (1938) had made an excoriating attack on the 'cynicism' and 'dishonesty' of the British government in turning a blind eye to Mussolini's imperialist ventures into first Ethiopia then Spain (Garratt 1938, 108, 237).[22] And most relevant here, both watched in dismay as Britain attempted to extend its 'sphere of influence' into Greece. E.P. Thompson records his brother's emotions from where he was working on the Greek desk in Cairo, as Frank seethed 'with the black reservoir of anger' at SOE's 'double-faced policy' towards the Greek partisans (1997, 72–73):[23]

> he soon discovered that he was part of an organisation in which the main interest of many of his superiors was in frustrating the genuine resistance movement of Greece and in dividing and discrediting the forces of E.A.M. [. . .] The whole treacherous business disgusted him. A friend of his speaks of Frank leaving the daily policy conferences in a 'state of apoplexy'. [24]

22   Mulgan's admiration for Garratt has been referred to in Chapter 1 here. For Thompson's, see T.J. Thompson and E.P. Thompson 1947, 134.

23   In their Introduction to the early memoir of Frank, his mother and brother record that Frank was finally 'unwilling to go to Greece as the agent of a double-faced policy' towards EAM and pressed for a transfer.

24   At the same time, they continue, his sense of urgency and his confidence in the ultimate outcome increased (T.J. Thompson and E.P. Thompson 1947, 16–17). From Alexandria on 29 August Frank, soon to leave for Cairo to join SOE, wrote to Iris Murdoch that he'd got an

It was this fury which changed Thompson's mind about going to Greece—and which led him to tell his parents in December that if he was still on the Greek desk by the spring, he'd 'probably [be] under close arrest' (F.T. Thompson and E.P. Thompson 1947, 165). Also relevant here is that in the period immediately following the time when Mulgan trained for SOE work, Frank Thompson was meeting frequently in Cairo with James Klugmann (whose influence at the SOE office in Cairo we have discussed in Chapter 3). We know very little about Mulgan's activities between June '43, when (as he told J.V. Wilson in the 20 April letter) he 'began to work with [the Greeks] in the Middle East', and mid September, when he left for Greece after training, but it's possible that he participated in what Conradi describes as the left-wing 'subculture' in Cairo, much of it centring around Klugmann, who was urging all on the left, communists and socialists, to form 'an alliance recalling the Popular Front in a war for "national liberation, peoples' liberation, colonial liberation"' (Conradi 2013, 268).[25] Klugmann, Conradi speculates, was almost certainly responsible for recruiting Thompson that September (268), which may well mean that he had a direct hand in recruiting Mulgan, via his influence on Keble. Where both the Thompson brothers' Eurocentric sympathies were in particular accord with Mulgan's was in their justification of local revolutionary movements in putting their own national interests first. In a wonderfully eloquent piece with elements of irony reminiscent of Mulgan's, E.P. Thompson attacks the dominant branch of Anglophone historiography, which assumes

> that it was somehow 'unfair' that partisans in the Balkans (or, for that matter, in Italy) should 'take advantage of the war' to

American speaker 'lined up for this Tuesday's lecture at one of the Services Clubs in the "The World We Want to See" series' (1947, 137).

25   Conradi is citing here from Basil Davidson's *Special Operations Europe* (1980). Frank Thompson first reported to SOE HQ in Cairo (the Rustum Buildings) on 13 September 1943 (Conradi 2013, 266); Mulgan had flown out three days before and was dropped into Greece on the night of the 10th–11th. Mulgan's letters home at the time return repeatedly to his inability to say anything about what he's doing, as well as to the fact that the work was 'near to the kind of work in war that I have always wanted to do' and that he was 'with very nice people, some of them old acquaintances from Oxford—I think perhaps I have moved up a grade in the world' (AGM 256).

effect revolutionary changes in the property statutes and the state organisations of their countries. They should have allowed themselves to be used loyally as 'instruments of pressure', thereby enabling the Western allies to defeat the German antagonist and then to restore the old order—the monarchy, the army, the police, the property statutes 'as a going concern'. I don't know why historians on this side of the Atlantic should be quite so confident about this attitude. I have heard—but perhaps this is only a myth—that revolutions and civil wars have occurred here also. In Europe, by contrast, the peasants and the poor had 'loyally' endured for centuries the demands of authoritarian masters. For most of Europe the first World War had been the dominating experience—their children had been sent out to death in myriads by their masters so that the old order could be restored. Why should another generation of the rural and urban poor young men and women, go out and face torture and death for Mr Churchill or General Donovan, but not for causes of their own? (96)

Stories untold or half told, or hinted at, were part of the fabric of conspiracy-ridden Cairo. Some are even darker than E.P. Thompson's about his brother. Fitzroy Maclean, Churchill's personal envoy to Tito's left-wing partisans in Yugoslavia, although no left-wing sympathiser himself, ended up at the time of his dispatch in mid 1943 caught between Foreign Office policy and SOE arrangements on the ground in Cairo, under the theoretical command of Lord Glenconner but the practical control of Keble. According to an article in the *Herald* (Scotland) in February 2000, newly released documents reveal that Maclean's mission to Tito was being sabotaged by SOE, which was anxious to guard its independence from Foreign Office intervention. Describing SOE Cairo as 'a byword for dirty tricks' and Keble as 'an expert in double-cross', the article argues that it was through disagreement over Maclean's role that Glenconner and Keble were removed from their posts (just as Mulgan was being sent in to Greece) and that as a result 'by October 1943 SOE, Cairo had been gelded' and placed under the control of General Henry Maitland Wilson. Maclean's mission finally went ahead, but according to his own testimony (and he had had plenty of secret service experience in SIS), he was careful not to take the first parachute offered him for his drop as 'one of the things the SOE did to people it wanted to get rid of was to put a blanket in their parachute.'[26]

How to separate rumours from facts? Mulgan was not the first SOE agent to die in mysterious circumstances or the first whose death raised suspicion. When Colonel Guy Tamplin, who had served as British representative of SOE in Russia and in the Polish section in Cairo, was found dead at his SOE desk in Cairo in November 1943, the official verdict was heart attack (Stirling et al. 2005, 185–86). Frank Thompson, working in the office at the time, described it in his diary like this:

> Perhaps the most real thing about Cairo is the sense of death. Even at G.H.Q. you can feel it. The other day some of us were going up one of the staircases when an urgent but solemn bustle surged down and pressed us against the balustrade. They carried a corpse past us, on a stretcher, covered with blankets. A Colonel had 'had it'—just stiffened out over his desk. But any day, as one walks those corridors, one expects the same thing to happen. (T.J. Thompson and E.P. Thompson 1947, 157)

One rumour was that Tamplin's boss, the same Brigadier Mervyn Keble, in the process of experimenting with new forms of poison, had committed the 'perfect crime' (Mace and Grehan 2012, 253). It is possible that Tamplin's Russian connections (he was born in Russia and married to a Latvian) were behind it. Myers revealed in the 1970s that Anthony Eden had demanded the removal of Tamplin on account of 'political taint' (Auty and Clogg 1975, 164). The Tamplin case continues to be debated.

26   'At War with the Enemy Within'. *Herald 26* Feb. 2000. heraldscotland.com/news/12200046. at-war-with-the-enemy-within/. Date of access 27 Sept. 2019.

The truth of fiction

Stories of conflicting interpretation and foul play in this atmosphere of international chaos have proved a rich source for novelists. Fiction by its nature has always served to unsettle 'facts', reminding us of their susceptibility to manipulation by forces beyond the individual's control. Modernist fiction, in particular, was predicated on the assumption that when it comes to human behaviour, 'facts' can only be approached from a multiplicity of different viewpoints— as Lawrence Durrell's *Alexandria Quartet* set out to demonstrate. As post-war publications continue to testify, the real-life stories of SOE agents' activities are often more surreptitious and suspenseful than a spy novel by John Le Carré. The world of SOE intelligence was in many ways already structured like a spy novel, where the protagonists seldom reveal what they know and the final outcome remains unpredictable. Unhampered by the Official Secrets Act and with the bigger historical picture in mind, writers were at liberty to take what they saw as the causes and consequences of events to their own reasoned-out conclusions. This doesn't mean taking to its extreme Nietzsche's famous remark that 'There are no facts, only interpretations',[27] but it does offer a salutary reminder of the way facts have an osmotic tendency to lose their hard-and-fast edges. Those associated with 'the firm' in Cairo, both in the field and back at headquarters, might have felt more at home in the conspiratorial world of Stratis Tsirkas's *Drifting Cities* (*Akyvernites Politeies*, 1960– 65) than in so-called ordinary life. This trilogy by the Cairene-Greek novelist, which has continued to act as a point of reference in Greek perceptions of Anglo-Greek relations during the war, layers one half-disclosed or misunderstood story upon another, in this way providing as good a picture as any of the atmosphere Mulgan inhabited in the final months of his life.

Of particular interest for our purposes is Tsirkas's account of the inside story of EAM and its developing conflict with the British.

27   Cited in Michael Wood, 'All the World's a Spy Novel', *London Review of Books* 42.15 (30 July 2020), 33.

Centred upon a group of left-wing activists in the Middle East from the spring of 1942 until the Lebanon Conference in May 1944, the three novels trace the progress of the movement through its optimistic inauguration, the establishment of PEEA, the rebellions in the armed forces, and then the 'betrayal' of Lebanon. Its central protagonist, Manos, is a Greek officer who has lived through the Metaxas dictatorship, the war in Spain and the defeat of the Italians in Albania but has left the Greek army to join the underground resistance against the two 'illegitimate' governments of Greece, the collaborationist government pandering to the Germans in Athens and the government-in-exile pandering to the British in Cairo. Much of what Manos thinks is very close to what Mulgan was half expressing at this time. One of many examples here is the trilogy's recording of what happened at the Lebanon Conference. There, Tsirkas writes, 'the old politicians' backing the government-in-exile at the conference (Kanellopoulos, Sofoklis Venizelos, Papandreou) 'took advantage of British protection […] to wash away the shame of their cowardly abstention from the struggle against the oppressor by heaping abuse on the Resistance' (Tsirkas 2015, 688). This assessment echoes precisely Mulgan's note in his diary at the time: 'Papandreou provides hell acct [account] of Elas from safe distance of Lebanon.'

Writing out of his own involvement with the Greek left in Egypt during the war, Tsirkas attempts a version of historical fiction in which fictional characters interact with well-known historical figures from both sides—such as Generals Maitland Wilson and Paget, and Prime Ministers Tsouderos and Venizelos. Others, like 'Eddie' Myers, Zervas and Aris, all part of Mulgan's landscape, drift in and out of the narrative. An interesting case here is that of the unnamed Greek 'General' who from his description—aged about 50, ex-military attaché in Paris, participated in the rebellion against Greek fascism in 1935, a Venizelist veering progressively to the left—is clearly a thinly disguised Sarafis. Even some of the phrases attributed to him, such as that the British are gradually placing a 'harness' on the Greek Brigades who fought well at El Alamein (Tsirkas 2015,

257),[28] seem to have been lifted out of historical accounts (Sarafis's knowledge of Woodhouse's plot). This blend of the factual and the fictional foregrounds a dominant theme of the trilogy: the difficulty of establishing the facts amidst a confusion of conflicting stories.

Tsirkas employs a myriad of different perspectives from both the Greek and the British sides, against the backdrop of his three chosen locations: Jerusalem, Cairo and Alexandria. These interwoven and often conflicting storylines reinforce the lack of consensus on either side, let alone between the two opposing ideologies, which could be summarised as imperialist and anti-imperialist. As readers we are often in the dark. Who is to be trusted? Who committed the (usually political) murder? Or, on a more basic level, who in fact *is* narrating at the moment? Changes in name and identity, essential for the leftists attempting to evade the British Secret Intelligence (or Greeks working for them), often produce an atmosphere of undecidability, which Tsirkas is happy to leave hanging. These out-of-control/rudderless ('Drifting') cities, providing hiding places and covers, are mirrored in the constantly changing policies of the EAM movement as it struggles to deal with British subversion. In between narratives of the characters' engagement with the local population in the three cities are the political debates among EAM members, who rarely agree, giving the sense of groping their way forward, making it up as they go along—recalling Mulgan's observation about the early stages in the communist movement, that 'for the most part it was evolutionary and tentative. It was feeling its way and trying to look for facts' (RE 169). The Greek left-wing resistance is by this time doubly besieged as in addition to the stated enemy—the Axis forces play a rather shadowy background role in the narrative—their supposed British allies, in possession of most of the weapons, are now the greatest threat. External models are of limited help. As Manos puts it, this was a specifically Greek 'liberation struggle on a strictly national level, devoid of class

---

28   It was even suggested, by Angelos Angelopoulos, a PEEA leader who became one of the six
      left-wing ministers in the short-lived Papandreou government in late 1944, that the British
      themselves were inciting these mutinies in order to justify the purges that were to follow. As
      evidence he cites from the diaries of ex-Prime Minister Tsouderos himself (Angelopoulos
      1994, 69).

implications' and therefore resistant to any question of entering a 'Soviet phase' (626). But in their insistence on full co-operation with PEEA as the only legitimate government, EAM was up against too powerful an enemy. Tsirkas charts the full irony and horror of the way 'barbed-wire cages full of Greek anti-Fascists rapidly cropped up all over the African continent' (688) after the April 1944 rebellion in the Greek armed forces. After this there is little room for debate among individual members of EAM. Collective action, avoiding factionalism, is their only option. Through Manos the intellectual, constantly accused of 'over-subjectivity' by his comrades, we are made to feel both the difficulty and the necessity of conformity and obedience to the movement.

After the 'honeymoon with the Allies is over' (437) from mid to late 1943 onwards (the dates and events are precisely rendered), the challenge of escaping from the 'labyrinth' of British intrigue takes the third novel, *The Bat*, into Gothic mode. Some of Tsirkas's flights of fantasy, especially his insistence on the vampiric excesses of female desire, stretch the metaphor too far. But the point can be taken, that within the final months of what was rapidly becoming the British occupation of Greece, the stakes were raised to a pitch of terror beyond the reach of realistic narrative. Spies, agents, informers, lies, secrecy, bluff, betrayal, defections, double-crossings, self-delusion, machinations, treacheries: it's as if Tsirkas has scoured a thesaurus to find as many words as he can to recreate the atmosphere. One murder whose perpetrators *are* revealed is that of Dr Robbie Richards, who teaches classics at Cairo University but meets a sticky end at the hands of British intelligence agents on account of his criticism of British policy. Shortly before his death he warns Manos to 'keep away from the quagmire of politics, my friend [. . .] You cannot possibly imagine the intrigue, the Machiavellian maneuvers that go on, the betrayals' (281). Behind their debate lies the recurrent theme of history writing, how to convey truth in this sort of environment in Cairo, 'where British foreign policy is formed, and [. . .] where everything is resolved in the end' (361). Engels's famous words to Bloch serve as an epigraph to the third volume:

> History makes itself [out of] innumerable intersecting forces,
> an infinite series of parallelograms of forces [. . .] what each
> individual wills is obstructed by everyone else, and what emerges
> is something that no one willed. (426)

Tsirkas's maze of narratives gives form to this insight, but in the final analysis it is Manos's idea of how 'truth' will emerge that the trilogy endorses. He'll write the history of it all one day, he tells a comrade, but the only way it can have any plausibility is if he 're-create[s] the truth with my imagination and mold[s] it into shapes that I can't possibly foresee at the moment' (394). Stubborn facts, even when accessible, are unlikely to provide the full picture. This debate has particular significance for the history of Anglo-Greek relations in this period, which is still in the process of being rewritten.

As a farewell to Mulgan's (and Greek history's) noble 'general', Stefanos Sarafis, it seems fitting to record here another particularly tragic 'sticky end', one consonant with the atmosphere of conspiracy and conjecture which dominates in Tsirkas's novels. According to the evidence of Stefanos's English wife, Marion, it took her several years to want to acknowledge, and then to piece together, the facts relating to his death on 31 May 1957. Following their daily routine after his return from work that day, the couple set off for the beach in the seaside suburb of Athens where they lived. As they were crossing the road, Sarafis was hit by a speeding car, which killed him almost instantly; Marion was badly injured beside him. By this time, the Americans had replaced the British in the role of caretakers of Greece. Agents of the CIA, she discovered, had been renting the house next to theirs and were proved to have been following their every move. The American serviceman driving the car was returned to the US straight away and seems to have escaped prosecution. Sarafis, after his release from internal exile, had become General Secretary of United Democratic Left (EDA), which actively opposed the presence of American military bases in the country.[29]

---

29   See also mixanitouxronou.gr/o-antras-mou-dolofonithike-ton-skotose-i-cia-to-periergo-troxaio-ston-alimo-me-odigo-amerikano-sminia-kai-thyma-ton-stratigo-stefano-sarafi-protagonisti-tis-ethnikis-antistasi/. Date of access 22 Dec. 2021.

This 'staged accident', Marion Sarafis suggests, was used a few years later for the assassination in Thessaloniki of another prominent EDA politician, Grigoris Lambrakis, whose story was told in the novel *Z* by Vasilis Vasilikos and later made into a well-known film by Costa-Gavras (1980a, xcviii-ci).

Reasons for optimism

It's sometimes argued that Mulgan committed suicide out of despair at the political outcome in Greece, what James Bertram referred to as 'the Greek debacle'. In an essay in 1969 he wrote that Mulgan

> learnt to do a number of difficult things with real expertise—journalism, publishing, soldiering—but none of them really satisfied the kind of commitment he had been looking for. Even fraternity, the last and most durable of the great watchwords of revolution, had become a tattered banner, when he had seen it torn apart by the blind fury of left and right alike. (Day 1977, 53–54)[30]

It could perhaps be contended, however, that this conclusion reflected not so much Mulgan's but rather Bertram's view, his own disillusionment with revolutionary politics a quarter century after the war. For all his membership of the October Club in Oxford, his long experience in China and later surveillance by the SIS, Bertram came to be very critical of the left. It's possible Mulgan too might have shifted his position in this direction as the Cold War deepened in the 1950s–60s. But at this stage, as his writings to those he most trusted indicate, he held firm to his beliefs. It seems equally likely that his despair was not *with* the left but *for* those on the left like Sarafis, Bakirtzis and Tsamakos, men who were at this very time, in early

---

30   This was also Paul Day's view in the *Dictionary of New Zealand Biography* in 1998, that Mulgan had become 'increasingly disillusioned [. . . with] what seemed to him the failure of socialism' (Day 1998). Martyn Brown traces the shift in Day's view of Mulgan's death, from the claim that it was an 'insoluble mystery' in his 1968 book, to this view decades later (Brown 2014, 13).

1945, being rounded up by government forces to be sent into exile.[31]

But it might also have seemed to Mulgan, as it did to many at this time, that there was much to look forward to. The day he died, 26 April 1945, was an auspicious moment on the world stage in relation to both the end of the war and international peace-keeping initiatives. On that day, at 4.40 pm, the Soviet forces of the 58th Guards Division of the Red Army finally met up with the US First Army near the medieval town of Torgau in Germany, just 70 miles south of Berlin. From that day the German capital was encircled; Hitler committed suicide in his bunker five days later. The scene, as described by many, was of 'the gayest fraternisation' between Soviets and Americans, signalling that 'the war appeared all but over' (Stafford 2007, 150–51). In his diary, Mulgan had charted the progress of the Soviets meticulously as they moved in a south-westerly direction[32]—with emotions, one would assume, rather different from the dread of those on the right. The other significant event on April 25 was the opening of the international conference in San Francisco for the purpose of founding the United Nations organisation on the basis of the Dumbarton Oaks and Yalta proposals. The delegates of 50 or so countries, as Mulgan may well have known, included New Zealanders Peter Fraser as well as Alister McIntosh and Joseph (J.V.) Wilson from External Affairs.[33] The occasion was not without tensions and conflicts: Poland, for example, had been excluded from representation, a further insult after its repeated betrayal by the Allies. But the meeting had high symbolic significance for the future of world peace.

On a personal level at this time, Mulgan's feelings about leaving

31   For a detailed analysis of the persecutions, which cites from a range of newspaper reports, see *Lefki Vivlos* 1945b, 51–86.

32   See Mulgan's diary entries in the memos for weeks ending 20 February, 27 February, 26 March ('Russians going full out for Rumanian frontier, implies belief Balkan crisis may be around the corner'), 2 April, 16 April ('Russians have taken Odessa & are near Sebastopol'), 18 June, 9 July ('Russians take Vilna [Vilnius, in Lithuania]'), 16 July ('Russians take Minsk [. . .] advance on Lvov').

33   In his 22 April report to J.V. Wilson (2), Mulgan describes examples of a particular type of communist he's known in Greece (clever, well-travelled, multilingual men), including 'Karageorgos' (Kostas Karagiorgis, real name Gyftodimos), who 'has left for San Francisco as a journalist to report the conference.'

Greece included a complex and deep-rooted sense of commitment. Towards the end of his life, he had many reasons to return to the idea of his 'regrettably intimate acquaintance' with Greece, with its heroic resistance. In the April 17 letter to Gabrielle, after describing the moving trip to Fafoutis's village in Evoia, he reiterated: 'I wish I didn't love this country so much, or so that I hate leaving it' (AGM 299). Perhaps the necessity to leave violated a sense of commitment to the country and its future, a sense that his political insights or actions might have made a small difference if he stayed. It was at this time as well that he wrote to J.V. Wilson that if he were a young man in Greece at that moment, he would have been tempted to join the Communist Party (KKE), with a view to reforming it from within. The regret, in other words, seems to have had as much to do with a reformist political commitment as it did with any romantic attachment to the country's people and places. Like Frank Thompson at the end of his short life, he may have discarded many of his illusions but at the same time continued to hold on to what Frank called 'the craziest of all, perhaps—that the whole of life can be cast anew and that it's worth trying' (T.J. Thompson and E.P. Thompson 1947, 166). All his forward-looking statements around this time echo this sentiment.

The last published letter Mulgan wrote to his parents, on April 6, raises issues characteristic of the ambivalence of so much of his writing, where your interpretation depends on your own point of view or bias. In our reading, naturally, we cannot claim to be free of this.

He begins by explaining why his present plans are rather 'fluid': that he's been 'immersed' in the work in the Athens office and thus hasn't transferred sooner to the New Zealand division. He then continues:

> I'm due to leave Greece some time about the end of this month and the British army will certainly demobilise me quickly once their demobilisation plan sets in. I've had about enough and on all counts it's time I came home. It has seemed simpler to carry on in

the work I've been doing.

Actually, though the war is ending, it's a most difficult business to dissociate oneself from Europe. We aren't going blithely into peace like last time but merging in my experience from occupation into something that is almost equally difficult. I've been very depressed lately at the trend of events around me. I know that it's partly because I'm close to a situation that I've come to know rather too well, and also that nothing is happening that we mightn't have anticipated, but it still doesn't save me from depression. So few people seem to have learned from the war. In Greece now there is a foolish right-wing set who have just succeeded in upsetting the fairly fragile Plastiras government. What they hope to gain by it I don't know but they're operating in a kind of vacuum, that has a radius of about five hundred yards from the hotel where I'm now living. In Greece as a whole there is a strong and intransigent communist organisation which still controls all the villages and probably most of the towns, though covertly. The mass of the people are bewildered and lost between these two extremes [. . .] they need a military government, preferably international. Myself I've reached depths of verbal irony lately that would have done Lord Birkenhead credit. As one example, a rich lady who had spent all the war in America returned to her handsome house, found British soldiers living in it, had them ejected, complained of the damage—half the houses in Athens are damaged one way or another. I offered to take her down to the cemetery in Phaleron where there are five hundred graves of English soldiers who were killed for some odd reason protecting her house from the communists. I hope our embassy which befriends her, didn't ever get to hear that I concluded this particular argument by saying that I hoped the next revolution would make a cleaner job. In fact, there's no use getting angry with people, the rich are children like the poor and just as ignorant. But when you know and like the simple, home-loving English soldiers that have been killed in these wild countries for no good reason, it's easy to become bad-tempered. (AGM 297–98)

What are we to take from this exasperated outpouring? Do we read the sentence 'I've been very depressed lately at the trend of events around me' as indicating a psychological state, supporting the suicide thesis? Or, knowing Mulgan's political engagement, do we place the emphasis on the object of his depression, the recent disastrous events in Greece? It's certainly these that he goes on to talk about. The short-lived Plastiras government which replaced that of Papandreou, set up with British backing, was brought down mainly by pressure from royalist groups and by the rise of the fascist 'X' organisation under Giorgios Grivas (Sweet-Escott 1954, 45–46). On April 7, the day after this letter, Plastiras was replaced by Petros Voulgaris (who would last only four months), the man responsible for suppressing the naval mutiny in the Middle East the year before.[34] These events should have been foreseen, Mulgan protests: 'nothing is happening that we mightn't have anticipated'. The right-wing government, he repeats here, is operating in a vacuum within a 500-yard radius (around Kolonaki Square), totally cut off from the 'strong' (anti-monarchist) political wishes of the rest of the country. The assessment of the communists as 'intransigent' applies here to the communists in the strict sense (the KKE, as opposed to EAM-ELAS in general). The split in the movement was becoming increasingly apparent after the *Dekemvriana*: his ELAS comrades in Thessaly, he told Gabrielle in late December, were not taking any part in the fighting in Athens (AGM 286). And then the affection for the 'simple, home-loving English soldiers' certainly chimes with feelings expressed elsewhere for these victims of mistaken national policies. The force of the criticism, in the final analysis, seems to be directed against privilege—the rich (Greek-American?) 'befriended' by the British Embassy, who has the presumption to request compensation. In a by now familiar aside, he hopes his bosses won't get to hear about his treasonous enthusiasm at the prospect of the next revolution

---

34   KKE, Sweet-Escott continues, regarded the Voulgaris government as a tool of the British. The 'shape of things to come', he notes, 'was shown by the rapid filling up of the prisons with alleged Communists' (1954, 45–46). In his report to J.V. Wilson (4), Mulgan refers to the rounding up of four men ('communists?') by 'a patrol of national guard' in the village he was staying in on Evoia. Between 1944 and 1952, there were 26 changes of government in Greece (Angelopoulos 1994, 190–91).

making 'a cleaner job' of demolishing her lavish house.

Is this suicidal despair, or political passion? The second alternative seems to us at least as likely as the first, given the context. Above all, given the depth of Mulgan's political sensibilities, his continued faith in a socialist brave new world, a defeatist gesture at the last seems right out of character. It's sometimes said that Mulgan dreaded peace as worse than war.[35] But this was roundly contradicted in a late letter to Gabrielle:

> no one around me [in Athens at the beginning of April] seems to feel much the better or happier or to look forward to peace with any exhilaration. I don't feel this way myself, and reckon the peace will be all right. In a way I think it's a good thing that the war is going to end without any clear-cut armistice, and it's a sign of hope that people don't expect the millennium to break when peace is declared. (AGM 295–96)

Then straight away, as so often, he moves to the topic of Greek communism, not this time to the 'intransigence' of party policies but rather to its promise, being 'as strongly established as ever with an organisation that I see no sign of anyone being able to break' (AGM 296). A fortnight earlier he wrote to her about his 'deep convictions about people and society and the way the world should be made to exist for us' (AGM 293).

This last statement comes in the letter accompanying the manuscript of *Report on Experience* he was sending Gabrielle. It is striking to find Mulgan writing so optimistically about the future at this stage, about his commitment to what he'd elsewhere called 'the concept of Europe in our day' (AGM 265); anyone reading the book through the lens of an imminent suicide will be inclined to bypass it as bluff, or at least a facile attempt to steer away from a depressing conclusion. But the terms of reference are highly consistent with Mulgan's 'deep convictions', the convictions that had shaped his

---

35   To support this, reference is sometimes made to Johnson's comment to O'Reilly at the end of *Man Alone*, that he'd 'been in wars, there's nothing in them. The peace is more dangerous' (Mulgan 2021, 221).

thought and action over the past decade: an optimistic sense of the
'chemical change [. . .] taking place in Europe', described by Frank
Thompson to his brother E.P. in late 1943 (T.J. Thompson and E.P.
Thompson 1947, 140) and published in the memoir of his life in the
same year as Mulgan's *Report on Experience*. These were ideals that
guided Mulgan through to the last. The penultimate paragraph of
his book reads as follows:

> For ourselves, we have been the gainers from this war. We have
> seen a good deal of death but have learnt by contrast to appreciate
> the living. Each spring now has promise for us. Not all of us were
> family men by instinct, but are friendly now and made happy by
> every small child that we see, for the new generations that are
> coming on to support us. The sparse green of Attica and rare fruit
> blossoms in the city of Athens never looked or smelled sweeter in
> all their long history than they did in the last spring of the great
> European War when we began to make plans for a new Europe
> and a new world. (RE 199)

If this optimism seems deluded and short-sighted in view of the
Cold War conditions ahead, it is important to remember the time
and place, the particularities of left-wing resistance ideology across
Europe that inspired so many. The persistence of Mulgan's optimism
through to 1945 was far from unique, as indicated in an assessment
by Neal Ascherson, reviewing a recent book on an SOE agent in the
French resistance:

> During the Second World War, Resistance movements throughout
> Nazi-occupied Europe shared a passionate 'never again' mood, a
> conviction that after this global nightmare everything would be
> changed and made new. No more government corruption, no
> more giant industrial trusts and monopolies, never again mass
> unemployment—all the laissez-faire compost thought to have
> bred fascism. For a few years, it seemed possible that Western
> and Central Europe might be restored by coalitions of democratic

socialists, communists and 'progressive' Christian Democrats—
movements that had co-operated in the underground struggle.
(2020, 28)

That Mulgan was anticipating this 'new Europe and a new world'
with such confidence makes his early death, like that of Thompson
and so many others, particularly tragic.

Appendix A: The suicide letter

My dear Dolbey,

I am sorry to leave this particular problem of liquidation on your hands. The fact is that when I came out from Greece last November, I found I was suffering from cancer of the throat—(I had been warned of this some years ago and gave up smoking and drinking for a long time without any effect except a diminution in the pleasures of life). As you know, this is an unpleasant disease and not very curable. Nor have I any desire to prolong my life for a few months or a year or two as an invalid. I have enjoyed life too much to want it in a reduced or a second-rate form. You'll forgive my quoting the classics to you on this occasion but Seneca remarked, dealing with this subject, that he was prepared to face pain but not a life which pain robbed of its full value.

If the war had gone on, I would have kept quiet and continued with it, but the fighting has almost ended and there is a need now for normal and well-balanced men with a sense of continuity and a belief in their own future as well as in the future of the world. I've got a good belief—more than yourself I suspect—in this latter project, but little for myself and would soon become a drag on those who have, as it is, plenty of work in front of them.

I don't know whether it will be possible, but would greatly appreciate it if you could present some 'cover story' to my wife and family. Tell them I died suddenly of a fever or took an overdose of morphine by mistake. I have a small son whom I've barely seen as a baby but who is now five years old and would prefer him to grow up without any shadow from his father to perplex him. It's partly for this reason that I don't want to go home to die slowly as an invalid. There isn't any question of my wanting an army pension, since I'm adequately insured and my wife and son will be all right, but if you could unofficially do this for me I would be very grateful.

I would have got killed more decently in war or manufactured for myself an accident in Greece but felt in the first place that officers who go around trying to get themselves killed are an unnecessary liability to their men, and secondly that Greece has enough troubles of its own without my own suicide on top of it all.

I've jotted down a few notes on the points we left outstanding to-day, I dont think [*sic*] there's much of importance. There are a lot of untidy ends that I'd like to have settled for you before I left Greece but the general outline is all right. In a short and not very productive life, I remember with fleeting pride that I managed to live in friendship with a lot of different and differing Greeks and hope a little of this wont [*sic*] have been entirely wasted.

Again with apologies,
Yours ever,
[signed] John Mulgan

(TNA FO 841/524)

Appendix B: Medical report by Dr (Major) Kennedy

CONFIDENTIAL   A.P.I.S.
The Commander,   G.H.Q., M.E.F.
Force 133, M.E.F.   25 June 1945

91369 – Lt.Col.J.A.E.MULGAN – Oxf. & Bucks.

In reply to your AQ/71OA, I have to state that, on his return from services in GREECE, I examined the above-named officer to determine whether he was suffering from any kind of strain as a result of his long period in enemy territory. This examination was not specially indicated in Lt. Col. MULGAN's case, but was a routine procedure for all officers coming out of the Field. It was carried out on 24.11.44 and on the same day he had a full medical examination by Capt. GRANT at my office.

I have followed Col. MULGAN's career in Force 133 as I also examined him before he went to GREECE. He was a man of remarkably high intelligence (actual Intelligence Tests were done although the fact was indicated by his academic career) who was outstandingly successful in the Field and who, on his return, showed no signs whatever of strain although quite a high proportion of officers who served in his area exhibited signs of anxiety. As a result of this examination I was able to recommend him with confidence from this psychological point of view for more than one appointment which was offered to him. It appeared that there was competition for his services.

While episodes of mild depression are not uncommon in men of his intellectual level, there was no evidence in Col. MULGAN's case at the time that he had ever suffered from such an attack and no evidence whatever that he was likely to entertain the idea of suicide. The result of the medical examination showed that he had

had malaria while we [*sic*] was in GREECE, but that this had been successfully treated. He was in excellent physical condition and no major abnormalities were found. He was regarded by Capt. GRANT as correctly placed in his medical category 'A'.

The notes of his examination are held by me should they be required in the future.

(sgd) A. Kennedy, Major

R.A.M.C.

(TNA FO 841/524)

Appendix C: Chronological outline

1911, December 31: John Alan Edward Mulgan (JM) born.

1933, October 10: JM leaves New Zealand to continue his studies at Oxford University.

1935, July: JM begins working at Oxford University Press.

1936, August 4: Greek Prime Minister General Ioannis Metaxas, with the consent of the Greek king, suspends the constitution.

1937, July: JM marries Gabrielle Wanklyn. Son Richard born March 1940.

1939, September: *Man Alone* published.

1939, September: outbreak of World War 2.

1939, September: JM called up to join the Oxfordshire and Buckinghamshire Light Infantry.

1940, October 28: Mussolini issues ultimatum to Greece to cede Greek territory; PM Ioannis Metaxas refuses. Greek army resists the offensive and forces the Italian army to retreat into Albania.

1941, January 29: Metaxas dies suddenly and the king, George II, appoints Alexandros Koryzis PM. Unable to control the state apparatus due to pro-Nazi fifth column, Koryzis commits suicide.

1941, February–April: New Zealand, Australian and British troops arrive in Greece to help resist the German invasion.

1941, April 6: Germans launch major attack against Greece across Yugoslavian and Bulgarian borders.

1941, April: A reduced Greek army at the borders collapses within a few days. Allied troops forced to retreat, fighting at several narrow passages on the mainland, and by end of month evacuate to Crete and Egypt.

1941, April 21: Emmanouil Tsouderos sworn in as PM.

1941, April 23: General Georgios Tsolakoglou signs capitulation of Greek army.

1941, April 27: Germans enter Athens.

1941, May 20: Offensive in Crete by airborne German forces defended by Allies and local recruits and civilians under General Freyberg. Evacuation of Allies to Egypt starts within six days.

1941, May 22: Greek king and his government depart Crete for Egypt, to set up government-in-exile.

1941, September 17: Communist Party (KKE), along with various small groups, forms National Liberation Front (EAM).

1941, autumn: Thanasis Klaras ('Aris Velouhiotis') sent by EAM to organise resistance groups in the mountains of Roumeli.

1942, February: EAM establishes its own army, ELAS.

1942, April: First and Second Greek Brigades formed in Egypt.

1942, May: JM transfers to Royal West Kents as second-in-command of 4th Battalion.

1942, September: JM's battalion suffers heavy losses in defence of El Alamein.

1942, October 23–24: Allied forces under Montgomery begin attack at El Alamein. Greek First Brigade participates.

1942, November 29: Small group of British-controlled saboteurs (including Woodhouse and New Zealanders Edmonds and Barnes), under Brigadier Eddie Myers, with help of both ELAS and EDES partisans, blow up Gorgopotamos viaduct. The 'British' team stays on to form core of SOE's British Military Mission (BMM).

1943, March–July: Two Greek Brigades in Egypt mutiny in rebellion against right-wing elements in their ranks and are put down by British forces.

1943, March 20: Napoleon Zervas, leader of EDES, sends message of loyalty to Greek king.

1943, late March: After complaints against his commanders, JM released from West Kents.

1943, May: JM begins training for SOE in Cairo and Haifa, Palestine.

1943, July: Mussolini falls from power and is replaced by General Badoglio.

1943, August–September: Myers (head of BMM) takes representatives of Greek resistance bands (EAM, EDES and EKKA) to Cairo for talks. They insist the Greek king pledges not to return before a referendum. King refuses and representatives return to Greece empty handed.

1943, September 8: Italian surrender.

1943, September 11: JM dropped by parachute into Greece.

1943, October 21: Fighting between EDES and ELAS.

1944, March 10: PEEA (Government of Free Greece in the Mountains) founded by EAM and calls for national unity.

1944, March 30: PM of government-in-exile, Tsouderos, refuses PEEA's demands. Rebelling Greek armed forces dissolved by British and replaced by brigade of right-wing officers and men.

1944, April 14: Tsouderos resigns and is replaced by Sofoklis Venizelos.

1944, April 26: Georgios Papandreou replaces Venizelos as PM.

1944, May 17–20: Lebanon Conference, chaired by Papandreou, where EAM-ELAS (initially) agrees to participate in government of national unity.

1944, October: German troops begin withdrawal from Greece.

1944, October 18: Government-in-exile, under PM Papandreou, returns to Athens.

1944, November 9: JM returns to Cairo.

1944, December 3: ELAS refuses to disband and EAM calls for demonstration in Athens. Police open fire on demonstrators.

1944, December–January 1945: *Ta Dekemvriana* ('December events')—British and right-wing Greek government forces battle ELAS in Athens and Piraeus. Defeat of ELAS forces.

1945, January 15: JM returns to Athens as head of the Liquidation Fund office (Adv. Force 133).

1945, February 12: Varkiza Agreement signed by the British-backed Greek government and EAM, after which ELAS relinquishes its arms and equipment.

1945, March: JM posts MS of *Report on Experience* to wife Gabrielle in New Zealand.

1945, April 19: JM leaves Greece for Cairo.

1945, April 26: JM, aged 33, found dead in his room at the Continental Hotel in Cairo.

1946–49: Civil War in Greece, ending with defeat of left-wing *Dimokratikos Stratos* (Republican/Democratic Army), with casualties exceeding 150,000 and 57,000 forced into exile.

Appendix D: Short biographies of main Greek figures

Aris, 'Aris Velouhiotis' (Thanasis Klaras) (1905–1945). Leading *Kapetanios* of ELAS forces. Born Lamia (in Roumeli), studied agriculture in Larissa. Joined Communist Party (KKE). Jailed several times, then on Aegina in late 1936 tortured under interrogation, methods used by the notorious Maniadakis for the Metaxas dictatorship. In July 1939 signed statement of 'repentance', denouncing the KKE, in order to be released: this left a stain on his reputation. In 1940 fought in Greek army on Albanian front. After German invasion sent by EAM to Roumeli to set up resistance, resulting in the formation of ELAS, which soon numbered thousands of (eventually over 100,000) fighters. Huge prestige in mountains; known for effective (sometimes brutal) discipline. Participated (with SOE & EDES) in destruction of Gorgopotamos viaduct in Nov. 1942. Before German evacuation in Oct. 1944, sent to Peloponnese where fought Security Battalions. Signed (with Sarafis) demobilisation of ELAS forces under Varkiza Agreement in Feb. 1945 but later refused to comply & took to mountains again to start insurgency against new government & its British allies. Denounced by KKE leader Zachariadis &, on the run, (probably) committed suicide in June 1945.

Bakirtzis, Evripidis (1895–1947). Hellenic Army officer before war. Awarded DSO at Battle of Skra (May 1918). Dismissed from army twice beacause of involvement in pro-republican coup attempts. Sentenced to death twice (in 1926 & 1935) but sentences commuted. During Axis occupation was first military liaison between Greeks & British & led clandestine network code-named Prometheus, which after the British evacuation in May 1941 sent information to SOE in Cairo via wireless transmitter. Forced to leave Athens in early 1942 when his cover blown. Returned in Sept. 1943 to join Psarros & resistance group

EKKA. Later joined EAM-ELAS after witnessing its success in the mountains. Helped found PEEA: initially President, then Vice President. With Markos Vafiadis, led ELAS units to liberate Thessaloniki in Oct. 1944. As ELAS officer, dismissed from Greek army after war. Exiled (with Sarafis & others) to island of Icaria in Sept. 1946. Found dead in his cell the following year.

Contomichalos, Paul (1920–2008). Egyptian Greek, grew up in the Sudan & Alexandria. Arrived in the Greek mountains in August 1943 & accompanied JM as interpreter in dealings with the *andartes*. Of Venizelist sympathies.

'Karagiorgis' (Gyftodimos), Kostas (1905–1954). Middle-class background, studied medicine & joined Young Communist League of Greece (OKNE). Worked as journalist & wrote for communist paper *Rizospastis*. After time in prison moved to Vienna, Paris, then (in 1934–36) to Moscow, where studied at Workers' University (KUTV) & became critical of Stalin's show trials. Imprisoned & exiled on return to Greece. Along with wife (also a KKE member), arrived in Thessaly in 1943. *Kapetanios* of 10th Division of ELAS. After liberation was chief editor of *Rizospastis*. When paper (& KKE) banned in 1947, fled to mountains & joined *Dimokratikos Stratos*. Blamed Zachariadis for its defeat in 1949 & dismissed from party. Imprisoned in Romania, where he contracted TB & died.

Papandreou, Georgios (1888–1968). Politician, served three times as Prime Minister of Greece. Of liberal democratic sympathies; fanatically anti-communist in 1940s. Installed by the British to lead government-in-exile in April 1944. After liberation in October, returned to Athens & served as PM for another two months.

Partsalidis, Dimitrios (1903–1980). Born in Pontos & came to Greece with exchange of populations in 1922. Studied at Workers' University (KUTV) in Moscow. Worked in tobacco cultivation in Greece. Joined KKE & in 1934 elected Mayor of Kavala. General Secretary of EAM 1944–48. Signatory (for EAM) of Varkiza Agreement in Feb. 1945. During Civil War succeeded

Markos Vafiadis as head of Provisional Democratic Government. In exile in USSR from 1949. Died in Athens.

Peltekis, Yannis (1904–69). School in Thessaloniki, studied law in Switzerland. Agent for the British, carrying out espionage & sabotage from early in the occupation with clandestine network code-named Apollo/Yvonne; one of the most successful early saboteurs in the Athens area. Accused (by the Foreign Office) of collaborating with EAM-ELAS; simultaneously accused of being a double agent but acquitted in British inquiry & enjoyed particular confidence of the British after the war. Worked with JM in office of Liquidation Fund in Athens. Minister of Mercantile Marine in unelected government of Sofoulis, 1945–46.

Psarros, Dimitrios (1893–1944). Graduated Greek Army Academy in 1916, when he joined Venizelist National Defence government. Saw service in WW1 & Greco-Turkish war (1919–22). Military studies in France. Participated in Venizelist coup attempt in 1935, court-martialled & dismissed from army. In April 1942, along with Georgios Kartalis, Bakirtzis & others, founded EKKA (fighting force 5/42 Evzone Regiment) which was to become third largest resistance organisation. The band, supported exclusively by the British, operated mainly in central Greece, in area of Fokida. Murdered, probably by Evthymios Zoulas, during conflict with ELAS forces. Death caused horror at PEEA HQ (& in JM) & damaged ELAS's reputation.

Sarafis, Stefanos (1890–1957). (JM's 'general'.) Born in Trikala. Studied law at University of Athens. Enlisted in army in Balkan Wars (Lieutenant in 1913). In France in 1924 for higher military studies: School of Officers at Versailles then Alsace. From Sept. 1931 to 1933, military attaché in Paris at rank of Colonel. Republican with socialist leanings. Took part in two Venizelist coup attempts in 1933 & 1935. Discharged from army & exiled to Milos, where met English archaeologist Marion Pascoe, later his wife. Early contacts with EKKA during occupation. Arrested by ELAS, whose organisation & strength impressed him. A month later accepted role of head of general staff of ELAS &

played leading role in Greek resistance over next 18 months, both as Commander-in-Chief of ELAS & as negotiator for its position in government of national unity. In internal exile 1946–48. Thereafter leading role in EDA (United Democratic Left). Killed when hit by speeding car of officer of US Air Force.

Siantos, Giorgios (1890–1947). Born in Thessaly of peasant background; worked in tobacco industry. In infantry in Balkan Wars & WW1. Leading role in tobacco workers' union. Exiled under Metaxas. Acting General Secretary of KKE while Zachariadis interned in Dachau. Opposed hard (Stalinist) line of party as represented by members like Ioannidis. Leading role in EAM Central Committee from time of its formation in Sept. 1941. Leading role in PEEA. Condemned by Zachariadis on his return for signing Varkiza Agreement in Feb. 1945. Died soon after of heart failure.

Svolos, Alexandros (1892–1956). Studied law in Constantinople & Athens. Taught at university; 1917–20 headed Labour & Social Policy Directorate in Ministry of Economy. 1929–46 Professor of Constitutional Law at Athens University, though dismissed in 1935 & 1936 & sent into internal exile. Strong socialist & democratic views but not member of KKE. Appointed President of PEEA in April 1944 to replace Bakirtzis, who became Vice President. Finance Minister in the short-lived Papandreou government. Resigned on Dec. 2, 1944, along with other EAM members. After war, with disintegration of EAM, formed new party ELD/SKE (Popular Democratic Union/Socialist Party of Greece).

Tsamakos, Konstantinos (1890?–?) Grew up in remote mountain area of Tzoumerka, Epirus. Enlisted in army & fought in Balkan Wars of 1912–13. Wounded in Battle of Skra in May 1918. Rose in military ranks but as Venizelist, participated in coup attempts in the 1930s & was discharged from army. Left leaning in sympathies but never member of KKE. Joined ELAS in 1943. Commander from Sept. 1943 of 16th Division of ELAS, which in March 1944 became a Brigade & was attached to 13th Division.

Promoted by PEEA to Major General in July 1944, then Director General to Secretariat for War. In this capacity welcomed eight Russian delegates at Neraida airstrip on 28 July. In Sept. appointed Commander of overall Mainland Group Divisions. In early 1945 instructed by ELAS to release the 1,100 British hostages held by ELAS. In Sept. 1946 sent into internal exile along with Sarafis & others. Later denounced by KKE for having made peace with Sofoulis's 'non-Communist left' government. Formal discharge from army on 1 Jan. 1948; retired in Athens & published stories about his native village.

Tsiminaki, Zoi (1906?–?). Long-term partner of Peltekis, with whom she collaborated in the Apollo/Yvonne network in Athens. Escaped with him to Middle East in mid 1943. Worked with JM in Liquidation Fund office in Athens. After war returned to her position in Bank of Greece.

Tzimas, Andreas ('Vasilis Samariniotis') (1909–1972). Of Vlach origins; grew up in Kozani. Studied law in Athens, joining OKNE (Young Communist League of Greece), then practised law in Florina. Elected to parliament in 1936. Internal exile (with Aris) during Metaxas dictatorship; released June 1941. Founding member of KKE & member of its Central Committee. Political advisor to EAM. Representing ELAS (with Sarafis), signed National Bands Agreement with British in June 1943. Strong supporter (with Aris) of the peasant guerrilla struggle, as opposed to the urban proletarian model supported by KKE & Central Committee of EAM. After war suspected as 'Titoist' by KKE; self-exile in Eastern bloc.

Zervas, Napoleon (1891–1957). Born Arta, Epirus. Enlisted in army & served in Balkan Wars & WW1. Appointed Lieutenant Colonel under government of Venizelos (1928–32). Along with other Venizelist/anti-monarchist officers founded EDES in Sept. 1941. Eventually (July 1942) bribed by SOE (with 24,000 sovereigns) to take to mountains in Epirus on western mainland, along with second-in-command Pyromaglou. In Nov. 1942 EDES participated (along with ELAS & British & New Zealand agents) in destruction of Gorgopotamos viaduct. Suspected by SOE of self-interest & slack command. Began to recruit royalists. In March 1943, under pressure from Woodhouse, sent message of loyalty to king. Strongly anti-communist. Conflicts with ELAS from 1943. Suspected of collaborating with Germans to overcome ELAS. In late 1944 EDES & British took over the Ionian coast, expelling the Muslim Cham Albanian minority (of around 20,000), many of whom had collaborated with Axis. During *Ta Dekemvriana*, EDES attacked by Aris's ELAS forces & expelled to Corfu. Dissolved EDES in Feb. 1945. Political activity after war included Minister for Public Order (until Aug. 1947), ordering mass arrests of communists.

Works Cited

Archival sources

ANZ. Archives New Zealand, Wellington.

ATL. Alexander Turnbull Library, Wellington.

BHA. Benaki Historical Archives, Kifissia, Athens.

DIS. Diefthynsi Istorias Stratou (Directorate of Military History), Athens.

LCP. Library of the Communist Party of Greece, Perissos, Athens.

KCLMA. Liddell Hart Centre for Military Archives, King's College London.

TNA. The National Archives/Public Record Office, Kew, London.

Mulgan's publications

Mulgan, John, ed. 1938. *Poems of Freedom.* Introduction by W.H. Auden. London: Victor Gollancz.

_____. 2010 [1947]. *Report on Experience.* Ed. Peter Whiteford. London: Frontline Books/Wellington: Victoria University Press/Annapolis, Maryland: Naval Institute Press. (Abbreviated as RE)

_____. 2011a. *A Good Mail: Letters of John Mulgan.* Ed. Peter Whiteford. Wellington: Victoria University Press. (Abbreviated as AGM)

_____. 2011b. *Journey to Oxford.* Ed. Peter Whiteford. Wellington: Victoria University Press.

_____. 2021 [1939]. *Man Alone.* Ed. Peter Whiteford. Wellington: Victoria University of Wellington Press.

_____and G.S. Cox. 1936–37. 'Behind the Cables', *Auckland Star.* paperspast. natlib.govt.nz/newspapers/AS19360212.2.41

Other published works

Adorno, Theodor W. and Walter Benjamin. 1999. *The Complete Correspondence 1928–1940.* Ed. Henri Lonitz. Trans. Nicholas Walker. Cambridge: Polity Press.

Akam, Simon. 2022. 'A Surfeit of Rank'. *London Review of Books* 44.5 (10 Match): 31–35.

Alexander, George. 1980. 'The Unnumbered Round'. In Marion Sarafis, ed., *Greece: From Resistance to Civil War*. Nottingham, UK: Spokesman. 43–51.

Ali, Tariq. 2022. *Winston Churchill: His Times, His Crimes*. London: Verso.

Andrews, Geoff. 2015. *The Shadow Man: At the Heart of the Cambridge Spy Circle*. London: I.B. Tauris & Co. Ltd.

Angelopoulos, Angelos T. 1994. *Apo tin Katohi ston Emfylio: I Megali Efthyni ton Symmahon*. Athens: Parousia.

Anglim, Simon. 2014. *Orde Wingate: Unconventional Warrior: From the 1920s to the Twenty-First Century*. Barnsley, South Yorkshire: Pen & Sword.

Ascherson, Neal. 2020. 'The Bad News about the Resistance'. *London Review of Books* 42.15 (30 July): 27–28.

Auden, W.H. 1938. 'Introduction'. In John Mulgan, ed., *Poems of Freedom*. London: Victor Gollancz. 7–9.

_____and Christopher Isherwood. 1958. *The Ascent of F6 and On the Frontier*. London: Faber.

Auty, Phyllis and Richard Clogg, eds. 1975. *British Policy towards Wartime Resistance in Yugoslavia and Greece*. London: Macmillan Press.

Bærentzen, Lars, ed. 1982. *British Reports on Greece 1943–44 By J.M. Stevens, C.M. Woodhouse & D.J. Wallace*. Copenhagen: Museum Tusculanum Press.

Bailey, Roderick. 2007. 'Communist in SOE: Explaining James Klugmann's Recruitment and Retention'. In Neville Wylie, ed., *The Politics and Strategy of Clandestine War: Special Operations Executive, 1940–1946*. London: Routledge. 66–89.

_____. 2009. *The Wildest Province: SOE in the Land of the Eagle*. London: Vintage Books.

Barker, Elisabeth. 1975. 'Some Factors in British Decision-Making over Yugoslavia 1941–4'. In Phyllis Auty and Richard Clogg, eds., *British Policy towards Wartime Resistance in Yugoslavia and Greece*. London: Macmillan Press. 22–58.

_____. 1980. 'Greece in the Framework of Anglo-Soviet Relations 1941–1947'. In Marion Sarafis, ed., *Greece: From Resistance to Civil War*. Nottingham, UK: Spokesman. 15–31.

Barnes, Katherine. 2015. *The Sabotage Diaries*. Sydney: Harper Collins.

Beaton, Roderick. 2019. *Greece: Biography of a Modern Nation*. London: Allen Lane.

Beevor, Antony. 1991. *Kriti: I Mahi kai i Antistasi*. Trans. Panayiotis Makridis. Ed. Aristeidis Prokopiou. Athens: Govostis.

Bekios-Lambros, Spyros. 1976. *Selides apo tin Ethniki Antistasi*. Athens: Velouhi.

Bell, Rachael. 2015. 'Evidence and Interpretation in New Zealand's Official History: The Battle for Crete, May 1941'. *War in History* 22.3: 364–81.

Bennett, Jack. 1947. 'Foreword'. In John Mulgan, *Report on Experience*. London: Oxford University Press. v–xi.

Bertram, James. 1985. 'John Mulgan: Between Two Wars'. *Flight of the Phoenix:*

Critical Notes on New Zealand Writers. Wellington: Victoria University Press. 38–42.

Bines, Jeffrey. 2018. *Poland's S.O.E.: A British Perspective*. London: Polish Underground Movement Study Trust.

Binney, Marcus. 2002. *The Women who Lived for Danger: The Women Agents of SOE in the Second World War*. London: Hodder & Stoughton.

Blaazer, David. 1992. *The Popular Front and the Progressive Tradition: Socialists, Liberals, and the Quest for Unity, 1884–1939*. Cambridge: Cambridge University Press.

Brown, Martyn. 2011. 'The Political Context of John Mulgan's Greek Wartime Life and Death'. *Journal of New Zealand Studies* NS 10: 89–113.

_____. 2014. 'Investigating the Death of a Legend'. *Modern Greek Studies, Australia & New Zealand* 16–17: 127–46.

_____. 2019. *Politics of Forgetting: New Zealand, Greece and Britain at War*. Melbourne: Australian Scholarly Publishing.

Bryant, Marsha. 1997. *Auden and Documentary in the 1930s*. Charlottesville: University Press of Virginia.

Byford-Jones, W. 1946. *The Greek Trilogy: (Resistance–Liberation–Revolution)*. London: Hutchinson & Co.

Capell, Richard. n.d. *Simiomata: A Greek Note Book 1944–1945*. London: Macdonald & Co.

Caute, David. 1966. *The Left in Europe since 1789*. London: Weidenfeld and Nicolson.

Churchill, Winston S. 1951. *Closing the Ring*. Volume 5 of *The Second World War*. Cambridge, Mass.: Riverside Press.

_____. 1953. *Triumph and Tragedy*. Volume 6 of *The Second World War*. Cambridge, Mass.: Riverside Press.

Clive, Nigel. n.d. *Empeiria stin Ellada 1943–1948*. Trans. Evangelos Pierris. Ed. Dionysios I. Tsourakis. Athens: Elliniki Evroekdotiki.

Clogg, Richard. 1975. '"Pearls from Swine": The Foreign Office Papers, S.O.E. and the Greek Resistance'. In Phyllis Auty and Richard Clogg, eds., *British Policy towards Wartime Resistance in Yugoslavia and Greece*. London: Macmillan. 167–205.

_____. 1981. 'The Special Operations Executive in Greece'. In John O. Iatrides, ed., *Greece in the 1940s: A Nation in Crisis*. Hanover: University Press of New England. 102–18.

_____. 2000. *Anglo-Greek Attitudes: Studies in History*. Houndmills, Basingstoke: Macmillan Press.

_____, ed. 2002. *Greece 1940–1949: Occupation, Resistance, Civil War: A Documentary History*. Trans. Richard Clogg. Houndmills, Basingstoke: Palgrave Macmillan.

_____. 2012. 'In Athens'. *London Review of Books* 34.13. lrb.co.uk/the-paper/v34/n13/richard-clogg/in-athens. Date of access: 30 January 2021.

Close, David. 1993. 'The Reconstruction of a Right-Wing State'. In David Close, ed., *The Greek Civil War, 1943–1950: Studies of Polarization*. London: Routledge. 156–89.

_____. 1995. *The Origins of the Greek Civil War*. London: Longman.

_____. 2004. 'The Road to Reconciliation?: The Greek Civil War and the Politics of Memory in the 1980s'. In Philip Carabott and Thanasis D. Sfikas, eds., *The Greek Civil War: Essays on a Conflict of Exceptionalism and Silences*. Aldershot, Hampshire: Ashgate. 257–78.

Collard, Anna. 1990. 'The Experience of Civil War in the Mountain Villages of Central Greece'. In Marion Sarafis and Martin Eve, eds., Volume 2 of *Background to Contemporary Greece*. London: Merlin Press. 223–54.

Conradi, Peter J. 2013. *A Very English Hero: The Making of Frank Thompson*. London: Bloomsbury.

Cooper, Artemis. 1989. *Cairo in the War 1939–1945*. London: Hamish Hamilton.

Couvaras, Costa G., OSS. n.d. 'With the Central Committee of EAM'. stanford. edu/~ichriss/Couvaras.htm. Date of access: 27 August 2020.

Crang, Jeremy. 2000. *The British Army and the People's War 1939–1945*. Manchester: Manchester University Press.

Crowdy, Terry. 2008. *SOE Agent: Churchill's Secret Warriors*. Oxford: Osprey Publishing.

Cunningham, Valentine, ed. 1986. *Spanish Front: Writers on the Civil War*. Oxford: Oxford University Press.

Davidson, Basil. 1980. *Special Operations Europe: Scenes from the Anti-Nazi War*. London: Victor Gollancz Ltd.

Davin, D.M. 1953. *Crete: Official History of New Zealand in the Second World War 1939–45*. War History Branch, Department of Internal Affairs. London: Oxford University Press.

_____. 1962. 'John Mulgan'. *Landfall Country: Works from Landfall*. Chosen by Charles Brasch. Christchurch: Caxton Press. 373–78.

Day, Paul W. 1968. *John Mulgan*. New York: Twayne Publishers Inc.

_____. 1977. *John Mulgan*. Wellington: Oxford University Press.

_____. 1998. 'Mulgan, John Alan Edward'. *Dictionary of New Zealand Biography*.   teara.govt.nz/en/biographies/4m68/mulgan-john-alan-edward Date of access: 26 November 2020.

De Bernières, Louis. 1995. *Captain Corelli's Mandolin*. London: Minerva.

Edmonds, Arthur. 1998. *With Greek Guerrillas*. Putaruru.: Arthur Edmonds.

Elliott, Murray. 1987. *Vasili: The Lion of Crete*. Auckland: Century Hutchinson.

Eudes, Dominique. 1972. *The Kapetanios: Partisans and Civil War in Greece, 1943–1949*. Trans. John Howe. London: NLB.

Evans, Trefor, ed. 1972. *The Killearn Diaries, 1934–1946: The Diplomatic and Personal Record of Lord Killearn (Sir Miles Lampson) High Commissioner and Ambassador, Egypt*. London: Sidgwick & Jackson.

Filippidis, Ilias A. 2007. *Kriti 1941: I 'Paradosi' tis apo ton Tsortsil sto Hitler*. Ed.

Dimitrios B. Stavropoulos and Kostas Kokkorogiannis. Athens: Iolkos.

Fleischer, Hagen. 1980. 'The Don Stott Affair: Overtures for an Anglo-German Local Peace in Greece'. In Marion Sarafis, ed., *Greece: From Resistance to Civil War*. Nottingham: Spokesman. 91–107.

————. 1981. 'Contacts between German Occupation Authorities and the Major Greek Resistance Organizations: Sound Tactics or Collaboration?' In John O. Iatrides, ed., *Greece in the 1940s: A Nation in Crisis*. Hanover: University Press of New England. 48–60.

————. 1997. 'I Syskepsi Myrofyllou-Plakas: Anastoli tou Emfiliou'. In Kleomenis Koutsoukis, ed., *I Prosopikotita tou Ari Velouhioti kai I Ethniki Antistasi: Ena Epistimoniko Symposio*. Athens: Filistor. 137–72.

Foot, M.R.D. 1966. *SOE in France: An Account of the Work of British Special Operations Executive in France 1940–1944*. London: Her Majesty's Stationery Office.

————. 2001. *SOE in the Low Countries*. London: St Ermin's Press.

————. 2008. *SOE: An Outline History of the Special Operations Executive 1940–1946*. London: The Folio Society.

————. 2010. 'Foreword'. In John Mulgan, *Report on Experience*. Ed. Peter Whiteford. London: Frontline Books/Wellington: Victoria University Press/ Annapolis, Maryland : Naval Institute Press. 11–16.

Freud, Sigmund. 2004. 'Mass Psychology and Analysis of the "I"'. In Sigmund Freud, *Mass Psychology and Other Writings*. Trans. J.A. Underwood. London: Penguin. 15–100.

Garlinski, Jozef. 1969. *Poland, SOE and the Allies*. Trans. Paul Stevenson. London: George Allen and Unwin Ltd.

Garratt, G.T. 1938. *Mussolini's Roman Empire*. Harmondsworth, Middlesex: Penguin.

Gerolymatos, André. 1992. *Guerrilla Warfare and Espionage in Greece 1940– 1944*. New York: Pella.

————. 2016. *An International Civil War: Greece, 1943–1949*. New Haven & London: Yale University Press.

Gorman, Anthony P. 2002. 'Egypt's Forgotten Communists: The Postwar Greek Left'. *Journal of Modern Greek Studies* 20: 1–27.

Goulter-Zervoudakis, Christina. 1998. 'The Politicization of Intelligence: The British Experience in Greece, 1941–1944'. *Intelligence and National Security* 13.1 (Spring): 165–94.

Gounelas, C.-D. 2018. *Neozilandoi stin Amyna kai sto Elliniko Andartiko 1941– 1945*. Thessaloniki: Epikendro.

Grigoriadis, Solon. 2011 [1973]. *Istoria tis Synhronis Elladas 1941–1974*. Vols. 1–4. Athens: Kyriakatiki Eleftherotypia.

Hajis, Thanasis. 1980. 'EAM-ELAS: Resistance or National Liberation Movement?' In Marion Sarafis, ed., *Greece: From Resistance to Civil War*. Nottingham: Spokesman. 63–72.

Hammond, Nicholas. 1983. *Venture into Greece: With the Guerrillas 1943–44*. London: William Kimber & Co. Ltd.

Hamodrakas, Fanis A. 2016. *Apo tin Ethniki Antistasi ston 'Kokkino Dekemvri': O Rolos tis Organoseos 'X' kai o Grivas*. Athens: Pelasgos.

Haralambidis, Menelaos. 2014. *Dekemvriana 1944: I Mahi tis Athinas*. Athens: Alexandria.

Harding, Jeremy. 2013. 'A Kind of Greek'. *London Review of Books* 35.5: 11–14. [Review of Peter Conradi. 2012. *A Very English Hero: The Making of Frank Thompson*. London: Bloomsbury.]

Hardt, Michael and Antonio Negri. 2004. *Multitude: War and Democracy in the Age of Empire*. New York: Penguin.

Haritopoulos, Dionysis. 2003. *Aris o Arhigos ton Atakton: Istoriki Viografia*. Athens: Ellinika Grammata.

Harrison, E.D.R. 2000. 'The British Special Operations Executive and Poland'. *Historical Journal* 43.4: 1071–91.

Hart, Janet. 1990. 'Women in the Greek Resistance: National Crisis and Political Transformation'. *International Labor and Working-Class History* 39: 46–62.

Hobsbawm, E.J. 1977. *Revolutionaries: Contemporary Essays*. London: Quartet Books.

_____. 2002. *Age of Extremes: The Short Twentieth Century 1914–1991*. London: Abacus.

Howarth, Patrick. 1980. *Undercover: The Men and Women of the Special Operations Executive*. London: Routledge & Kegan Paul.

Hynes, Samuel. 1976. *The Auden Generation: Literature and Politics in England in the 1930s*. London: Bodley Head.

Iatrides, John O. 1972. *Revolt in Athens: The Greek Communist 'Second Round', 1944–1945*. Princeton: Princeton University Press.

_____, ed. 1980. *Ambassador MacVeagh Reports: Greece 1933–1947*. Princeton: Princeton University Press.

Inventory of War Events of the Greek Nation (Evretirio Polemikon Gegonoton tou Ellinikou Ethnous). 1989. Athens: Ekdosi Diefthynseos Istorias Stratou (Directory of Military History).

Jones, Matthew. 2007. '"Kipling and all That": American Perceptions of SOE and British Imperial Intrigue in the Balkans, 1943–1945'. In Neville Wylie, ed., *The Politics and Strategy of Clandestine War: Special Operations Executive, 1940–1946*. London: Routledge. 90–108.

Jordan, William. 1969. *Conquest without Victory*. London: Hodder and Stoughton.

Judt, Tony. 2000. 'The Past is Another Country: Myth and Memory in Postwar Europe'. In Istvan Deak, Jan T. Gross and Tony Judt, eds., *The Politics of Retribution in Europe: World War II and its Aftermath*. Princeton, NJ: Princeton University Press. 293–323.

Kailas, Dimitris. 2005. *Kato apo tis Simaies tou Laikou Stratou: Ellines Monimoi Axiomatikoi stis Taxeis tou Ellinikou Laikou Apeleftherotikou Stratou—ELAS*.

Athens: Synhroni Epohi.

Kalyvas, Stathis N. 2008. 'Armed Collaboration in Greece 1941–1944'. *European Review of History* 15.2: 129–42.

Kanellopoulos, Panayiotis. 2012 [1964]. *Ta Hronia tou Megalou Polemou 1939–1944.* Athens: I Ellada Avrio.

Kasparek, Christopher. 2004. 'Krystyna Skarbek: Re-viewing Britain's Legendary Polish Agent'. *Polish Review* 49.3: 945–53.

Kazantzakis, Nikos. 2012. *The Selected Letters of Nikos Kazantzakis.* Trans. and Ed. Peter Bien. Princeton, NJ: Princeton University Press.

Kedros, Andreas. 1980. 'The Mistakes of the Allies and the Mistakes of the Resistance'. In Marion Sarafis, ed., *Greece: From Resistance to Civil War.* Nottingham: Spokesman. 52–62.

Kelly, Saul. 2007. 'A Succession of Crises?: SOE in the Middle East, 1940–1945'. In Neville Wylie, ed., *The Politics and Strategy of Clandestine War: Special Operations Executive, 1940–1946.* London: Routledge. 130–53.

Klugmann, James. 1979. 'The Crisis of the Thirties: A View from the Left'. In Jon Clark et al., eds., *Culture and Crisis in Britain in the Thirties.* London: Lawrence and Wishart. 13–36.

Kontis, Vasilis and Spyridon Sfetas, eds. 2011. *Emfilios Polemos: Engrafa apo ta Yiougoslavika kai Voulgarika Arheia.* Athens: To Vima.

'Krystyna Skarbek/Christine Granville'. 2011. youtube.com/watch?v=UeKH4N-YIE8. Date of access: 29 December 2019.

Lefki Vivlos: Mais 1944–Martis 1945. 1945a. Athens: Ethniko Apeleftherotiko Metopo (EAM).

Lefki Vivlos: Paravaseis tis Varkizas (Flevaris–Iounis 1945). 1945b. Athens: Politikos Synaspismos ton Kommaton tou E.A.M.

Leigh Fermor, Patrick. 1983. *Roumeli: Travels in Northern Greece.* London: Penguin.

Lenin, V.I. 2010 [1916]. *Imperialism: The Highest Stage of Capitalism: A Popular Outline.* London: Penguin.

Liddell Hart, B.H. 2011. *History of the Second World War.* London: Pan Books.

Mace, Martin and John Grehan. 2012. *Unearthing Churchill's Secret Army: The Official List of SOE Casualties and Their Stories.* Barnsley, South Yorkshire: Pen & Sword.

Macintyre, Ben. 2010. *Operation Mincemeat: The True Spy Story that Changed the Course of World War II.* London: Bloomsbury.

Mamarelis, Argyrios. 2014. 'The Special Operations Executive in Greece 1941–1944: The Case of the 5/42 Regiment of Evzones'. lse.ac.uk/europeanInstitute/research/hellenicObservatory/pdf/1st_Symposium/Mamarelis.pdf. Date of access: 15 June 2019.

Marvell, Andrew. 1976. *Selected Poetry.* Ed. Frank Kermode. New York: New American Library.

Masson, Madeleine. 1975. *Christine: A Search for Christine Granville O.B.E., Croix De Guerre.* London: Hamish Hamilton.

Maule, Henry. 1975. *Scobie: Hero of Greece: The British Campaign 1944–5.* London: Arthur Barker.

Mazower, Mark. 1995. 'The Cold War and the Appropriation of Memory: Greece After Liberation'. *Eastern European Politics and Societies* 9.2: 272–94.

_____. 1997. 'Policing the Anti-Communist State in Greece, 1922–1974'. In Mark Mazower, ed., *The Policing of Politics in the Twentieth Century.* Providence, RI: Berghahn Books. 129–50.

_____, ed. 2000. *After the War was Over: Reconstructing the Family, Nation, and State in Greece, 1943–1960.* Princeton: Princeton University Press.

_____. 2001 [1993]. *Inside Hitler's Greece: The Experience of Occupation, 1941–44.* New Haven: Yale University Press.

McClymont, W.G. 1959. *To Greece. Official History of New Zealand in the Second World War 1939–1945.* Wellington: War History Branch, Department of Internal Affairs.

McDonald, Gabrielle. 1991. *New Zealand's Secret Heroes: Don Stott and the 'Z' Special Unit.* Auckland: Reed Books.

McGlynn, M.B. 1953. *Special Service in Greece.* Wellington: War History Branch, Department of Internal Affairs.

McNeill, Dougal. 2012. 'Man Alone/Mulgan/Marxism'. *Journal of New Zealand Studies* NS 13: 2–10.

McNeill, William Hardy. 1947. *The Greek Dilemma: War and Aftermath.* London: Victor Gollancz Ltd.

McNeish, James. 2003. *Dance of the Peacocks: New Zealanders in Exile in the Time of Hitler and Mao Tse-tung.* Auckland: Vintage Books.

Meletzis, Spyros. 1982. *Me tous Andartes sta Vouna.* Athens: Kallitehnikes Ekdoseis S. Meletzi-E. Papadaki.

Mihiotis, Harilaos. 2005. *Dramatiki Poreia: Apo tin Apeleftherosi 1944 stin Tragodia tou Dekemvri kai sti Varkiza.* Athens: Kastalia.

Milne, Seumas. 2000. 'Greek Myth'. theguardian.com/books/2000/jul/29/fiction.features?CMP=Share_iOSApp_Other. Date of access: 15 September 2022.

Mortimer, Gavin. 2013. *The SBS in World War II.* Oxford: Osprey Publishing.

Moss, W. Stanley. 1956. *Gold is Where You Find It: What Happened to the Reichsbank Treasure?* London: Andre Deutsch.

Mulgan, Alan. 1959 [1958]. *The Making of a New Zealander.* Wellington: A.H. & A.W. Reed.

Mulgan, Richard. 2010. 'Preface'. In John Mulgan, *Report on Experience.* Ed. Peter Whiteford. London: Frontline Books/Wellington: Victoria University Press/Annapolis, Maryland: Naval Institute Press. 7–10.

Mulley, Clare. 2012. *The Spy Who Loved: The Secrets and Lives of Christine Granville, Britain's First Female Special Agent of the Second World War.* London: Macmillan.

_____. 2013. 'Christine Granville's Exploits in the Second World War'.

Talk (29 August) at the National Army Museum, London. youtube.com/watch?v=tDuaF29QZXs. Date of access: 6 January 2017.

Myers, E.C.W. 1975. 'The Andarte Delegation to Cairo: August 1943'. In Phyllis Auty and Richard Clogg, eds., *British Policy towards Wartime Resistance in Yugoslavia and Greece*. London: Macmillan. 147–66.

_____. 1985. *Greek Entanglement*. Gloucester: Alan Sutton.

Nalmpantis, Kyriakos. 2010. *Time on the Mountain: The Office of Strategic Services in Axis-Occupied Greece, 1943–1944*. PhD thesis. Kent State University.

Nefeloudis, Vasileios. 1981. *Ethniki Antistasi sti Mesi Anatoli*. 2 vols. Athens: Themelio.

Nowicki, Ronald. 2005. 'Krystyna Skarbek: A Letter'. *The Polish Review* 50.1: 93–101.

O'Connor, Bernard. 2018. *Sabotage in Greece during the Second World War*. n.p.: Bernard O'Connor.

O'Connor, Brian. 2000. 'Introduction'. In Brian O'Connor, ed., *The Adorno Reader*. Oxford: Blackwell. 1–19.

Ogden, Alan. 2012. *Sons of Odysseus: SOE Heroes in Greece*. London: Bene Factum.

_____. 2014. 'Afterword. Billy Moss: Soldier, Writer, Traveller—A Brief Life'. In W. Stanley Moss, *A War of Shadows*. London: Bene Factum. 284–323.

Ondaatje, Michael. 2018. *Warlight*. London: Jonathan Cape.

Orwell, George. 1970. *As I Please 1943–1945*. Volume 3 of *The Collected Essays, Journalism and Letters of George Orwell*. Ed. Sonia Orwell and Ian Angus. Harmondsworth, Middlesex: Penguin Books.

_____. 1971. *My Country Right or Left 1940–1943*. Volume 2 of *The Collected Essays, Journalism and Letters of George Orwell*. Ed. Sonia Orwell and Ian Angus. Harmondsworth, Middlesex: Penguin Books.

_____. *Homage to Catalonia*. 2000 [1938]. London: Penguin Books.

O'Sullivan, Vincent. 2003. *Long Journey to the Border: A Life of John Mulgan*. Auckland: Penguin. (Abbreviated as LJB)

Papandreou, Georgios. 1963. Vol. I. *Keimena 1913–1942*. Vol. II. *Keimena: Katohi—M. Anatoli—Apeleftherosis*. Athens: Biris.

Papastratis, Prokopis. 1980. 'The British and the Greek Resistance Movements'. In Marion Sarafis, ed., *Greece: From Resistance to Civil War*. Nottingham: Spokesman. 32–42.

_____. 1984. *British Policy towareds Greece during the Second World War 1941–1944*. Cambridge: Cambridge University Press.

_____. 1997. 'I Ethniki Antistasi: Symmahikes Skopimotites kai Antidraseis'. In Kleomenis Koutsoukis, ed., *I Prosopikotita tou Ari Velouhioti kai i Ethniki Antistasi: Ena Epistimoniko Symposio*. Athens: Filistor. 121–35.

Parianou, Mairi. 2007. *Martyries apo tin Antistasi kai ti Filaki (1941–1945)*. Ed. Maria Spiliotopoulou. Athens: Filippoti.

Parker, Dean. 1998. 'Elusive Objectives: The Bitter Deaths of Two New Zealand

Marxists'. *New Zealand Political Review* 7.2 (June/July): 16–19.

Parkin-Gounelas, Ruth, ed. 2012. *The Psychology and Politics of the Collective: Groups, Crowds and Mass Identifications*. New York and Oxford: Routledge.

Pashalidis, Nikos. 1997. *Vretaniki Diamahi kai Elliniki Antistasi: Anatomia Enos Ainigmatos*. Thessaloniki: Kyromanos.

'Polish Contribution to World War II'. wikipedia.org/wiki/Polish_contribution_to_World War_II. Date of access: 18 August 2018.

Ponder, John. 1997. *Patriots and Scoundrels: Behind Enemy lines in Wartime Greece 1943–44*. South Melbourne: Hyland House.

Pyromaglou, Komninos. 1978. *O Doureios Ippos*. Athens: Dodoni.

Rattenbury, Arnold. 1997. 'Convenient Death of a Hero'. *London Review of Books* 19.9. lrb.co.uk/the-paper/v19/n09. Date of access: 22 February 2021.

Richter, Heinz. 1980. 'The Battle of Athens and the Role of the British'. In Marion Sarafis, ed., *Greece: From Resistance to Civil War*. Nottingham, UK: Spokesman. 78–90.

_____. 1985. *British Intervention in Greece: From Varkiza to Civil War*. Trans. Marion Sarafis. London: Merlin Press.

_____. 1997. *I Epemvasi ton Anglon stin Ellada: Apo ti Varkiza ston Emfylio Polemo, Fevrouarios 1945–Avgoustos 1946*. Trans. Periklis Vallianos and Giorgos Giannaris. Ed. Giorgos Giannaris. Athens: I.D.Kollaros.

_____. 2009. *I Ethniki Antistasi kai oi Synepeies tis*. Trans. Eliza Panagiotatou, Fani Gaidatzi and Anna Markoulidaki. Athens: Mesogeios.

Romeos, Georgios. 2019. 'I Apelasi tou Nikou Kazantzaki apo tin Anglia'. In Ioanna Spiliopoulou and Nikos Hrysos, eds., *O Nikos Kazantzakis kai i Politiki*. Athens: Kastaniotis. 137–46.

Ross, Ken. 2019a. 'John Mulgan: New Zealand Wants You'. *New Zealand International Review* 44.1: 16–19.

_____. 2019b. 'John Mulgan: The Turnbull Library Solves an Inexplicable Death?' *Turnbull Library Records* 51: 70–79.

Sakkas, John. 2012. '*The Times* and the British Intervention in Greece in December 1944'. imxa.gr. Date of access: 30 May 2020.

Sampatakakis, Theodoros. 2006. *Taftotites Praktoron kai Kodika Onomaton: I Drastiriotita ton Vretanon Yperesion Pliroforion stin Ellada (1939–1944)*. Athens: Filistor.

Sarafis, Marion. 1980a. 'Stefanos Sarafis 1890–1957'. In Stefanos Sarafis, *ELAS: Greek Resistance Army*. Trans. Sylvia Moody. London: Merlin Press. xi–ci.

_____, ed. 1980b. *Greece: From Resistance to Civil War*. Nottingham: Spokesman.

_____. 1990. *O Stratigos Sarafis opos ton Gnorisa*. Athens: Kastaniotis.

Sarafis, Stefanos. 1980. *ELAS: Greek Resistance Army*. Trans. Sylvia Moody. London: Merlin Press.

Schmitt, Carl. 2004 [1963]. *The Theory of the Partisan: A Commentary/Remark on the Concept of the Political*. Trans. Alfred Clement Goodson. Michigan:

Michigan State University Press.

Scott, Sid. 1945. 'Preface.' *The Truth About Greece.* Auckland: In Print Publishing. 4.

Seaman, Mark. 2006. '"A New Instrument of War": The Origins of the Special Operations Executive'. In Mark Seaman, ed., *Special Operations Executive: A New Instrument of War.* London: Routledge. 7–21.

Seferis, Giorgos. 1993. *Meres.* Vol. IV (1 January 1941–31 December 1944). Athens: Ikaros.

Sfikas, Thanasis D. 2004. 'A Prime Minister for All Time: Themistoklis Sofoulis from Premiership to Opposition to Premiership, 1945–49'. In Philip Carabott and Thanasis D. Sfikas, eds., *The Greek Civil War: Essays on a Conflict of Exceptionalism and Silences.* Aldershot, Hampshire: Ashgate. 75–99.

Sinclair, Keith. 1980. *History of New Zealand.* Harmondsworth: Penguin Books.

Skalidakis, Giannis. 2015. *I Eleftheri Ellada: I Exousia tou EAM sta Hronia tis Katohis (1943–1944).* Athens: Asini Publisher.

Soulogiannis, Efthymios. 2009 'Oi Ellinikes Paroikies stin Aigypto kata ti Neoteri kai Synhroni Epohi'. parathemata.com/2009/11/blog post_104. html. Date of access: 30 September 2013.

Spencer, Floyd A. 1952. *War and Postwar Greece: An Analysis Based on Greek Writings.* Washington: Library of Congress: European Affairs Division.

Stafford, David. 1983. *Britain and European Resistance 1940–1945: A Survey of the Special Operations Executive with Documents.* London: Macmillan Press.

_____. 2000. *Secret Agent: The True Story of the Special Operations Executive.* London: BBC.

_____. 2006. 'Churchill and SOE'. In Mark Seaman, ed., *Special Operations Executive: A New Instrument of War.* London: Routledge. 47–60.

_____. 2007. *Endgame 1945: Victory, Retribution, Liberation.* London: Little Brown.

Stead, C.K. 2013. 'John Mulgan: A Question of Identity'. *Kin of Place: Essays on 20 New Zealand Writers.* Auckland: Auckland University Press. 156–96.

Stirling, Tessa, Daria Nalecz and Tadeusz Dubicki, eds. 2005. *Intelligence Co-Operation between Poland and Great Britain during World War II: The Report of the Anglo-Polish Historical Committee.* Volume I. London: Vallentine Mitchell.

Stroggilis, Apostolos. 1996. *Treis Morfes tis Antistasis: Sarafis–Kartalis–Karagiorgis.* Athens: Filistor.

Stroud, Rick. 2015. *Kidnap in Crete: The True Story of the Abduction of a Nazi General.* London: Bloomsbury.

Stuart, Duncan. 2006. '"Of Historical Interest Only": The Origins and Vicissitudes of the SOE Archive'. In Mark Seaman, ed., *Special Operations Executive: A New Instrument of War.* London: Routledge. 217–29.

Svoronos, Nicolas. 1981. 'Greek History, 1940–1950'. In John O. Iatrides, ed., *Greece in the 1940s: A Nation in Crisis.* Hanover: University Press of New England. 1–14.

Sweet-Escott, Bickham. 1954. *Greece: A Political and Economic Survey 1939–1953*. London: Royal Institute of International Affairs.

_____. 1965. *Baker Street Irregular*. London: Methuen & Co. Ltd.

_____. 1975. 'S.O.E. in the Balkans'. In Phyllis Auty and Richard Clogg, eds., *British Policy towards Wartime Resistance in Yugoslavia and Greece*. London: Macmillan Press. 3–21.

Thompson, E.P. 1997. *Beyond the Frontier: The Politics of a Failed Mission; Bulgaria 1944*. Suffolk: Merlin Press.

Thompson, T.J. and E.P. Thompson, eds. 1947. *There is a Spirit in Europe . . .: A Memoir of Frank Thompson*. London: Victor Gollancz Ltd.

Tillotson, Michael, ed. 2011. *SOE and the Resistance: As Told in* The Times *Obituaries*. London: Continuum.

Tsakalotos, Thrasyvoulos. 1978–79. *1946–1949: Dimokratia kai Oloklirotismos: To Hroniko tou Symmoritopolemou*. Athens: Ethnkon Idryma Amynis.

Tsamakos, Kostas. 1949. *O Tsaous' Hasan Agas ki Alla Ipeirotika Diigimata*. Athens: n.p.

Tsirkas, Stratis. 2015. *Drifting Cities [Akyvernites Politeies*, 1960–65]. Trans. Kay Cicellis. Athens: Kedros.

Tsoutsoumpis, Spyros. 2016. *A History of the Greek Resistance in the Second World War: The People's Armies*. Manchester: Manchester University Press.

Vlavianos, Haris. 1989. 'The Greek Communist Party: In Search of a Revolution'. In Tony Judd, ed., *Resistance and Revolution in Mediterranean Europe 1939–1948*. London: Routledge. 157–212.

Voglis, Polymeris. 2002. *Becoming a Subject: Political Prisoners during the Greek Civil War*. New York: Bergham Books.

_____. 2004. 'Becoming Communist: Political Prisoners as a Subject during the Greek Civil War'. In Philip Carabott and Thanasis D. Sfikas, eds., *The Greek Civil War: Essays on a Conflict of Exceptionalism and Silences*. Aldershot: Ashgate. 141–57.

_____and Ioannis Nioutsikos. 2017. 'The Greek Historiography of the 1940s: A Reassessment'. *Südosteuropa* 65.2: 316–33.

Vulliamy, Ed and Helena Smith. 2014. 'Athens 1944: Britain's Dirty Secret'. *The Observer*, 30 November theguardian.com/world/2014/nov/30/athens-1944-britains-dirty-secret. Date of access: 20 May 2020.

Walton, Calder. 2013. *Empire of Secrets: British Intelligence, the Cold War and the Twilight of Empire*. London: Harper Press.

Ward, Michael. 1992. *Greek Assignments: SOE 1943–1948 UNSCOB*. Athens: Lycabettus Press.

Whiteford, Peter. 2010. 'Introduction: The Textual History'. In John Mulgan, *Report on Experience*. Ed. Peter Whiteford. London: Frontline Books/Wellington: Victoria University Press/Annapolis, Maryland: Naval Institute Press. 17–28.

Widdowson, Peter. 1979. 'Between the Acts?: English Fiction in the Thirties'. In

Jon Clark et al., eds., *Culture and Crisis in Britain in the Thirties*. London: Lawrence and Wishart. 133–64.

Windmill, Lorna Almonds. 2008. *A British Achilles: The Story of George, 2nd Earl Jellicoe KBE, DSO, MC, FRS: Soldier, Diplomat, Politician*. Barnsley: Pen & Sword.

Woodhouse, C.M. 1948. *Apple of Discord: A Survey of Recent Greek Politics in Their International Setting*. London: Hutchinson & Co.

————. 1971. 'Early British Contacts with the Greek Resistance in 1942'. *Balkan Studies* 12.2: 347–63.

————. 1982. *Something Ventured*. London: Granada.

————. 2002 [1976]. *The Struggle for Greece 1941–1949*. London: Hurst & Company.

Woods, Christopher. 2006. 'SOE in Italy'. In Mark Seaman, ed., *Special Operations Executive: A New Instrument of War*. London: Routledge. 91–102.

Wylie, Neville. 2007a. 'Introduction: Politics and Strategy in the Clandestine War—New Perspectives in the Study of SOE'. In Neville Wylie, ed., *The Politics and Strategy of Clandestine War: Special Operations Executive, 1940–1946*. London: Routledge. 1–14.

————. 2007b. 'Ungentlemanly Warriors or Unreliable Diplomats?: Special Operations Executive and "Irregular Political Activities" in Europe'. In Neville Wylie, ed., *The Politics and Strategy of Clandestine War: Special Operations Executive, 1940–1946*. London: Routledge. 109–29.

Index

*Numbers in **Bold** indicate entry in Appendix D (Short biographies of main Greek figures)*

338